GW00787928

THE SOUTH OF FRANCE

John Ardagh

Second
edition
of the
American
Express
Pocket
Guide

Mitchell Beazley

The Author

John Ardagh is a journalist, broadcaster, noted authority on France and the French, and the author of several important studies of contemporary French life, *The New France* (1968), *France in the 1980s* (1982), *Rural France* (1983) and *The Collins Guide to France* (editor: 1986). He has also worked on the staff of the *Observer* and *The Times* and for two years was managing editor of *The Good Food Guide*.

Acknowledgments

The author and publishers would like to thank the following for their invaluable help and advice: Pauline Hallam and Martine Williams of the French Government Tourist Office in London, Marek Obbink and Véronique Seban of the Délégation Régionale du Tourisme in Nice and Paul Coué of the DRT in Marseille, Josiane Mérino of the Société des Bains de Mer in Monaco/Monte-Carlo, Pamela Fiori, Martin Grafton, Ila Stanger, Jenny Towndrow.

Quotations

The author and publishers are grateful to those listed below for their kind permission to reprint the following extracts: The Bodley Head (UK) and Charles Scribner's Sons (US) for the quotations from *Tender is the Night* by F. Scott Fitzgerald (pages 97, 103, 150), Curtis Brown Ltd (UK, USA) for the quotations from *Aspects of Provence* by James Pope-Hennessy (pages 17, 28, 85), Faber and Faber Ltd. (UK) and Viking Penguin Inc. (US) for the quotation from *Monsieur* by Lawrence Durrell (page 75).

Few travel books are without errors, and no guidebook can ever be completely up to date, for telephone numbers and opening hours change without warning, and hotels and restaurants come under new management, which can affect standards. While every effort has been made to ensure that all information is accurate at the time of going to press, the publishers will be glad to receive any corrections and suggestions for improvements, which can be incorporated in the next edition.

Series Editor   David Townsend Jones
Editor (first edition 1983)   Fiona Duncan
Editor (second edition 1987)   Christopher McIntosh
Art Editor   Eric Drewery
Designer   Sarah Jackson
Illustrators   Jeremy Ford and Industrial Art Studios (David Lewis Artists), Illustrated Arts, Rodney Paull
Production   Androulla Pavlou

Edited and designed by
Mitchell Beazley International Limited
Artists House, 14–15 Manette Street,
London W1V 5LB

Maps in 4-colour by Clyde Surveys Ltd,
Maidenhead, England, based on
copyrighted material of IGN-Paris 1982;
authorization no. 99-0595; extracts from
maps of the Institut Geographique
National-France.

Typeset by Vantage Photosetting Co.
Ltd, Eastleigh, England.
Printed and bound in Hong Kong by
Mandarin Offset International Ltd

Contents

How to use this book

The American Express Pocket Guide to the South of France is an encyclopaedia of travel information, organized in the sections listed on the previous page. There is also a comprehensive **index and gazetteer** (pages 245–256), and there are full-colour **maps** at the end of the book.

For easy reference, the *South of France A–Z* and other sections as far as possible are arranged alphabetically. For the organization of the book as a whole, see *Contents*. For individual places that do not have separate entries in the *A–Z*, see the *Index*.

Abbreviations

As far as possible only standard abbreviations have been used. These include days of the week and months, points of the compass (N, S, E and W), street names (Av., Bd., Pl.) Saint and Sainte (St and Ste), rooms (rms), C for century, and measurements.

Bold type

Bold type is used in running text primarily for emphasis, to draw attention to something of special interest or importance. It is also used in this way to pick out places – shops or minor museums, for instance – that do not have full entries of their own. In such cases it is usually followed in brackets by the address, telephone number, and details of opening times, printed in italics.

Cross-references

A special type has been used for cross-references. Whenever a place or section title is printed in sans serif italics (for example *Nice* or *Basic information*) in the text, this indicates that you can turn to the appropriate heading in the book for further information. For added convenience, the running heads, printed at the top corner of the page, always correspond with these cross-references.

Cross-references always refer either to sections of the book –

How entries are organized

Martigues

Map 10G5. 40km (25 miles) w of Marseille. 13500 B.-du-R. Population: 38,350 i Quai Paul-Doumer
☎ *(42) 80–30–72.*

The former fishing village has today grown into a sizeable dormitory town, owing to its proximity to the new oil-based industries of Lavéra and Berre Lagoon (see *Berre, Étang de*). But its old quarter, where pretty houses line the canals, has not lost the charm that drew Ziem and Corot to paint it in the 19thC. The prettiest spot is the **Pont St-Sebastien** on the central Ile de Brescon, where there is also the 17thC **church of Ste-Madeleine**, fronted by Corinthian pillars, and with a fine organ loft and Baroque decor.

In the w suburbs, an imposing modern suspension bridge, 292m (330yd) long, carries an autoroute over the canal. Just N of the town, above a new hospital, the **chapelle de Notre-Dame-des-Marins** stands alone on a hilltop; from here there are views over the vast industrial complex of Berre/Fos and the limestone ranges beyond.

Basic information, *Planning*, *Biographies* – or to individual entries in the *A–Z*, such as *Avignon*, *Cannes* or *Nice*. Ordinary italics are used to identify sub-sections. For instance: See *Area planners and tours* in *Planning*.

Map references

Each page of the colour maps at the end of the book has a page number (**2–16**) and each map is divided into a grid of squares, which are identified vertically by letters (A, B, C, D, etc.) and horizontally by numbers (1, 2, 3, 4, etc.). A map reference identifies the page and square in which the town or place of interest can be found – thus **Agay** is located in the square identified as Map **13G13**.

Price categories

Price categories are denoted by the symbols ⬜ 🔲 🔳 ▮▮ and ▮▮▮ which signify cheap, inexpensive, moderately priced, expensive and very expensive, respectively. In the cases of hotels and restaurants these correspond approximately with the following actual prices, which give a guideline at the time of printing. Although actual prices will inevitably increase, in most cases the relative price category – for example expensive or cheap – will be likely to remain more or less the same.

Price categories	Corresponding to approximate prices	
	for **hotels** *double room; single room not significantly cheaper*	for **restaurants** *meal for one with service, taxes and house wine*
⬜ cheap	under 150 francs	under 60 francs
🔲 inexpensive	150–350 francs	60–100 francs
🔳 moderate	350–550 francs	100–200 francs
▮▮ expensive	550–1,000 francs	200–400 francs
▮▮▮ very expensive	over 1,000 francs	over 400 francs

—— Bold blue type for entry headings.

—— Blue italics for address, practical information and symbols, encapsulating standard information and special recommendations. For list of symbols see p6.

—— Black text for description.
Bold type used for emphasis.
Sans serif italics used for cross-references to other entries.

Entries for hotels, restaurants, —— shops, etc. follow the same organization, and are usually printed across a narrow measure.
In hotels, symbols indicating special facilities appear at the end of the entry, in black.——

🐦 Liautaud
2 Rue Victor-Hugo, 13260 Cassis
☎(42) 01–75–37 🔲 *to* 🔳
32 rms 🛏 *32* 🍽 🏠 ═ 🏠
June–Sept.
Location: Very central, on the quayside. A busy and friendly holiday hotel, much modernized in recent years, but run by the Liautaud family for a century. The adjoining bar-café is popular with locals, so not all bedrooms are totally quiet, but the front ones have balconies facing the harbour. (See restaurant.)
🛝 🕭 🖼 🍷 🎿 🐦 👥

5

Key to symbols

☎ Telephone	🏖 Beach holiday hotel
⑩ Telex	✤ Tennis court(s)
★ Not to be missed	✓ Golf course
☆ Worth a visit	⚞ Riding facilities
✿ Good value (in its class)	⚓ Fishing facilities
_i_ Tourist information	🏛 Conference facilities
⟞ Parking	⚊ Restaurant
⚘ Hotel	⚬ Simple (restaurant)
⬛ Simple (hotel)	△ Luxury (restaurant)
▥ Luxury (hotel)	▭ A la carte available
▭ Cheap	▤ Set (fixed price) menu available
▯ Inexpensive	
▥ Moderately priced	▥ Good for wines
▥ Expensive	◒ Open-air dining available
▥ Very expensive	🏛 Building of architectural interest
▭ Rooms with private bathroom	† Church or cathedral
⊟ Air conditioning	◻ Free entrance
⬛ Residential terms available	◼ Entrance fee payable
AE American Express	■■ Entrance expensive
CB Carte Blanche	🚫 Photography forbidden
⊕ Diners Club	K Guided tour available
⬛ MasterCard/Eurocard	🎫 Guided tour compulsory
VISA Visa/Carte Bleue	▣ Cafeteria
▭ Secure garage	✳ Special interest for children
⬛ Meal obligatory	
▱ Quiet hotel	☿ Bar
⬆ Lift	◉ Disco dancing
♿ Facilities for disabled people	▰ Nightclub
▭ TV in each room	⚜ Casino/gambling
▱ Telephone in each room	♫ Live music
▱ Dogs not allowed	♪ Dancing
⚘ Garden	▨ Revue
⚟ Outstanding views	⊠ 'Adults only'
⇄ Swimming pool	▤ Members only
	▤ Temporary membership

6

Before you go

Documents required

A valid national passport is all British citizens need. No visas are required; and no health or vaccination certificates are required for entry into France or re-entry into Britain.

If arriving by car, you need a valid driving licence (not provisional). An international driving licence is not required. You also need the vehicle registration certificate (logbook), a national identity plate or sticker displayed at the rear of the vehicle, and a certificate of insurance proving that you have third party insurance. Though the green card insurance certificate is no longer necessary for members of EEC countries, it is still advisable to have it, as it is the most effective way of proving that you have reliable cover. Details of these and other requirements can be obtained from the AA or RAC.

Travel and medical insurance

It is advisable to travel with an insurance policy which covers loss of deposits paid to airlines, hotels, tour operators, etc., the cost of dealing with emergency requirements, such as special tickets home and extra nights in a hotel, as well as a medical insurance policy. Be especially careful about insurance cover if you are going skiing.

There is a reciprocal agreement between EEC countries whereby visitors, who are entitled to full UK benefits, can obtain emergency medical treatment for the same amount as the nationals themselves. In order to benefit from this you must have form E111. To obtain this form, ask your local Department of Health and Social Security office for leaflet SA28/30, Medical Treatment During Visits Abroad, and fill in form CMI on the back page. For instructions on how to use the form in France, ask for leaflet SA36 and take it abroad with you. In France you are entitled to a refund of approximately 75% of the medical services expenses you are charged, and about 70% of the medicinal costs incurred, so it is wise to be insured privately as well.

Money

The unit of currency is the franc (f), which consists of 100 centimes (c). There are coins for 5c, 10c, 20c and ½f, 1f, 2f, 5f and 10f, and notes for 20f, 50f, 100f, and 500f. There is no limit to the amount of currency you can bring into France, but you can take out no more than 5,000f when you leave, unless large sums are declared on entry.

Travellers cheques issued by American Express, Thomas Cook, Barclays and Citibank are widely recognized; make sure you read the instructions included with your travellers cheques. It is important to note separately the serial numbers of your cheques and the telephone number to call in case of loss. Specialist travellers cheque companies such as American Express provide extensive local refund facilities through their own offices or agents.

Major international credit cards such as American Express, Diners Club, Eurocard (MasterCard) and Carte Bleue (Visa), are widely accepted – but do not assume that your card will always be accepted. British citizens can make use of the Eurocheque Encashment scheme whereby they can cash personal cheques with a Eurocheque Encashment Card.

Basic information

Customs

If you are visiting France for less than six months, you are entitled to bring, free of duty and tax, all personal effects, except tobacco goods, alcoholic drinks and perfume, which you intend to take with you when you leave. Make sure that you are carrying dated receipts for more valuable items such as cameras and watches, or you may be charged duty.

In the following list, the figures in brackets are the increased allowances for goods obtained duty and tax paid in the EEC. In all cases the limits apply only to travellers over 17 years old.

Tobacco If you live in an EEC country, you are allowed 300 cigarettes *or* 150 cigarillos *or* 75 cigars *or* 400g of tobacco. If you live outside Europe, you are allowed 400 cigarettes *or* 200 cigarillos *or* 100 cigars *or* 500g tobacco; however, if you live in a non-EEC European country you are allowed half this amount.

Alcoholic drinks 1(1.5) litres spirits (over 22% alcohol by volume) *or* 2(3) litres of alcoholic drinks of 22% alcohol or less; *plus* 2(5) litres still wines.

Perfume 50g/60cc/2 fl oz (75g/90cc/3 fl oz).

Other goods Commodities and articles to the value of 300f (2,000f); 150f(400f) for travellers under 15.

Certain prohibited and restricted goods cannot be imported, such as narcotics, gold, copyright infringements and weapons (other than arms for sport and target shooting). A more detailed list can be obtained from the French Government Tourist Office.

Getting there

By air: The Nice-Côte d'Azur Airport is one of the busiest and most important in France. There are daily flights between London and Nice with British Airways and Air France. It is also possible to fly to several other major towns within the area (see *Getting around* opposite); this often means changing planes, usually at Paris, and using France's internal airline, Air Inter. International car-hire companies offer an efficient fly-drive service whereby your car is waiting for you.

By train: There is a frequent and excellent train service from Paris (Gare de Lyon) to Marseille by the *TGV* (*Train à Grande Vitesse*) and thence along the coast and into Italy. The fastest train in the world, the *TGV* takes under 5hr from Paris to Marseille and under 8hr to Nice, or you can take one of the slower trains which stop at many of the resorts along the Riviera. The most comfortable way to travel by train is overnight: in a couchette, which has six berths to a compartment if you are travelling second class, four if travelling first class (there is no sex segregation). Alternatively, you can have a sleeping car with berths for one, two or three. Only some trains have a buffet car or trolley. There is a Motorail service (*trains autos couchettes*) exclusively for passengers who wish to transport their cars to their destination by train. The SNCF office in London (☎(01) 409–1224) will give information and make arrangements for you.

By bus: If coming from London, International Express Eurolines (☎(01) 730–0202) have buses leaving on Mon, Wed and Fri at 15.00 and arriving the following evening (Marseille at 17.30, Nice at 20.15); seats have to be booked in advance.

By car: If you are not in a hurry, there is no more enjoyable a way of travelling than through the countryside on the minor roads. Alternatively, the region is well served by autoroutes. Paris to Marseille can be accomplished in about 7hr, and Paris to Nice in 9hr via the A7 to Aix-en-Provence and then the A8. The toll is expensive however, so keep plenty of loose change handy. Remember that from July 14 until the end of Aug, the French holiday period, the traffic is very heavy, especially at weekends. The alternative direct route to the autoroute, though much slower, is the N7. Or you can follow the special alternative summer routes marked with green arrows.

Climate
During the summer the average temperature on the coast is 24°C(75°F) and the average temperature of the sea is 19°C(66°F). There is very little rain, and the vegetation is arid. This is the time when fires can ravage the pine forests, so be particularly careful to obey the rules of fire prevention.

Even in late Oct it can still be bikini weather, although the hot spells are often punctuated by spectacular storms. The average temperature on the coast in Jan is a warm 9°C(48°F). The hills behind the coast, however, are cold and snow-covered.

In spring, heavy but short showers encourage the flowers to burst into colour, and the weather is warm and pleasant, except when the annoying Mistral begins to blow, when, for days on end, powerful swirling gusts of wind prevail.

Clothes
The Riviera is informal but very fashion-conscious and in all the main cities and towns you will find the classic French *chic* to live up to. In winter, be prepared for both warm and cold weather, taking both light shirts and skirts as well as jeans and sweaters.

Poste restante
You can have letters sent to the central post offices of most major towns. The envelope should be addressed as follows: name (the inclusion of words such as 'Esq.' can cause confusion), *poste restante*, *poste centrale*, postcode (if possible) and town, France. You will need identification when you collect your post and a small fee may be charged. Travel companies, such as American Express and Thomas Cook, will also hold mail.

For post codes see *A–Z* entries.

Getting around

The South of France is adequately served by public transport, but in the hinterland it is a real bonus to have a car.

Flying
There are airports at Nice, Marseille, Toulon, St Raphael/Fréjus and Nîmes, although it is only possible to fly with Air Inter, France's domestic airline, between Nice, Marseille and Corsica within the region. Nice Airport and Cannes Airport also cater for private planes and Nice Airport offers a helicopter service to Monaco.

If arriving at Nice-Côte d'Azur Airport, there is a regular bus service (as well as taxis) to the centre of Nice and also to the resorts along the coast. There is a bus service from Marseille Airport to the Gare St-Charles in the city centre.

Buses

The bus service in general does not compete with the railway,
but links villages with larger towns. Local buses, running from
the coastal towns to the hinterland, are infrequent and
crowded, so it is advisable to have a car if you are based inland.
If you are based in one of the resort towns and want to see the
hinterland in relative comfort, SNCF runs excursions which
can be booked at railway stations. It is wise (and often
obligatory) to reserve a seat in advance.

For more detailed information and for a complete set of
timetables, see a copy of the booklet *Plaisir de Voir*, distributed
by SNCF.

Railway services

Coastal resorts are linked by a good train service. There is also a
service from Nice to Tende, and a private service taking
passengers through the charming mountain region between
Nice and Digne. From Digne, it is possible to go to Aix and on
further into Provence.

Although some lines, particularly in Provence, have closed, a
bus service, operated by SNCF, now calls at the disused railway
stations thus continuing the service.

When travelling by train, you must validate your ticket by
stamping it at a machine at the entrance to the platform. If you
fail to do this, you may be treated as if you were intending to
travel without a ticket, and you will have to pay a surcharge of
20%.

Getting around by car

Driving in France is, for the most part, a pleasant experience;
almost all roads are well surfaced, and mountain roads are
exceptionally well-engineered. The main drawback to driving
in the South of France, however, is the exceptionally heavy
traffic in summer.

Speed limits are 130kph(80mph) on toll autoroutes,
110kph(68mph) on free autoroutes and dual carriageways,
90kph(56mph) on other roads, 60kph(37mph) in built-up
areas. Police can, and often do, impose heavy on-the-spot
speeding fines. In the case of a more serious driving offence they
are entitled to confiscate your licence and impound the vehicle.
Wearing seat belts is compulsory.

Parking is not easy in big towns, especially in summer.
Beware of parking on a street marked *stationnement gênant*
(obstructive parking); your car is liable to be towed away. Car
break-ins are rife; never leave visible objects in the car and try to
park overnight in a well-lit main street.

Renting a car

Most international car rental companies have branches in the
region, particularly at airports and major railway stations, and
there are also many reliable and often cheaper local firms.
Payment by credit card avoids the need for a large cash deposit.
A current driver's licence is required, and the minimum age is
usually 21, although some companies have raised it to 25. Make
sure the car is fully insured, even if it means making separate
arrangements for insurance against damage to other vehicles
and injury to your passengers.

With some car rental firms you can arrange to leave your car
at your destination without having to return it, and fly-drive
arrangements can also be made.

On-the-spot information

Public holidays
New Year's Day, Jan 1; Easter Monday; Labour Day, May 1;
VE Day, May 8; Ascension Day (sixth Thurs after Easter);
Whit Monday (second Mon after Ascension); Bastille Day, July
14; Assumption, Aug 15; All Saints' Day, Nov 1;
Remembrance Day, Nov 11; Dec 25. Most museums close but
many shops and restaurants remain open.

Time zones
Like most Western European countries, France is 1hr ahead of
GMT in the winter and 2hr ahead in summer, i.e. 1hr ahead of
the UK most of the year.

Banks and bureaux de change
Normal banking hours are Mon–Fri 9.00–12.00, 14.00–16.00.
However, in big towns, such as Nice and Marseille, some
central banks have now reduced their lunch closure to
12.30–13.30. In provincial towns, banks are often closed on
Mon, and in small villages they may only be open one or two
days a week. Money can also be exchanged outside banking
hours at *bureaux de change* found in hotels, travel agencies,
railway stations and airports.
  See *Money p7* for more details.

Shopping and business hours
Because of the Mediterranean climate, a siesta is usually taken
somewhere between 12.00–15.00, when only bars and
restaurants will be open. To compensate, shops often open
early in the morning (7.00 or 8.00) and close late (19.00 or
20.00). Food shops tend to close at 13.00, and in large towns
they often stay open until 22.00; they also stay open on Sun
morning. Many shops are closed on Mon (although some may
be open during the afternoon) and open on Sat. Department
stores and supermarkets do not close for lunch and stay open
late on certain evenings. Many towns have fruit and vegetable
markets from Tues–Sat.

Post and telephone services
Post offices are marked by a blue bird on a white disc or by the
letters PTT, and are open Mon–Fri, 8.00–19.00, Sat
8.00–12.00 (small branches may have shorter hours and close
for lunch). Stamps can be bought from cafés, *tabacs*, hotels and
newsagents and from yellow coin-operated vending machines.
Letter boxes are also yellow and marked *boîte aux lettres*. Allow
7–10 days for a letter to travel between France and the US or
Canada, 2–3 days for a letter between France and the UK.
  Telegrams can be sent from a post office or over the
telephone.
  Public telephones are found in post offices and cafés as well as
in the streets. They take 50c, 1f and 5f pieces. **When dialling a
number, even a local one, you must now use all eight
figures, including the two-figure prefix shown in
brackets in this book.** The ringing signal is a shrill
intermittent tone, the engaged signal less shrill and more rapid.

Electric current
The electric current in France is 220V (50 cycles AC), although
a few country areas are on 110V AC. Plugs are usually standard
European two-pin, but occasionally you will find three-pin
sockets, so it is advisable to take an adaptor and a non-electric
razor with you.

11

Laws and regulations

There are no particularly surprising laws in France; laws against drug abuse are as strongly enforced as elsewhere, with greater penalties for the buying and selling of drugs. Naturism is allowed on certain beaches, and topless sunbathing is common on others. Hitch-hiking is forbidden on motorways, although it is tolerated on other roads.

Customs and etiquette

The French are among the most manner-conscious of all nations, and observe a rather rigid code of behaviour in personal relationships which is, however, just beginning to be broken down by the younger generation. This consciousness is exemplified by the *vous* and *tu* forms of address; the former applying to everyone except relations, close friends and children. Handshaking is common when greeting or saying goodbye among friends, as well as between acquaintances and strangers. When addressing someone, it is customary to say 'Madame' or 'Monsieur' without using a surname.

Tipping

Tipping is still widely practised in France, although most bars, restaurants and hotels include 15% service and taxes in their prices (*service compris*). If a meal or the service has been particularly good, you can show your appreciation by leaving a small tip for the waiter. For *service non compris*, a tip of 12–15% is advisable.

Small tips of up to a few francs should be given to cloakroom attendants, tour guides, doormen, hairdressers and cinema usherettes. Airport and railway porters have a fixed charge per item, while taxi drivers expect about 10–15%.

Disabled travellers

Special facilities for the disabled are becoming more and more usual in France and the French Government Tourist Office has some useful leaflets describing them. They also indicate, in their regional lists, which hotels are accessible to wheelchairs. The *Comité National Français de Liaison pour la Réadaptation des Handicapés* (38 Bd. Raspail, 75007 Paris) will give general advice and guidance to the handicapped person travelling in France. *RADAR* (25 Mortimer St., London W1) will also provide useful information.

Local publications

As well as the FGTO publications that can be obtained before departure you will find more specialized publications in *Syndicat d'Initiative* offices. Several local French newspapers such as *Nice-Matin* for the Côte d'Azur, *Le Provençal* and *Le Méridional* for Marseille, and *Le Mois à Aix* for Provence (published by the tourist office) also include up-to-date information.

Addresses and telephone numbers

Tourist information

An *Office de Tourisme* or *Syndicat d'Initiative* can be found in most towns and is there to help the visitor with travel and accommodation problems, and to supply local information. Tourist offices are indicated in this book by the symbol *i*.

These offices are open Mon–Fri 9.00–12.00, 14.00–18.00, and often during the weekends in the summer. They can be easily identified by the 'SI' sign. Some are combined with *Acceuil de France* offices and can make hotel reservations in other regions of France as well as in their own.

See *A–Z* for addresses of tourist offices of specific regions.

Telephone services

Weather   Alpes-Maritimes region ☎(93) 83–91–11 (for snow report ☎(93) 71–01–21); Marseille ☎(91) 90–35–00
Speaking clock   Nice ☎(93) 53–36–99; Marseille ☎(91) 91–84–00
Traffic report   Marseille ☎(91) 78–78–78; for all of France ☎(1) 48–58–33–33

Airlines
Marseille
Air France   Reservations: 14 La Canebière ☎(91) 54–92–92; Terminal: Gare St-Charles, Av. Pierre-Sémard ☎(91) 50–59–34
Air Inter   8 Rue des Fabres ☎(91) 54–77–21
Nice
Air France   Reservations: 7 Av. Gustave-V ☎(93) 21–32–32/ 83–91–00
Air Inter   4 Av. de Suède ☎(93) 31–55–55

Motoring organization
Touring Club de France
11 Allée Lion-Gambetta, Marseille ☎(91) 64–73–11

Tour operators
Tourist offices have details of local tours. The following companies in Marseille and Nice organize tours and provide information.
C.I.T.   3 Pl. Général-de-Gaulle, Marseille ☎(91) 33–66–00
Havas Voyages (American Express representatives)   20 La Canebière, Marseille ☎(91) 33–61–00
American Express   11 Promenade des Anglais, Nice ☎(93) 87–29–82
French Riviera Tours   38 Av. Auber, Nice ☎(93) 87–22–59

Main post offices
1 Rue Lapierre, Aix-en-Provence ☎(42) 27–68–00
13 Rue Henri-Barbusse, Marseille ☎(91) 00–50–00
Pl. Wilson, Nice ☎(93) 85–94–20

Major places of worship
There are, of course, many Catholic churches throughout the South of France. There is also a reasonable selection of Anglican churches which hold English services for the Anglo-American community.
   The major ones are as follows.
All Saints   Rue de Belloi, Marseille
Holy Trinity Anglo-American Church   11 Rue de la Buffa, Nice
St John   Av. Carnot, Menton
St John the Evangelist   Av. Paul-Doumer, St Raphael
Synagogues
117 Rue Breteuil, Marseille
7 Rue Gustave-Deloyé, Nice
1 Rue Boissy-d'Anglais, Nice

Basic information

Consulates

Austria★ 27 Cours Pierre-Puget, 13006 Marseille
☎(91) 53–02–08
Belgium★ 62 Cours Pierre Puget, 13286 Marseille
☎(91) 33–83–89/33–25–26
Canada 24 Av. du Prado, 13006 Marseille ☎(91) 37–19–37
Denmark★ 2 Rue Henri-Barbusse, 13001 Marseille
☎(91) 90–80–23
Finland 22 Quai de Lazaret, 13002 Marseille ☎(91) 91–91–62
Germany (West)★ 338 Av. du Prado, 13295 Marseille
☎(91) 77–60–90
Greece★ 538 Rue Paradis, 13008 Marseille ☎(91) 77–54–01
Italy★ 56 Rue D'Alger, 13005 Marseille ☎(91) 47–14–60
Japan 352 Av. du Prado, 13008 Marseille ☎(91) 71–61–67
Netherlands★ 25 Boulevard Edouard Herriot, 13008 Marseille
☎(91) 71–47–84
South Africa★ Le Gellion, 17 Bd. Augustin-Cieussa, 13007
Marseille ☎(91) 77–00–20
Spain★ 38 Rue E. Delanglade, 13006 Marseille
☎(91) 37–60–07
Sweden★ 376 Av. du Prado, 13008 Marseille ☎(91) 76–30–14
Switzerland★ 7 Rue D'Arcole, 13291 Marseille
☎(91) 53–36–65
UK★ 24 Av. du Prado, 13006 Marseille ☎(91) 53–43–32/
37–66–95
USA★ 13 Boulevard Paul Peytral, 13286 Marseille
☎(91) 54–92–00
★Also represented in Nice. (There is no representation for
Australia, Ireland and New Zealand.)

Conversion tables

Length								
cm	0	5	10	15	20	25	30	
in	0 1 2 3 4 5 6 7 8 9 10 11 12							
metres	0		0.5		1		1.5	2
ft/yd	0 1ft 2ft 3ft(1yd) 2yd							

Distance		
km	0 1 2 3 4 5 6 7 8 9 10 11 12 13 14 15 16	
miles	0 1 2 3 4 5 6 7 8 9 10	

Weight	(¼kg)	(½kg)	(¾kg)	(1kg)
grammes	0 100 200 300 400 500 600 700 800 900 1,000			
ounces	0 4 8 12 16 20 24 28 32			
	(¼lb) (½lb) (¾lb) (1lb) (1½lb) (2lb)			

Fluid measures			
litres	0 1 2 3 4 5	litres	0 5 10 20 30
imp.pints	0 1 2 3 4 5 6 7 8	imp. gallons	0 1 2 3 4 5 6
US pints	0 1 2 3 4 5 6 7 8	US gallons	0 1 2 3 4 5 6 7

Temperature chart		
°C	–15 –10 –5 0 5 10 15 20 25 30 35 40	100
°F	0 10 20 30 40 50 60 70 80 90 100 105	212

Emergency information

Emergency services
Police ☎17
Ambulance ☎18
Fire (*Sapeurs pompiers*) ☎18
There is no unified ambulance service – the operator will
offer you the numbers of several companies.

Other medical emergencies
Marseille hospital casualty wards operate on a rota system;
see a local paper for details. In Nice, go to *Centre Hospitalier
St-Roch*, 5 Rue Pierre-Devoluy ☎(93) 55–91–50, or
83–01–01 for a 24hr doctor service. Elsewhere, if you dial
for an ambulance, the driver will know where to take you.

Late-night chemists
Chemists in large towns stay open on a rota basis; see the
window of any chemist or a local paper for a list.
    There are all-night chemists at: *Pharmacie du Chapître*, 10
Sq. Stalingrad, Marseille ☎(91) 62–54–76, and *Pharmacie
Principale*, 10 Rue Masséna, Nice ☎(93) 87–85–48.

Motoring accidents
—Do not admit liability or incriminate yourself.
—Ask any witness(es) to stay and give a statement.
—Contact the police.
—Exchange names, addresses, car details and insurance
  company details with any other drivers involved.
—In serious accidents, ask the police to contact the sheriff's
  clerk (*huissier*) to make out a legally acceptable account of
  the incident. You will have to pay for his services, but in
  any dispute his report will be accepted as authoritative.

Car breakdowns
—Put on flashing hazard warning lights, and place a
  warning triangle 50m (55yd) behind the car.
—Telephone police, who will arrange a breakdown van to
  collect you; ring the *Touring Club de France* if you are a
  member of a motoring club affiliated to this association.
  Either the police or the *Touring Club de France* will advise
  you on the nearest appropriate garage. If in a hired car,
  ring the number you have been given.

Lost passport/travellers cheques
Passport: Contact the local police immediately, and your
nearest consulate who can give you emergency travel
documents. (See *Consulates* opposite.)
Travellers cheques: Contact the local police immediately,
and your consulate if you are stranded with no money. Not
all banks issue on-the-spot refunds for lost travellers
cheques. Your travellers cheques will include instructions
on how to proceed if you lose them.

Emergency phrases
Help! *Au secours!*
There has been an accident. *Il y a eu un accident.*
Where is the nearest telephone/hospital? *Où se trouve le
téléphone/l'hôpital le plus proche?*
Call a doctor/ambulance! *Appelez un médecin/une
ambulance!*
Call the police! *Appelez la police!*

Introduction

When non-Frenchmen speak of "the South of France" they are usually referring to that celebrated easterly corner, the true name of which is Provence – the old Roman *Provincia*. And Provence is the subject of this book: the 320km (200 mile) stretch of coast, plain and mountain from the Rhône delta to the Alps.

It is enchanted ground. Art and landscape, wine and sunshine, ancient history and modern sophistication fuse into an alchemy that makes a heady impact on mind and senses alike. No other part of Europe, nor perhaps of the world, offers so dazzling a density and variety of interest in one relatively small area. For 2,500yr Provence has been a meeting place of civilizations and each has left a strong imprint, so that almost every bend in the road reveals something surprising and different – be it medieval abbey or modern art museum.

This is the land where the Roman legions passed, leaving behind them the Pont du Gard, and the great arenas at Arles and Nîmes. It is the land where the troubadours sang in the gaunt castle of Les Baux, and where the Popes held sway in their palace at Avignon; the land, too, where the crowned heads of Europe came to gamble at Monte-Carlo in the Belle Époque – now as much a part of history as Romans or troubadours – and where Picasso painted in the castle at Antibes. Today, Provence is more than ever a land of contrasts: oil refineries and nuclear power stations in the lower Rhône valley; remote medieval mountain villages; Cannes and Nice with their traffic jams and tower blocks of modern luxury flats; St-Tropez with its trendy youth.

O, for a draught of vintage! that hath been
Cool'd a long time in the deep-delved earth,
Tasting of Flora and the country green,
Dance, and Provençal song, and sunburnt mirth!
John Keats, *Ode to a Nightingale*

Unlike the rest of France, save neighbouring Languedoc, Provence is quintessentially Mediterranean. Drive down from the north, over the mountains or via the Rhône valley, and you cross that mysterious cultural frontier that separates Europe's north from its south. Suddenly the sun beats stronger, the light is clearer, the air drier. Hills terraced with vines and olives roll to blue horizons; the air carries the scent of pines, or maybe a hint of wild thyme or lavender; a lone cypress stands by a stone barn against the skyline. In village squares, under shady plane trees, old men play *boules* or drink *pastis* with black olives; and out in the fields the special white light of Provence dazzles and reflects on the chalky hillsides. Even in winter the air is usually clear and bright – but Provence then is whipped periodically by its icy north wind, the Mistral. It is the price that nature exacts for so much idyllic beauty.

The scenery is extremely diverse. To the w, on either side of the Rhône, the country is mostly flat and fertile, covered with olive groves, orchards and vineyards, though the plains are broken by several ranges of barren limestone hills. Further E, much of Provence is wild and mountainous, from the rocky plateau of Vaucluse to the sub-alpine slopes behind Nice that rise up to the snow-capped Alps along the Italian frontier. Nearer the coast, hilly forests of pine, oak and cork alternate with luxuriant valleys which in spring are carpeted with flowers, especially with fragrant mimosa. The coast itself from Marseille to Italy is one of Europe's most beautiful, a succession of rocky headlands and wooded coves, strung with palm and cypress trees, exotic cacti and bright flowers. This is the famous *Côte d'Azur*. But nothing is more striking in Provence than the contrast between this hectic, crowded coast and the silent hinterland, serene and unspoilt, that begins just a few miles inland.

The strongest memories of Provence are colour-memories. It is a country in which colour seems more important than form.
James Pope-Hennessy, *Aspects of Provence*, 1952

Upon this landscape, history lies in dense layers. Ancient Celto-Ligurian tribes, Greek colonizers, Roman conquerors, destructive barbarians, all came here in their turn. Provence in the past 30yr has been swept forward by a great tide of modernization and growing prosperity – even if, as in other countries, this has levelled off in the past few anxious years. Improvements in farming have led to a huge rural exodus: only some 10% of people today work on the land, against 35% in 1945. The overall population has been growing fast, too, due to the sunny south's appeal to migrants from Paris and elsewhere, but also to the return from Algeria in 1962 of nearly a million French colonists, about a third of whom settled in Provence, where the towns have mushroomed in size with large new suburbs. Today, despite the strength of its peasant roots, Provence is above all a sophisticated urban society – and this is not confined to the chic resorts of the coast: in their way, towns to the W such as Aix and Avignon are sophisticated too. And everywhere, for better or for worse, are the trappings of modernity – gigantic supermarkets, new student campuses outside Aix and Marseille, and (all too apparent) one of Europe's highest levels of car-ownership. Even the French telephone service, that old bad joke, has suddenly become ultra-modern.

The people and their language
These material changes have little affected the basic character and temperament of the Provençaux. Like other meridionals, they are less reserved, more instinctive and passionate, than Parisians or other northerners. A Provençal may quickly fly into a temper, but without malice, and minutes later he will have his arm round your shoulder, offering to buy you a drink. He has the quality known as *"bon enfant"*, a good-natured ability to make quick human contact; rather in the Italian manner, he enjoys endless feuding but without taking it entirely seriously. He works hard (the French, even in the south, have never been lazy people) but is not too bothered with punctuality and is adept at twisting or quietly ignoring rules. These traits are true especially of Marseillais with their earthy, plebeian humour; also of some country areas where the tempo of life is still agreeably slow. In the cosmopolitan resorts such as Cannes and Nice, people do, however, tend to be rather more reserved, like Parisians – maybe made blasé by so much tourism.

The people of Provence are usually dark, often swarthy, and stockily-built. They speak French with the twangy accent of the south (*"Bong-jourr!"*), harsh and grating in the cities, more melodious in country areas. In olden times their daily language

17

Culture, history and background

was Provençal, which is a version of Occitan, the common
tongue of southern France in the Middle Ages; the Papal court
at Avignon used Provençal. But after c.1550 pressures from
Paris enforced the introduction of French, and by the mid-
19thC Provençal had disappeared from daily use except in
country districts. The poet Mistral then made efforts to revive
it, but had little success outside literary circles. Today, as in his
day, there is a vogue among local intellectuals for the study of
Provençal, helped by the fact that government curbs are now
eased (it can even be taught in schools). But the Provençaux
seldom respond: they find it far more practical to speak French.
Today very few of them use Provençal as a daily tool, while not
many even understand it. Its preservation has become artificial
– a pity, for it is a beautiful language.

Farming, industry and tourism
The economy of the region relies heavily on produce from the
land, on new industries and, of course, on holiday-makers.
Agriculture is very varied. Sunshine, a fertile soil and good
irrigation conspire to make the lower Rhône valley the foremost
market garden of France, exporting its early fruit and
vegetables to Paris and many parts of Europe – melons,
strawberries, peaches, asparagus, and much else. In the
Camargue, rice is cultivated. The chalky soil of Provence is
good terrain both for vine and olive: some 450,000 acres are
under vine, mostly in the Rhône valley and the Var, while
Provence is France's leading producer of olives and olive oil, as
well as of almonds. In the lush valleys behind Cannes, flowers
are cultivated on a massive scale (mainly roses, jasmin, violets,
carnations), for the cut-flower markets of Europe and to make
essences for the perfume industry of Grasse. Lavender grows on
the hills further w, while lemons are a speciality of the sheltered
coast at Menton. All along the coast, the fishing ports are active.
Many upland areas are used for sheep-grazing, and bulls are
reared on the plains of the Camargue: however, Provence is not
a major livestock-breeding region.

Everywhere in country areas you will see the traditional
Provençal farmsteads and villas. They have roofs of red terra
cotta tiles and stone walls; the main doors and windows face s,
while northern walls are often blind, as a protection against the
Mistral. A farmhouse, large or small, is called a mas (from the
Latin mansum, like 'mansion' and 'maison'). Rather similar to it
is the bastide, a small country house, usually square. Inside
these buildings, typical Provençal decor consists of red-tiled
floors, beamed ceilings, sturdily handsome wooden furniture,
and stone walls often hung with copper pots. This rural style
today is studiously imitated by a great many modern hotels,
restaurants and villas, alike in their architecture and decor: the
results may be monotonous, but at least in keeping with
tradition.

Only since the war has Provence been developed on any scale
as a region of modern advanced industries. But it has long had
its traditional industries based on the exploitation of local
resources – bauxite mining at Brignoles, ochre quarrying near
Apt, cork production in the Maures forests, and salt-works at
Hyères and on the edge of the Camargue. All these are still
active – and so, more than ever, is the pastis (aperitif) industry
of Marseille.

Marseille, La Ciotat and Toulon have long been centres of
shipbuilding and repairing, but these industries are today in

18

decline. The Marseille area still has a number of engineering and food-processing firms. But since the war the industrial centre of gravity has shifted westward, to the lake of Berre and the new port and manufacturing centre of Fos. Here are some of France's main oil refineries, as well as chemical works and Europe's largest helicopter factory. The new steelworks at Fos have inevitably been hit by the European steel crisis.

In the Durance valley, and beside the Rhône, N of Avignon, there are several important nuclear stations and hydro-electric works: they do not always enhance the landscape, nor please ecologists, but they help provide Provence with the energy it needs. Over to the E, the Nice/Cannes area has found an entirely new vocation to complement high-class tourism, for it is now marked out as a pilot zone for high technology research. In the mid-1970s the government created an 'international scientific park' at Valbonne, near Antibes, where several firms have now built advanced laboratories; and IBM has a large research centre nearby, at La Gaude. Companies do not find it hard to persuade their scientists and executives to come and work on the *Côte*.

Tourism, none the less, still takes pride of place in Provence. The Alpes-Maritimes (along the E part of the *Côte d'Azur*) has over four million visitors a year, half of them foreign. The tourists come to bathe or to gamble, to ski or water-ski, to explore the museums or enjoy Provençal cooking – or maybe for all this at once. They stay in luxury hotels or country inns, in rented farmsteads up in the quiet hills, or herded together in the ritzy camping-sites along the coast where the pine groves in summer are studded with blue and orange tents. The *Côte d'Azur* has changed radically since the 19thC when its mild winter climate first made it fashionable as Europe's leading playground of the rich. Until the 1920s, winter was the smart season on the coast, when the leisured and titled would come with their retinues to escape the foggy northern climate; in summer, tourists were few. Today, it is almost the reverse: the coast is crowded in summer, half dead in winter. However, some larger resorts do remain busy all year thanks to the recent development of so-called 'business tourism', the congress trade. What better pretext for combining work with pleasure than to be flown by your firm, all expenses paid, to attend some seminar or conference in out-of-season Cannes or Monte-Carlo? These towns today depend heavily on this trade.

The *Côte's* five main resorts are intriguingly different, each with its own persona. Flowery Menton, favoured by the elderly, has a cosy feminine prettiness and a genteel, old-fashioned air. Monte-Carlo, just 8km (5 miles) away, is a total contrast: very up-to-date, brashly glamorous, more than a little Americanized, a town of skyscrapers and publicity-conscious jetsetters. Nice, the *Côte's* largest city by far, has a lively, year-round commercial and social life of its own. Cannes is much smaller than Nice but smarter, an efficient and glittering showcase of up-market tourism. And St-Tropez, newest of the big resorts, is an unclassifiable hotch-potch of picturesque fishing port, fashion venue and gaudy bazaar. So has mass tourism spoilt the *Côte d'Azur*, as some people feel? Or is the tourist invasion all part of the fun, the latest of Provence's many fascinating layers of civilization? Each visitor has his or her own response. If you hate the crowds, then leave for the hinterland, as unruffled and majestic as the days before the Roman legions came.

19

Time chart

Greek and early Roman period

c.600BC   Greeks from Asia Minor founded Massalia (Marseille), their first colony in Provence, then inhabited by primitive Ligurian tribes.

540BC   The Carthaginians occupied Marseille.

480BC   The Greeks of Massalia created trading posts at Glanum, Antibes, Nice, and other towns.

218BC   Hannibal crossed the Alps into northern Italy, via Upper Provence (Sisteron area).

123BC   The Romans under Sextius destroyed the Celto-Ligurian stronghold at Egremont, N of Aix, then founded a thermal station at Aix.

102BC   The Roman general Marius defeated the invading Teuton hordes near Aix.

51BC   Julius Caesar conquered Gaul and founded the major
–49BC   port of Fréjus.

49BC   In the civil war, Marseille sided with Pompey against the victorious Caesar, and was made to suffer for it.

19BC   Agrippa built the Pont-du-Gard.

Later Roman period

1st–   Roman civilization spread over Provence, with the
2ndCAD growth of important towns at Cimiez (Nice), Antibes, Fréjus, Marseille, Arles, Nîmes, Glanum (St-Rémy), Orange, Vaison-la-Romaine, Riez. The Emperor Aurelius built the Aurelian Way from Rome through Provence into Spain.

313   The Emperor Constantine, converted to Christianity, gave full freedom to Christians under the Edict of Milan.

400   Arles, now at the height of its glory, was made capital of the 'Three Gauls' (France, Spain, Britain) by the Emperor Honorius.

4th–   Christianity took root in Provence; St-Cassien
5thC   founded the abbey of St-Victor at Marseille (413).

476   Fall of the Roman Empire.

Dark Ages, Middle Ages and Renaissance

5th–   Provence was invaded successively by Vandals,
6thC   Visigoths, Franks, and other barbarian hordes, causing much devastation.

597   At Arles, St Augustine was consecrated first Bishop of England by the Bishop of Arles. The Saracens (Moors) from North Africa repeatedly invaded Provence, laying waste many coastal towns.

800   In Rome, Charlemagne was crowned Emperor of the West.

843   By the Treaty of Verdun, Charlemagne's empire was split up between the three sons of Louis the Debonair: Lothaire, the eldest, received Provence as well as Burgundy and Lorraine.

855   Lothaire elevated Provence into a kingdom, and his son Charles was crowned.

962   Creation of the Holy Roman Empire.

10th–   After frequently changing hands, Provence joined the
11thC   Holy Roman Empire. But the Counts of Provence retained a high degree of autonomy.

12thC   Aix became capital of the Counts of Provence. Their realm fell under the sway of the Counts of Toulouse, and later of the Counts of Barcelona.

1226– 70	Reign of St Louis, King of France, who embarked for the seventh Crusade at Aigues-Mortes (1248) and returned from it to Hyères (1254).
1308	A member of the Grimaldi family bought Monaco from the Genoese, thus making it into an independent lordship.
1388	Nice detached itself from Provence and joined the Earldom of Savoy, in Italy.
1409	Founding of Aix University.
1434– 80	The 'Good King René' ruled at Aix as Count of Provence, ushering in a golden era of prosperity.

Reunion to Revolution

1481	René's nephew, Charles of Maine, bequeathed Provence to Louis XI of France. In 1488, Provence's incorporation into the kingdom of France was ratified.
1501	The Parliament of Provence was set up at Aix, with some regional autonomy in matters political and judicial.
1545	The Vaudois, Protestant heretics of the Lubéron, were massacred on the orders of François I.
1562– 98	The eight 'Wars of Religion' between Catholics and Protestants, resulting from the Reformation.
1632	Richelieu destroyed the ramparts and castles at Les Baux, Beaucaire, Uzès, and other towns with Protestant sympathies.
1660	Louis XIV, the Sun King, visited Marseille after crushing revolts there.
1713	The Dutch House of Nassau ceded Orange to France, under the Treaty of Utrecht.
1720	A great plague, contracted from Syria, killed some 100,000 people in Provence, half of them in Marseille.
1746	In the War of the Austrian Succession, the Austro-Sardinian armies advanced as far as Antibes, but were then turned back.
1763	The English novelist Tobias Smollett spent a year in Nice, thus starting the English vogue for tourism on the Riviera.
1789	Mirabeau's election to the States-General, as deputy for Aix, helped pave the way for the Revolution. The beginning of the French Revolution: the storming of the Bastille on July 14 in Paris.

Napoleonic Wars and the 19thC

1790	The Revolutionary Government deprived Provence of its semi-autonomy and carved it up into three *'départements'* of the new centralized France.
1791	Avignon and the Comtat Venaissin, hitherto a Papal protectorate, were incorporated into France.
1792	500 Marseillais volunteers marched through Paris singing the *Battle Hymn of the Army of the Rhine* which thus became *La Marseillaise.*
1793	Execution in Paris of Louis XVI. Napoleon first won fame at the Siege of Toulon. Nice was re-attached to France.
1799	After the fall of the government of the Directoire, Napoleon became First Consul of France.
1804	Napoleon assumed the title of Emperor.
1805	The British defeated the French fleet at Trafalgar.
1812	Napoleon defeated the Russians at Borodino, captured Moscow, but was later forced to retreat.
1814	Napoleon abdicated, on April 6; and sailed from

	St-Raphael for exile on Elba on April 28.
1815	Napoleon returned from Elba, landing at Golfe-Juan on March 1. He marched N along the Route Napoléon, but was defeated at Waterloo on June 18.
1822	British residents at Nice financed the building of the Promenade des Anglais, named after them.
1834	Creation of the Félibrige, Provençal literary movement, by Frédéric Mistral and his friends.
1860	Nice was finally re-attached to France.
1865	The Monte-Carlo Casino was opened.
1869	The opening of the Suez Canal set Marseille's commerce booming.
1870– 71	Franco-Prussian War: end of the French monarchy, and birth of the Third Republic.

The 20thC

1910	Opening of Monaco's Oceanographic Institute.
1932	Paul Ricard created his *pastis* firm at Marseille.
1934	King Alexander of Yugoslavia was assassinated in Marseille.
1939	Inauguration of the Cannes Film Festival.
1940	After the German victory in June, France was divided into two, with Provence forming part of the Non-Occupied Zone ruled from Vichy.
1942	Nov: after the Allied occupation of North Africa, the Germans at once seized Provence and the rest of the Vichy Zone, but Vichy's fleet eluded them by scuttling itself at Toulon.
1944	Aug 15: the Allied Armies landed on the *Côte d'Azur*, and liberated all Provence within two weeks. Creation of the Fourth Republic.
1947	Jean Vilar founded the Avignon Theatre Festival.
1952	Le Corbusier's avant-garde Unité d'Habitation building at Marseille was completed.
1953	Gaston Defferre elected Mayor of Marseille.
1954	Start of the Algerian War.
1956	Prince Rainier III of Monaco wed Grace Kelly.
1957	Treaty of Rome was signed, giving birth to the European Economic Community.
1958	De Gaulle returned to power; Fifth Republic born.
1959	Malpasset dam disaster at Fréjus: hundreds perished.
1962	Algeria won independence after 8yr of war; some 800,000 French colonists returned to France, many of them settling in Provence.
1965	Work started on the port and industrial complex at Fos.
1969	De Gaulle resigned; Pompidou elected President.
1970	Paris-to-Marseille autoroute completed.
1973	Under Pompidou's reforms, an indirectly elected Council with some limited powers was set up in Provence, as in the other 21 French regions.
1974	The death of Pompidou; Giscard d'Estaing elected President.
1977	Marseille's Metro was opened.
1981	François Mitterrand elected President. New Socialist Government granted some internal autonomy to Provence and the other regions.
1986	March: the Right won general election; Jacques Chirac appointed Prime Minister. Provence, too, turned Right, electing conservative majority for its first directly-mandated Assembly.

Architecture

The architecture of Provence is marvellously varied. Most of the major styles are represented, from Roman to ultra modern. The buildings, made mostly of local limestone, harmonize not only with each other but with the landscape.

Roman (1stC BC to 3rdC AD)

Western Provence, the heart of the Roman *Provincia* of Gaul, contains the best-preserved assortment of Roman buildings outside Italy. There are massive, grandiose public buildings such as the theatre of *Orange* and the arenas at *Arles* and *Nîmes*, and a fine example of Roman engineering in the magnificent *Pont-du-Gard* aqueduct. The Romans were also capable of finesse, as can be seen in the elegant proportions of the Maison Carrée temple at *Nîmes* and the carvings on the triumphal arches at *Carpentras*, *Orange* and *St-Rémy*. At *Vaison-la-Romaine* you can study the remains of Roman domestic architecture.

Gallo-Roman and Merovingian (5th–8thC)

Virtually all that survives are some octagonal baptistries, such as those at *Aix*, *Fréjus*, *Riez* and Venasque (see *Carpentras*).

Romanesque (11th–12thC)

The 12thC was the golden age of Provençal architecture, producing a style of Romanesque that is readily distinguishable from its Norman counterpart and seen at its purest in the Cistercian abbeys of *Sénanque* and *Thoronet*. The influence of Roman antiquity is clearly visible in the fine limestone masonry (sometimes incorporating fragments from Roman ruins) and some of the carvings. The churches are generally in the form of a cross, with a semi-circular apse at the end of a broad nave, which often has no side aisles. The few small windows barely dissipate the austere, sparsely decorated gloom, but the tall pillars and barrel vaulting give a sense of space. West fronts are sometimes richly sculpted, as at St-Sauveur (see *Aix*), St-Trophîme and St-Gilles (see *Arles*). Magnificent carved capitals can be seen in the cloister galleries of St-Trophîme, Montmajour (see *Arles*) and *St-Rémy*.

Gothic (12th–15thC)

The Gothic style, which originated in northern France, is marked by more ornate decoration and the use of pointed arches, ribbed vaulting and flying buttresses. These new techniques made it possible to liberate space for larger windows (often of stained glass), reducing the solidity of the walls and flooding the interior with light. The overall effect is of a soaring, vertical quality, in contrast to the horizontal and rounded lines of the Romanesque. The Gothic style is not well represented in the region apart from the cloisters at *Fréjus* and the Basilica of St-Maximin (see *St-Maximin-la-Ste-Baume*). The final phase, ornate and exuberant, is known as Flamboyant Gothic because of its flame-like window tracery and columns, best seen in the facades of St-Siffrein at *Carpentras* and St-Sauveur (see *Aix*). Other notable Gothic buildings are the abbey at *St-Maximin* and the newer part of the Papal Palace at *Avignon*.

Military architecture

In the Middle Ages, kings and feudal lords built castles for protection, usually on hill tops (for example, *Sisteron*) but sometimes on the plain (as in *Tarascon*). Each castle has a keep (*donjon*), turreted battlements, often with machicolation (parapets with apertures for dropping missiles or molten lead on assailants), and maybe a moat too if it is on a plain. Some early

23

churches, such as those at *Les Stes-Maries* and *Marseille* (St-Victor), have battlements and a fortress-like look, for they were constructed partly as a refuge against Saracen and other invaders. *Aigues-Mortes* is a perfect example of a medieval walled city. In the 15thC the arrival of heavy cannons made this kind of defence obsolete, but in the 17thC Louis XIV's great military architect, Vauban, built a series of far more impregnable forts; some can be seen above *Toulon*.

Renaissance and Classical (*16th–18thC*)
The Renaissance style in France, a synthesis of French medieval and Italian Renaissance, is marked by a return to Greek and Roman forms, with Classical columns, balustrades and pediments. Despite the proximity of Italy, however, it never caught on widely in Provence, although its influence can be seen in some facades, courtyards and stairways, as in the ducal palace at *Uzès*. The more ornate Classicism of the 17thC and the 18thC left a much stronger mark, notably in the many *hôtels* (mansions) in the heart of *Avignon* and *Aix*. Mansart built the town halls at *Marseille* and *Arles*.

Eclecticism (*19thC*)
The 19thC was an age of stylistic revivals, reflecting the opulent

The Roman arena at Nîmes, one of the best preserved in the world, still gives a vivid picture of what life was like in those days.

Lacking the heaviness of much Roman architecture, Nîmes' **Maison Carrée** is one of the most beautiful Roman temples surviving today.

The pointed arches of the lower arcade in the **cloister** at Fréjus are one of the few signs in Provence of Gothic architecture.

Aigues-Mortes, chosen as a port for the Crusades, is a marvellous example of a perfectly preserved medieval walled city.

self-confidence (and dubious taste) of that age. *Marseille* contains good examples: the New Cathedral and the Basilica of Notre-Dame-de-la-Garde (both Neo-Byzantine) and the Palais Longchamp (Neo-Baroque). In the Belle Époque (late 19thC, early 20thC) the growth of aristocratic tourism on the Riviera produced a number of equally grandiose buildings.

Post-1945

Le Corbusier, France's most famous modern architect and a specialist in low-cost housing, designed one seminal work in Provence: the Unité d'Habitation at *Marseille*, a huge block of flats on massive supports which was to form part of the never-completed Cité Radieuse. The 'neo-gigantism' in vogue in France in the 1960s and early 1970s produced a more dubious legacy, as exemplified by the pyramid blocks of the Marina-Baie-des-Anges near *Antibes*. Rather more tasteful and imaginative new trends include some cleverly designed museums of modern art (notably the Fondation Maeght at *St-Paul-de-Vence* and the Fondation Vasarely at *Aix*) and the large-scale holiday complexes of *Port-Grimaud* and Port-la-Galère (see *Théoule*), built in a pastiche vernacular style to blend harmoniously with the landscape.

The **Château du Duché**, or Ducal Palace, at Uzès is a mixture of styles, but the stately facade of the living quarters shows a Renaissance influence.

The Neo-Baroque **Palais Longchamp**, which houses two of Marseille's foremost museums, is an example of the overblown architecture of the 19thC.

Le Corbusier's controversial **Unité d'Habitation** (1952) is part of the abandoned **Cité Radieuse** project, in Marseille.

The arts in Provence

Across the centuries a number of great artists and writers – the troubadours, Mistral, Fragonard, Cézanne – have emerged from Provence. The region is even more important, however, as a place of inspiration for outsiders. From Petrarch to Picasso, countless artists and writers, and musicians too, have been seduced by the beauty of Provence, by the brilliant light and vivid colours, by the people and their traditions, and, in the 1920s and 30s, by the glamour and sparkle of the Riviera. The spell that it has cast, for whatever reason, on so dazzling an array of great painters – Picasso, Matisse, Van Gogh, Chagall, Renoir, to name but a few – has left the region with a marvellous heritage of paintings in its museums, while the writings of Petrarch, Mistral, Daudet, Fitzgerald, Durrell and others capture in words its magical appeal.

Art: The Provençal schools

Influenced by the Italian Renaissance, Provence developed its own schools of religious painting. In the late 15thC a school of 'primitives' flourished at Nice, led by the prolific Louis Bréa, his brother and nephew. Their works, mainly retables (painted wooden screens above the altar) can be seen in many churches of the Nice hinterland (often far-flung ones since they were commissioned mainly by monks). Perhaps the best examples of their work are in the church at Lucéram. In the same period, Enguerrand Charenton (or Quarton) was working at Avignon (his masterly *Coronation of the Virgin* is at nearby Villeneuve), while Nicolas Froment was King René's court painter at Aix (his extraordinary *Burning Bush* is in the cathedral there). These two artists were among the founders of the so-called Avignon school which continued in various guises until the 19thC. In the 17thC its leading lights were Nicolas Mignard and the Parrocel family, whose works are in many local churches.

In the 17thC Provençal artists began to turn to secular as well as religious subjects. Pierre Puget of Marseille, Provence's greatest sculptor, chose Greek classical themes, like Bernini, to whom he is sometimes compared. His best works are in Paris and Italy, but there are others at Marseille and Toulon. The Van Loos, a Dutch family who lived and worked at Aix and Nice in the 18thC, are known for their vividly coloured portraits and *genre* paintings: the Musée Cheret at Nice has a particularly good collection. Provence's greatest native painter of the 18thC was an emigrant, Pierre Fragonard. Though born in Grasse, he spent most of his working life in Italy and Paris, concentrating on frothy and sensuous subjects that delighted a frivolous age.

Impressionism and beyond

Ever since Impressionism changed the face of art in the 1870s Provence has been a constant magnet for painters. The Impressionists were much concerned with the effects of light, and under the Mediterranean sun they found an unsurpassed clarity and luminosity. Paul Cézanne (later to diverge from the Impressionists both in ethos and technique) was born in Aix in 1839, and spent much of his later life there painting the landscape he loved: chalky hills, lone cypresses and red-roofed farmsteads. His searching analysis of colour and tone led him to paint again and again, in varying lights, the glowering pyramid of Mont Ste-Victoire. Van Gogh too was inspired to a savage passion by the sun, sky and scenery around Arles and St-Rémy where he spent the last 2yr of his life, in and out of mental institutions. His northern Protestant soul, however, never took to the local lifestyle which he called "rather squalid". None of his work, and more surprisingly, very little of Cézanne's – is in local museums.

Towards the turn of the century artists moved towards the increasingly popular *Côte d'Azur*. In 1892, the Neo-Impressionist Paul Signac settled in the then unknown fishing village of St-Tropez, thus setting a trend. Bonnard, Matisse, Dunoyer de Ségonzac and others would spend their summers in this little port, the museum of which today houses much of their lively land- and seascapes. Further along the coast, at Cagnes-sur-Mer, Renoir spent the last 12yr of his life until 1919, and though by then crippled with arthritis he painted joyously until the end.

After 1918, leading artists formed a virtual colony on the *Côte*. Matisse lived at Cimiez (Nice) and Vence from 1917 until his death in 1954. His feeling for colour matured here and it was in his studio at Cimiez that he painted the odalisques and still-life subjects that form his main *oeuvre*.

Picasso did not settle in Provence until 1945, but his short period at Antibes, 1946–47, was among the most creative of his long career, and works such as *Ulysses and the Sirens* were clearly inspired by the setting. His move to the nearby pottery centre of Vallauris brought a new outlet for his versatile genius and he devoted much of his later life to ceramics.

Marc Chagall, likewise, did not move to the *Côte* till late in life but found there a new inspiration: witness the luminous Mediterranean colours of the *Biblical Message* in his museum at Nice, painted at Vence when he was in his seventies. Léger and Vasarely are other artists who have lived or worked in Provence, though its influence on their work is less direct. (The Musée Léger is at Biot, Vasarely at Gordes and Aix.) Cocteau, however, was romantically fascinated by the life of Provençal fisher folk, as can be seen by his murals at Menton and Villefranche. Dufy, too, never failed to catch the dash and vivacity of the *Côte d'Azur*, especially Nice, where he lived.

Literature: The Provençal masters

The region's earliest known writers were the troubadours, lyric poets of the 12th and 13thC. The vogue for troubadours flourished all over southern France, more in Gascony and Languedoc than in Provence itself where the main centre was the feudal castle of Les Baux. They wrote and sang in Occitan, the old language of the South of France; court poets and musicians attached to noble families, their theme was love – patient, chaste and courtly love for beautiful women (often their employers' wives).

For centuries after the troubadours had flourished, Provence produced no dominant writers, save Nostradamus, the prophet and astrologer, in the 16thC. It was not until 1854 that cultural life in the region was revitalized: a group of young poets in the Avignon/Arles area, led by Frédéric Mistral, founded a movement which they named the Félibrige, after a Provençal folk tale. These poets were not nationalists in a political sense, but they resented the suppression of Provençal culture by Napoleon's new centralized France, and passionately they embarked on a crusade to renew local interest in the region's history, customs, spirit and language. Their success in

Provence was only modest, though they did promote a new
regional awareness. And they caused a great stir in French
literary circles, for Mistral himself was a poet of undoubted
genius who some critics – including Lamartine – equated with
Homer and Dante. The judgement is not easy to assess, for he
wrote only in Provençal, abhorring French. *Miréio* (*Mireille* in
French), the tale of a girl's tragic love affair in the Camargue, is
one of the most celebrated of his epic poems of Provençal rural
life. Romantic, full-blooded, handsome and generous, he was
able to fire any visitor with his own fervent love for the land
where he spent all his life (in a village s of Avignon). In his
lifetime a cult grew around him, which is still alive today. He
was awarded the Nobel Prize for Literature in 1904.

To Mistral western Provence was enchanted ground. He had
felt for it from childhood just as violently as Sir Walter Scott had
felt for the Border country, and like him he harvested the
folk-tales, compounds of historic incident and pure legend, and
wove his poems from them, peopling a whole countryside with
imaginary characters, witches, magicians, lovers and antique
heroes. He had the same burning regional patriotism as Sir
Walter, the same wildly romantic reactions to some ruined keep
or Roman stone. As Scott cared for the old Border ballads, so
Mistral cared for the traditional love songs of Provence, in many
of which could be heard echoes of the melodies of the
troubadours . . . He did, like Scott, succeed in making a whole
countryside vocal, and in forcing upon the attentions of the
outside world the existence of Provence, and its intense
individuality.

James Pope-Hennessy, *Aspects of Provence*, 1952

The Provençal influence

The first of an illustrious line of non-Provençal writers
influenced by the region was the Italian poet Petrarch. He
moved with his parents to the Papal court at Avignon when he
was a child in 1312, and though he hated Avignon itself and its
corrupt court he was inspired by the nearby Fountain of
Vaucluse where he spent 16yr, by the abbey of Sénanque, and
by his pure passion for Laura, a lady of Avignon.

In the 18thC, well-known English travellers such as Tobias
Smollett and Arthur Young wrote vividly about Provence.
Then, when the Riviera grew fashionable, it began to attract the
writers of all nations – and Cannes, Nice and 'Monte' became
the settings of a multitude of novels both good and bad.
Somerset Maugham lived a long while at Cap Ferrat, and
Katherine Mansfield a short while at Menton: both set some of
their best stories on the *Côte*. Aldous Huxley lived at Sanary,
Gertrude Stein at St-Rémy, Colette at St-Tropez. In the 1930s,
Cyril Connolly set his cutting novel *The Rock Pool*, at Cagnes-
sur-Mer; and in *Tender is the Night* Scott Fitzgerald described
his life among the debauched American socialites of Cap
d'Antibes. Today, Anthony Burgess lives near Grasse and
Lawrence Durrell near Nîmes (his novel, *Monsieur*, was set at
Avignon), while the eminent French novelist J.M.G. Le Clézio
has his home at Nice. And to prove that the region still exerts
influence on literature, though not necessarily for the same
reasons, a recent work by Graham Greene, who lives in
Antibes, is *J'Accuse*, a dossier of corruption and gang warfare in
Nice.

Provençal folklore and traditions

It is inevitable that many of the traditions so beloved of Mistral are no longer a part of daily Provençal life. Even in Arles the old costumes have disappeared from the streets. However, as in other parts of France today, efforts are being made to revive the traditions – if only for special occasions or festivals. Scores of new folk groups have been formed in recent years, and if the revival is sometimes less spontaneous than self-consciously cultural, it is better than letting the old customs disappear.

One tradition that has never died out is the *fête*, held annually in almost every town and village, and often on various saints' days at other times of the year. On these occasions there is much dancing and festivity and colour. The *farandole* may be danced to the sound of *tambourins* (narrow drums) and *galoubets* (three-holed flutes). Old traditions are best preserved in western Provence, where three or four day festivals that include bull races and horse displays as well as dancing take place at Nîmes, Arles, Les Saintes-Maries-de-la-Mer and other larger towns. East of Marseille there are carnivals known as *bravades*, notably at St-Tropez and, E again, around Nice, there are flower battles and flower parades. (See *Calendar of events* in *Planning* for all main dates.)

Cribs and santons

The Christmas crib arrived from Italy in the 17thC and has been popular ever since. In the 18thC puppetry was very popular and the 'talking crib' came into vogue. This was a mechanized puppet show of the Nativity story accompanied by words and carol-singing. In the late 18thC the *santon* ('little saint') was invented in Marseille and enjoyed a huge vogue throughout the 19thC. *Santons* are costumed clay figurines, usually some 46cm (18in) high. Initially they represented just the figures of the Nativity story, but soon the range was widened to include Provençal stock types such as the drummer, the *gendarme*, the drunkard, the Camargue cowboy. Many a family still has its *santon* collection, either for a crib at Christmas in the *salon* or purely as secular ornaments; and *santons* today are still widely manufactured, for sale to local people as well as tourists – Marseille has its *santon* fair every Dec. In many churches from Christmas to late Jan you will find prettily-lit cribs full of *santons*. And the folklore museums of Aix, Arles, Marseille and Monaco have remarkable historic displays of *santons* and cribs.

In just a few villages – notably Les Baux – the tradition of a 'live crib' survives: this is a Midnight Mass on Christmas Eve in the form of a Provençal pageant of the Nativity, with villagers dressed up as the Holy Family and other figures. And in summer some villages still have their annual pilgrimages – a colourful procession to the local shrine of a saint.

Boules

Of all the old traditions, *boules* is one that has not been allowed to disappear from daily life: it is still the most popular of games, all over southern France. It is a version of bowls, played with small metal balls on an earth pitch – and everywhere, in dusty village squares, even by smart promenades, you see the locals playing it intently. There are two teams, each of three or four players; as in bowls, a team must get its balls as close as possible to the jack without hitting it. *Pétanque*, a local variant of *boules*, is played on short pitches with the players standing in a circle.

29

Orientation map: west Provence

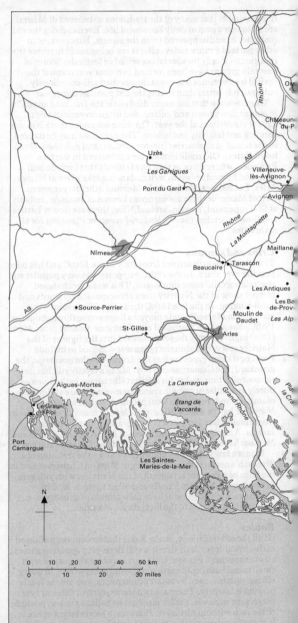

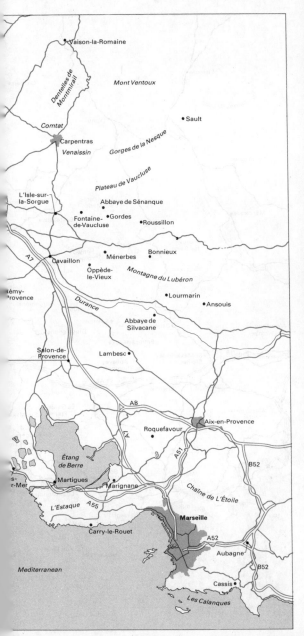

Orientation map: Côte d'Azur an

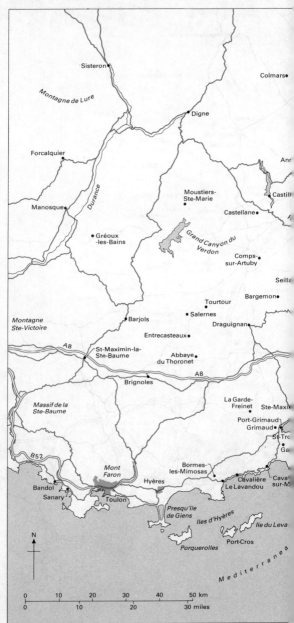

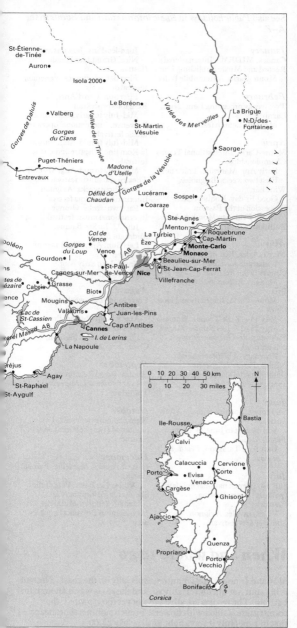

Provençal hinterland

St-Étienne-de-Tinée
Auron•
Isola 2000•
Le Boréon•
Gorges de Daluis
•Valberg
Gorges du Cians
Vallée de la Tinée
Valée des Merveilles
La Brigue
• N.D.-des-Fontaines
St-Martin Vésubie
Saorge•
Puget-Théniers
Madone d'Utelle
ɪ T A L Y
Entrevaux
Gorges de la Vésubie
Défilé de Chaudan
Lucéram•
Sospel•
•Coaraze
Ste-Agnes•
Menton
•poléon
Col de Vence
Gorges du Loup
La Turbie
Roquebrune
Cap-Martin
Gourdon•
Vence
Èze•
Monte-Carlo
Monaco
ns
Cagnes-sur-Mer
St-Paul-de-Vence
Beaulieu-sur-Mer
St-Jean-Cap-Ferrat
tes de ʒzaire•
Cabris•
Grasse
Nice
ance
Biot•
Villefranche
Mougins•
Antibes
•Lac de St-Cassien
Vallauris•
Juan-les-Pins
arel Massif A8
Cap d'Antibes
Cannes
La Napoule
I. de Lerins
réjus
Agay
St-Raphael
St-Aygulf

0 10 20 30 40 50 km
0   10   20   30 miles
N

Ile-Rousse
Bastia
Calvi
Calacuccia
Cervione
Porto
•Evisa
Corte
Venaco
Cargèse•
Ghisoni•
Ajaccio•
Quenza•
Propriano•
Porto-Vecchio
Bonifacio•
Corsica

Calendar of events

See also *Public holidays* in *Basic information* and *Events* in the *A–Z*.

January
Cannes. MIDEM – International Record and Music Publishing Fair
Monte-Carlo. Automobile Rally

February
Two weeks preceding Lent. Nice. Carnival
Menton. Lemon festival

April
Monte-Carlo. International Tennis Championships
Early Apr. Marseille. Trade fair
First two weeks. Brignoles. Wine fair
Good Friday. Roquebrune. Procession of the Passion
Easter Friday to Monday. Arles. Bullfight festival

May
May 1. Arles. Fête of Camargue *gardians*
Cannes. Film Festival
Monaco. Automobile Grand Prix
Monte-Carlo. International Dog Show
May 16–18. St-Tropez. *Bravade*
May 23–27. Les Saintes-Maries. *Pèlerinage des Gitanes* (gypsy celebration)
Five days of Whit weekend. Nîmes. *Feria de Pentecôte* (bullfights, folklore events, concerts, etc)

June
St-Tropez. Spanish *bravade* – folk festival
Sun nearest to June 24. Signes. *Fête de St-Eloi*
Last Sun. Tarascon. *Fête de la Tarasque*

July
July 14. French national holiday (parades, street dancing, fireworks)
Villeneuve-lès-Avignon. Summer arts festival

Juan-les-Pins. Jazz festival
Nice. Grand Jazz Parade (festival)
First Sat. Martigues. Venetian festival on canals
First Sun. Cap d'Antibes. Religious procession
Mid-July to early Aug. Aix-en-Provence. International opera and music festival
Mid-July to mid-Aug. Vaison-la-Romaine. Theatre and music festival
Mid-July to mid-Aug. Sisteron. Theatre and music festival
Last three weeks. Avignon. International drama festival
Last two weeks. Orange. International music festival
July 22. La Ste-Baume. Midnight Mass
Last Sun. Apt. Pilgrimage of Ste-Anne
End July to early Aug. Beaucaire. Fête of the Fair

August
Entrevaux. Two-week music festival
Aug 5. Roquebrune. Procession of the Passion
First two weeks. Menton. Chamber music festival

September
Cannes. Royal Regatta
Last two weeks. Marseille. Trade fair

October
Weekend nearest Oct 22. Les Saintes-Maries. Fête of St Mary Salome

December
Last two weeks. Marseille. Fair of *santons*
Dec 24. Les Baux. Fête of the Shepherds, Midnight Mass
Dec 24. Séguret. Midnight Mass, famous Provençal mystery play

When and where to go

May and June are ideal months, especially on the coast. The sun is hot, but not uncomfortably so, and the sea is warm enough for bathing. The resorts are alive but not yet too crowded; the countryside is filled with flowers. French summertime means that in June/July it stays light until nearly 23.00.

The French holiday season is from July to Aug. During this time the tourist industry swings into top gear, and many resorts offer their full amenities, such as outdoor discos, only in those months. But the crowds are dense, especially on the coast with its tedious traffic jams. Sept is a good month. The sun is still hot, but the crowds are thinning out. In the w, however, the cold north wind known as the Mistral has begun to blow. Sept to Oct can be a good period for cultural sightseeing.

Until the 1930s, winter was the fashionable season on the Riviera, its resorts – such as Cannes and Menton – favoured for their sheltered, mild climate. Today they are still quite active in winter, with their own select clientele. This can be a good time for a visit if you don't expect to sunbathe, and there's the advantage of skiing just inland. And the indigenous life of the towns, stripped of their tourist facade, is revealed at this time of the year. But the resorts further w, like St-Tropez, all but close down in winter, as do many of the hotels in rural areas.

Whatever time of year you go, you will find Provence a region of dazzling variety where it is possible to have many different kinds of holiday in one. Medieval mountain villages lie 16km (10 miles) from glamorous resorts. There are great castles and cathedrals as well as casinos and palace hotels.

Broadly speaking, the western part of the region is richer than the eastern zone in history and culture. In and around the lower Rhône valley, there are Roman remains and gracious medieval and Renaissance cities, full of museums and fine buildings. The landscape is relatively flat, broken by ranges of limestone hills.

To the E, the 240km (150 miles) of coast from Marseille to Menton is hilly, indented with capes and coves, and mostly very beautiful. But its popularity has brought problems. It is heavily built up, and in places spoilt by recent eyesores. This is the French Riviera, today better known by its French name, *La Côte d'Azur*. The eastern part (Cannes, Nice, Monte-Carlo, Menton) has for more than a century been Europe's leading "playground of the rich". Its resorts, though today more democratized, remain smart and sophisticated. This coast is one string of towns. Yet only a few miles behind, in striking contrast, lie isolated hill villages and a wild hinterland.

Provence stretches inland for some 160km (100 miles). From the snowy Alps in the E to the Cévennes uplands w of the Rhône, this is a vast undulating territory of wooded or vine-clad valleys and limestone plateaus cut by deep gorges. It contains much of interest, from lonely mountain chapels, decorated with vivid medieval frescoes, to modern art museums surprisingly located in old castles.

Area planners and tours

Though it is made up of several large *départements* (Alpes-Maritime, Var, Bouche-du-Rhône, etc) for the visitor's purpose, Provence is best divided into a few large geographical areas: western Provence, Marseille and the western *Côte d'Azur* as far as Fréjus, the eastern *Côte d'Azur* from Fréjus to Menton, the Nice hinterland and the central and western hinterland.

(To refer to places printed in bold type – as opposed to cross-references in italics – you should use the index.)

Western Provence The rich historical heritage of this area
includes the Roman monuments at *Orange, Pont-du-Gard,
Nîmes, Arles* and *St-Rémy*; these are all within a 32-km
(20-mile) radius. You should also visit the museums, palaces
and churches of Provence's three proudest cultural cities, the
three As: *Aix, Arles, Avignon* (it is only an hour by autoroute
from Avignon to Aix). And do not miss some smaller, equally
historic towns: *Aigues-Mortes, Tarascon, Uzès, Villeneuve-
lès-Avignon*.

The *Camargue*, a strange marshy plain full of birds, bulls
and wild horses, is like nowhere else in France. *Les Baux*, a
ruined hill-top feudal stronghold, is one of France's most
remarkable sights; nearby, the white rocky spurs of Les Alpilles
are worth exploring. Lastly, those interested in modern France
may care to visit the big new oil-based industries of *Étang de
Berre* and **Fos** nearby.

Marseille and the western Côte d'Azur A 128-km (80-mile)
stretch of fascinating coast. The seaport of *Marseille*, second
city of France, may be strident and shabby; but it is lively and
full of historic interest. *Cassis* and *Bandol* are the best of the
resorts just to its E: visit the creeks (*calanques*) near Cassis.
Toulon, France's leading naval base, is unexpectedly absorbing
and strikingly situated, with grandiose scenery to its N. Off the
coast further E lie the lovely islands of Hyères (see *Hyères, Îles
d'*) which can be visited by boat. The Maures coast, between
Toulon and *Fréjus* is beautiful too, backed by the wooded
Maures massif. One of its resorts is the flamboyant *St-Tropez*, a
byword for the sybaritic life. In its hinterland are some smartly-
restored hill villages. And don't miss *Port-Grimaud*, that
modern miracle of pastiche.

Eastern Côte d'Azur: Fréjus to Menton One of the world's
most luxurious strips of coast, saturated with glamour but
interesting for other reasons as well. *Fréjus* is worth a visit,
more for its cathedral ensemble than its Roman ruins. To the E
lies the startling Esterel Coast with its jagged red rocks. Then at
Cannes the classic Riviera begins where each resort is a house-
hold name – and each one different. First, Cannes itself, glossy
and cosmopolitan, a small-scale Paris-on-Sea; a little to the E is
the youthfully boisterous *Juan-les-Pins*. Next, by contrast, is
the leafy elegance of exclusive *Cap d'Antibes*; then *Antibes*, an
old seaport. From here to *Nice* the coast is ugly: but in the hill
villages just behind (*Vallauris, Biot, St-Paul-de-Vence,
Cagnes-sur-Mer*) are museums devoted to the work of the great
artists who lived in this area, such as Picasso and Renoir. Nice,
the *Côte d'Azur's* capital, is a sophisticated city of multifold
fascination. *St-Jean-Cap-Ferrat*, to its E, is worth a visit too.
The tiny state of *Monaco* is a must for its museums, princely
palace and the pleasure haunts of *Monte-Carlo*. Beyond lies the
wistfully old-fashioned resort of *Menton*. The steep coast
between Nice and Menton is of spectacular beauty and includes
two fine hill villages, *Èze* and *Roquebrune*.

Nice's hinterland Travel just a dozen miles inland from the
crowded coast, and you enter another world – a wild,
mountainous environment in the foothills of the Alps, where
old hill villages and scattered holiday chalets are almost the only
signs of habitation. One good excursion is to *La Brigue* and the
curious **Vallée des Merveilles** cradled by snowy Alps. Further
W, there is fine sub-alpine scenery around *St-Martin-Vésubie*.
Inland from *Cannes*, you should visit *Grasse*, the perfume
town, and the hill villages nearby. The immediate hinterland of

Cannes is beautiful, though rather over-built. However, further N you come to wild, grandiose scenery: take the route of the clues from *Vence*, and on to picturesque *Entrevaux* and the **Cians gorges**. Further W is more fine, open country, all the way to *Sisteron* and its stern citadel.

The central and western hinterland This is the broad swathe of attractive hill country E of *Aix* and *Avignon*, and inland from *Toulon* and *St-Tropez*: you can reach any of it easily in one- or two-day trips from these or other towns. It has, first, some splendid scenery: the *Verdon Grand Canyon*, *Mont Ventoux*, the *Lubéron* mountain, and the haunting *Ste-Baume massif*. Secondly, it contains some lovely and interesting buildings: the 12thC Cistercian sister abbeys of *Sénanque*, *Silvacane* and *Thoronet*, the abbey at *St-Maximin*, the cathedral at *Carpentras*, and the Roman town at *Vaison*. Lastly, it has some surprising curiosities; these include the gushing waters of the *Fontaine de Vaucluse*, the odd stone-dwellings of **Les Bories** at *Gordes*, and a museum in the castle at **Entrecasteaux** devoted to the work of the Scottish Surrealist Ian McGarvie-Munn.

Hill villages The mountainous parts of inland Provence are dotted with hundreds of ancient fortified villages either perched on the crests of hills or terraced along mountain sides. They were built there for protection, first against the Saracen pirates of the 8th–10thC, then against the marauders of the Middle Ages. The peasants would live within the safety of their walls, venturing out by day to work in their fields. Then in the 19thC, with the coming of peace and order, they began to move down into the valleys. So today many of the more remote of these villages, such as **Evenos**, are wholly or partially abandoned, and it is fascinating to wander in their ruins.

However, the past 50yr or so have seen an entirely new trend which is bringing some villages back to life. A few, such as *Èze* and *Les Baux*, have been taken over by the tourist trade and are now filled with cafés and souvenir shops which give them the semblance of being lived in. Many others – especially near the coast – have been engulfed by the post-war fashion for buying up rural cottages and converting them as weekend or summer homes. Such villages are now smartly restored, their alleys neatly paved, their stone walls adorned with creepers and flower-pots – an artificial revival, maybe, but better than letting them fall into ruin. Colonies of artists and craftsmen have settled in some villages.

Whether restored or still un-restored, the hill villages are well worth exploring. Often you must go on foot, for the alleys are too steep and narrow for cars. You will find a maze of winding stone stairways and vaulted archways, shadowy arcades and tiny squares where fountains play. The villages are built of the local stone, so that some, like *Gourdon*, seem to merge into the hillside. Some of them still have their old ramparts.

Here are some villages that are particularly worth visiting.

Most spectacularly situated: *Les Baux*, **Evenos**, *Èze*, *Gourdon*, **Ste-Agnes** and *Saorge*.

Haunts of artists and artisans: **Haut-de-Cagnes**, *Roussillon*, *St-Paul-de-Vence*, **Séguret** and *Tourette-sur-Loup*.

Restored, smart, residential: some of those above, also **Auribeau**, **Bormes-les-Mimosa**, *Cabris*, **Le Castellet**, **Gassin**, *Gordes*, *Grimaud*, *Mons*, *Mougins*, **Peille**, *Peillon* *Roquebrune*, **Seillans** and *Tourtour*.

Still lived in by villagers, and largely unrestored: *Coaraze*, **Fox-Amphoux**, *Lucéram*, **Roure**, *Utelle*.

Planning

Routes

The following suggested tours by car are best accomplished at leisurely speed, stopping for lingering lunches and for the night at suitable places. Details of hotels and restaurants can be found under the name of the town in the *A–Z*.

The six routes take four main tourist centres as starting points – *Avignon*, *Aix*, *Cannes* and *Nice*. They are all circular, and can be joined at any suitable point. Between them they cover all the places of most interest in the region. If you devoted your entire holiday to following the six routes, you would gain the greatest possible knowledge of Provence. But be warned: don't just turn up on spec at hotels in summer months, but book well ahead.

Route 1: The Rhône estuary

From *Avignon*, cross the Rhône to explore *Villeneuve-lès-Avignon* on the other bank. From here take the N100, soon passing on your right the hilly forest of Rochefort and the vineyards of Tavel (famous for its rosé). At Remoulins, turn right down the D981 to *Uzès*. You might make a detour here to **Arpaillargues**, 4.75km (3 miles) to the w, for a luxury meal or night stop, or else strike s from Uzès by D979, down into the rocky **Gardon Gorge**, then up over the *garrigue* (semi-arid hills) – and so to Roman *Nîmes*.

Leave Nîmes by the N113 to the sw. After 16km (10 miles) you can make a left detour to visit the **Perrier** mineral water factory. Turn left along the D979, via Aimargues, where you enter the marshy, salty plain bordering the *Camargue*. Next stop, and not to be missed is *Aigues-Mortes*, a walled medieval city. Finally the D979 brings you to the sea at the pretty fishing

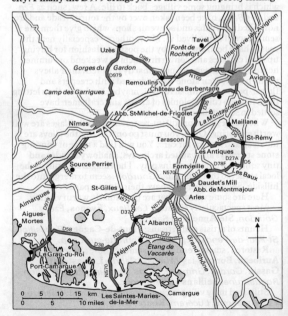

port of **Le Grau-du-Roi**. Turn left here to explore the
modernistic sailing resort of **Port-Camargue**, where there is a
reasonable hotel.

Return to the major road junction 2km (1¼ miles) NE of
Aigues-Mortes, where you turn right along the D58, through
vineyards producing grey-pink Listel wines. Cross the Petit
Rhône, and you are in the mysterious Camargue. Continue via
the D38 and N572 to *Les Saintes-Maries* (good hotels here).
After perhaps taking time to explore the Camargue by horse or
boat, go N along the N570, either direct to *Arles* or via one of the
following two detours: from l'Albaron you can either turn left
along the D37 and N572 to visit **St-Gilles** with its remarkable
church, or turn right along the D37 to the pleasure ranch of
Méjanes, then travelling E along the D37 for views of the lake of
Vaccarès, finally reaching Arles by turning back N along the
D36.

Leave Arles by the N570 to the NE, turning right along the
D17 to visit **Montmajour Abbey** and *Fontvieille*, where you
can see Daudet's mill. Then turn left along the D78F to
enchanted (and gastronomic) *Les Baux*. Leaving the village by
the D27A, by going left along the D5, you come next to the
Roman remains just S of *St-Rémy*. From this town, drive W
down an avenue of plane trees to *Tarascon*, through a typical
sun-baked Provençal landscape of the kind Van Gogh loved and
painted. Alternatively, there is a possible detour going N from
St-Rémy via the D5, to **Maillane** and its Mistral museum. After
visiting Tarascon's romantic castle, return to Avignon, not by
the main N570 but by the D35 between the **Montagnette** hill
and the Rhône, stopping if you wish at the abbey of **St-Michel-
de-Frigolet** and the château of **Barbentane**.

Route 2: Mountains, forests and vineyards
Leave *Avignon* to its NE by the D225, then N7; just N of
Sorgues turn left down the D17 to **Châteauneuf-du-Pape**
(famous for its wine of the same name) and on by the D68 to
Roman *Orange*. From here the D975 cuts NE across the plain,
past other famous vineyards to the right (*Gigondas*), to more
Roman remains at *Vaison*. A detour off the D975, via D8 and
D23, leads E to the quaint hill village of **Séguret**; there is good
eating here and fine views of the craggy **Dentelles de
Montmirail**.

Take the D938 SE from *Vaison-la-Romaine*, turning left at
Malaucène for the long haul up the D974 to the summit of *Mont
Ventoux* where you will have another superb view. Then
descend the far side by the D974 and D164 to *Sault*. There is a
possible detour here to the wild **Nesque gorge** to the SW. From
Sault drive 64km (40 miles) through wild country, by the D942,
D542, D546 and D946, to *Sisteron* and its citadel. Retrace your
tracks for about 8km (5 miles) up the D946, turning left along
the D53 past Valbelle for the looping ascent through vast
woodlands to the lofty **Signal de Lure** (more stunning views).
Zig-zag down through more beautiful forests to *Forcalquier*
(with its lovely cemetery) where the N100 highway whisks you
to *Apt*.

From Apt you can explore the strange *Lubéron* mountain,
first climbing SE by the D48 to the Mourre Nègre peak for yet
another mountain-top panorama. Here a narrow road winds
down to Cucuron by its S slopes, where you go W by the D56 to
Lourmarin (castle), then up into the Lubéron again by the
D943, turning left down the D36 to **Bonnieux** (make sure you

39

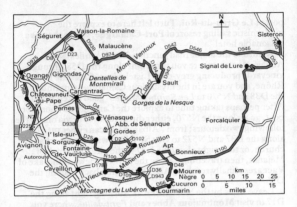

see the 15thC paintings in the New Church). A detour
leads through a forest of giant cedars to glorious uplands above
Cavaillon. Otherwise you keep on the D109 to **Ménerbes** (ideal
for a greedy lunch) and the gaunt rock village of **Oppède-le-
Vieux**.

Drop down to the plain by the D178, go back E along the
N100, then turn left up the D104 to rose-red *Roussillon* and its
weird crags. Follow the signs to fashionable *Gordes* (by the D2)
where there is much to see, notably the abbey of *Sénanque* by a
detour of 4km (2½ miles) to the NW. Strike SW from Gordes by
the D2, then W via Cabrières to *Fontaine-de-Vaucluse* with its
(sometimes) surging waters. Go W by the D25 to survey the
calmer, surer waters of **l'Isle-sur-la-Sorgue**, then drive N by
the D938 via pretty **Pernes** to *Carpentras* and back to
Avignon. Alternatively, take a detour, E from Pernes by the
D28 to **Vénasque** with its 7thC baptistry, reaching Carpentras
by the D4.

Route 3: The western Côte d'Azur

Take the A51 autoroute from *Aix* to *Marseille*. After exploring
that great city, travel over the arid limestone hills to picturesque
Cassis; be sure to visit its *calanques* (creeks). Hug the coast to
smart *Bandol*, from there you can take an excursion to the **Ile
de Bendor**, then either go direct to *Toulon* or take one of two
detours: either turn right just beyond Sanary, down the D616 to
tour hilly Cap Sicié, where a fine view can be obtained from the
chapel of Notre-Dame-du-Mai; or, in *Sanary*, turn left to
Ollioules to explore the savage scenery of **Le Gros Cerveau**,
Evenos and **Mont-Caume**, entering Toulon from the N
(D62).

Mont-Faron and the harbour should be visited in Toulon,
where you can eat well too. Continue on the coast road, the
N559, to **Hyères-Plage**, where you turn right along the D97
past the salt works to the **Giens peninsula**: leave the car at La
Tour-Fondue for a 20min boat trip to lovely **Porquerolles** (see
Hyères, Iles de). Return by the D97 to visit *Hyères*, then drive
E along the N98 where the wild *Maures massif* rises on your
left. Turn right down the N559, then left up to **Bormes-les-
Mimosas**, a hill village as pretty as it sounds and a good place
for a meal. From here there is a possible detour to the N, into the
heart of the massif to places like **Collobrières** and **Chartreuse-
de-la-Verne**.

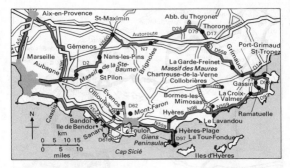

From **Bormes**, drop down to *Le Lavandou* for a 45min boat trip to luxuriant **Port-Cros** island (which has a romantic hotel) and maybe also to its neighbour, the **Ile du Levant**, popular for nude bathing. Back at Le Lavandou, continue E along the beautiful Maures coast. At **La Croix-Valmer**, turn right up the D93 to visit the even lovelier **Ramatuelle peninsula**, hilly, wooded and vine-clad. Turn left off the D93 for the hill villages of **Ramatuelle** and **Gassin** and the panorama point of the **moulins de Paillas**. Further along the D93, all lanes lead right to *St-Tropez*, with golden beaches and unclad *jeunesse dorée*.

From St-Tropez – if you can tear yourself away from its pleasure-seeking atmosphere – skirt the gulf of the D98A to *Port-Grimaud*, a skilful, modern imitation of an old fishing village, then strike inland by the D14 to hilltop **Grimaud** – and so over the Maures massif by the D558 via **La Garde-Freinet**. At the N7 highway, turn right, then promptly left down the D17 to the serene 12thC abbey of *Thoronet*, light years away from St-Tropez. Then drive W through a vine-clad valley by the D79 and D24 to *Brignoles*.

Go on W by the N7 to *St-Maximin* with its splendid church and medieval basilica. Then drive SW by the N560 and D80, via **Nans-les-Pins**, where the road winds up through glorious woods to the strange, spectacular heights of the *Ste-Baume massif* (excursion on foot to the summit of **St-Pilon** and its sacred grotto: superb views). Loop down past gaunt white crags to **Gémenos**, where you can either return due W via **Aubagne** to Marseille, or NW to Aix by the N96 or the autoroute.

Route 4: Central coast and hinterland
Leave *Cannes* by the coastal N559 for *La Napoule*, with its sandy beaches and restored castle, now an art gallery; then take the N98 along the spectacular Esterel coast with its red rocks, passing the Gaudi-esque new holiday estate of **Port-la-Galère**. At *Agay* you can make a detour into the heart of the *Esterel massif* – there are fine views from its peaks. If you carry on down the N98 you will come to *St-Raphael*, with good beaches, then to *Fréjus* with its Roman remains and nearby zoo. From there go S by the N98 to the first stretch of the lovely Maures coast where umbrella pines stand above secluded coves. Beyond *Ste-Maxime*, drive round the azure gulf to the tarnished Eldorado of *St-Tropez* and the **Ramatuelle peninsula** (from here to the abbey of *Thoronet* follow Route 3).

From Thoronet, zig-zag NW via the D84, D562, D31, through rolling vineyards to **Entrecasteaux**. Continue N by the D31 via the tile-making town of *Salernes* to **Aups**; then N again

41

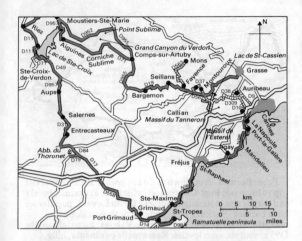

by the D957 through hilly woodlands, bearing left along the
D49, D71 and D111 to **Ste-Croix-de-Verdon** which commands
fine views over **Ste-Croix** lake. Join the D11, and you reach
Riez (which has Roman and early Christian remains). The D952
then leads NE to the capital of Provençal faïence, **Moustiers-
Ste-Marie**. From here travel SE to admire the *Verdon Grand
Canyon*, France's most grandiose gorge. Drive either along its S
cliff, via **Aiguines** and the Corniche Sublime (D957, D71 to
Comps), or by the N cliff, via the Route des Crêtes and the Point
Sublime (D952, then right down the D955, also to **Comps-sur-
Artuby**).

Sated with gorges, you may be ready for another kind of
gorging at Comps' good *auberge*. Then go S by the D955, across
a rocky plateau with a military camp, turning left along the
D19. Suddenly the scenery changes – from arid limestone
heights to a land of gentle, verdant valleys W of Grasse, their
slopes lined with hill villages. On the D19, **Bargemon** and
Seillans are two such villages, elegantly restored and
possessing good restaurants. Continue on the D19 past
Fayence, then along the main D562. There are possible detours
here to other hill villages: **Mons**, N of Fayence by the D563;
Callian and Montouroux, off the D562 to the N. Turn right off
D562 down by the D37 to visit the artificial but scenic lake of
St-Cassien, then turn left (D38) up into the wild and wooded
Tanneron massif, possibly making a detour to another pretty
hill village, **Auribeau**, to the N. Descend to Mandelieu by the
D9 or by the D309 and D109, and thence back with a jolt from
the wild hinterland to the dazzling concrete jungle of Cannes.

Route 5: Inland from Cannes

Leaving *Nice* by the N7, turn right in *Cagnes-sur-Mer* to visit
Renoir's house and **Haut-de-Cagnes**. Then go N by the D36,
turning off left to explore artistic *St-Paul-de-Vence*, reaching
Vence by the D2. Drive W from Vence by the scenic D2210, via
Tourette-sur-Loup, a great centre for artists and craftsmen,
Pont-de-Loup in its deep valley, and **Le Bar**, the church of
which contains a remarkable 15thC painting of a *Dance of
Death*. South of Le Bar, turn sharp right (D3) to climb up to
hill-top *Gourdon* where you will get an outstanding view and,

the chances are, a near-outstanding lunch too.

Continue on the D3, above the vertiginous gorge of the Loup. At the junction with the D2, turn left and follow the wild and spectacular **circuit of the clues** (see *Vence*) via **Gréolières**, the **Col de Bleine**, the **Clue d'Aiglun**. Just w of **Roquesteron**, turn left up the D17 to the **Clue du Riolan**, and so by the D2211A to the N202 highway at *Puget-Théniers*. If you want to make an optional loop to the N, go E to the D28 and through the **Cians Gorge** to *Valberg*, returning to the N202 down the **Daluis gorge**.

Otherwise, from Puget-Théniers drive w along the N202 to explore ancient *Entrevaux*; further on, turn right down the D908 for a look at pretty *Annot* which has a fine *auberge*. Back on the N202, go w as far as the artificial lake of Castillon. Turn left along its shore following D955 which brings you to *Castellane*. Then go SE down the N85 (the old Route Napoléon), over empty, mountainous country as far as **St-Vallier-de-Thiey** where there is a splendid *auberge*. Turn along the D5 to **St-Cézaire** for views over the **Siagne gorge**; then go E by the D13 (a short detour by the N leads to the **St-Cézaire caves**) through glorious country to the elegant hill village of **Cabris** where there is good bed and board to be had. Just 4.5km (3 miles) more, and you're in *Grasse*.

After visiting Grasse, leave by the D2085 to the E, turning right along the D3 to *Valbonne*. Farther along the D3, turn left down D103 to the new 'scientific park' of **Sophia-Antipolis**. At the junction with D35, turn right past the smart Cannes golf club, then up left to equally smart (and very gastronomic) *Mougins*. If you wish, drop down to *Cannes* from here. If not, retrace tracks along the D35, turning right (D135) to *Vallauris*, a world-famous pottery centre where Picasso had a ceramics studio. The road goes down to the sea at **Golfe-Juan**, where you turn left into hedonistic *Juan-les-Pins*, then take the idyllic coastal route round *Cap d'Antibes* before reaching

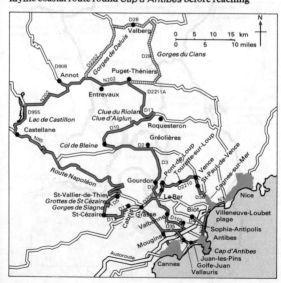

Antibes itself. From here go N by N7, making a short detour
inland (D4) to *Biot* and the Léger museum. Return to Nice by
the coast road, past the controversial pyramids of the **Marina
Baie des Anges** at *Villeneuve-Loubet*.

Route 6: Nice's dramatic hinterland

Go W from *Nice* to the airport, where the fast N202 leads N up
the Var valley. It is flat and ugly, but you are soon past it and
into breathtaking scenery. Turn right down the winding
Vésubie gorge (D2565); at its far end, turn sharp right again, up
the D19, as far as the **Saut des Français** viewpoint high above
the gorge. Return down the D19, turning left at **St-Jean-la-
Rivière**, up the looping mountain road (D32) to *Utelle*, then on
to the **Madone d'Utelle** where there is a superb panorama.
Retrace your tracks to St-Jean, then go up the Vésubie valley
(D2565) to *St-Martin-Vésubie*, where two side excursions can
be made: by the D31 to the hill village of *Venanson*; or by the
D89 to *Le Boréon*, at the edge of the **Parc de Mercantour** in
the Alps (fine hiking country).

Return S from *St-Martin*, turning left up the D70 to the **Col
de Turini**, amid glorious sub-alpine scenery. Take the D2566
to the S, via **Peïra Cava**, where there are more lovely views, and
Lucéram, where there is a good-value restaurant, and on to
Escarène. From here turn left up the main D2204 which
zig-zags over the **Col de Braus** to *Sospel* where you will find a
good hotel. Once you are over the next pass you will find
yourself on the N204, which leads through the wild gorges of
the **Roya valley**, past *Saorge* perched dramatically up on your
right. At St-Dalmas-de-Tende, turn right along the D43 to *La
Brigue* and the lonely, lovely chapel of **Notre-Dames-des-
Fontaines**. Back at St-Dalmas go W by the narrow D91 into
sub-alpine country at **Casterino** with its good quality *auberge*
(see *La Brigue*). This is a good base for a visit by jeep or on foot

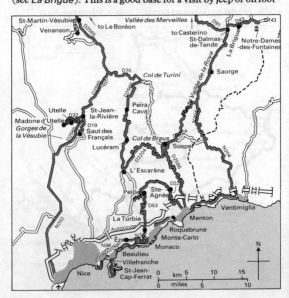

to the weird, aptly-named **Vallée des Merveilles** in its cradle of mountains.

Retrace tracks down the Roya valley. From here you can get to *Menton* via Sospel and the D2566: but the quicker, better route is along the N204 into Italy at Ventimiglia (there is a superb market on Fri) where you turn left along the coast. After savouring Menton, with its lush, tropical vegetation, go back briefly into the wild hinterland: first up the D22 to hill-top **Ste-Agnès** (ideal for lunch), then through wild uplands to **Peille**, another hill village, and along the D53 to *La Turbie* on the upper corniche where there is a Roman monument and a striking panorama.

The rest of the circuit is pure *Côte d'Azur*. Go E along the corniche to visit *Roquebrune* and its castle; then turn sharp right down to the middle corniche to explore *Monaco/Monte-Carlo*. Leave the principality to visit the hill village of *Èze*. Then go back E along the N7, taking the first on the right, a minor road zig-zagging down to the lower corniche; here you turn right to *Beaulieu*. Explore the glorious *St-Jean-Cap-Ferrat* peninsula to the s, then continue w on the N98 to *Villefranche* and Nice.

Accommodation

Hotels in the South of France range from the ultra-luxurious palaces that line the smart promenades of the Riviera, to the functional urban hotels of the kind that are found all over France, comfortable but with no special ambience, to be used purely as a convenient base. In between are the traditional country inns (*auberges*), many simple, some extremely plush.

Suitable more for an overnight stay than a full holiday, but none the less excellent, are the recently built chains of utility hotels, usually located by main roads or on the outskirts of towns. Though some are more enticing than others, they are all reliable. The principal chains are **Frantel** (■■■), **Ibis** (□■ to ■■), **Mercure** (■□), **Novotel** (■□), **Sofitel** (■■). Many privately-owned hotels have grouped themselves into associations for joint promotion, and are of comparable quality as they submit to mutual inspection. The most reliable are: **Logis de France** (□ to ■□), in the country or in small towns; **Mapotel** (■□ to ■■■), mostly in towns; **Relais et Châteaux** (■■ to ■■■), rural.

Reservations

In season (Easter, and mid-June to mid-Sept) it is essential to book well in advance at the better holiday hotels. In July and Aug, if you try to tour without prior bookings you might well end up spending the night in the car or on the beach. Out of season, things are easier; but many holiday hotels, on the coast and in rural areas, tend to close from about Nov–Mar.

Prices

These tend to be highest in smart resorts such as Cannes and Monte-Carlo, and lowest in the hinterland. The apparent price category of a hotel can be deceptive, for most hotels have a choice of bedrooms of different kinds across a wide price range; under the same roof, you can pay three times as much for a large room with balcony facing the sea as for a small one at the back with no bath. So, when booking, it is wise to specify the kind of room you want, and then check the price. Moreover, you are charged for the room rather than per head; thus two people occupying one room pay only slightly more than one person would, especially if it is double-bedded, as is usual, rather than twin-bedded.

Comfort

Standards of comfort in French hotels have greatly improved in the past 20yr, and the days of primitive French plumbing are gone. Even our cheapest recommendations have at least some rooms with bath or shower. And if you want to economize by forgoing this amenity, you will always find a communal bathroom down the corridor. Pillows may at first present a problem, for many hotels provide merely a long, sausage-like bolster. But, if you ask, the hotel will usually supply a softer cushion-type pillow.

Meals in hotels

Especially in country areas, food in hotels tends to be every bit as good as in restaurants; in many cases, the *patron* of an *auberge* sees himself foremost as a restaurateur and only secondly as a hotelier. In season, most holiday hotels require residents to take at least one main meal a day (*demi-pension*), if not both meals (*pension complète*), and it is wise to check this when booking, especially if your intention is to have a culinary spree and eat out frequently. The *menu pension* included in these terms may well be simpler, and with less choice, than the hotel's more elaborate menus, but at an extra charge you can order special dishes.

The French tend to be rather frugal when it comes to breakfast; most hotels provide just coffee, bread, croissants and small pre-packed portions of butter and jam. Fruit juice or a boiled egg will come if you ask, but you must pay extra. A few more modern hotels are moving over to a Dutch-style help-yourself buffet-breakfast with cold meat, cheese, cereals and fruit, but this is still fairly rare.

Food and drink

Of the great regional *cuisines* of France, *provençale* is probably the one with the strongest personality. It is a spicy Mediterranean *cuisine* of bold, clean flavours, leaning heavily on garlic, on local herbs such as thyme, basil and fennel, and on olive oil which generally replaces butter in cooking. The garlic enhances the natural flavours of the food, but is used so carefully that it rarely leaves its usual unpleasant mark.

The cooking is wonderfully varied – a blend of the traditions of mountain people and fisher folk, as befits an area where the Alps sweep down to the sea. In a region richly endowed by nature, it draws lavishly on local produce: fish of all kinds, game from the hinterland, and an abundance of fresh fruit and vegetables in season, for Provence is France's foremost market garden. Artichokes, asparagus, aubergines and tomatoes are especially delicious.

Some typical dishes

As an appetizer, a meal might begin with *tapenade*, a purée of chopped black olives and anchovies. Starters include a range of salads and *crudités*, the commonest being *salade niçoise*, a rich mixture of eggs, olives, anchovies and tomatoes. At lunch some restaurants offer a help-yourself buffet of spicy hors d'oeuvres; others bring a basket of crispy raw vegetables with mustard and vinaigrette dips. The best soups are *pistou*, a thick vegetable soup with a paste of garlic and basil, and the ubiquitous *soupe de poissons*, made of a pungent stock of many fish including shellfish, and served with toast crusts, grated cheese and *rouille*, a strong garlic sauce. At its best, probably in some unpretentious bistro near the fishing boats, it can be superb.

On and near the coast, fish holds pride of place. *Bouillabaisse*, star of the Provençal kitchen, is a garlicky stew made from various rock and shellfish; *rascasse*, a spiky fish unique to this part of the Mediterranean, is the essential ingredient, also saffron. The delicate taste depends on the right combination of the fish, and on the amalgamation of oil and water by correct boiling. The result looks alarming, as the fish in their orange, saffron-flavoured stew are gruesomely cadaverous, and the strong taste might scare the novice, though he will soon succumb to its spell. The true home of *bouillabaisse* is Marseille, but you can find it elsewhere. It usually needs to be ordered in advance, for very few restaurants keep it on their daily *cartes*, so hard is it to prepare. Be warned: it is very expensive, as are many other of the best fish dishes, such as *bourride*, a simpler garlic stew made with white fish, and *loup au fenouil*, sea bass grilled with fennel. Cheaper fish are *rouget* (red mullet) and *daurade* (John Dorey), usually cooked richly with tomatoes and herbs; inland you find trout and *écrevisses* (crayfish), the latter often in a rich sauce. To tackle this dish you are usually swathed by the waiter in a white napkin to catch the drips. At least once you must try *aioli*, a garlic mayonnaise, the very name of which sends the Provençaux into fits of lyricism (the poet Mistral once founded a local paper called *L'Aioli*), and which often forms the main dish at village feasts; it is served either as a sauce with boiled cod and vegetables, or pounded into a purée with the cod when it is called *brandade de morue*.

Local variations

In the hinterland, meat predominates. Here you will find *agneau de Sisteron* – lamb, the aromatic flavour of which comes from grazing on wild herbs on its upland pastures. Like beef, it is often served grilled on a wood fire, with more herbs sprinkled on it. Rabbit is common, cooked either in a mustard sauce or *à la provençale* (in a tomato and garlic sauce); chicken and frogs' legs also come *à la provençale*. In winter, wild game is prepared in scores of ways – try *civet de lièvre* (jugged hare) and *pâté de grives* (thrush pâté). And all year, as in some other French country areas, you will find meat stewed deliciously in red wine and herbs, such as *boeuf en daube* or (in the Camargue area) *boeuf gardianne*. Arles is famous for its salami-style sausages, while Marseille offers *pieds et paquets*, a kind of tripe – which can be an acquired taste.

Within the Provençal tradition, the Nice area has its own distinctive *cuisine*. It is closer to the Italian style, reflecting the town's former association with Italy. Many of its special dishes are served, like pasta, as starters: *anchoiade* (anchovy tart), *pissaladière* (a kind of pizza), *socca* (a pancake of ground chick-pea), *tian* (a grill of rice, vegetables and grated cheese), and ravioli, more delicate than the Italian kind. *Mesclun* is a dressed salad of coarse lettuce and dandelion. And *ratatouille* (a stew of aubergines, peppers and other vegetables in olive oil) is a local dish which – like *salade niçoise* and *soupe au pistou* – has spread far outside the Nice area.

Provence's cheeses are few, and not among France's greatest but pleasant in their way; try *cachat*, made from sheep's milk and often marinated in brandy and herbs, or *banon*, soaked in wine and wrapped in chestnut leaves. Desserts, except in some luxury restaurants, lack imagination or finesse; but fresh fruit is plentiful in season – notably the sweet pink melons of Cavaillon, the sweet green figs of the Marseille area, and local cherries, peaches and grapes. Apt is known for its crystallized fruits, and Aix for its *calissons* (tiny almond cakes).

Nouvelle cuisine

Although the true *cuisine bourgeoise* of Provence is still the norm in most restaurants, a number of more ambitious or modish places have in recent years become more influenced by the vogue for the new style of cooking, aptly called *nouvelle cuisine*, that has swept France since the 1960s. *Nouvelle cuisine* marks a return to a lighter, purer manner, spurning most heavy sauces and relying on very fresh ingredients, rapidly cooked in their own juices, almost in the Chinese manner, to bring out their full flavours; vegetables are served crispy, half-cooked. The chef is encouraged to deviate from classic recipes and try out daring new blends.

In the wrong hands, the results can be absurd, with ridiculous combinations of ingredients and niggardly portions. But France's best modern chefs have worked wonders with *nouvelle cuisine*, and some of its leading exponents are in the region: notably Roger Vergé at Mougins, Louis Outhier at La Napoule and Jacques Maximin at Nice. These chefs are true masters, and at their restaurants you will sample marvellously inspired food using the local produce of the region. In fact, while some of Provence's grandest restaurants stick within the classic repertoire, a majority today are to some degree flirting with *nouvelle cuisine*, which almost always is expensive; you will not find it in a modest *auberge*.

Nouvelle cuisine is not so much a break with the classic tradition as an adaptation of it, to suit a calorie-conscious age. Similarly, it is not so much turning its back on regional *cuisine* as seeking to re-explore it. Thus, in Provence, many of the best chefs are using traditional Provençal dishes as a basis for their own innovations – and the results, at their best, are a subtle blend of the old and the new. They give their dishes long and complex names, and are constantly changing their menu or adding new inventions: so the specialities we quote for restaurants can be no more than a rough guide. The *patron* or his staff will usually be eager to unravel for you the mysteries of his baffling bill of fare.

In the restaurant

Generally it is far better value to choose a fixed-price menu than to eat *à la carte*, where exactly the same dishes can cost twice as much. In provincial restaurants, much more than in Paris, the French still expect to eat a *prix fixe* meal of four or even five courses; the only exceptions are in modern downtown brasseries or snack-bars or, at the other end of the spectrum, in some luxury restaurants where special dishes are often only on the *carte*. Restaurants generally display their menus outside, and may offer three or four different *prix fixes*, varying greatly in price. No one will mind if you order the cheapest; on the other hand, the best specialities (notably fish) may well be only on the dearest. For an inexpensive, light snack, there are plenty of pizzerias and *crêperies* (pancake houses), while most larger cafés serve simple hot snacks such as *croque monsieur* (toasted cheese) or *un sandwich* (half a French loaf, sliced down the middle and filled with perhaps cheese, pâté, ham or salami).

Although southerners, the Provençaux tend to lunch early, unlike the Spaniards. Service begins at 12.00 or so, and in most places ends at 14.00. As for dinner, many places in large resorts are open till midnight, though many rural restaurants stop serving as early as 21.00. Most restaurants have space for eating outdoors, but at the first breath of a cold wind they will close their terraces or gardens and make you eat indoors.

The menu

The most noticeable difference on a French menu is that cheese is eaten before dessert. Meat is not smothered indiscriminately with several vegetables in the Anglo-Saxon manner, but is usually served with just one vegetable which the chef has specially selected to give his dish the right balance of tastes. If you want another vegetable, it will come later as a separate course. As for steak, the French prefer to eat it rare (*saignant*) or semi-rare (*à point*), and a serious restaurateur may even refuse to serve a "barbarian" who insults him by asking for it well done (*bien cuit*).

Wines of Provence

Though the region has few great wines compared with Burgundy or Bordeaux, there is a fine variety, and nearly all local wines are palatable. In the Rhône valley, Châteauneuf-du-Pape red wine is warm, full-bodied and long-lived. The white is heavy: at best rich, almost sweet. Some of the nearby Côtes-du-Rhône are excellent too, notably the red Gigondas. Tavel, NW of Avignon, produces a strong, dry rosé, rather expensive; cheaper and lighter is Listel gris-de-gris, a cloudy rosé from vines growing on sand near the sea S of Nîmes.

From the area E of Marseille come two fruity reds, Bandol and Château Simone, as well as the dry white wine of Cassis, ideal for drinking with shellfish or *bouillabaisse*. North of Toulon is the Côtes-de-Provence sector: here Pierrefeu and Château Minuty are labels to look for, while Ott is a prolific but reliable grower. The hill slopes of Nice itself produce Bellet, a rare, select and fashionable wine which comes as red, rosé or white. The white is dry, and goes well with shellfish.

Remember that although you can buy a perfectly reasonable bottle of local wine for a very few francs in a shop, the mark-up in a restaurant can often be outrageous, and better known non-Provençal wines will be much more expensive. In order to pick a good bottle at a fair price, it is wise to know something of the classification of French wines.

The four classifications of wine are *Appellation Contrôlée*, VDQS (*Vins Delimités de Qualité Superieure*), *Vin de Pays* or *Vin de Table*. None of these are a guarantee of quality, but simply mean that each category must conform to certain criteria of origin, vinification and grape variety. The criteria are more strict for *Appellation Contrôlée* than VDQS, and so on down the scale, and prices reflect this. Good value, however, can be found in each category.

The reputation of the grower, château or *négotiant* is another extremely important criterion, particularly with Burgundies. If a name is not familiar, it is often wiser to choose according to the year because a good vintage VDQS can often be better quality, and value, than a mediocre vintage of an *Appellation Contrôlée*. Most wine in the lower categories is blended by the shippers and does not carry vintage dates. *Vin de Table* is commonly served in carafes or jugs called *'pichets'* and it is a simple matter to order a small *pichet*, then a second if it is good.

Apart from buying wine from shops and supermarkets, you can purchase from *Vinicoles* where different wines are blended. A *cubitaine* is usually good value from one of these co-operatives. The sign *'vente au détail'* at vineyards means you can purchase the château bottled wine retail at source.

Among aperitifs, by far the most popular local drink is *pastis*, aniseed flavoured, not unlike the *ouzo* of Greece. It is drunk diluted with water and ice, which makes it go cloudy, and on a hot day it is most refreshing – as well as being heady stuff. Ricard and '51 are both dry; their rival Pernod is sweeter.

Vintage chart
Provençal wines

Châteauneuf-du Pape, 1976, 1979, 1983; Château Rayas, 1978; Château Simone, drink youngest available; Château Vignelaure, 1978, 1980, 1984; Tavel, drink youngest available; Listel, drink youngest available; Côtes-du-Rhône-Villages, 1978, 1983; Côtes du Lubéron, drink youngest available.

	1977	1978	1979	1980	1981	1982	1983	1984	1985
Red Bordeaux									
Médoc/Graves	○*	●	●	●*	◐*	●*	●	●	◐
Pomerol/St-Emilion	○*	●	●	●*	◐*	●*	●	●	○
White Bordeaux									
Sauternes & sweet	○*	●*	◐*	○*	●*	●	○*	◐	◐
Graves & dry	◐*	●*	●	○*	◐*	●	◐*	●	◐*
Red Burgundy and neighbours									
Côte d'Or	○*	●	●	◐*	●*	○*	●*	◐*	●
Beaujolais	○*	●*	●	◐*	○	●*	●	◐*	●*
White Burgundy and neighbours									
Côte d'Or	◐*	●	●	◐*	○	●*	○*	●*	●
Chablis	◐*	●*	●	◐*	◐	●*	◐*	●*	●
Alsace	○	●*	●*	●	◐*	◐*	◐*	●*	●
Rhône	◐*	●*	●	●	◐	●	◐	●	●

Above-average vintages of other white wines
Mâcon-Villages, 1982, 1983, 1985; **Loire** (sweet – Anjou, Touraine), 1976, 1978, 1979, 1982, 1984; **Upper Loire** (dry – Pouilly-Fumé, Sancerre), 1981, 1983, 1984; **Muscadet** the newest vintage is best.

Key: ● above average to outstanding   ◐ average
      ○ acceptable   * for drinking now

Shopping

As befits France's affluent society, every main town of Provence has modern shops, to meet all daily needs. In some resorts, such as Cannes, the boutiques are among the smartest in Europe. See *Basic information* for shopping hours.

More than any other European country, France has followed the American model of giant supermarkets on the outskirts of towns. The French call them *hypermarchés*. The range of goods is wide, with seductively lavish food counters. All have free parking lots, and many stay open till 22.00. **Carrefour** and **Casino** are the leading chains in Provence.

Open-air markets are a lively aspect of the local daily scene. Virtually every town, large or small, has its outdoor market in some shady square or avenue, where farmers come in to sell their produce. Some markets are open daily, some weekly, (notably on Sat); most operate in the mornings only. Their food is often fresher and a little cheaper than in the shops. Prices are marked, and bargaining will not often bring dividends.

Regional specialities

Provence's main specialities are: ceramics, glasswork, olive-wood sculpture, silk-painting, weaving, and *santons*. Villages with boutiques selling local products include: *Biot* (pottery, glassware); *Cabris* (olive-wood sculpture, *santons*); **La Cadière-d'Azur** (pottery, weaving); *Coaraze* (enamel sun-dials); **Cogolin** (carpets, furniture, pipes); *Èze* (jewellery, ironwork); *Gordes* (stained glass); **Moustiers-Ste-Marie** (faïence); *St-Paul-de-Vence* (murals); *Salernes* (enamel tiles); **Seillans** (pottery); *Sospel* (olive-wood sculpture); *Tourette-sur-Loup* (ceramics, silk-painting, puppets, etc); *Vallauris* (pottery). Many boutiques in the towns, too, sell the villages' output, but often at higher prices.

Clothing sizes
When shops give clothing sizes in centimetres, use the following conversion scale to determine the correct size

12 *in*	16	20	24	28	32	36	40	44	48
30 *cm*	40	50	60	70	80	90	100	110	120

When standardized codes are used, although these may be found to vary considerably, the following provides a useful guide.

Women's clothing sizes

UK/US sizes	8/6	10/8	12/10	14/12	16/14	18/16
French sizes	38/34N	40/36N	42/38N	44/40N	46/42N	48/44N
Bust *in/cm*	31/80	32/81	34/86	36/91	38/97	40/102

Men's clothing sizes

European code (suits)	44	46	48	50	52	54	56
Chest *in/cm*	34/86	36/91	38/97	40/102	42/107	44/112	46/117
Collar *in/cm*	13½/34	14/36	14½/37	15/38	15½/39	16/41	16½/42
Waist *in/cm*	28/71	30/76	32/81	34/86	36/91	38/97	40/102
Inside leg *in/cm*	28/71	29/74	30/76	31/79	32/81	33/84	34/86

Men's and women's shoe sizes

UK/US sizes	3/4¼	4/5¼	5/6½	6/7½	7/8½	8/9½	9/10½	10/11½	11/12½
European	36	37	38	39	40	41	42	43	44

South of France A–Z

The A–Z section is orientated particularly towards major resorts and the best of the hinterland towns and villages within Provence. Major geographical sights such as the Maures massif and Verdon Grand Canyon also have their own entries, and many more sights are described as *Places nearby* under the major entries. These are all listed in the index.

The basic information at the beginning of each entry gives map reference, postcode and *département* (Alpes-Mar is an abbreviation for Alpes-Maritime, Alpes-de-H.P. is an abbreviation for Alpes-de-Haute-Provence), population and tourist office (*i*). Full hotel entries give the full postal address; brief hotel entries and restaurants give only the street. All telephone numbers include the regional code (in brackets).

Sights and places of interest – a selection

Natural sights

Les Baux
Les Calanques
  See *Cassis*
La Camargue
Esterel massif
Fontaine de Vaucluse
Hyères, Iles d'
Lubéron, Montagne du
Maures massif
Ste-Victoire, Mont
  See *Aix*
Ste-Baume, massif de la
Ventoux, Mont
Verdon, Grand Canyon du
Vésubie, gorges de la

Best resorts

Antibes, Cap d'
Bandol
Cannes
Cassis
Menton
Monte-Carlo
Nice
St-Jean-Cap-Ferrat
St-Tropez
Villefranche

Most attractive hill villages

Les Baux
Cabris
Coaraze
Èze
Fox-Amphoux
  See *Salernes*
Gassin
  See *St-Tropez*
Gordes
Gourdon
Grimaud
Haut-de-Cagnes
  See *Cagnes-sur-Mer*
Mons
Mougins
Peille
  See *Peillon*
Peillon
Roquebrune

Roussillon
St-Paul-de-Vence
Ste-Agnes
  See *Menton*
Saorge
Tourette-sur-Loup
Tourtour

Art museums

Annonciade, Musée de l'
  See *St-Tropez*
Art Moderne Méditerranée
  See *Cagnes-sur-Mer*
Calvet, Musée
  See *Avignon*
Chagall, Musée
  See *Nice*
Chéret, Musée
  See *Nice*
Granet, Musée
  See *Aix*
Grobet-Labadié, Musée
  See *Marseille*
Léger, Musée
  See *Biot*
Maeght, Fondation
  See *St-Paul*
Matisse, Musée
  See *Nice*
Picasso, Musée
  See *Antibes*
Réattu, Musée
  See *Arles*
Tapisseries, Musée des
  See *Aix*
Vasarely, Fondation
  See *Gordes* and *Aix*

Historic buildings

Chartreuse
  See *Villeneuve-lès-Avignon*
Château
  See *Tarascon*
Citadelle
  See *Sisteron*
Duché
  See *Uzès*
Palais des Papes
  See *Avignon*

Agay
Map **13***G13. 9km (5¼ miles)* E *of St-Raphael. 83700 St-Raphael, Var* **i** *Bd. Mer, N98* ☎ *(94) 82–01–85.*

An animated bathing resort on the Esterel coast, set in a deep bay with gently sloping sides crowned by the red crags of the Rastel d'Agay. The bay makes a perfect anchorage, and Roman pottery dug up from the sea bed indicates that it has harboured boats for well over 2,000yr. A long sandy beach curves round the bay, and there are several smaller creeks and coves. At **Le Dramont**, 1km (⅔ mile) to the SW, a tablet by the main road marks the landing at this spot of the 36th US Infantry Division on Aug 15, 1944. To the E of Le Dramont beach is a headland surmounted by a semaphore from where there is a spectacular view of the coast and the red Esterel massif behind.

☎ Beau Site
Camp-Long, Agay, 83700 St-Raphael ☎ *(94) 82–00–45* ▥ *24 rms* ▤ *14* ⬛ ▦ ▧ ☰ ☰ *June–Oct* AE ⓦ *Closed mid-Oct to Feb.*
Location: *Just* S *of Agay, across main road from an attractive sandy cove.* A spruce, German-owned pension; most guests are German. The leafy forecourt has a replica of Brussels' *Manneken Pis*. No lunches.
⬜ ⚲

☎ Sol e Mar
Le Dramont, Route de la Corniche d'Or, 83700 St-Raphael ☎ *(94) 95–25–60* ▥ *to* ▥ *46 rms* ▤ *46* ⬛ ☰ *Closed mid-Oct to Mar.*
Location: *Right by the sea at Le Dramont, 1.5km (1 mile)* SW *of Agay.* A very good new hotel, relatively secluded. There is a superb view from its panoramic restaurant, which has a sliding sun-roof. The pleasant rooms have balconies facing the sea. Amenities include a sea-water swimming-pool and a well-equipped private beach.
♨ ⬜ ⚓ 《 ≈ ⚲ ☏ ⚲

Restaurant nearby
Anthéor *(4km (2¼ miles)* E *of Agay).*

Les Flots Bleus ✿
☎ *(94) 44–80–21* ▥ ▭ ⬛ ⬛ *Last orders 21.00. Closed mid-Oct to Feb, Mon from Mar–May, Sept–Oct.*
Here are some reasonable fish soups, as well as tasty local fish dishes. A good place to stop for lunch, where you can eat under plane trees on a pleasant outdoor terrace in summer.

Aigues-Mortes
Map **8***F2. 42km (26 miles)* SW *of Nîmes. 30220 Gard. Population: 4,350* **i** *Pl. St-Louis* ☎ *(66) 53–73–00.*

Approached from the D979, built on the site of the original causeway to the town, Aigues-Mortes presents an unexpected and extraordinary sight: a perfect example of a medieval fortified town, still completely enclosed by four walls, above which no building or church spire is visible. This strange, lovely and rather melancholy town stands amid flat salty marshes and lagoons (the name means dead water, from the Roman *Aquae Mortuae*) and the only external aspect that has changed is the moat, now filled in. Inside, the ancient streets preserve their original grid pattern, though the population has dropped from 15,000 in the days of the Crusades to approximately 4,000 today.

The development of Aigues-Mortes from a sleepy fishing village – in those days it was by the sea, but the waters have since silted up, and it lies some 8km (5 miles) inland – came when Louis IX, St Louis, chose this spot from which to set sail on the

Aigues-Mortes

Seventh Crusade in 1248. While preparing for the voyage he built the city keep, the **Tour de Constance**. After his death from the plague on the Eighth Crusade (also begun from Aigues-Mortes), his son, Philip the Bold, completed the main ramparts. In the **Pl. St-Louis** there stands a statue of his father.

Tour de Constance et Remparts Ⅲ ☆
X July–Aug. Open Oct–Mar 10.00–12.00, 14.00–17.00; Apr–Sept 9.00–12.00, 14.00–18.00.

The imposing circular keep is 27m (90ft) high, and consists of two vaulted rooms, one above the other. In the lower room, the **Oratory of St Louis** is built into the 5.5m (18ft) thick walls; here a showcase holds early illuminated manuscripts and other documents of St Louis at Aigues-Mortes.

The upper room is devoted to souvenirs of the long period between the 14th–18thC when the tower was used as a political prison, first for Templars, later for Huguenots and victims of religious oppression. You can see the brave inscriptions left on the walls by the 18thC Huguenots: notably the words '*au ciel, résistez*', carved by Marie Durand, who entered the prison aged eight and was released 38yr later, physically a wreck but morally triumphant. The Protestants of the Nîmes area still venerate this tower for the sufferings of their martyrs. The summit of the tower affords a fine view over the strange countryside around, and from the tower you can walk round the ramparts.

Les Remparts
6 Pl. Anatole-France, 30220 Aigues-Mortes ☎ (66) 51–82–77 ▯ to ▮▮ 18 rms ☰ 18 ◻ ⊕ ⊚ VISA Closed Nov to mid-Dec.
Location: Just inside the ramparts, facing the Tour de Constance. An 18thC mansion has been converted into a sophisticated little hotel of character (though the ambience is slightly frosty) with comfortable period furniture offsetting the grey stone walls. (See restaurant.)
⌂ & ⎙

La Camargue
19 Rue de la République ☎ (66) 51–86–88 ▯ to ▮▮ ◻ ▬ ⌂ ⊕ Last orders 22.00. Closed Tues (except July–Aug). Nov to mid-Dec.
Very well known, very touristy, but fashionable too, La Camargue has hit on a sure-fire formula for revelry by night: a gargantuan six course set menu – *crudités* with *bagna cauda*, fish with *rouille*, log-fire-grilled steaks and chops, salad, cheeses, homemade tarts, wine ad lib – eaten by candlelight in the 17thC stone walled house to the vibrant accompaniment of gypsy guitarists and singers, often including Manitas de Plata. The name plates on the *banquettes* bear witness to the famous faces that have dined there; Pompidou, Romy Schneider, Alain Delon, Princess Radziwill and others. Lunches are simpler and quieter.

Les Remparts
Address and ☎ as hotel ▯ to ▮▮ ◻ ▬ ⌂ AE ⊕ ⊚ VISA Last orders 22.00. Closed Wed (except July–Aug), mid-Nov to mid-Dec, last two weeks in Jan.
The *carte* here is over-priced, but the set menu is much better value, with various local dishes. You can choose between eating in the elegant dining-room, or on the terrace with a view of the ramparts. (See hotel.)

Places nearby
Le Grau-du-Roi (*6km (4 miles) to SW*) A charming old fishing village, crowded in summer. Cheap, fairly good restaurants line its quays.
Port-Camargue (*10km (6 miles) to SW*) The most easterly of the chain of modernistic resorts along the Languedoc coast. (**La Grande Motte** is another, only 8km (5 miles) from Aigues-Mortes, but not within Provence.) Carved out of a marshy strip of deserted coast in the 1970s, it is a vast residential marina for 3,000 boats, so designed that every villa has its own mooring.

Whereas *Port-Grimaud* is in mock traditional style, Port
Camargue is unashamedly modern, and more spacious. (*For
villa hire and boat moorings apply to: Carrefour 2000 BP49, 30240
Port-Camargue* ☎ *(66) 51–41–71.*)

🛏 **Le Spinaker**
Pointe du Mole, 30240 Port-Camargue ☎ *(66) 51–54–93* ⬜⬜ *20 rms*
⬜ *20* 🚗 🛏 ≍ 🍽 *July–Aug* VISA *Closed Jan to mid-Feb.*
Location: On a broad grass jetty in the heart of the marina. This well
designed and cheerful little hotel would make a good base for a sailing
holiday (it has ten moorings, free to residents). The Cazals are charming
hosts, and each bedroom has its own terrace, with a view of the port.
& 🖼 ⬅ ≋

🍽 **Le Spinaker**
Address and ☎ *as hotel* ⬜⬜ 🍽 🚗 *July–Aug* 🚗 VISA *Last orders 21.00.*
Closed Sun dinner, Mon (Oct–May), Jan to mid-Feb.
Excellent fish dishes from Jean-Pierre Cazals in the light dining-room
overlooking the port. Buffet lunches served by the pool in summer.
Specialities: *Escalope de mérou poêlée au basilic, bouillon de crustacés à
l'estragon.*

Salins du Midi (*Just s of Aigues-Mortes*) These huge
saltworks produce 500,000 tons of salt from the surrounding
marshes. (*Visits July–Aug, Tues–Fri afternoons.*)

Aix-en-Provence

Map **10***G7. 31km (19 miles)* N *of Marseille. 13100 B.du-R.
Population: 114,000* ⓘ *Pl. du Gén.-de-Gaulle*
☎ *(42) 26–02–93.*

Aix is many people's favourite French town. More than any
other in the French provinces, it has the same kind of
aristocratic grace as certain noble Italian cities, say Florence or
Verona. From the 12th–18thC it was Provence's brilliant
capital: today, capital no more, it is still a centre of learning and
the arts, and still wears a proud patrician air. Its many lovely
buildings of the Classic period somehow harmonize with its
modern student ambience; and so intense and vivid is the life of
its womb-like nucleus of narrow streets that you hardly notice
its wider setting – on the edge of the plain of the Rhône delta,
with Cézanne's beloved hills rising steeply from its eastern
suburbs.

As at other towns called Aix, such as Aix-les-Bains, its name
(pronounced 'aches') comes from the Latin *aquae*, for there are
springs here, and in 123BC the Roman consul Sextius, after
subduing a local Ligurian tribe, founded a thermal station and
called it after himself, *Aquae Sextiae*. Aix soon became a major
Roman centre and for a while was capital of this part of Gaul.
But then it went into a long decline, to revive in the 12thC when
the Counts of Provence made it their capital. It was in the 15thC
that Aix knew its greatest splendour, under 'Good King René'
from 1442–80. He was really a count, but as exiled King of
Naples and Duke of Anjou he kept his royal title. Patron of
music and the arts, linguist and mathematician, René was a true
Renaissance man. He did much for Provence's economy,
introducing the silkworm and the muscat grape. He was also a
genial man with the common touch, who loved chatting with his
subjects and organizing festivals for them. Today he still enjoys
popularity and is something of a cult-figure in Aix: you will see
shops, cafés, even driving-schools and dry-cleaners, called '*Au
Roi René*'.

Soon after his death Provence was united to France, but until 1790 it retained much autonomy: Aix was the seat of its parliament and courts of justice. This is how it acquired its elegant 17thC and 18thC mansions, built by wealthy nobles, magistrates and prelates. Then in the 19thC with the rise of Marseille, Aix went into relative decline, and today is a mere sub-prefecture. But its population has grown enormously since 1945, with new suburbs and industries spreading across the plain. The new campuses of its important university (founded in the 15thC) are also in the suburbs.

The old part of the town is compact, a mere 730m (800yd) across, and is best visited on foot. Its central avenue, and focus of local life, is the famous **Cours Mirabeau**. Here, even outside university term, the sidewalks and terrace cafés are crowded with people who seem to retain a rare natural grace. The Aixois seem in many ways more northern Italian than French: they are relaxed, they dress with chic, they have pride. It is a town that exudes culture, and a deeply-rooted stylishness very different from the imported gloss of, say, Cannes.

Events: Last fortnight in June, street festival of free outdoor concerts. From mid-July to mid-Aug, Aix stages one of the leading annual music festivals in Europe. For details apply to Bureau du Festival, Palais de l'Ancien Archevêché, 13100 Aix ☎(42) 23–11–20.

Sights and places of interest
Atelier Cézanne
9 Av. Paul Cézanne ☎ *(42) 21–06–53* 🔲 🗺 *Open June–Sept 10.00–12.00, 14.30–18.00; Oct–May 10.00–12.00, 14.30–17.00. Closed Tues.*

Cézanne's austere, obsessive personality emerges forcefully in this untidy studio, which has been reconstructed just as it was at his death in 1906. He lived down in the city, at 23 Rue Boulegon: but each day he would come to paint in the first floor room of this small house in the N

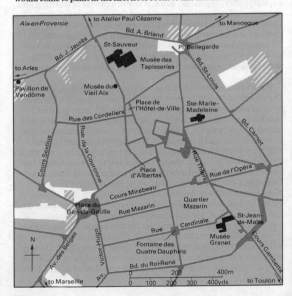

suburbs, with its wide N-facing windows. Of his own works there are just two drawings and a gouache: but you can see his easel and palette, his chair, hat and cloak, clay pipe and other personal effects, as well as photos and letters. Here too are some of the actual objects that he painted: wine-glasses, bottles, and skulls (only the onions are recent). The effect is more than a little macabre, far removed from the sense of family warmth and life-affirming lyricism that pervades Renoir's house at *Cagnes-sur-Mer*.

Cours Mirabeau ☆

Aix's central avenue, built in the 17thC on the site of the old ramparts, and later named after the Marquis de Mirabeau, is still one of France's noblest streets, though a mere 450m (500yd) long. It is shaded by four rows of tall plane trees which meet above to form a green arbour. The N side is lined with bookshops and cafés, of which the smartest is **La Belle Époque**, at no.31 (Le Quick Burger, at no.37, somewhat lets the tone down). The s side, though now infiltrated with banks, cinemas and estate agents, is still mainly a preserve of 17th and 18thC mansions: note the bearded, half-naked atlantes supporting the balcony of **no.38**, now a university building.

The Cours has four fountains. To the w, the giant three-tiered **Fontaine Grande**, with traffic swirling round it in the wide Pl. du Général-de-Gaulle; then the **Fontaine des Neufs-Canons** (1691); then the squat, moss-covered **Fontaine d'Eau Chaude**, with running warm spring water; lastly, the **Fontaine du Roi René**, with a 19thC statue of the king holding muscat grapes.

Granet, Musée ☆

Pl. St-Jean-de-Malte ☎ (42) 38–14–70 ▓ Open 10.00–12.00, 14.00–18.00. Closed Tues.

This former Priory of the Knights of Malta (17thC) now houses one of the most excellent and varied art collections in Provence. The museum is named after the early 19thC Aixois painter François Granet, who was a leading donor. On the first floor are French paintings of the Renaissance and of the Fontainebleau and Provençal schools. Provence is represented notably by Granet himself, as well as Van Loo and Le Nain, and by a large colourful 19thC canvas of *King René Signing a Reprieve*, by Guillemot.

The few Cézanne canvasses are minor works. But there is a fine Ingres: *Jupiter and Thetis* (1811). On the second floor: mainly Dutch and Flemish works, including a de Hooch interior, a small Rembrandt self-portrait, Teniers' charming *Night Fête in a Village*, and Vinckeboons' strange *Wedding in Cana*. The museum mounts special exhibitions each year, for example, in 1981, a superb 'King René and his Times'.

The large archaeology room on the ground floor has Greek and Roman sculptures, and Egyptiana, including a mummy of the Twelfth Dynasty with elaborate coloured inscriptions. There is also a unique collection of Celto-Ligurian sculptures from Egremont, mostly excavated in the 1940s. They include deathmasks, low-reliefs and warriors' torsos, all very primitive but detailed in their carving; the earliest known pre-Roman sculptures in France.

Mazarin Quarter

Just SE of the Cours Mirabeau, this once aristocratic quarter was built in the 17thC by Michel Mazarin, Archbishop of Aix: it is a grid of narrow streets, harmonious but severe. Worth seeing: the 17thC **Fontaine des Quatre Dauphins**; the **Musée Paul Arbaud** (▓ *open 14.00–17.00, closed Sun*) of local art and history; and the lovely 13thC interior of the **St Jean-de-Malte church**, next to the **Musée Granet**.

Ste-Marie-Madeleine †

Pl. des Prêcheurs. Closed Sun afternoon, Mon–Sat 11.30–15.00.

This large 17thC church has a dull modern w façade, but inside is very ornate. There are paintings by Rubens and Van Loo, and an 18thC marble *Virgin* by Chastel at the far end of the right aisle. The treasured work of art is the 15thC *Annunciation*, believed to be the work of Jean Chapus of Avignon: it is the centrepiece of a triptych, the side-panels of which are in Belgium and in the Netherlands (but copies are here in the sacristy).

St-Sauveur, Cathédrale ▥ † ☆

Rue J-Laroque. ▥ Open daily 8.00–12.00, 14.00–18.30.

A cathedral rich in works of art, and in a great jumble of styles, from the

5th–16thC. The right aisle was the nave of an old Romanesque church, later incorporated into the Gothic cathedral. Thus the w facade, too, has a Romanesque section on the right while the rest is 16thC Flamboyant Gothic. Of its original sculptures, all were destroyed in the Revolution save the central *Virgin*, spared because someone stuck a cap of Liberty on her head. The other statues are 19thC replacements.

The cathedral's main treasures are kept locked for safety: the sacristan will open them up and explain them. First, the elaborate 16thC wood carvings on the w doors, depicting 12 pagan sibyls and four prophets. Next, Nicolas Froment's famous triptych, *The Burning Bush* ☆ painted for King René in 1475.

The cathedral's magnificent set of 15 Brussels tapestries are not now in view, alas. They were woven in 1511 for Canterbury Cathedral, then sold by Cromwell, and finally bought by a canon of Aix for a paltry 2,200 *écus*. Off the right aisle is a large 5thC Gallo-Roman baptistry, similar in style to that at *Fréjus*.

Beside the cathedral is its delightful Romanesque **cloister**. Unlike those of *Arles* and Fréjus it is roofed over.

Tapisseries, Musée des
Ancien Archevêché ☎ (42) 23-09-91 ■■ ☆ 🌂 ✗ *Open June to mid-Oct 10.00–12.00, 14.00–18.00; mid-Oct to May 10.00–12.00, 14.00–17.00. Closed Tues.*

The former archbishop's palace, with its chandeliers and marble walls, houses this celebrated collection of 18 Beauvais tapestries of the 17th–18thC. They were discovered in the roof in 1849, possibly having been hidden there during the Revolution. Nine of them, from designs by Natoire, are lively scenes from the life of Don Quixote, a gangling figure with startled eyes.

Vasarely, Fondation ☆
Av. Marcel-Pagnol, 4km (2½ miles) wsw of Aix ☎ (42) 20-01-09 ■■ *Open 9.30–12.30, 14.00–17.30. Closed Tues.*

This ultra-modern museum stands alone on a hill in the w suburbs. The Hungarian-born artist, not the most modest of men, created it himself in 1975 to house his own works, and has included tributes to his 'genius' by Le Corbusier and other contemporaries. It is very striking, and will fascinate admirers of Vasarely's idiosyncratic innovations. Seven open-plan hexagonal cells, cleverly lit, display a range of his huge geometric murals as well as tapestries, rotating glass sculptures, polychromatic tiled mosaics and much else. Dazzling colours integrate with mathematical complexities, to provide insights into Vasarely's experiments with the illusions of light and movement. Upstairs, a set of automatic sliding panels explain his *oeuvre* to the uninitiated (as in his museum at *Gordes*). The Foundation also acts as a research and seminar centre.

Vendôme, Pavillon de
32 Rue Célony ☎ (42) 21-05-78 ■■ *Open June–Sept 10.00–12.00, 14.00–18.30; Oct–May 10.00–12.00, 14.00–17.00. Closed Tues.*

Lying just outside the Old Town, this gracious mansion with its formal garden was built in 1667 as a summer home of the Cardinal of Vendôme, governor of Provence. It later belonged to the Aixois painter Van Loo. The facade, a fine example of the 17thC local style, has atlantes supporting its balcony. Inside are furniture and paintings of the period, and an imposing double stairway.

Vieil Aix ☆
The oldest part of Aix, between the Cours Mirabeau and the cathedral, is a delightful place for a walk, especially as many of its narrow streets are now closed to traffic. Though lined with lovely old buildings, it is more than a museum piece – it is a vibrant centre of the city's present-day life, full of smart shops and shoppers. Here the comparison with Florence is most apt.

Of the many fine 16th–17thC houses, several are now museums. The **Hôtel Boyer d'Eguilles** (*6 Rue Espariat*) now houses the **Muséum d'Histoire Naturelle** (■■ *open 10.00–12.00, 14.00–18.00, closed Sun*). Next door, the calm and enchanting little **Pl. d'Albertas** ☆ is a tiny cobbled square with a fountain in the middle, lined with grey 18thC houses, with not a shop or café.

To the N, via the Rue Aude and Rue Foch, is the **Pl. de l'Hôtel-de-Ville** with its colourful flower market. The former corn-market building, now a sub-post office, has splendid 18thC carvings by the sculptor

Chastel. The **Hôtel de Ville** itself (17thC), with its fine wrought-iron entrance gate, houses the famous **Méjanes library** of 300,000 volumes bequeathed in the 18thC by the Marquis of Méjanes: its many rare books of the 15th–16thC are kept locked away, but can be consulted by scholars who should write in advance to the curator. In one wing of the town hall, the **Fondation St-John Perse** is devoted to this poet's life and works and contains a legacy of his own letters, photographs and manuscripts.

The early 16thC **tour de l'horloge** beside the town hall is unusual, for in the belfry at its top are four statues representing the seasons which rotate, each one showing its face in turn for three months. From here it is just a few yards to the **Musée du Vieil Aix** (see below), the cathedral of **St Sauveur**, and the **Musée des Tapisseries** (see left). In the NW corner of the old town is a spa centre, built in the 18thC beside the old Roman baths. It is still used for treating arthritis and bad circulation.

Vieil Aix, Musée du ☆▥
17 Rue Saporta ☎ *Open daily Apr–Sept 10.00–12.00, 14.00–18.00; Oct–Mar 10.00–12.00, 14.00–17.00. Closed Mon.*

Occupying the ground floor of a fine 17thC mansion, this is one of the best folklore museums in Provence. It is notable for its collections of *santons*, nativity cribs, and mechanical dolls and puppets, all once used in local traditional *fêtes*. The *santons* are of clay and the puppets of cardboard: but all are so richly costumed you can hardly spot the difference. At the back is a pretty boudoir with a frescoed ceiling: in it is a chest which Louis XIV left behind on a visit to this house. Note also the unique paintings worked on velvet by the Aixois artist Grégoire (1751–1846).

Hotels

Caravelle ✿
29 Bd. de Roi-René, 13100 Aix-en-Provence ☎ *(42) 62–53–05*
▯▯ to ▯▯▯ *30 rms* ▭ *24* ⊕ ⊚
[VISA]
Location: Fairly central, on a main street SE of the Cours Mirabeau. This neat, modern hotel makes a useful base for a visit to Aix. Its staff are attentive and helpful and its prices remarkably modest for such comfort.
‡ ▱

Cézanne ▥
40 Av. Victor-Hugo, 13100 Aix-en-Provence ☎ *(42) 26–34–73*
▯▯▯ to ▯▯▯ *44 rms* ▭ *44* ▤ ▭
[AE]
Location: Central, on a main street facing the station. The Cézanne justifies its prices, for it has real character, as well as being friendly and very well run. Each bedroom is strikingly different, some modern, some in classic style; some even have the added luxury of four-poster beds.
‡ ▱ ✇

Nègre Coste
33 Cours Mirabeau, 13100 Aix-en-Provence ☎ *(42) 27–74–22*
▯▯▯ to ▯▯▯ *37 rms* ▭ *37* ▭ [AE]
⊕ ⊚ [VISA]
Location: Central. This 18thC residence is now a sedate little hotel, the discreet elegance of which is fully suited to Aix's

famous main avenue. The spacious bedrooms are decorated, somewhat dully, in Louis XV style, and much of the hotel's ornate furniture is made up of genuine period pieces.
‡ ⟡ ▭ ▱

Le Pigonnet ✿
Av. du Pigonnet, 13100 Aix-en-Provence ☎ *(42) 59–02–90*
▨*410629* ▯▯▯ to ▯▯▯ *50 rms* ▭ *50*
▭ ▭ ⇌ [AE] ⊕ ⊚ [VISA]
Location: Towards the outskirts. Part of the long-established PLM chain, this is Aix's most seductive hotel: a handsome creeper-covered mansion with true Provençal decor and an air of intimate chic. Bedrooms are spacious, with pretty wallpaper and antique furniture; some have large balconies, facing the hills that Cézanne loved. The large, ornate garden with its fountains and rose arbours could belong to some grand Edwardian villa, and is suffused with romantic melancholy. (See restaurant, Le Patio.)
▱ ‡ ⟡ ▭ ▱ ❦ ≈ ☗

Other recommended hotels:
Novotel Aix Est *(3km (2 miles) SE beside A8* ☎ *(42) 27–47–50* ▯▯); **Novotel Aix Sud** *(same location* ☎ *(42) 27–90–49* ▯▯); **Le Prieuré** *(2km (1.25 miles) NE on Route de Sisteron* ☎ *(42) 21–05–23* ▯ *to* ▯▯).

Restaurants

L'Abbaye des Cordeliers
21 Rue Lieutaud
☎*(42) 27–29–47* ◻ *to* ◼◻ ▭
▰ *Last orders 21.00. Closed
Mon–Thurs (Oct–Feb).
Tues–Wed (Mar–Sept).*
A quiet and select establishment,
housed in a former abbey. Reliable
traditional cooking.

Auberge d'Aillane
Zone industrielle Les Milles
☎*(42) 24–24–49* ◻ ▭ ▰
Closed eve, Sat and Sun.
The Curto family have turned their
own attractive home into a
restaurant, where the parents cook
and their three charming daughters
serve. Tasty Provençal cuisine. In
summer you dine in a courtyard
amid flowers and fountains. The
atmosphere is relaxed and friendly
and the service good-natured.

Les Caves Henri IV
32 Rue Espariat
☎*(42) 27–86–39* ◼◻ ▭ ▰
▦ *Last orders 21.30. Closed
Sun, Mon (lunch), one week in
early Mar, three weeks in Aug.*
The *caves* are a 16thC cellar with
vaulted stone ceiling, in the heart
of Vieil Aix. The conversion has
been tastefully done, though some
might find the setting a shade
claustrophobic. Jean-Marc Banzo,
the young *patron* and chef, learned
his craft by working in some of the

region's top restaurants, such as
Hiély at Avignon; and now he is
eagerly putting into action his own
nouvelle cuisine ideas, usually with
success and adhering closely to
local produce. Menus change
frequently but you may find the
following dishes particularly good.
Specialities: *Salade d'écrevisses à la
crème d'anis, aiguillettes de canette à
la compôte d'oignons.*

Al Dente
14 Rue Constantine
☎*(42) 96–41–03* ◻ *Last orders
22.00. Closed Sun, Mon lunch.*
Quick service and very reasonable
prices at this lively Italian
restaurant, popular with young
people. ***Specialities:*** *Various kinds
of fresh pasta.*

Le Patio
Address and ☎ *as Hôtel Le
Pigonnet* ◼◻ *to* ◼◼◻ ◻ ▭ ▰
▱ ◉ ◎ ▨ *Last orders
21.00. Closed Sun dinner
(Nov–Mar).*
The dining-room is elegant but
somewhat formal, but on fine days
it is a delight to dine out on the
wide terrace under the chestnut
trees. Service is polished, and the
classic *cuisine* very reliable.
Specialities: *Terrine de St-Pierre,
aiguillettes de canard aux griottes,
estouffade de boeuf provençal.* (See
hotel, **Le Pigonnet**.)

Nightlife
Casino Municipal (*Bd. de la République* ☎ *(42) 26–30–33,
open 15.00–2.00*); **Le Vendôme** (☎ *(42) 26–01–00*) for dinner
dances on Sat; and **Cardinal** (☎ *(42) 26–30–03*) for *thés-
dansants*. All are part of the casino, smart and conventional.

Aix has over 25 discos; try the **Mistral Newby Street** (*3
Rue Mistral*). **Célony** is one of Provence's best jazz clubs and
often has famous performers.

Shopping
Several streets in the old town, N of the Cours Mirabeau, are full
of antique shops and boutiques selling Provençal handicrafts
and food specialities (Rue Saporta, Rue Granet, Rue Jaubert,
Rue Mathéron, Pl. des Cardeurs).

La Reine Jeanne (*32 Cours Mirabeau*) and **Brémond Fils**
(*36 Cours Mirabeau*) are two *pâtisseries* specializing in *calissons*,
the marzipan biscuits for which Aix is famous.

There is a delightful open-air **food market** in the Pl. des
Prêcheurs on Tues, Thurs, and Sat mornings.

Places nearby
Aqueduc de Roquefavour (*11km (7 miles) W of Aix*)   This
vast three-tier edifice was built in 1842–47 to carry the waters of
the Durance to Marseille. It is nearly twice as high as the *Pont
du Gard*, and 90m (100yd) longer.

Entremont *(3km (2 miles) N of Aix)* In pre-Roman days, a group of Celto-Ligurian tribes had their base on this plateau. Recent excavations have revealed the remains of their sizeable oppidum, sacked by Consul Sextius in 123BC. Parts of the ramparts, a gateway, and some house walls are visible.
Meyrargues *(20km (13 miles) NE of Aix)* A village in the Durance valley, dominated by its 12thC château/hotel.

♔ Château de Meyrargues
13650 Meyrargues ☎ *(42) 57–50–32* ▮▮▯ *14 rms* ▭ *14* ◂▪ ▭ ≈ ⌂
AE ⊙ *Closed Dec–Jan.*
Location: Perched on a high hill above the village, amid its own 12-acre park. The perfect place for lovers of baronial grandeur, this may look like the set of an old Charlton Heston sword-duel movie, but it's real. The stately 12thC château, restored in the 17thC, has been converted into an elegant little hotel, with all the right touches – tapestries, beamed ceilings, genuine Louis XV furniture in the bedrooms, and lordly stone chimney-pieces where log fires are lit on chilly days. The entrance is high romance: a steel flight of steps, a massive stone gateway, and a charming inner courtyard, open on one side to a dizzy view across the valley below. The *patronne*, Jeanne Drouillet, has the ideal *châtelaine*-like presence for running her domain with stylish authority, but she also enjoys informality: guests are invited to pay their bills in the kitchen.
⌂▭ ⚓ ⟨⟨ ☺

Ste-Victoire, Mont *(8km (5 miles) E of Aix)* This high limestone ridge is the mountain that Cézanne loved and painted so often, in so many varied hues. Seen head-on from Aix, as he saw it, it looks like a great white cone. In reality, as seen from the A8 autoroute to the S, it is a long 16km (10 mile) wall of rock, rising to over 1,000m (3,300ft). From Aix take the D10 toward Vauvenargues. Just beyond a string of artificial lakes leave the car at Les Cabassols for a stiff 2hr hike up a mule track past the chapel of Ste-Victoire to the monument of **Croix de Provence** on the summit (superb views, from the Alps to the sea). At **Vauvenargues** is the 17thC château owned for a while by Picasso; he lies buried in its park. Near **Pourrières**, at the E end of the ridge, is the site of the Roman general Marius' victory over the Teuton hordes in 102BC: 100,000 invaders are said to have been slain, hence, so it is thought, the mountain's name.

Annot
*Map **14**D12. 32km (20 miles) NE of Castellane. 04240 Alpes-de-H.-P. Population: 885* ℹ *Pl. du Revely* ☎ *(92) 82–23–03 (winter), (92) 83–21–40 (summer). Inquiries also at Mairie* ☎ *(92) 83–22–09.*
Annot has attracted many a painter, for this graceful little town has much charm and is one of the most pleasant summer resorts of the eastern hinterland. Stroll down the winding, neatly-paved alleys of the Old Town, full of little streams, ancient archways and tall Renaissance houses. The main square, archetypically Provençal, is shaded by lofty veteran plane trees. Annot lies in a valley which in summer is full of scents and colours – lilac and lavender, lime and chestnut. The hills close by, easily reached on foot, are famous for their curious sandstone rock formations, eroded into bizarre shapes.

♔ Auberge La Cigale
04240 Annot ☎ *(92) 83–20–24* ▭ *116 rms* ▭ *116* ≈ ⌂ ▪▪ ⌴
Location: Thirty metres from the main square of the town. A simple but sympathetic little country inn, with two dining-rooms, a room for dancing and a terrace for eating outdoors in summer. Generous helpings.
Specialities: *Pâté de truite, filet de sanglier ou de chevreuil (in season).*

Ansouis

≈ **Honnoraty**
Les Scaffarels, 04240 Annot ☎ *(92) 83–22–03* ☐ *12 rms* ☐ *3* ⊷ ≈
◼

Location: 2km (1.25 miles) from Annot on the Nice road. A modest family
hotel of no great pretensions but with perfectly comfortable rooms. There
is a serviceable restaurant with a choice of two cheap menus.

≈ Other simple hotels include: **Avenue** (☎ *(92) 83–22–07* ☐);
Beauséjour (☎ *(92) 83–21–08* ☐).

Places nearby
Méailles (*8km (5 miles) NW of Annot*) An attractive hilltop
village, beyond which there are good views from the **Col de la
Colle-St-Michel**, leading into the upper Verdon valley toward
Colmars. To the E of Annot, along the N202, lies *Entrevaux*, to
the SW, the *Verdon Grand Canyon*.

Ansouis
*Map 5E7. 29km (18 miles) N of Aix. 84120 Vaucluse.
Population: 500.*
A tiny hill village, just S of the *Lubéron* mountain, which is
dominated by its **Château de Sabran** (◼ *open 14.30–18.30,
closed Tues from Oct–June*). Heavily fortified, part medieval
and part 17thC, the château has belonged to the same ducal
family since the 13thC. The interior is baronial and impressive,
notably the dining-hall with its Flemish tapestries and the
guardroom with its armour. Do not miss the curious hanging
gardens.
   The village **church** is an old Romanesque fortified chapel.
Nearby the little **Mazoyer museum** of Provençal furniture,
paintings and also seashells – an odd subject for a hill village
(*open 14.00–19.00, closed Tues*).

Places nearby
La Tour d'Aigues (*8km (5 miles) E of Ansouis*) In the village
are the ruins of a fine moated 16thC castle, burned in 1780. The
stately Corinthian entrance gate gives some idea of the
building's quality in its heyday. Attractive views.

≈ **Hostellerie du Château** ✿
Pl. du Château ☎ *(90) 77–43–55* ☐ ☐ ☐ *Last orders 21.00. Closed
Sun dinner, Mon, early June to early July.*
A simple, typical *auberge* in 'rustic' style, on the first floor of a house
opposite the castle. The cooking is faultlessly professional and the
helpings plentiful. Sound country food. *Specialities: Cuisses de
grenouilles, civet d'agneau.*

Antibes ☆
*Map 15F14. 11km (7 miles) NE of Cannes. 06600 Alpes-Mar.
Population: 56,300 ℹ 11 Pl. de Gaulle* ☎ *(93) 33–95–64.*
Founded by the ancient Greeks as a trading-post, Antibes today
is still bustling and commercial, with sprawling suburbs and
dense traffic. The Greeks called it Antipolis, 'the city opposite',
as it faced their colony at Nice across the Baie des Anges; this
geographical fact has dominated much of the town's history.
From the late 14thC Antibes was the frontier fortress town of
the Kings of France when their enemies, the Dukes of Savoy,
held sway in Nice; of the town's fortifications only the sea-front
and the giant 16thC Fort Carré, situated just N of the harbour,
remain. As a young patron in command of coastal defences,
Napoleon lived here with his family in 1794 – in penury it

62

seems, for his revolutionary masters were slow with their pay cheques. Today you can walk along the sea ramparts with their fine views of the coast, of Nice and the Alps. Behind them is the famous **Musée Picasso**, and the narrow streets of the **Vieille Ville**, full of atmosphere and charm. Antibes is not the best choice for a beach holiday (though the shingle to the E here turns to sand and the beach is usually very crowded), but culturally it is fascinating.

Sights and places of interest
Archéologique, Musée
St-André Bastion 🔳 *Open 9.00–12.00, 14.00–18.00. Closed Tues, Nov.*

In this museum just s of the Château Grimaldi, 4,000yr of the town's history are revealed in pottery, money and other finds.
Cathédrale †
Antibes' parish church is still referred to as a cathedral, though the bishopric was removed to Grasse as far back as 1244 and is now at Nice. The building is mainly 17thC, but dates originally from the 12thC. It stands right by the sea wall on what is thought to be the site of a Roman temple. Inside, the elaborate altarpiece at the end of the right aisle is probably by Louis Bréa (c.1500).
Picasso, Musée ☆
Château Grimaldi, Vieille Ville ☎ *(93) 33–67–67* 🔳 ✗ *Open summer 10.00–12.00, 15.00–19.00, winter 15.00–18.00. Closed Tues, Nov.*
The 13th–16thC castle of the Grimaldis, for centuries the rulers of Antibes, is today a municipal museum, housing one of the world's finest Picasso collections.

After spending the bleak war years in Paris, Picasso returned to his adored Mediterranean in 1945, but he was handicapped by the lack of a proper studio – until the curator offered him the museum for this purpose. Here Picasso worked for several months with joyous inspiration, and afterwards, in gratitude, he left his entire prodigious output of that period on permanent loan to the museum, together with some 200 of the vivid ceramics he later produced at nearby *Vallauris*.

The museum's first floor is filled with works inspired by the sea and Greek mythology: here are numerous centaurs, fauns, fish and fishermen, and some of the artist's famous large-scale paintings such as *Ulysse et Les Sirènes* and *La Joie de Vivre*, an exuberant fantasy with dancing satyrs.

The second floor houses temporary exhibitions as well as works by other modern artists, including tapestries by Léger and Lurçat. On the terrace facing the sea are four statues by Germaine Richier.

The museum also includes archaeological exhibits dating from the Roman occupation of Antibes.

🕰 Bleu Marine
Rue des Quatre-Chemins, 06600 Antibes ☎ *(93) 74–84–84* ☐ *to* ▥ *18 rms* 🛏 *18* 🚭 ᴀᴇ 𝘝𝘐𝘚𝘈
Closed Dec to mid-Jan.
Location: *2km (1.25 miles) N of Antibes, between N7 and the sea.* A brand-new hotel, most of its rooms with sea-facing balconies. No restaurant.
✚ ☐ ☛ ❧ 🐾

🕰 First Hotel
21 Av. des Chenes, 0660 Antibes ☎ *(93) 61–87–37. 16 rms* 🛏 *12* 🚭
Location: *200m (220yds) from a sandy beach.* A former villa converted into a comfortable modern hotel with a family

atmosphere. Meals in the garden summer.
🕭 ☐ ☛ ❧ 🐾 🚗

🕰 Mas Djoliba
29 Av. de Provence, 06600 Antibes ☎ *(93) 34–02–48* ▥
14 rms 🛏 *14* 🚗 🛏 🚼 ᴀᴇ ⊕
Location: *In a quiet street in the s suburbs, near the beach.* This villa-hotel, which has recently changed management and undergone substantial refurbishing, stands in its own large garden and has something of the air of a private house. Rooms are comfortable, but service has been known to be vague. No lunches; dinners served in a vine arbour in fine weather.
☁ ☛ ❧

Antibes

➤ L'Ecurie Royale
33 Rue Vauban ☎ *(93) 34–76–20
or 61–07–99* ▥▥ *to* ▥▥▥ AE ⊕ VISA
*Closed Sun for lunch, Mon, Tues
mid-Oct to May, mid-Nov to
December.*

A Belgian couple, the Xhauflairs,
show flair indeed in running their
rustic-style restaurant, warm and
welcoming, with excellent cooking.
Specialities: *Foie de canard au
torchon maison, suprême de pintade
aux épinards.*

➤ La Marguerite ✿
11 Rue Sadi-Carnot
☎ *(93) 34–08–27* ▥▥ ▭ ▬ CB
⊕ *Last orders 21.30, Closed Sun
dinner, Mon, Tues lunch in
summer, mid-Apr to mid-May.*

In a dull part of Antibes near the
station, a small restaurant with a
romantically pretty interior, and
some of the best cooking in town.
Specialities: *Fresh fish, depending
on season and availability.*

➤ La Paille en Queue
42 Bd. Wilson ☎ *(93) 34–39–89*
▥▥ AE ⊕ VISA *Last orders 22.00.
Closed Sun dinner, Wed.*

The decor is Louis XVI, and the
owners, the Niesor brothers, come
from the island of La Reunion,
which explains the spicy exoticism
of some of their dishes.
Specialities: *(Réunion) agneau au
massalé, samoussas sambos; (French)
brouillade d'aubergine à la menthe
fraiche.*

➤ Other good restaurants in the
Old Town are: **Auberge
Provençal,** *(Pl. Nationale*
☎ *(93) 34–13–24* ▭ *to* ▥▥);
L'Oursin *(16 Rue République*
☎ *(93) 34–13–46* ▭).

Restaurant nearby
La Brague *(4km (2½ miles) N of
Antibes).*

La Bonne Auberge ⌂
RN7, La Brague
☎ *(93) 33–36–65* ⑩*470989* ▥▥
▭ ▬ ☎ AE ⊕ *Last
orders 22.00. Closed Mon lunch,
Mon dinner Sept to June, mid-
Nov to mid-Dec.*

Under the supervision of its
brilliant *patron* and chef, Jo
Rostang, this spacious pink
auberge just N of Antibes has moved
up to near the top of the *Côte's*
gastronomic league, and is
besieged by the rich and famous. A
bouquet of flowers on each table, a
shady arbour for summer dining –
all is near perfection, including the
food. Big picture windows separate
kitchen from dining-room, so that
some tables have a front-row view
of the high drama of the *maître* and
his acolytes preparing their
delights. These are inventive and
varied in the *nouvelle cuisine*
fashion. **Specialities:** *Terrine
de foie de canard au bavarois d'ail
chaud, feuilleté d'asperges au
sabayon de verveine, aiguillette de
canard poivrade.*

Nightlife
The best nightlife in the Antibes area is to be found at **La Siesta**
(*N559, La Brague, 4km (2½ miles) N of Antibes*
☎ *(93) 33–31–31* ▾ ⊙ ♪ ☺ ✻ *open June to mid-Sept
10.00–5.00, dancing from 21.00*), a huge and exotic beach
nightclub attracting the *Côte's jeunesse dorée.* By day it's a lido
(every watersport, specially imported sand, supervised
children's area, even a restaurant for dogs), by night a network
of open-air bars and dance floors with waterfalls illuminated by
flaming torches. Extraordinary wave-shaped casino.

Shopping
La Colombelle, opposite the Musée Picasso, sells good, locally
made jewellery, pottery and handicrafts. Just behind, in the Pl.
Masséna, is the open-air fruit, vegetable and fish **market**, open
every morning except Mon. The Rue James Close has many
little boutiques.

Places nearby
Marineland ☆ (*RN7, La Brague* ☎ *(93) 33–49–49* ▬ ▬
✱) Performing dolphins, sealions and huge Icelandic orcas.
The zoo also contains penguins and an aquarium, and there's a
children's play area. Amusing and crowded.

64

Antibes, Cap d' ☆
Map **15***F15. 2km (1 mile) s of Antibes. 06600 Alpes-Mar* **i** *11*
Pl. de Gaulle, Antibes ☎ *(93) 76–95–64.*

The name Cap d'Antibes refers to the whole of the beautiful
pine-forested peninsula to the s of Antibes and *Juan-les-Pins*,
though the Cape proper is its southern-most tip. A haven of
calm, it is, like *St-Jean-Cap Ferrat*, a favourite haunt of the
rich, and much of it is divided into private estates with imposing
villas and sub-tropical gardens. But there is much for the
ordinary visitor too: sandy beaches, splendid views, reasonably
priced hotels and restaurants, botanical gardens and other
curiosities. The best beaches charge a fee: to the E **Plage de la
Garoupe**; to the w, **Port Gallice**.

Sights and places of interest
La Garoupe, Sanctuaire de ☆
La Garoupe ⛪ *Open Easter to Sept, 9.30–12.30, 14.30–19.00; Oct
to Easter 10.00–12.00, 14.30–17.00. Ask porter for key.*
Standing by a lighthouse on a hill in the centre of the peninsula, this
curious sailors' chapel is famous for the ex-votos with which its walls are
hung: paintings by amateurs, executed in fulfilment of a vow or in
thanksgiving for deliverance from death. Their naiveté is fascinating and
rather touching. One aisle is filled with sailors' ex-votos, including a
self-portrait by a convict seen giving thanks to Our Lady for helping him
escape to Martinique from Toulon gaol. The second aisle is devoted to
the miraculous escapes of land-lubbers: a man falling from a tree in 1865,
another from a ladder, another saved from an irate dog. A particularly
vivid one depicts a road accident. The car lies on its back in a ditch while
the family, somewhat foolishly one might think, kneel in the middle of
the road and give thanks to Our Lady who has appeared in the sky.

The diffused magic of the hot sweet South had withdrawn into
them – the soft-pawed night and the ghostly wash of the
Mediterranean far below – the magic left these things and
melted into the two Divers and became part of them.
                    F. Scott Fitzgerald, *Tender is the Night*, 1939

After this high drama, it may come as an anti-climax to learn that the
chapel also has a fine 14thC Russian ikon and a Russian silk painting –
spoils of the Crimean War.
    Next to the chapel is a vista point with marvellous views of the coast.
The lighthouse is one of the most powerful on the Riviera.
Naval et Napoléonien, Musée
Batterie du Grillon 📷 *Open 10.00–12.00, 15.00–19.00
(14.00–17.00 in winter). Closed Tues, Nov to mid-Dec.*
Models of men-o'-war and mementoes of Napoleon's landing at nearby
Golfe-Juan on his return from Elba in 1815. Views of the Alps and
Corsica on a clear day from the top of the tower.
Thuret, Jardin
*w of La Garoupe Chapel. Open 8.30–12.00, 14.00–17.30. Closed Sat,
Sun.*
Containing a fine array of exotic trees and flora, the gardens were
founded in 1856 by Thuret as one of the first centres in Europe for the
acclimatization of tropical vegetation, much of which is now established
on the coast.

🍴 **Cap d'Antibes** 🏨
*Bd. Kennedy, 06600 Cap
d'Antibes* ☎ *(93) 61–39–01*
📞*470763* **IIII** *90 rms* 🛏 *90* 🔲
🍽 🔲 🔲 ⇌ *Closed Nov to
Easter.*
Location: *At the s tip of the peninsula
in its own 15-acre park.* There are
more famous ghosts than

bedrooms to haunt, at this, the
proudest and most stylish of all the
Riviera's luxury palaces. It was the
original hotel in Scott Fitzgerald's
Tender is the Night; and from its
opening in 1870 until recent times
it was the very smartest rendezvous
for royalty and celebrities alike,
from Haile Selassie to Betty Grable

and J. F. Kennedy to G. B. Shaw.

Today Le Cap's Swiss owners have married tasteful, modern decor with the opulence of a bygone age: marble floors, airy salons, spacious bedrooms, and, beneath the handsome cream-coloured palace, a splendid garden of flowers, pines and palms that sweeps down to the sea. (See restaurant, **Pavillon Eden Roc**.)
🛏 🔔 🚗 📺 🌊 ⚓ 🛶 ⛷ ⛵
🏌 🚴 🚣 🎾 *out of season.*

🐾 La Gardiole
Chemin de la Garoupe, 06600 Cap d'Antibes
☎ (93) 61–35–03 ▮▮ *20 rms* 🛏
20 🍴 🚗 AE ⊕ ⊙ VISA *Closed Dec to mid-Feb.*
Location: High in the centre of the peninsula, with a sandy beach close by. Set amid a pine wood in its own flowery garden, this is a delightful medium-priced hotel with a civilized family ambience (though service can be a little disorganized). Rooms are simple and fresh, many with private terraces. (See restaurant.)
🛏 🔔 🚗 📺 🍴 🚴 🎾

⟀ Bacon 🍴
Bd. de Bacon ☎ (93) 61–50–02
▮▮ to ▮▮ AE ⊕ *Last orders 21.00. Closed Mon, Sun dinner, mid-Nov to Jan.*
Many connoisseurs consider the *bouillabaisse* here to be the finest E of Marseille. Prices are high, but they are justified by the quality of

the fish cookery and by the luxurious setting with wide views of the Baie des Anges and the Alps. *Specialities: Salade de poisson cru, langouste 'nage de légumes'.*

⟀ La Gardiole ✿
Address and ☎ as hotel ▮▮
🍴 🚗 AE ⊕ ⊙ VISA *Last orders 22.30. Closed Dec to mid-Feb.*
The hotel's large terrace, overhung with wisteria and surrounded by flowers, is a lovely setting for a meal in fine weather. Service may be slow, but the Provençal cooking is copious and good value. *Specialities: Soupe de poissons, papillote de saumon.* (See hotel.)

⟀ Pavillon Eden Roc
Address and ☎ and ⊕ as Hôtel Cap d'Antibes ▮▮▮ 🍴 🚗 📛 🚣 *Last orders 22.00. Closed Nov to Easter.*
The Cap d'Antibes' famous restaurant stands apart from the hotel at the foot of the garden, overlooking the rocky shore and glittering sea. Here the bright young things of the 1920s had some of their wildest times. Today's ambience is more sober, but the idyllic setting can still set the head spinning, whether you dine on the terrace or just take a drink at the open bar. The food has never been remarkable, but it has recently been revitalized by a new chef, and includes a lavish buffet. (See hotel, **Cap d'Antibes**.)

Apt
*Map **5**D7. 52km (33 miles) E of Avignon. 84400 Vaucluse. Population: 11,600 **i** Pl. de la Bouquerie ☎ (90) 74–03–18.*
A busy town set in the valley N of the *Lubéron* mountain, and now creeping up the surrounding hillsides with new high-rise blocks of flats. Apt is a centre for ochre quarrying (see also *Roussillon*) and also makes crystallized fruits and lavender essence. It was an active place in Roman days too, and traces remain: Roman baths lie beneath the sub-prefecture, while part of the Arena can be reached underground from the museum.

St Anne, mother of the Virgin, has long been venerated in Apt, for according to legend her body was brought here. The town was the site of the first shrine dedicated to her in France, and there is still an annual pilgrimage (last Sun in July). In the apse of the 11thC **ex-cathedral of St Anne** is a 14thC stained-glass window representing the saint, a reliquary bust of her is above the altar in the first chapel of the N aisle. This chapel's **sacristy** (*open July, Aug 14.30–17.00, closed Sun, Mon*) houses treasures including 11thC and 12thC manuscripts, 12thC and 13thC enamel reliquaries, and the 'shroud of St Anne', and an 11thC Arab standard brought back from the First Crusade.

The musée archéologique (*Pl. Carnot* 🔟 *open summer 10.00–12.00, 14.30–17.30; winter 10.00–12.00, 14.30–16.30*) contains Roman objects found in local excavations: coins, pieces of mosaic, sarcophagi, oil lamps of the 2ndC BC. There is also Provençal faïence of the 17th–19thC.

🐾Le Ventoux

67 Av. Victor-Hugo, 84400 Apt ☎ (90) 74–07–58 🔟 13 rms 🛏 13 ➡ 🏠 ⬛ 📶 Jul–Aug 🗛 ⓟ ⓒⓓ 🆅🆂🅰 Closed Jan.

Location: 1km (⅓ mile) w of town centre, on the Avignon road. The best hotel in Apt, quite simple, but clean and comfortable. Much used by businessmen. Hardly a holiday place but fine for a stopover.
⬛ 🖼

═ Le Ventoux ✿

Address and ☎ as hotel 🔟 to 🔟🔟 ⬜ 🍴 ➡ 🗛 ⓟ ⓒⓓ 🆅🆂🅰 Last orders 21.30 (summer), 20.30 (winter). Closed Jan.

The cheerful little dining-room has an attractive balcony-bar. Gérald Folco, *patron* and chef, is a dedicated cook, and serves copious helpings of dishes both local (*lotte aux écrevisses*) and not so local (*coquelet au whisky*).

Places nearby

Colorado de Rustrel (*11km (7 miles) NE of Apt*)   This is a series of enormous ochre quarries, some still being exploited. To view the unusual sight, leave the car on the main road, D22, and walk for about 50min to reach the terraces overlooking the partially man-made canyon.

Arles ★

Map **9**F4. 36km (22 miles) sw of Avignon. 13200 B.-du-R. Population: 50,340 **i** Palais de l'Archevêché, Esplanade Charles-de-Gaulle ☎ (90) 96–29–35.

Mellow Arles stands astride the wider of the two arms of the lower Rhône, on the N edge of the plain of the *Camargue*. It is a museum town *par excellence*. Though no individual building can equal say *Avignon*'s **Palais des Papes** or *Orange*'s **Théâtre Antique**, its ensemble of Roman and early Christian splendours is as rich and varied as that of any French city. It is also the capital of Provençal folk tradition.

Arles is so fortunately placed, its commerce is so active and merchants come in such numbers that all the products of the universe are channelled there; the riches of the Orient, perfumes of Arabia, delicacies of Assyria.

Honorius, Roman Emperor, writing in AD418.

Arles became a key Roman centre thanks to its geographical position. After the consul Marius dug a canal to the sea near Fos, in c.100BC, it grew into a major maritime port. Being at the southernmost point where the Rhône was bridgeable, it also carried much of the land traffic from Italy to Spain, and was at the junction of the Aurelian Way leading w and the Agrippan Way leading N to Lyon. When Julius Caesar punished Marseille for siding with Pompey, Arles supplanted it in influence and for a while it was capital of Roman Provence. Under the later Roman Empire, it grew into an important industrial and trade centre: Constantine the Great built himself a palace here in the 4thC, and in AD400 the Emperor Honorius made Arles the capital of the 'three Gauls' (France, Spain and Britain).

After the Roman era Arles became a vital focus of early

Christianity: here in 597 St Augustine was consecrated first
Bishop of Canterbury by the Bishop of Arles. But the town
suffered terribly from the barbarian invasions of the Dark Ages
and never recovered its status, even though in the 9th–10thC it
was the capital of a kingdom of Provence, and from that date
played a minor role compared with Aix or Avignon.

In more modern times, Arles has held a strong appeal for
writers, artists and musicians – for Bizet, for example, who
wrote the music here for Daudet's play *l'Arlésienne*, and for Van
Gogh who lived in Arles between 1888–90, painting with a
furious fecundity and subsiding into madness; it was here that
he cut off his ear. Alas, the Arles that he painted has also been
disfigured: his *Café du Soir*, on the E side of the Pl. du Forum, is
now a furniture shop below the Vaccarès restaurant. The house
that he shared with Gauguin in the Pl. Lamartine, and painted
as *The Yellow House*, was bombed in 1944. And his bridge, the
Pont de Langlois, S of Arles, was pulled down in 1926, though a
copy has since been built at Port-de-Bouc, near Martigues.

This country seems to me as beautiful as Japan for clarity of
atmosphere and gay colour effects. Water forms patches of
lovely emerald or rich blue in the landscape, just as we see it in
the crape-prints. The pale orange of the sunsets make the fields
appear blue.

Van Gogh, Letters, 1888–90

Today, artists in Arles are few, and folklore is for museums
and festivals: the lovely old costumes and bonnets of the
Arlésiennes are no longer part of daily wear. As a modern town,
Arles, except for its tourist trade, is a quiet place, with little of
the intense inner-city animation of Aix or Avignon. But its old
streets have their own sleepy charm. Apart from the **Alyscamps**
to the SE, all the main sights are close together in the town
centre, between the **Bd. des Lices** and the broad majestic
Rhône (there is a promenade above the river, past the back of
the **Musée Réattu**). The heart of the town is the **Pl. de la
République**, where stand the **cathedral** and Mansard's
imposing 17thC **Hôtel de Ville**. Just to the N, the small **Pl. du
Forum** is not quite on the site of the old Roman forum: but the
two Corinthian columns at its SE corner are the remains of a
temple that adjoined the forum. In the square is a statue of the
poet *Mistral*, around whom the tiresome north wind of the same
name often swirls in Mar and Apr.

Events: On May 1, a fête of Camargue *gardians* (people who
tend the wild horses and bulls).

In July, an international festival of music, dance and drama
in the Roman Theatre. Also in July, an international
photography festival.

From mid-Dec to mid-Jan, a trade fair of *santons* is held in the
town.

Bullfights are held in the Roman arena approximately two
Suns in every month, Apr–Nov. There is a four-day bullfight
festival from Easter Friday to Monday.

Sights and places of interest
Les Alyscamps
Rue Pierre-Renaudel ▦ *Open 8.30 or 9.00–12.00, 14.00–17.30,
18.30 or 19.00 depending on season. A single ticket for admission to
any sight in Arles, except St-Trophîme and the Muséon Arlaten, is
available.*
This wide path lined with sarcophagi, in the SE suburbs, is the remnant of

what was formerly one of Christendom's greatest cemeteries. The
Romans first established it as a necropolis on the Aurelian Way (the name
is thought to mean 'Elysian fields'), then during early Christian days it
became a prestigious burial ground, and remained so until the 12thC.
Almost 2km (1 mile) long and half as wide, it contained thousands of
tombs. Many of the finest were given away as gifts during the
Renaissance, but some have found their way into Arles' museums.
Today a few second-rate ones remain on the site, which preserves a
strange faded and peaceful atmosphere, even though factories and a
railway now insensitively abut on to it. At the end of the path is the
ruined Romanesque church of **St Honorat**.

Arènes ⅢⅢ ☆

*Rond Point des Arènes. For entry details and opening times see Les
Alyscamps.*

Built in 46BC, this is one of the earliest arenas of the Roman world, as well
as one of the largest: it could hold some 25,000 spectators. Fights with
wild beasts were often held here, as is clear from the height of the wall
surrounding the ring, and from the tunnels that led to their cages. For
gladiatorial combats, a raised wooden floor was temporarily inserted, to
give the lower spectators a better view (you can still see the sockets of its
supports in the wall).

After the fall of the Empire the arena was turned into a fortress, with a
church and some 200 houses inside. Its own stones were used for this, so
that it suffered badly, and was not restored until the 19thC. Today it is in
fairly good shape, though unlike the Nîmes' arena it lacks its third storey
which held a canopy-like roof. The three towers were added as a defence
in the 12thC: from the top of the one by the entrance you get a good bird's
eye view of the arena, and of Arles and the country around.

Today bullfights and festivals are frequently held here (see events in
introductory text).

Arlaten, Muséon ☆

*Rue de la République ▦ ▨ Open Apr–Sept 9.00–12.00,
14.00–18.00; Oct–Feb 9.00–12.00, 14.00–16.00; Mar 9.00–12.00,
14.00–17.00. Closed Mon.*

This marvellously vivid and varied museum of Provençal traditional life
was founded in 1896 by the poet Frédéric Mistral who installed it in this
16thC Gothic house. He spent many years building up his great

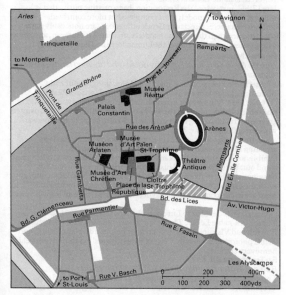

collection, helped at the end by the money from his 1904 Nobel Prize; and many of the exhibits are labelled and explained in his own hand. The museum is an intensely personal creation: every one of its 30 rooms is suffused with Mistral's passion for the people, language and culture of his native Provence.

The whole museum, particularly the first floor, holds a splendid profusion of exhibits, which merit hours of study. From traditional costumes and coiffures, to a green spiky monster from the famous procession at *Tarascon* and from lifesize tableaux of traditional scenes to the golden tresses of a girl found in a tomb at *Les Baux*, the museum is a marvellous insight into the culture and traditions of Provence.

Art Chrétien, Musée d' (*Christian Art, Museum of*) ☆
Rue Balzac. For entry details and opening times see Les Alyscamps.

Housed in a former 17thC Jesuit chapel, this collection of richly-carved early Christian sarcophagi is the world's finest after that of the Lateran Museum in Rome. In the centre of the nave are three splendid 4thC tombs found in 1974 at Trinquetaille in the N suburbs of Arles: most fascinating is the tomb of a married couple known as the **tomb of the Trinity**, with a medallion of the couple below friezes of Old Testament scenes. Round the walls are sarcophagi from the Alyscamps.

From the museum, steps lead down in to the remarkable **Cryptoporticus** ☆ – a vast U-shaped basement gallery built by the Romans underneath their Forum. They used it as a granary for storing wheat milled in the nearby Alpilles, part of which was shipped to feed the population of Rome.

Art Païen, Musée d' (*Pagan Art, Museum of*) ☆
Rue de la République. For entry details and opening times see Les Alyscamps.

A deconsecrated church containing a rich collection of Greek and Roman art – statues, tombs, mosaics – all found locally. As in the Musée d'Art Chrétien, all is fully and clearly explained. The fine sarcophagus of **Hippolytus and Phaedra**, a Greek work from the 2ndC AD, comes from the villa excavated at Trinquetaille. The statue of *Augustus* stood at the back of the stage of the **Théâtre Antique**. The two statues of *Venus* are casts of the famous **Venus of Arles**, also found in the theatre, in 1651, broken in three pieces and with both arms missing. The original, much restored, is in the Louvre. Of the two copies here, the one made in the late 17thC, just before the Restoration, has a pristine purity that is missing in the later model, more complete but more contrived.

The works here, Grecian or Greek influenced, are noticeably more sophisticated than those in the parallel Christian Art museum, and show a far greater understanding of the human form and how to portray it.

Réattu, Musée ☆
Rue de Grand Prieuré. For entry details and opening times see Les Alyscamps.

Formerly the Priory of the Knights of Malta, this graceful 15thC building belonged for a while to the local painter Jacques Réattu (1760–1833). It is now a spacious museum of art, varied and eclectic, and uneven in quality. Many of the works by minor 19thC and 20thC painters are mediocre, including most of those by Réattu himself. But there are wonderful things, too.

On the ground floor, pieces of Roman masonry stand beside an arresting modern tapestry by the Spaniard, Grau Garriga. Most of the exhibits are in a suite of 12 rooms on the first floor. Here two collections stand out: first, five 17thC **Brussels tapestries** showing a quirkily imaginative view of five of the seven Wonders of the World; second, an intriguing set of coloured sketches by Picasso, donated by him in 1971. Most are in cartoon style, like playing card figures, with an impish sense of humour.

One room is devoted to Lurçat, with a fine tapestry, *Early Dawn*. There is a notable Léger, *The King of Hearts*, and works by Gauguin, Rouault and Vlaminck. The second floor houses a display of 19thC and 20thC photographs, mostly views of Arles. Special exhibitions are held here every summer.

St-Trophime ⅢⅢ † ☆ *Rue de l'Hôtel-de-Ville. Open 10.00–12.00, 16.00–19.00.*
This former cathedral, now demoted to a church, is dedicated to St Trophime, said to have been sent by St Peter to evangelize Provence.

Though much rebuilt in the 11th, 12th and 15thC, the original church was Carolingian, as is evident from the w facade where the lowest part is Carolingian while the 12thC **portal** above is purest Provençal Romanesque in startling contrast to the plainness of the upper façade. The stone carvings, though sombre and weather-beaten, are amazingly rich. Above a row of stern-looking saints is a curious frieze: to the left, a row of the elect, fully clad, advance towards Christ in the centre; to the right, the damned are led off naked and chained together, to be cast into hell.

Inside, the Romanesque nave is unusually high and narrow for Provence: its simplicity contrasts with the Gothic flamboyance of the choir. In a chapel off the N aisle is a 4thC sarcophagus now used as a font; further on, another sarcophagus, representing the crossing of the Red Sea, is now an altar. Note also two paintings by Finsonius: an *Annunciation*, in the left transept, and an *Adoration of the Magi* in a chapel off the s aisle.

Cloître St-Trophime (St-Trophîme Cloister) 𝕀𝕀𝕀 ☆
Pl. de la République. Entrance through the porch next to the Palais de l'Archevêché.

Its serene beauty, and its ornate and detailed carvings, have made this the most renowned of all the cloisters in Provence. Its graceful arcades with their slender marble pillars surround a little garden of cypresses. The N and E arcades, 12thC, have barrel vaulting while those to the w and s, with ogival arches, are 14thC Gothic. The capitals are decorated with scenes from the Bible and even from Provençal legends (including the strange low-relief of St Martha and the Tarasque on the s side, see *Tarascon*), while the pillars themselves carry elaborate carvings of Christ and saints: those at the NW and NE corners are the richest.

A chapel off the N side contains three superb 17thC Aubusson tapestries of the *Life of the Virgin*, and three smaller 17thC Flemish tapestries of the Hebrews.

Théâtre Antique (Roman Theatre)
Rue du Cloître. For entry details and opening times see Les Alyscamps.

Built under Augustus, the theatre today is far more of a ruin than the arena. In the Dark and Middle Ages it was pillaged and used as a quarry for building churches, houses and the city ramparts. Of its stage wall, once so sumptuously elaborate with its rows of statues, just two tall columns survive and a few lesser fragments: but the stage's foundations are still visible. Twenty rows of seats survive too, from a theatre that once held nearly 7,000 people; and open-air spectacles are held here in summer (see events in introductory text).

Thermes de la Trouille, Palais Constantin (Trouille Baths, Constantine's Palace) 𝕀𝕀𝕀
Rue D. Maïsto. If doorkeeper is absent, apply to Musée Réattu.

These Roman baths, the largest in Provence, are all that visibly survives of Constantine's great imperial 4thC palace. Though partly ruined, the sheer size, 98m (320ft) by 45m (148ft), is impressive. Unlike earlier Roman buildings, the baths are constructed of narrow alternate layers of brick and stone.

Hotels

d'Arlatan ✿
26 Rue du Sauvage, 13200 Arles ☎ *(90) 93–56–66* ▥
46 rms ▭ *44* ⊟ ⒶⒺ ⓪
Location: In a quiet side street, in the Old Town. ". . . . an enclosed and enchanted garden, not overlooked by any window in the heart of that grey city" – Evelyn Waugh's celebrated vision of romantic Oxford, in *Brideshead Revisited*, applies with uncanny appropriateness to this, one of the loveliest hotels in Provence. Its Arcadian garden is overlooked by the high Roman wall of

Constantine's palace; beside it is an equally charming patio where breakfasts and drinks are served. The building, 15th–17thC, was the ancestral home of the Counts of Arlaten, and has been converted with consummate taste by the Desjardin family, who run the hotel with the civilized and friendly warmth that the setting deserves. The red-tiled floors, beamed ceilings and 18thC furniture, all so common in Provence, are most elegant; the bedrooms are delightfully decorated.
▱ ⚓ ♨

Le Cloître
16 Rue du Cloître, 13200 Arles
☎ *(90) 96–29–50* ▯ *33 rms* ▭
25. Closed mid-Nov to mid-Mar.
*Location: Very central, in a narrow
street of the Old Town.* Some
bedrooms of this quiet little hotel
overlook the lovely cloister of St-
Trophîme. The hotel has few
amenities, but is efficient and
comfortable enough.
◌ ▱

Jules César ▥
Bd. des Lices, 13200 Arles
☎ *(90) 93–43–20* ▯*400239* ▥
60 rms ▭ *60* ▭ ☲ ☲ AE ⊕ ⊙
VISA *Closed Nov to mid-Dec.*
*Location: On the town's main
boulevard.* A 17thC monastery is
now a sedate hotel, particularly
popular with well-to-do
Americans. Its best feature is the
flowery tree-lined cloister garden,
where you can take breakfast or
bask in the sun. There are some
lapses of taste, though: the too-
grandiose foyer, the phoney
'imperial Roman' façade (though
the Baroque chapel is genuine
enough); bedrooms lack character,
too. But the hotel is very well run,
and the food is varied and
excellent. (See restaurant, **Lou
Marquès**.)
& ▭ ▭ ▱ ☙ ✤

Mireille (*2 Pl. St-Pierre*
☎ *(90) 93–70–74* ▯); and
Le Forum (*10 Pl. du Forum*
☎ *(90) 93–48–95* ▯ *to* ▯) are
also worth recommending.

Restaurants

Hostellerie des Arènes ● ✿
62 Rue du Réfuge
☎ *(90) 96–13–05* ▯ ▰ *Last
orders 21.00. Closed Wed, mid-
Jan to mid-Feb.*
Tourists and Arlésiens alike crowd
out this simple family-run *auberge*
opposite the Arena. It's a bit
crushed, but the value is
remarkable and the food excellent.
*Specialities: Canard braisé au
poivre vert, pintadeau aux morilles,
carré d'agneau provençale.*

Lou Marquès
Address and ☎ *as Hôtel Jules
César* ▯ *to* ▥ ▭ ▰ ☲ ⊖
▰ AE ⊕ ⊙ VISA. *Last orders
21.30. Closed Nov to mid-Dec,
Tues (early Jan to mid-Mar).*
Alas, the waitresses no longer wear
Arlésian costume, but their service
remains skilled and smiling, and a
meal here is a joy, either in the
spacious dining-room or
(especially) on the front terrace.
The chef, Roland Petrini, was
trained in the 1950s by Fernard
Point of La Pyramide, Vienne, the
first great innovator of *nouvelle
cuisine*; today he presents guests
with his own light and subtle
variations on the classic cooking of
Provence, and the results are
superb. *Specialities: Baudroie à
l'aïgo sau, magret de canard aux
figues, saumon mariné à l'huile
d'olive.* (See hotel, **Jules César**.)

Le Tambourin
65 Rue Amédée-Pichot
☎ *(90) 96–13–32* ▯ ▭ ▰
*Last orders 22.00. Closed Sat,
Feb.*
A place with friendly service,
soft lighting and family cooking.
Try *boeuf gardian.*

Le Vaccarès
Pl. du Forum ☎ *(90) 96–06–17*
▯ *to* ▯ ▭ ▰ ⊖ *Last
orders 21.30. Closed Mon, Sun
(dinner), mid-Dec to mid-Jan.*
Le Vaccarès is a lake in the
Camargue and Bernard Dumas'
excellent and varied *cuisine* closely
reflects the traditional dishes of the
region, as well as including some
flourishes of his own. Equally
excellent is the wine list, well
balanced and very reasonably
priced. The chic and spacious
restaurant faces the remains of the
Roman Forum, with a small
outdoor terrace. *Specialities:
Soupière de baudroie camarguaise,
pieds et paquets, filets de sandre à la
poutargue.*

Shopping
E. Ferriol (*2 bis, Chemin de Barrol*) makes and sells *santons*;
workshop open to visits 10.00–20.00, except Sun. **M. Deville**
(*66 Rue de Chartreuse*) sells ceramics.

Places nearby
Montmajour, Abbaye de ▥ ✝ (*5km (3 miles)* NE *of Arles, beside*

D17 to Fontvieille 🚗 *open Apr–Sept 9.00–11.45, 14.00–19.00, Oct–Mar 9.00–11.45, 14.00–17.00, closed Tues, Wed)*   The former Benedictine abbey of Montmajour was founded in the 10thC, on a low hill which then was an island surrounded by marshlands beside the Rhône. In the Middle Ages it was rich and powerful, owning priories all over Provence: its annual *pardon* would draw up to 100,000 pilgrims. But it gradually fell into decline, and after the Revolution it was sold off cheaply by the State and partially pulled down. Today it is partly ruined, partly restored. The towering crenellated *donjon* dates from the 14thC and was built for defence against marauders. Below it stands the 12thC Romanesque church of **Notre-Dame**, cross-shaped, with an unusually wide nave. From here steps lead down into the crypt, partly raised and partly built out of the rock. The **cloister** with its marble pillars and its ancient well is most charming: note the carvings of bears, camels and other animals on the capitals of the columns.

The unusual little burial ground chapel of **Ste-Croix** lies 180m (200yd) along the Fontvieille road: it is in the form of a Greek cross, surmounted by a campanile (*keys at the abbey*).

St-Gilles (*15km (9 miles) w of Arles, on N572*)   In the Middle Ages this town on the edge of the Camargue was an important centre for pilgrims, who came to venerate the tomb of St Gilles the Hermit. It was also a staging-post en route to Santiago de Compostela, and a port of embarkation for the Crusades.

An abbey was founded here by St Gilles in the 7thC, but the present abbey church dates from the 12thC. It was badly knocked about during the Wars of Religion, but its broad **west front** ☆ survives as one of the finest ensembles of medieval sculpture in Provence – three arched portals, decorated with scenes from the life of Christ and with animals such as lions, camels and even a centaur. The central doorway was carved by 12thC artists from Toulouse; those on the side are the work of early 13thC sculptors from the Paris area.

The abbey church's 11thC **crypt** is a spacious Romanesque church in its own right, one of the earliest in France to have ogival vaulting. Here the **tomb of St-Gilles** (who has also given his name to Edinburgh's cathedral) was unearthed in 1865 and is believed to be authentic. The E part of the abbey church is in ruins, save for a solitary bell-tower: this contains a famous spiral staircase, known as **Le Vis**, unusual because the steps are roofed over with stone, giving the effect of a curving funnel (*crypt and staircase* 🚗 📷 *on the hour 9.00–11.00, 15.00–18.00, half-hourly July–Aug, closed Jan–Feb*).

Nearby is a **museum**, with lapidary remains from the church.

Auron

*Map **15**B14. 98km (61 miles) NW of Nice. 06660 St-Étienne-de-Tinée, Alpes-Mar* **i** *Town square* ☎ *(93) 23–02–66.*

Auron is a natural choice for the creation of a winter ski resort and has a genuinely alpine flavour. It stands imposingly on a circular plateau at 1,600m (5,250ft) and is surrounded by an amphitheatre of peaks rising to 2,474m (8,100ft). The resort has a feeling of space and grandeur that the other 'Ski Azur' villages of *Valberg* and *Isola 2000* lack. Various hotels, snack bars and shops have grown up around the large informal square and there are plenty of facilities behind the square such as tennis courts, swimming pool and cinema. Despite these, and other summertime activities, Auron remains very much a winter resort, and most of the hotels are closed in summer.

St-Érige, Chapelle † ☆

Just off main square. Apply to tourist office for key.

Legend has it that this richly decorated chapel, established in a place
previously only inhabited by a few shepherds in summer, marks the spot
where the mount of St Érige, Archbishop of Gap, landed when taking a
short-cut home: when returning from Rome in the late 6thC the horse
evidently tired of the journey and leaped over the Tinée valley in a single
bound. In fact the chapel, dating from the 12thC, is another sign that
St-Étienne-de-Tinée was an important religious centre. It has a simple
larch interior with two parallel apses covered in arresting and
wonderfully vivid 15thC frescoes depicting St Mary Magdalene (said to
have lived in Provence – see *Ste-Baume, Massif de*), St Denis (martyred
in Paris in AD250), and St Érige. Best of all is the fresco of Christ, wearing
a mantle decorated with birds and animals.

☜ St-Érige

06660 St-Étienne-de-Tinée, Auron ☎ *(93) 23–00–32* ▥ *20 rms*
▭ *20* ⬛ ⇌ *Closed May–Nov.*

The St-Érige has the advantage of being run by the friendly and homely
Mme Rubini and her family, who built the hotel over 29yr ago. The
bedrooms, though small, have a pleasant, old-fashioned feel about them,
and you can eat heartily in the wood and stone 'hunting lodge' dining-
room, complete with assorted stuffed beasts. Mme Rubini adores
animals, and welcomes pets.

🖭 ⫶

☜ Other recommended hotels in Auron are: **Las Donnas**
(☎ *(93) 23–00–03* ▯ *to* ▥); **L'Heure Mauve** (☎ *(93) 23–00–21* ▯
to ▥); **Le Pilon** (☎ *(93) 23–00–15* ▯ *to* ▥).
The **Piscine Restaurant** provides reasonable food.

Sports and activities

With 120km (74 miles) of pistes over the steep-sided slopes of
two valleys, Auron offers far more adventurous skiing than its
main rival, *Isola 2000*. It has the advantage of plenty of sun,
with the drawback that good snow is not always guaranteed.
Whereas Isola and *Valberg* are good for beginners, Auron is the
choice for more advanced skiers.

In summer Auron has good pony-trekking with guides; also
walking and climbing. A cable car rising nearly to the summit of
Las Donnas, 2,256m (7,400ft), where the views are excellent,
operates in summer as well as winter (*daily 9.00– 17.30, closed
May, June, Oct, Nov*).

Avignon ★

*Map 9D4. 100km (63 miles) nw of Marseille. 84000
Vaucluse. Population: 93,000* ℹ *41 Cours Jean-Jaurès*
☎ *(90) 82–65– 11.*

Avignon, like *Aix*, is a sophisticated modern city with a glorious
historical legacy. But whereas Aix's history focuses on the
intimacy of the 17thC, Avignon's great period was the
grandiose 14thC. Today, the full circuit of the ramparts above
the Rhône remains, even if four-fifths of the town spreads
outside them. Dominating all is the colossal palace that the
Popes created here, perhaps the most impressive medieval
building in Europe.

Well placed at the confluence of the Rhône and Durance,
Avignon had been a trading centre since pre-Roman times. Yet
mere chance led to it becoming a major city, for it was chance
that led the Papacy to move here in 1307, when it found that life
in Rome was becoming impossible owing to the endless feuding
between rival noble families. The Papacy already possessed the
lands of the Comtat Venaissin just to the N but these had no
town suited to be its capital. Avignon was in the earldom of

Provence, then on friendly terms with the Church; and it was in fact the French king, Philippe-le-Bel, who persuaded the newly-elected Clément V, a French Pope, to make the move here, in the hope of increasing French influence over the Papacy.

Clément and his successor ruled from the Episcopal palace. Then Benedict XII, elected in 1334, decided to make the move from Rome more permanent by building the **Palais des Papes**, which was completed in 1352 by his successor, Clément VI. Thus began Avignon's brief golden age as the capital of Christendom, at a time when Papacy enjoyed pomp and high living, flaunted its great wealth ostentatiously, and was tolerant of fleshly weaknesses. Avignon became a town of gaiety and luxury, even of vice and crime – to the horror of some of the more straight-laced members of the Papal entourage, including the Italian poet Petrarch: ". . . . an abode of sorrows, the shame of mankind, a sink of vice . . . . a sewer where all the filth of the universe has gathered. There God is held in contempt, money is worshipped, and the laws of God and man are trampled underfoot. Everything there breathes a lie: the air, the earth, the houses and above all the bedrooms."

By 1377 seven Popes had ruled in Avignon, all of them French, then at last Gregory XI was persuaded to return to Rome. But some Cardinals disputed the move and decided to remain in Avignon where they elected their own Pope – or Antipope. Thus began the Great Schism of the West, as Popes and Antipopes flung insults and excommunications at each other and wrangled over Papal lands and revenues. Avignon's last Antipope was expelled by force in 1403, but he continued the fight in his native Spain and the Schism did not end till 1449. Avignon was then governed by a Papal legate until the Revolution, when it was finally united to France.

I climbed the green-fringed ramps which led up into the marvellous hanging gardens of the Rocher des Doms. From this vantage point one can look down on three sides to see the loops and curls of the Rhône carving out the embankments of its bed in the carious limestone, sculpting the soft flanks of the nether hills. A frail sun shone upon distant snowlines leading away towards the Alps. Mont Sainte-Victoire stood up in the distance, erect as a martyr tied to its stake of ice.

Lawrence Durrell, *Monsieur*, 1974

The town's focus of life today is still the area within the ramparts, which were built in the 1350s by Innocent VI, then much restored by the architect Viollet-le-Duc in the 19thC. As Avignon lies on a plain surrounded by suburbs and other towns, it is less spectacular as a walled city than Carcassonne or *Aigues-Mortes*. But the network of old streets within the ramparts are fascinating and full of animation. Here the main avenue is the **Rue de la République**, leading from the station to the **Pl. de l'Horloge**, centre of social life. Avignon is one of the most fashionable French towns outside Paris: the shops are smart, and so are the people, who since Papal days have kept their reputation for ebullience and gaiety. The town lives late: even out of season, the cafés in the Pl. de l'Horloge are crowded long past midnight with young people. And Avignon's July theatre festival is one of Europe's great annual cultural events.

Events: At the end of January is the Cheval Passion, a three-day horse festival. In February there is a dance festival, and in August a jousting tournament on the Rhône, which makes a

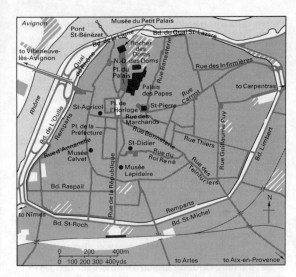

colourful and exciting spectacle. In the last three weeks of July an international drama festival takes place, one of Europe's leading events of its kind, created after the war by Jean Vilar and Gérard Philippe. Some 50 productions in all, including many 'on the fringe'. Main productions are staged in the Great Courtyard of the Palais des Papes. Apply: Bureau du Festival, BP 92 84006 Avignon ☎ (90) 86–24–43.

Sights and places of interest

Calvet, Musée
Rue Joseph-Vernet ☎ *(90) 86–33–84* 🏛 🎫 *Open 9.00–12.00, 14.00–18.00. Closed Tues.*

The ground floor of this 18thC mansion houses an oddly diversified museum of art. One large room contains hundreds of pieces of wrought-iron and locksmith's work – one of Europe's leading collections of its kind. Next door is the Hellenic room: vases, sculptures and steles dating back to the 4thC BC. The lion's share of the museum is given over to a display of French painting from the 16th–20thC (as well as two Brueghels), remarkable more for its range than its high quality. The early Avignon school is here in force, led by Mignard and de Chalons; landscapes by the 18thC Joseph Vernet of Avignon share rooms with Géricault, Toulouse-Lautrec, and a good Corot. Of the modern artists, Vlaminck, Dufy and Utrillo are outshone by a lesser-known painter, Albert Gleizes, whose three vivid canvasses recall Picasso. The museum lies round a courtyard full of peacocks, where – so says an inscription – Stendhal liked to stroll.

Lapidaire, Musée
27 Rue de la République 🏛 *Closed Tues.*

Housed in a former 17thC Jesuit chapel, the museum contains a few Renaissance sculptures, but is devoted mainly to local Roman and pre-Roman remains. Note especially the *Venus of Pournières*, found near Aix, and the *Tarasque of Noves*, a statuette of a man-eating lion, dating from the Second Iron Age.

Palais des Papes 🏛 † ★
Pl. du Palais 🏛 🎫 *Open daily. Guided tours only Oct to Easter hourly 9.00–11.00, 14.00–16.00; Easter–June open for guided or unguided visits 9.00–11.30, 14.00–17.30; July–Sept likewise 9.00–18.00. Multi-language guided tours available.*

At first sight, with its massive walls and turreted towers rising to 45m

(150ft), this great building looks more like a fortress than a palace of the Church. Inside, it is a labyrinth of halls, chapels, corridors. It is really two adjacent palaces, built within 20yr by two very different Popes. The **Old Palace** to the N, is simple and sober, reflecting the austere spirit of Benedict XII, a former Cistercian monk. The **New Palace** to the s, built by Clément VI, a lover of the arts and of high pomp, is far more ornate.

During the Revolution, the building was damaged and its furniture removed; from 1810 until 1906 it served as barracks, and many of the frescoes were vandalized. Today it has been restored as far as possible; but it is still bare of much of the sumptuous decor and furnishings that must have lent it such splendour in its great days.

The conducted tours commence in the **Grand Courtyard** and proceed first to the **consistoire**, where the Pope received important visitors, conferred with his cardinals, and passed judgement in trials. Little is left of its lavish decoration, save for some fine but faded frescoes by Simone Martini of Siena. It is now hung with 18thC portraits of the nine Avignon Popes. Off this room is the **chapel of St Jean**, its upper part covered with bright frescoes showing scenes from the lives of the two St Johns, by Matteo Giovanetti, Pope Clément's painter.

The tour then leads upstairs to the long **Banqueting Hall** (Grand Tinel) where 150 people would sit down to a meal which lasted as long as 8hr, accompanied by minstrels and jugglers. The hall today is hung with six Gobelins tapestries: the best, early 18thC, are based on works by Raphael. Off the hall is the tiny **chapel of St Martial**, its upper walls and ceilings lined with beautiful dark-blue frescoes by Giovanetti, showing the miracles of St Martial.

Steps lead down from the hall to the **Papal Anti-Chamber**, where traces remain of the original vaulted roofing, badly damaged by a fire in 1413. This room contains a scale model of the palace as it was in the 14thC. The Pope's **bedroom** ✩ is small and richly decorated. Note that its blue and gold frescoes of birds, squirrels and foliage are entirely secular: so they probably date from Clément VI, not Benedict XII. The brightly-coloured tiled mosaic floor is a recent copy of the original which was found beneath existing flooring and is now in the palace museum.

Pope Clément's study is known as the **Room of the Deer** ✩ because of its intriguing frescoes of hunting and fishing scenes, bathing and games – more evidence of the worldly tastes of Clément and his court. Steps lead to the N sacristy of the **Grand Chapel**, containing statues of Popes, cardinals and kings, copies of originals in various museums. The Grand Chapel itself has 17thC paintings by Mignard and Parrocel. In its s sacristy are casts of the tombs of *Clément VI* and other Popes.

The tour here ends, and the visitor is left to explore other rooms himself. At the top of the staircase leading from the Grand Chapel is the **Indulgence Window** where the Pope would give his blessing to pilgrims down in the courtyard. The stairs lead down to the **Grand Audience Hall**, a majestic state room where tribunals were held. On the way out, do not miss the lovely vaulted **Gallery of the Conclave** which leads to the Conclave itself where the cardinals were locked up to elect a new Pope – just as in the Vatican today.

Petit Palais, Musée du ✩
Pl. du Palais ☎ *(90) 86–44–58* ▪ *Open daily 9.00–12.00, 14.00–18.00. Closed Tues.*

Built in 1317, this is the former palace of the Archbishops of Avignon whose famous guests included Cesare Borgia and François I. It is now a museum with 20 rooms, very well laid out, housing a remarkable collection of 13thC to 16thC works of art of the Avignon and Northern Italian schools. Avignon is represented by frescoes and sculptures and by two rooms of paintings, notably a beautiful retable by Enguerrand Charenton. Especially impressive are the compelling Italian primitives: a *Virgin and Child* by Taddeo di Bartolo of the Siena school; and a *Virgin in Majesty* by an unknown Pistoia artist. There is a room of fine Florentine paintings (note the lovely triptych by Lorenzo Monaco, the vividly-coloured miniatures by Ambrogio di Baldese, and Botticelli's *Virgin and Child*), while among the best of the Venetian works are a triptych by Antonio Alberti and a *Holy Conversation* by Carpaccio.

Also in the Pl. du Palais is the cathedral of **Notre-Dame-des-Dômes**, dating from the 12thC. It contains an archbishop's throne in white marble, and, in a chapel off the sacristy, the Flamboyant Gothic tomb of *Pope John XXII*. The gilt *Madonna* on the steeple was added in 1859.

Avignon

Just to the N of the cathedral and Palais des Papes is the **Rocher des Doms**, a rocky plateau overlooking the Rhône, which has been transformed into an attractive, rose-filled garden with a little lake and fine views. Also in the Pl. du Palais is the **Hôtel des Monnaies**, a large 17thC mansion with a highly decorated facade.

Pont St-Bénézet

Built in the late 12thC, this famous bridge originally stretched for 900m (1,000yd) across the river to the foot of the Tower of Philippe-le-Bel in *Villeneuve-lès-Avignon*. As one of the very few solid bridges over the lower Rhône in those days, it helped bring prosperity to the town. But most of it was carried away by floods in the 17thC, and today just four arches remain, on the Avignon side. Beside one of them is the small **chapel of St Nicolas**, Gothic above, Romanesque below.

This is the 'Pont d'Avignon' of the ancient song. Built for pedestrians and horses, it was, in fact, far too narrow for people to 'dance in a circle' on it: more probably the dancing was *'sous le pont'*, on the Ile de la Barthelasse, a traditional recreation place for the Avignonnais.

Vieille Ville

The central district of Avignon, within the ramparts, is best explored on foot, for parking is not easy. Its honeycomb of narrow streets contains a number of churches and mansions: some date from the period of the Popes, and some from the 16thC when this was a prosperous city under the tolerant rule of the Papal legates. Most of the churches and chapels have paintings by Parrocel and the Mignards, of the Avignon school.

To the E of the Papal Palace, the **Chapelle des Pénitents Gris** (*Rue Banasterie, ask for key at tourist office*) has a facade, remodelled in 18thC, with ornate sculptures of angels carrying the head of John the Baptist; inside are more rich carvings, in wood and marble. The **church of St Symphorien** (*Pl. des Carmes*) is notable for its 16thC gilded wood sculptures. To the S of the Palace, the **Fondation Jean Vilar** (*Hôtel de Crochans, Rue de Mons*) is a small museum likely to appeal to anyone interested in post-war French theatre: it was inaugurated in 1981, in honour of the great director who founded the Avignon Festival and led the French drama revival of the 1950s. To the E, the **church of St-Pierre** has sumptuous Renaissance carvings on its interior folding doors, and fine sculptured woodwork in the choir. To the S, the **Rue des Marchands** and other little streets nearby are now an elegant pedestrian zone full of smart shops.

Turning E of the Rue de la République, the 14thC **church of St-Didier** has superb late 14thC frescoes. In the first chapel on the right is the famous **retable** ☆ of the *Bearing of the Cross* (15thC), by Francesco Laurana of Dalmatia, with movingly realistic looks of anguish on the faces of the Virgin and other bystanders. To the E of the church, the **Rue Roi René** and the **Rue de la Masse** have several imposing 17thC and 18thC mansions. East again is the charming **Rue des Teinturiers**, an old cobbled street beside the river Sorgue: the old paddle-wheels were still used until the late 19thC to power the local textile workshops.

The **Musée Louis-Vouland** (*17 Rue Victor-Hugo*), on the W side of the town, is a new museum of local ceramics and furniture of the 17thC and 18thC.

Hotels

Angleterre
29 Bd. Raspail, 84000 Avignon
☎ (90) 86–34–31 ▥ 34 rms ▭ 31 🛏

Location: Fairly central, on a quiet boulevard within the ramparts. A cut above the average utility town-centre hotel; sprucely modernized.

⬍ 🖾 ♨

Bristol Terminus
44 Cours Jean-Jaurès, 84000 Avignon ☎ (90) 82–21–21
☎432730 ▥ to ▥ 85 rms ▭ 85 ▭ AE ⊙ ◉ *Closed Nov–Feb.*

Location: Very central, on the main street. The bedrooms are comfortable and the staff friendly, so do not be put off by the hotel's humdrum appearance and graceless decor. It is much in demand by foreign tourist groups.

⬍ 🖾 ♨

Central
31 Rue de la République, 84000 Avignon ☎ (90) 86–07–81
☎431532 ▥ to ▥ 29 rms ▭ 23 ▤▤ AE ◉ VISA

Location: Off the main street, at the

back of a courtyard. Central it is, but not noisy, for the hotel is set well back from the street, and its quiet patio is a pleasant place for breakfast or a drink. Bedrooms are clean and modern, if without a great deal of individuality or charm.

⭑ ◻ ◲ ⩇

Europe 🏨

12 Pl. Crillon, 84000 Avignon
☎ (90) 82–66–92 ☎ 431965 ▥
65 rms ▭ 60 ◳ ▱ ◲ ◱ AE ⊕

Location: A square just inside the ramparts, near the Palace. This 16thC nobleman's house was already in use as a hostelry when Napoleon stayed here in 1799, the year he became First Consul. It is Avignon's only classic hotel of real character, and is beautifully kept up: the spacious bedrooms have beamed ceilings and period furniture, mostly Louis XV. The formality of the public rooms, with their marble floors, may not suit all tastes: but the Gobelins tapestries lend a touch of softness, while the piano-bar adds a cheerful, individual note. (See restaurant, **Vieille Fontaine**.)

⭑ � & ◲ ◱ ⛿

Novotel

Route de Marseille, 84000 Avignon ☎ (90) 87–62–36
☎ 432878 ▥ to ▥ 79 rms ▭ 79
◳ ▱ ▤ AE CB ⊕

Location: Outskirts. Frequented by businessmen and tour groups but equally good for holiday-makers.

⭑ & ◻ ◲ ⩘

Sofitel Pont d'Avignon

Quartier de la Balance
☎ (90) 85–91–23 ▥ 86 rms
▭ 86 AE ⊕ VISA

Location: Central; in side-street behind Petit Palais museum. An efficient upper-medium-priced modern hotel, part of one of the leading French hotel chains. Efficient service and good sound-proofing. The hotel has no restaurant.

Nearby hotel

Noves (*13km (8 miles) SE of Avignon*).

Auberge de Noves 🏨

13550 Noves ☎ (90) 94–19–21
☎ 431312 ▥ to ▥ 22 rms ▭ 22
◳ ▱ ◲ ◱ ◱ *Closed early Jan to mid-Feb.*

Location: In its own wooded park off D28, 4km (2½ miles) W of Noves. André Lallemand, a cultured and amiable host who speaks perfect English, is justly proud of his chic and intimate country hotel, a converted 19thC manor. Its rambling garden is oddly unkempt, but inside all is stylishly welcoming: caged singing birds in the foyer, and a lounge with ravishing pale-green decor – its cosy modern sofas make a change from the usual formal, stiff-backed Louis XV chairs. The large bedrooms, too, are in pleasing pastel shades, and have very modern bathrooms. (See restaurant.)

◲ & ◻ ◲ ⛿ ⫷ ⩘

Restaurants

Café des Artistes

Place Crillon ☎ (90) 82–63–16
◻ to ◻ ◻ ▦ AE VISA *Last orders 22.00. Closed Dec 22–Jan 7.*

A modish, informal bistrot where in fine weather you can eat outdoors in a pretty square. Reliable cooking.

La Férigoulo

30 Rue Joseph-Vernet
☎ (90) 82–10–28 ◻ to ▥ ◻
AE *Last orders 22.00. Closed Mon (Oct–Mar), Sun last two weeks of Jan and June.*

Here is the kind of post-1960s *'bistro'* one associates with St-Germain-des-Prés or Chelsea – modern decor, and informal service; youthful clientele. The food is traditional and rather good. **Specialities:** *Truite aux amandes, daube Avignonnaise.*

La Fourchette ✿

7 Rue Racine ☎ (90) 82–56–01
▥ *Last orders 21.00. Closed Sun, Mon, mid-June to early July, two weeks in Oct.*

Robert Hiély (brother of Pierre Hiély, see over) proves that a stylish setting plus really good food need not necessarily equal high prices: so it is small wonder that his delightful restaurant is usually booked up days or sometimes even weeks ahead. The building is old, but the pretty decor is breezily modern; flowers and creepers lend it a rural air. Three, graceful young ladies serve Avignon's *beau monde* with a set menu that is not only great value but full of interest and originality: M. Hiély blends local tradition with his own innovations. **Specialities:** *Haricots blancs en anchoiade, terrine à la confiture* *d'oignons, boeuf cuit à la manière des anciens mariniers du Rhône, glaces, sorbets.*

Hiély ♣
5 Rue de la République
☎ (90) 86–17–07 ▇▇▇ ▄▄ ▬ ≡ ▇
Last orders 21.30. Closed Mon (except July, Aug), Tues.

Avignon's best restaurant is designed for the dedicated gourmet: a simply but tastefully furnished first-floor room in the heart of town, where the service is impeccable and Madame Hiély's welcome always courteous. Her husband Pierre remains loyal to his family's 60yr tradition of serving a single set menu with wide choice, and no *carte:* his *cuisine* is classic but not too conventional and its quality sublime. ***Specialities: Cassoulet de moules aux épinards, tourte chaude et cailles au foie gras, râble de lapereau farci, desserts.***

Le Vernet
58 Rue Joseph-Vernet
☎ (90) 86–64–53 ▇▇▇ to ▇▇▇ ▭
▄▄ ▬ ▲ ▨ᴬᴱ ▨ⱽᴵˢᴬ Last orders 22.30 May–Aug, 22.00 Sept–Apr. Closed Sun (except May–Aug), mid-Nov to mid-Dec.

It's evident that Claude Chareton, the ambitious young *patron*, wants to be a great restaurateur, and there is just a hint of pretentiousness about his admittedly very elegant new restaurant in an 18thC mansion. The intimate dining-room achieves its effect with soft lights, low recorded music, and romantic modern paintings on the wall. For summer, there is a shady and spacious garden, complete with a statue of *Diana*. As in many restaurants of this kind, the *cuisine* blends the *nouvelle* with the regionally traditional, usually with great success. The menu *gastronomique* comes with English and German translations. ***Specialities: Terrine de St-Pierre et de vive à la crème d'ourins, jambon d'agneau à la fleur de thym garniture 'aigre doux'.***

Vieille Fontaine △
Address and ☎ *as Hôtel Europe* ▇▇▇ ▭ ▄▄ ▬ ▲ ▨ᴬᴱ ▨ Last orders 22.00. Open for dinner only. Closed Sun.

In summer you can dine beside the restaurant's namesake, an old fountain in a lovely courtyard, where lamps glow on every table. The indoor *salle* is more severely classical. The *cuisine*, too, is of the classical variety and hard to fault. (See hotel, **Europe**.)

(See hotel, **Europe**.)

Restaurants nearby
Bellevue-lès-Angles *(4km (2¼ miles) w of Avignon).*

L'Ermitage Meissonnier △ ♣
Route de Nîmes, Bellevue-lès-Angles ☎ (90) 25–41–02 ▇▇▇ to ▇▇▇ ▭ ▄▄ ▬ ▨ Closed Sun dinner (winter), Mon.

Paul Meissonnier has been teetering on the verge of perfection for some years and his third coveted star and the accompanying glory cannot be far away now. L'Ermitage-Meissonnier is a hard-working family affair (Paul's son, Michel, is as accomplished a chef as he), and the restaurant lacks the haughty atmosphere of some top-class establishments. The prices don't preclude all but the rich, for the set menus start at a very reasonable level. There are some excellent Côtes du Rhône on the wine list, the cheeses are marvellous, and the food, apart from the occasional slip, is light, inventive and delicious. ***Specialities: Sorbet au basilic, bisquebouille d'Avignon.***

Noves *(13km (8 miles)* SE *of Avignon).*

Auberge de Noves △
Address ☎ *and* ⑬ *as hotel* ▇▇▇ to ▇▇▇ ▭ ▄▄ ▬ ▲ ▬ Last orders 21.30. Closed Wed (mid-Oct to mid-June), early Jan to mid-Feb.

The bright, elegant dining-room is so full of flowers that if the Mistral blows one hardly feels disappointed at being deprived of the lovely shaded terrace. Superb wines – and some of the finest cooking in Provence, supervised by M. Lallemand but mainly the work of his young chef, Claude Aubertin. Their *cuisine* marries *nouvelle* and regional. ***Specialities: Filets de rougets aux oursins, caneton en papillotte, agneau à la ficelle.*** (See hotel.)

Nightlife
Bar: **Pimm's** *(24 Pl. de l'Horloge)*, piano and saxophone every night; full orchestra Fri and Sat; very lively.

Cabaret: **Ambassy** (*Rue Bancasse* ☎ *(90) 86–31–55*), cabaret and striptease.
Discos: **Les 2G** (*Bd. St-Michel*); **Galaxie** (*Route de Montfavet*).

Shopping

Good boutiques and shops include: for regional fabrics and clothing, **Souleiado** (*Rue Joseph-Vernet*); for local food products, **Les Olivades** (*Rue des Marchands*); for *santons* and other local handicrafts, **Gattini** (*Rue de la République*); and an attractive antiquarian bookshop, **Roumanille** (*19 Rue St-Agricole*). There are also numerous antique shops off the Rue Joseph-Vernet.

Place nearby

Barbentane (*10km (6 miles) sw of Avignon*)   An old fortified village on the N slopes of the Montagnette hills. Its handsome 17thC **château** (◨ *open mid-Mar to Nov, daily except Wed in Mar–May, Oct; Nov to mid-Mar, Sun only*), owned by the Duc de Barbentane, is more in the style of the Ile-de-France than of Provence; rooms are sumptuously decorated.

Bandol

Map 11I9. 17km (11 miles) w of Toulon. 83150 Var.
Population: 6,200 **i** *Allées Vivien* ☎ *(94) 29–41–35.*

Bandol is a delightful and sophisticated resort with a style of its own; it has sandy coves, a lively yacht and fishing harbour, and an elegant palm-lined promenade with a fashionable café.
The only blemish is the ugly new row of concrete holiday flats on the hill behind.

Sights and places of interest

Jardin Éxotique et Parc Zoologique ☆
Beside the B52 autoroute 3km (2 miles) NE of Bandol (clearly signposted) ▨ ✦ *Open 8.00–12.00, 14.00–19.00. Closed Sun mornings.*

Not a large zoo, but arguably the most attractive and well-kept of the dozen or so on the *Côte*. The animals look happy and well cared-for. They share their habitat with a variety of exotic plants and pretty trees, spread across a carefully landscaped garden. There are no large animals here, but plenty of small species such as monkeys and lemurs, as well as brightly-coloured birds; and there are charming puppy-like Saharan fennecs with their big ears, and, rolling in the mud, two hideous Vietnamese pigs called Romeo and Juliet.

⬱ La Brunière
Av. Louis-Lumière, 83150 Bandol
☎ *(94) 29–52–08* ▢ *to* ▥
16 rms ▭ *16* ⬥ ⬠ ⇌ 🖃
May–Sept.

Location: On a wooded headland just above the sea, close to town centre. A demure and simple little residential hotel set in its own garden with slender pines. Service can be rather *distrait*, but the bedrooms combine homely comforts with a fine view of the sea.
⬕ ◲ ⬦ ⬱

⬱ La Ker-Mocotte
Rue Raimu, 83150 Bandol
☎ *(94) 29–46–53* ▥▥ *19 rms*
▭ *19* ⬥ ⇌ 🖃 *mid-June to mid-Sept* *VISA* *Closed Nov-Jan.*

Location: On a cliff 45m (150ft) above the beach, in the quiet w part of the town. This beguiling beach hotel was built as a private villa by the great Provençal actor Raimu. The hotel's name was his own in-joke, for his wife was *bretonne*, and *ker* is Breton for 'house', while *mocotte* is Provençal slang for inhabitants of Toulon, Raimu's home town. Today the large pink villa is run by a sophisticated Alsatian couple, the Goetzes, who are specialists in ambience. In summer there are *soirées* for the residents while watersports are on hand at the hotel's private beach (children can be left with a trained *moniteur*).
⬕ ▢ ◲ ⬰ ⬦ ⬱ ⬗ ⬩ ⬛

Bandol

☞ PLM Ile Rousse 🏨
Bd. Louis-Lumière, 83150 Bandol
☎ (94) 29–46–86 Ⓣ 400372 ▥▥▥
55 rms 🛏 *53* ▦▦ 📺 🅿
July–Aug AE 💳 ◉ 🅒 VISA
Location: On a narrow isthmus, just off the town centre. This is a stylish luxury holiday hotel in the modern idiom: every amenity is on hand, soft pop music plays in the spacious salon, bedrooms are in period style, some with four-poster beds. The *maître d'hôtel* is conjuror and comedian Charles Roux who entertains in the bar after dinner. The restaurant, Les Oliviers, tends to be too ambitious. In summer there are two cheaper restaurants on the beach.
🍽️ 🏊 ♿ 📷 《 ⇆ 🐾 👙

☞ Other good hotels in Bandol include: **Les Galets** *(2km (1 mile)*

E of town ☎ *(94) 29–43–46* ▮▯);
La Baie *(62 Rue Docteur-Marçon*
☎ *(94) 29–40–82)*.

🍴 La Grotte Provençale ✿
Rue Docteur-Marçon
☎ *(94) 29–41–52* ▯ 🗋 ▮▮ ▦▦
Last orders 22.30 (summer), 21.30 (winter). Closed Wed, Dec, Jan.
A cheerful if cramped little *auberge* serving good Provençal food at very reasonable prices. The owner's white cat, Modeste, surveys proceedings majestically from his perch behind the bar.

🍴 Other restaurants are:
Auberge du Port *(9 Allée Jean-Moulin* ☎ *(94) 29–42–63* ▮▯); **La Marmite** *(1 Rue Pons*
☎ *(94) 29–44–88)*; **Réserve** *(Rte de Sanary* ☎ *(94) 29–42–71* ▮▯).

Nightlife

Two bars are worth mentioning. **Tchin-Tchin** (*Allée Jean-Moulin*) is a highly sophisticated place with soft lights and a smart clientele. Whisky, champagne and cocktails are the only drinks served; also *foie gras* and caviar. **Le Bistrot du Port** (near the *Mairie*), is a bar which has a lively terrace and a jolly atmosphere.

There is a nightclub, **Stars Circus**, at the Casino. Another, much in vogue, is the **Maï Taï**, on the Sanary road (*booking advised*).

Sports and activities

Circuit Paul Ricard, motor racing track (*18km (12 miles)* N *of Bandol, just off N8*). Motor racing is one of the great passions of Paul Ricard, who has built the best track in Provence; it stages several major races each year, notably the Moto Journal 200 (early Apr) and the Bol d'Or (mid-Sept). Nearly every weekend there is an event of some kind. The circuit also includes a museum of vintage racing cars, and a karting centre. Anyone can run their own car or motor-bike on the track for an hourly fee. For details apply: Circuit Paul Ricard, 83330 Le Beausset ☎ (94) 93–55–19.

OK Corral (*RN8 Cuges-les-Pins, 28km (17 miles)* N *of Bandol* ▦ ▯ ✳ *open daily Apr–Sept 10.00–18.30, Wed, Sat, Sun only Mar–Oct, closed Nov–Feb*). A Dutch-owned amusement park with ghost train, Wild West train, shooting galleries, big wheel etc, as well as live shows where actors play out the exploits of Buffalo Bill and other heroes. Plenty of excitement and fun for kids.

Places nearby

Bendor, Ile de (*Frequent boat trips from Bandol*) This tiny island 2km (1 mile) from Bandol was rocky and deserted until 1955 when it was bought by Paul Ricard, the flamboyant *pastis* tycoon. He transformed it into a tourist-cum-cultural centre.

The boat moors beside an imitation Provençal fishing port, a miniature forerunner of *Port-Grimaud*. Close by is an 'artisans' village' with potters, jewellers and lacquer painters, and also an excellent art gallery devoted to exhibitions of contemporary artists. The island's *pièce de résistance*, however, is its **World Museum of Wines and Spirits** (⊡ *closed Wed*) which has a collection of wines from 50 nations, and a fine array of glasses.

Paul Ricard has a villa on Bendor, and his island is now attractively planted with pines, flowers and creepers. It has three hotels, restaurants, a conference centre and thriving **Nautical Club** (*apply Ile de Bendor, 83150 Bandol* ☎ *(94) 29–47–15*).

⌨ Delos 🏨
Ile de Bendor, 83150 Bandol ☎ *(94) 29–42–33* 📞 *40083* ▥ *19 rms* ▭ *19* 🅐 ⚌ ⚌ *June–Sept* 🅐🅔 ⓘ ⓒ🄳 *VISA* *Closed mid-Dec to mid-Feb.*
Location: On the rocks above the sea, on the E tip of the island. Pseudo-Moorish clashes with pseudo-Classical at this bizarrely decorated 1960s hotel. If you can take the surroundings, you'll find the service attentive, and the rooms comfortable and romantically situated, waves lashing on the rocks below.
🛏 ☐ ☒ 🐎 ⚤ ⟨⟨ ≈ 🐟 ♒ 👥

La Cadière d'Azur (*9km (6 miles) N of Bandol*) An unspoilt hill village where dogs laze in the sun, fountains play and bead curtains rustle in the shop doorways. Several artists work and sell their goods here, notably **Martine Kistner** (*Route de St-Côme*) for pottery and weaving. All around is a lush landscape of vine, olive, pine and cypress.

⌨ Hostellerie Bérard
Rue Gabriel, 83740 La Cadière d'Azur ☎ *(94) 29–31–43* ▯ *to* ▥▯ *40 rms* ▭ *40* 🅐 ⚌ ⚌ *Closed Nov.*
Location: Near the village centre, overlooking the valley. René and Danièle Bérard run one of the best country hotels in the area: a 19thC *auberge*, with red-tiled floors and white vaulted ceilings. The bedrooms are well-modernized, especially those in the annexe, a converted monastery. Good Provençal cooking and a log fire for spit roasts.
☒ ⚤ ⟨⟨ ≈ 👥

Le Castellet (*11km (7 miles) N of Bandol*) Perched high on a hilltop, close to La Cadière, this ancient village is more a half-deserted showpiece, and less lived in than its neighbour.

⚌ Castel Lumière ✿
Le Castellet ☎ *(94) 90–62–20* ▥▯ ▯ ☐ ▰▰ 🚪 *Last orders 21.30. Closed Tues (Oct–Mar), last two weeks in Nov.*
An elegant little restaurant, beside the medieval gateway to the village. There are lovely views over the valley both from the outdoor patio and from the indoor *salle* with its Provençal antique furniture. *Patron* and chef Jean Matheron's cooking is well above average. The dearer *'menu mediéval'*, being mainly classical, is a misnomer – there is nothing medieval about *soupe de poissons*.
⌨ The restaurant also has five pleasant rooms (▥▯ 🅐🅔 ⓘ).

Embiez, Ile des (*Just offshore from Le Brusc*) This 240-acre island also belongs to the Paul Ricard empire and has been developed as a sea-sports centre. It has a big modern marina for sailing and powerboats, a repair shipyard, a luxury hotel and flats, and sports facilities. Above all, the island houses the **Fondation Océanographique Ricard**, a research centre directed by Alain Bombard, the famous marine biologist, with a small museum and aquarium. (*i Ile des Embiez, 83140 Le Brusc* ☎ *(94) 25–02–49*).
Les Lecques (*10km (6 miles) NW of Bandol*) A family resort with a good sandy beach. **Musée le Tauroentum**, built on the

foundations of a Roman villa, has 1stC mosaics and other
Gallo-Roman relics.

≈› Grand (☎ *(94) 26–23–01* ▮▮▯ *to* ▮▮▮▮).

Sanary *(5km (3 miles) SE of Bandol)*   A pleasant sailing and
fishing port, with a sandy beach and some modest family hotels.
Aldous Huxley used to live here. Further S, **Le Brusc** is a
not-too-spoilt village amid a landscape of rocky cliffs and pines.

Barjols
*Map 12F10. 22km (14 miles) NW of Brignoles. 83670 Var.
Population: 2,100.*
A small market town enclosed by hills and full of fountains,
running springs and shady trees. The plane tree by the town
hall, 12m (40ft) in circumference, is said to be the largest in
France. The church, founded in 1060, rebuilt in the 16thC, has
an early 12thC tympanum on its Gothic facade.

   Barjols is the only French town still to make the traditional
galoubets (three-holed flutes) and *tambourins* (narrow drums)
that accompany Provençal dances.
   Event: On Jan 16, the Fête du St-Marcel is celebrated every
fourth year, with dancing inside the church.

≈› Pont d'Or ▟ *(Route St-Maximin (94) 77–05–23* ▢).

Les Baux ★
*Map 9E4. 19km (12 miles) NE of Arles. 13520 B.-du-R.
Population: 350 i ☎ (90) 97–34–39.*
Les Baux, most celebrated of all Provençal hill villages, stands
on a southerly spur of the craggy limestone range of Les
Alpilles. It is a haunting, mysterious place – a half-ruined,
half-deserted village, nestling below the grisly remains of a
castle with a long and tormented history. The best views of Les
Baux are from the hill road to the NW (D27) or the valley road to
the E (D5): here the whitish-grey castle walls seem to be part of
the great white rock on which it stands. The name Les Baux
comes from the Provençal *baou*, meaning rock, and has given its
name to bauxite, first discovered here in 1822 but quarried no
longer.

At other times we would arrange to meet at the town of Les
Baux, that dusty pile of ruins, sharp rocks, and old emblazoned
palaces, crumbling, quivering in the wind like high eagles'
nests. . . .
   Alphonse Daudet, *Letters from my Windmill* 1868, translated
by Frederick Davies

   From the 11thC the lords of Les Baux were among the
strongest and most arrogant feudal families of France, claiming
descent from the *magus* Balthazar. At one time their realm
extended over 79 townships of Provence, including *Orange*,
and as far afield as Sicily and Albania. In the 13thC Les Baux
was a great 'court of love' where troubadours played for lovely
women. But in 1372 it fell under the rule of the sadistic
Viscount Raymond de Turenne, a high-class brigand whose
favourite sport was to kidnap people from neighbouring towns,
then force them to jump to their deaths from his clifftop castle.
The sight of their agony made him weep with laughing. Finally,
in 1400, the king led an army to crush this "scourge of

Provence" who was encircled near *Tarascon* and drowned while trying to cross the Rhône.

Incorporated into the earldom of Provence in the 15thC, Les Baux later became a Protestant enclave under its seigneurs, the de Manvilles. Such private strongholds displeased Louis XIII and Richelieu, who, in 1632, demolished the castle and ramparts and fined the citizens 100,000 livres. Thus ended the great days of Les Baux, which in its prime had 6,000 inhabitants, and today just over 350. But over a million tourists a year now invade this eyrie, crowding its crumbling alleys, jostling its souvenir stalls. You would be advised to come very early in the day, or right out of season – or, best of all, explore the ghost realm by moonlight.

Les Baux is terrifyingly lonely: the midnight silence is shattered merely by the baying of some stray dog at the moon, or by the echo of a church bell as the church clock strikes the hour. Below you in the valley you can hear the gross coarse croaking of the bull-frogs in the ponds.

James Pope-Hennessy, *Aspects of Provence*, 1952

Park in the valley below, and enter the village on foot by the Porte Mage. The 16thC **Hôtel de Manville** houses a **Musée d'Art Moderne**. All round are other half-ruined Renaissance mansions, such as the **Hôtel des Porcelets**, now the **Musée Archéologique**; above it is the former **Protestant chapel** (1571) built by the de Manvilles. Overlooking the tiny Pl. St-Vincent is the charming 12thC church of **St Vincent**, the scene of the famous Shepherds' Festival (see event below).

From the terrace by the church, the view extends over the valley, with its row of luxury hotels. Among them, incongruously, is the tiny **Pavillon de la Reine Jeanne** (accessible by a path from the Porte Eyguières), built in 1581 in memory of the second wife of King René, who owned Les Baux for a time before the de Manvilles.

The narrow **Rue Turcat**, hewn out of the rock, leads up to the 14thC **Tour de Brau**, now a small **Musée Lapidaire** with a well-presented display of locally excavated finds. Here you buy tickets for the castle ruins. First, a path leads to the barren s end of the spur, where a memorial stands to the Provençal poet *Rieu*: here the view offers a dramatic contrast between the wild peaks of the Alpilles and, at their feet, a lush pastoral landscape of vines and olive groves. The path then doubles back to the N end of the spur and the castle ruins, crowned by the 13thC keep where de Turenne watched his victims leap into the abyss. Even without this memory, the acres of gaunt wreckage are a macabre spectacle.

Event: Every year since the 16thC a Midnight Mass in the form of a Provençal pageant of the Nativity has been held in the church of St Vincent on Christmas Eve. It is still enormously popular, and you should arrive early.

☙ Benvengudo
13520 Les Baux
☎ *(90) 54–32–54* ▮▮ *16 rms*
▭ *16* ⬥ ⇌ *Closed Nov to mid-Dec.*

Location: In glorious country, 2km (1 mile) sw of Les Baux, off D78F. An old creeper-covered farmhouse, now an elegant little hotel with more than a touch of glamour. Excellent for a quiet but civilized rural holiday: idyllic garden, snug Provençal salon with log fire for winter, bedrooms ravishingly decorated with local furniture; and owned and run by a friendly local family, the Beaupieds.
⌂ ☑ ⬇ ⪍ ⇌

Les Baux

🍴 La Cabro d'Or

*Les Baux-de-Provence, 13520
Maussane* ☎ *(90) 54–33–21*
📞*401810* ▥ *19 rms* 🛏 *19* 🗏
🍴🛋🚻🍽 AE ① ⑩ CO VISA *Closed
mid-Nov to Dec 20, Mon, Tues
lunch (winter).*

*Location: In the open valley SW of Les
Baux.* For those who cannot quite
manage **Oustau de Baumanière's**
prices (see below), M. Thuilier also
runs the Golden Goat. It is a
spacious modern hotel, built to
resemble a Provençal *mas*;
bedrooms, furnished in period
style, are in villas spread around
the huge ornate garden where
swans glide in neat pools. The
accent here is on sport: tennis, a
riding club, and large, luxurious
swimming pool. Service is
attentive and the ambience, though
sophisticated, is a little more
informal than the Baumanière's.
The food, while not in the same
class as the Baumanière's, is still
distinctive.
🍴🛋🖾🚻 ⬇ ⟨⟨ ⇌ ♨ ✔ 🐾
🎖

🍴 Oustau de Baumanière 🏆

*Les Baux-de-Provence, 13520
Maussane* ☎ *(90) 54–33–07*
📞*420203* ▥ *15 rms* 🛏 *15* 🗏
🍴🛋🚻🍽 AE ① ⑩ CO VISA *Closed Feb.*

*Location: At the foot of craggy cliffs,
where the valley narrows into a gorge
NW of Les Baux.* Proven to be a
place fit for a queen when
Elizabeth and Prince Philip dined
here on their state visit to France in
1972, L'Oustau (hostelry) de
Baumanière has long held a place of
honour among French hotels and
restaurants, as has its veteran
owner, the seignurial Raymond
Thuilier. His pampered guests
stroll in the cypress groves of his
large garden, bask by the fine pool,
or sip cocktails on the elegant
terrace. They may find the ornate
salon somewhat sombre, but will

be impressed by the *mis-en-scène*
that includes a discreet
floodlighting at night of the rocks
behind the hotel. Bedrooms are
suitably regal. It is also possible to
rent flats within the hotel itself.
(See restaurant.)
🍴🛋🖾🚻⬇ ⟨⟨ ⇌ ♨ ✔ 🐾

🍽 Benvengudo

Address and ☎ *as hotel* ▥
🍴🛋🍽 — *Dinner only. Last
orders 21.30. Closed Nov to
mid-Dec.*

Dinner is served on the beautiful
patio, gently lit at night, or in the
rustic-style dining-room, with
rather too ornate furniture. In
either setting, Daniel Beaupied's
brief set menu is always pleasing,
while his *carte* is more ambitious.
*Specialities: Mousse de rouget, tête
de veau, pintadeau à la crème
d'echalotes.* (See hotel.)

🍽 Oustau de Baumanière 🏅

Address ☎ *and* ① *as hotel* ▥
🍴🛋🚻🍽 AE ① ⑩ VISA *Last
orders 21.30. Closed mid-Jan to
Feb, Wed, Thurs lunch (winter).*

Luxury is the keynote here,
whether in the vaulted *salle* amid
tapestries, silver candlesticks and
bouquets of flowers, or on the
lovely shaded terrace; and service
is suitably stylish. In the 1950s and
'60s *patron* and chef Raymond
Thuilier built this into one of the
world's greatest restaurants.
Today some would say that his
cooking, traditional in style, is no
longer at the height of its glory. But
it is still among the best in France.
The *cave* comprises 35,000 bottles
and includes an 1865 Château
Lafite Rothschild. *Specialities:
Filet de rouget au vin rouge, gigot
d'agnelet en croûte.* (See hotel.)

Other recommended hotel

Mas d'Aigret, just below the old
town.

Places nearby

Les Alpilles Les Baux lies on the S edge of this range of arid
hills that run for 32km (20 miles) from the Rhône to the
Durance. Nowhere do the hills rise above 450m (1,500ft)
though the jagged white peaks give a mountainous and pre-
historic air. On the lower slopes are olive and cypress trees, and
higher up scrub and rough grass where sheep graze.
    The highest point is **La Caume**, with fine views. The
approach is a road which leads up off the D5, S of St-Rémy.
Some of the wildest scenery is in the **Val d'Enfer** (hell's valley),
a rocky gorge 2km (1 mile) NW of Les Baux.
Maussane (*5km (3 miles) S of Les Baux*) A small village on the
S edge of Les Alpilles.

➫ L'Oustaloun ✿
Pl. de l'Eglise, 13520 Maussane-les-Alpilles ☎ *(90) 97–32–19* ▯ *to*
▮▯ *12 rms* ▭ *7* ▬ ▭ ▭

Location: A square in the village centre. After the glamour and formality of
the establishments around Les Baux, it is pleasant to find this modest but
comfortable *auberge*. A converted 16thC chapel, it is run by the charming
and cultivated Bartolis, new to the hotel trade. In the dining-room (lined
with Emma Bartolis' own paintings) there is sound country cooking,
delicious chocolate cake, and homemade jam for breakfast.
▱ ✖

Beaucaire
Map **9***E4. 25km (16 miles)* sw *of Avignon. 30300 Gard.*
Population: 13,000 ℹ *Rue de l'Hôtel de Ville*
☎ *(66) 59–26–57.*

Beaucaire and *Tarascon*, each with its mighty castle, face each
other across the Rhône, linked by a long bridge. For centuries
the towns were rivals, for Beaucaire historically is in
Languedoc, as Tarascon is in Provence.

Beaucaire's castle was built in the early 13thC by Count
Raymond VI of Toulouse, who also instituted the town's annual
Trade Fair which became the greatest in w Europe, drawing as
many as 300,000 people and 800 boats, every July, from all over
the Mediterranean and much of Europe. It survived till the
mid-19thC, when it died out at the onslaught of the railway age.
The fairground was in the broad meadow between the castle
and the river.

Event: An annual fête at the end of July to early Aug
commemorates the old fair.

Bullfights are held occasionally in summer in the bullring
below the castle.

Château
▦ ▮ *Open Apr–Sept 10.00–12.00, 14.00–19.00; Oct–Mar*
10.00–12.00, 13.30–17.30. Closed Tues.

The castle is reached via a steep flight of steps, leading to a promenade
above the town. Partially demolished by Richelieu in 1632, the castle is
half-ruined and little attempt has been made to restore it. But its high
donjon (keep) still stands, and you can still climb up inside to the top of its
unusual triangular tower. Here there are fine views, though in the
foreground the romantic towers of Tarascon Castle are hardly less
noticeable than the tall chimneys of two huge factories by the river.

The **vieille ville**, below the castle, is attractive: note the late 17thC
Hôtel de Ville, and the 18thC church of **Notre-Dame-des-Pommiers**.
The **Musée du Vieux Beaucaire** (*27 Rue Barbès* ▦ *opening times limited
and variable*) contains souvenirs of the history of the fair. The **Musée
Lapidaire** (*Rue de Nîmes*) contains local Roman finds.

➫ Robinson
Route du Pont du Gard, 30300 Gard ☎ *(66) 59–21–32* ▯ *to* ▮▯
30 rms ▭ *25* ▬ ▭ ▭ *Closed Feb.*

Location: In a garden beside wooded hills, 2.5km (1½ miles) NW *of the town,
just off the D986.* A spacious family hotel, neither smart nor alluring, but
with a large garden and plenty of amenities. Most bedrooms are in
annexes round the garden. Better for a short stay than a full holiday.
▭ ▱ ❧ ≈ ✂

≕ Robinson ✿
Address and ☎ *as hotel* ▯ *to* ▯▯ ▭ ▬ *Last orders 21.15. Closed
Feb.*

The hotel's emphasis is on food, which it serves at amazingly low prices
in a huge, rather soul-less dining-room. Locals pack out the place and are
served reliable *cuisine familiale* by the unflappable Blanc family and their
staff.

Beaulieu-sur-Mer

Map 15E15. 10km (6 miles) NE of Nice. 06310 Alpes-Mar.
Population: 4,300 **i** *Pl. de la Gare* ☎ *(93) 01 – 02 – 21.*

Once one of the most fashionable resorts on the coast, Beaulieu
has lost much of its glamour but, with its floodlit palms, still
retains a certain elderly chic. Handsome villas abound: the **Villa
Namouna** belonged to Gordon Bennett, the owner of the *New
York Herald* who commissioned Stanley to find Livingstone;
the **Villa Léonine** was designed and built by the British prime
minister, the Marquess of Salisbury. Open to the public is **Villa
Kérylos** ☆ (☎ 🖬 *open July, Aug 15.00 – 19.00, Sept – June
14.00 – 18.00, closed Mon, Nov*). Standing in its little headland,
it is a faithful reconstruction of an ancient Greek villa, and was
built between 1902 and 1908 by archaeologist Theodore
Reinach. The **library** contains a collection of ancient art.

Beaulieu's sheltered setting makes it one of the warmest
places on the *Côte d'Azur*, especially in winter. To keep one
amused there is a lively **casino** (🌑 *open daily 15.00 – 3.00*) and a
large marina; but the beach is stony. By the Promenade
Maurice-Rouvier at the w end of the Baie des Fourmis you can
walk along the sea to *St-Jean-Cap-Ferrat*.

🍴 Don Gregorio
*5 Bd. Maréchal-Joffre, 06310
Beaulieu-sur-Mer*
☎ *(93) 01 – 12 – 15* ☎ 97044 ▮▮▮
70 rms ▭ 70 ▭ AE ⊕ ⊙ VISA
*Location: In the main street, near the
station and 320m (350yd) from the
sea.* The hotel is somewhat formal,
but is smoothly run and fully
equipped, many of the bedrooms
with small balconies. There is a
swimming pool at the rear.
♨ ⬜ ▭ ≈ ⚓

🍴 Métropole ▮▮
*Bd. Maréchal-Leclerc, 06310
Beaulieu-sur-Mer*
☎ *(93) 01 – 00 – 08* ☎ 470304 ▮▮▮
50 rms ▭ 50 ▤▤ ▭ ▭ ▮▮▮
Closed Nov to mid-Dec.
*Location: In the town, but secluded
and overlooking the sea and own
private beach. A fin-de-siècle hotel,*
modernized with great sensitivity.
Spacious, bright and luxurious, it
is set in a large neat garden, and has
a delightful heated swimming pool
alongside the private beach (which
is sheer stone). The bedrooms and
bathrooms are elegant with
beautiful views, the service smooth
and polished. (See restaurant.)
▱ ♨ & ⬜ ▭ ⬇ ≪ ≈ ⚓

🍴 La Réserve ▮▮▮
*Bd. Maréchal-Leclerc, 06310
Beaulieu-sur-Mer*
☎ *(93) 01 – 00 – 01* ☎ 470301 ▮▮▮▮
53 rms ▭ 53 ▤▤ ▭ ≡ *Closed
Dec to mid-Jan.*
*Location: In the town centre and right
on the sea.* When it was founded by
Gordon Bennett 100yr ago, La

Réserve was one of the half dozen
most exclusive hotels on the *Côte*.
For today's tastes its ambience may
be somewhat stiff, and the rival
Métropole has a more relaxed
atmosphere, but it remains
flawlessly luxurious, with fine sea
views. (See restaurant.)
▱ ♨ ▭ ⬇ ≪ ≈

≡ African Queen
Port de Plaisance
☎ *(93) 01 – 10 – 85* ▯▯ AE ⊕ VISA
🚗 ▭
A lively, popular place by the port,
with views of the yachts alike from
its terrace and from indoors.
*Specialities: Curry de poissons avec
des legumes crus, salade de ratatouille
froide au jambon de canard.*

≡ Métropole △
Address and ☎ as hotel ▮▮▮ ▭
▮▮ ▭ ▭ *Last orders 23.00.*
Closed Nov to mid-Dec.
In the gracious dining-room of the
Métropole, with its large terrace
overlooking the sea, some of the
finest *cuisine* on the coast can be
sampled. Though the dishes are
classic, they are far from heavy,
and combine *nouvelle cuisine's*
lightness of touch with traditional
French cooking. *Specialities:*
*Soupe de poissons de roche, court-
bouillon de la mer à la crème
d'oseille.* (See hotel.)

≡ La Pignatelle ❀
10 Rue de Quincenet
☎ *(93) 01 – 03 – 37* ▭ ▮▮ 🚗
*Last orders 21.00 (winter), 22.00
(summer). Closed Wed, mid-Oct*

to mid-Nov.
A very popular little *auberge* in the town centre with a pretty patio for dining out of doors. Honest Niçois family cooking is served at very reasonable prices for this part of the coast.

➤ **La Réserve** ⌂
Address ☎ *and* ⓣ *as hotel* ▥▥▥ *to* ▥▥▥ ▭ ▤ ▬ ▱ ▱ *Last orders 22.00 (winter), 22.30 (summer). Closed Dec to mid-Jan.*

The formal Renaissance-style dining-room, with its chandeliers and huge Venetian mirrors, looks right on to the sea. Both *cuisine* and service are in the grand old style – in short, little has changed over the years but for a discreetly less conventional menu under the guidance of Gilbert Picard, a *Meilleur Ouvrier de France.*
Specialities: *Brouillade aux fruits de mer, escalope de saumon frais aux chablis, carré d'agneau.* (See hotel.)

Berre, Étang de
Map **10**G6. *32–40km (20–25 miles)* NW *of Marseille. B.-du-R.*

This vast and placid salt water lake, separated from the sea by the Estaque mountain range, covers 155sq. km (60sq. miles) yet is only 10m (30ft) deep. Its shores have been colonized since Greek and Roman days. Today they are heavily industrialized, especially on the SE and SW sides, where the glittering factories and blazing flares make a powerful sight at night. There are four big oil refineries, as well as factories for petro-chemicals and other derivatives; and the terminal of the South Europe Pipeline, carrying crude oil to the refineries of E France and SW Germany.

Interesting places near the lake include the following.
Marignane Marseille's international airport is situated here. Next to it is Europe's largest helicopter factory, part of the State-owned Aerospatiale group: it is famous in France for having successfully pioneered a new system of labour relations based on small autonomous work groups, rather like the Volvo and Fiat ventures. The town of Marignane has an interesting château and church.

➤ Good hotels at Marignane include: **Novotel** (*9km (5 miles)* N *on* N113 ☎ *(42) 89–90–44* ▥▥); **Sofitel** (☎ *(42) 89–91–02* ▥▥▥).

Martigues Here a 6km (4 mile) canal links the lake to the sea at the giant oil complex of Port-Lavéra.
Miramas-le-Vieux A village on a rocky spur at the N tip of the lake, with good views; 15thC church and 13thC ruined castle.
Pont-Flavien A fine 1stC Roman bridge.
St-Blaise Beside a 12thC chapel is a major archaeological site: excavations have revealed a Greek fortress of the 7thC BC, possibly the oldest Greek colony in France. There are traces too of an early Christian settlement.

Places nearby
Fos ☆ *(10km (6 miles)* W *of the lake)* This gigantic modern port and industrial estate, covering 103sq. km (40sq. miles) and able to handle ships of up to 400,000 tons, has been developed since 1965 by the Port of Marseille Authority. It is in fact an extension of *Marseille*'s own port, 40km (25 miles) to the E, cramped for space and now in decline. In the boom years before 1973, Fos was a trail-blazer of France's role as New Industrial Super-Power: after this, it was hit by the world recession and has not grown as fast as planned. Even so, it has a number of sizeable refineries, steelworks, and chemical and other factories.

At **La Fossette** (*8km (5 miles) inland beside the* N568 *to Arles*).

Le Centre de la Vie is an information and exhibition centre (*open Mon–Fri 9.00–12.00, 13.00–17.00*), with large-scale models of Fos and details of its activities. It will lay on guided tours of Fos with prior warning (☎ *(42) 05–03–10*).

Biot

Map 15F14. 8km (5 miles) NW of Antibes. 06410 Alpes-Mar. Population: 2,750 i Pl. Chapelle ☎ (93) 65–05–85.

Overlooking a valley growing table grapes, carnations and roses for the market, Biot is a lively and attractive village with an arcaded square and 16thC gates and ramparts. The church contains two 15thC retables of the Nice school; one, depicting *Our Lady of Mercy* in eight panels, is by the prolific Louis Bréa.

Due to the rich clay deposits around Biot, the village has since ancient times been a major centre of pottery and ceramics. The industry is thriving, as is an old Provençal tradition of glass-making. One of the best glassworks is **Novaro** – opposite the turning to the **Musée Léger** on the D4. Also worth a visit is the **Verrerie de Biot**, at the entrance to the village.

Fernand Léger, Musée ☆
Open Apr–Sept 10.00–12.00, 14.30–18.30; Oct–Mar 10.00–12.00, 14.00–17.00. Closed Tues.

Built by Léger's widow Nadia soon after his death in 1955, this was the first major museum in France created specifically to house the work of one artist. The handsome building stands on a hillside among pines and cypresses, the front facade dominated by a startling, vividly-coloured mosaic representing sport. The interior is functional and spacious, with large windows designed to attract the maximum of sunlight. Over 300 of Léger's distinctive works are displayed here, a dazzling array of cubes, cogs, girders, machines and massive, robot-like figures frozen in movement. Léger's evolution – from his early dabblings with Impressionism (*Portrait de l'Oncle*, 1905), through his creation, with Picasso and Braque, of Cubism (*La Femme en Bleu*, 1912, *Contrastes des Formes*, 1913), to his increasing preoccupation with machinery, its harsh impersonality, ordered movements and primary colours – can be traced through the permanent collection of paintings. Later in life his canvasses became jollier, though still involving mechanics (*Les Loisirs sur Fond Rouge*, 1949, *Les Oiseaux sur Fond Jaune*, 1955). In the garden are a number of large mosaics and sculptures, executed to Léger's design by his followers.

☎ Café des Arcades 🏠
16 Pl. des Arcades, 06410 Biot ☎ (93) 65–01–04 ▯ 10 rms 🛏 5 🚪 ⚍ Closed Nov.

Location: In a small arcaded square in the village centre. Owner André Brothier sets the tone for the truly Bohemian atmosphere at his 16thC inn which also acts as an art gallery and a lively meeting place for locals. The bedrooms, with their antique furniture and views of the hills and sea, are charming, and although the trappings are old, the plumbing is modern.
▢ ⚔

⚍ Café des Arcades
Address and ☎ as hotel ▯▢ ▭ ▰ 🪑 Last orders 21.00. Closed Sun dinner, Mon, Nov.

Brothier is a friend and collector of modern artists and, among others, Braques and Miròs adorn the walls of the simple, countrified dining-room; or you can eat under the arcades on the pavement. Visitors have sometimes found the approach too take-it-or-leave-it. But they are rewarded by sound Provençal cooking.

⚍ Auberge du Jarrier
30 Passage de la Bourgade ☎ (93) 65–11–68 ▯▮ to ▮▮▮ ▭ ▰ 🪑 AE ⓉD VISA Last orders 21.15. Closed Mon dinner, Tues, mid-Nov to mid-Dec.

Delicious *nouvelle cuisine* and a friendly welcome at this charming auberge, which has a garden. The *patron/chef*, Christian Metral, spent five years with the great Alain Senderens in Paris. **Specialities:** *Gâteau chaud de foies de volaille, pigeonneau rôti aux pois gourmands et aux fèves.*

Brignoles
*Map **12**G10. 57km (36 miles) E of Aix. 83170 Var. Population: 10,500 **i** Pl. St-Louis ☎ (94) 69–01–78.*

Wines, bauxite and marble have brought affluence to this busy little market and industrial town on the old N7 Aix-Nice highway. It lies in a valley full of vineyards and is one of the main wine-producing centres of Provence. It is also France's leading centre for bauxite extraction (2 million tons a year), and white marble has been quarried nearby since Roman days.

In the *vieille ville*, the remains of the 11thC château of the Counts of Provence today house the small **Musée du Pays Brignolais** (☎ *closed Mon, Tues*), with a 3rdC sarcophagus. The church of **St Sauveur**, has a fine Romanesque doorway and a *Descent from the Cross* by Parrocel, much of whose work can be seen at Avignon, but who died at Brignoles.

Hotel/restaurant nearby
Flassans-sur-Issole (*12km (8 miles) E of Brignoles*).

☜ La Grillade au Feu de Bois
RN7, Flassans-sur-Issole, 83340 Le Luc ☎(94) 69–71–20 ■□ 7 rms
■□ 7 ☞ ☰ AE ⊕ VISA

Location: Secluded in its own wooded park 3km (2 miles) NE of Flassans, just off N7. Jacques and Germaine Babb, an enterprising couple, have turned this 18thC farmhouse into an unconventional small hotel. Mme Babb not only does the original cooking – she is also a weaver, and an antique dealer, specializing in doors, and she will gladly sell you a hand-woven coverlet, or a carved 18thC door. Her husband meanwhile farms his 110-acre estate surrounding the hotel. Yet the Babbs still have time for their guests, whom they treat more as friends than paying clients. Bedrooms are spacious, the Provençal furnishings are elegant, and the ambience is one of civilized rural informality.
⌂ ‡ □ ☞ ⍚ ⌖ ⇌

☰ La Grillade au Feu de Bois
Address and ☎ as hotel ■□ □ ■ ☞ ☜ AE ⊕ VISA Last orders 21.00.

You can eat in the garden under a 300yr-old mulberry tree, or in the old vaulted dining-room with its big open fireplace. Here log-fire grills are a speciality, as the hotel's name implies. Mme Babb also provides copious helpings of simple, well-cooked local dishes. **Specialities:** *Daube à la provençale, tarte tatin, fromage de chèvre à l'huile et au marc.*

Place nearby
Montagne de la Loube (*8km (5 miles) SE of Brignoles*) A strenuous 70min walk from the D5 brings you to the summit, from where there are views of the whole region and far beyond.

La Brigue
*Map **16**C17. 39km (24 miles) NE of Sospel; 82km (51 miles) NE of Nice. 06430 Tende, Alpes-Mar. Population: 500.*

Once the private hunting ground (for chamoix and wild boar) of the kings of Italy, the region round La Brigue and Tende was ceded to France as recently as 1947. The unrestored medieval village of La Brigue has vaulted and cobbled streets, and a Romanesque church with a Lombard belfry, with two good primitive paintings, by Bréa and Fossano. Above the village is the ruined castle of the Lascaris, local *seigneurs* until the 18thC.

Cabris

Notre-Dame-des-Fontaines, Chapelle de ☆
4km (2½ miles) E of La Brigue. Ask at any hotel in La Brigue for key.
Standing alone in a fertile mountain valley full of streams, orchards and
grazing sheep, this beautiful sanctuary is the goal of pilgrims and tourists
alike. The exterior is quite plain but, stepping inside, one is
overwhelmed by the richly decorated interior. The walls are covered
with 15thC frescoes by Giovanni Canavesio, a Piedmontese priest,
depicting with realism and poignancy the Life of Christ. Most
memorable is the agonized portrayal of *Judas Iscariot.*

☜ Mirval 🏠
06430 La Brigue, Alpes-Mar ☎ *(93) 04–63–71* ☐ *20 rms* 🛏 *14* 🛏
🏠 ☲ 🗚 🗔 🗚 *Closed Nov–Feb.*
Location: *On W edge of the village, across the river from the main road.* The
friendly and helpful owners, M. and Mme Dellepiane, are busy
modernizing their simple, unpretentious country hotel. The bedrooms
are fresh and neat, some with fine, upland views.
🏠 🏠 🏊 🐾 ⛷

☲ Mirval
Address and ☎ *as hotel* ☐ 🗚 🏠 🛏 🗚 🗔 🗚 *Last orders*
20.30. Closed Nov–Feb.
Sound country cooking from M. Dellepiane, including homemade pasta
and fresh trout.

Places nearby
Vallée des Merveilles ★ *(24km (15 miles) W of La Brigue,
signposted roads to near valley, then well-marked paths – no guide
needed; jeeps can be hired from any hotel in the region, but this is
expensive; the valley is only accessible June–Oct, owing to
snow)*   The aptly named Valley of the Marvels is one of the
most haunting and bizarre places in all France. Set beneath the
eerie Mont Bégo in a majestic circle of the Alps, the forbidding
rock-strewn landscape makes the visitor feel very remote from
the South of France. Yet more mysterious are more than 30,000
engravings of bulls, daggers and totems cut all over the rock
faces. Discovered in 1896 by an American archaeologist, they
are believed to have been made by Iron or Bronze Age
tribesmen who came in pilgrimage to Mont Bégo and its valley.
   If you decide to see the valley properly on foot, you should
allow 8hr for the round trip. The Valmasque path leads past a
string of deep alpine lakes, each, strikingly, a different colour.
   Although now on the tourist track, there is a remarkable
feeling of awe and isolation when ascending to this remote
domain. At the S end of the valley is a **climber's hostel**, with
dormitory beds and simple food *(open July to mid-Oct).*

☜ Auberge Marie Madeleine 🏠
Casterino par 06430 St-Dalmas-de-Tende ☎ *(93) 04–65–93* ☐
11 rms 🛏 *4* 🛏 🏠 ☲ 🛏 *Closed Nov–May.*
Location: *8km (5 miles) NW of Vallée des Merveilles at Casterino.* An
excellent place to stay on a visit to the *vallée*: a simple alpine inn, in a
glorious open setting amid pastures and wooded hills. Friendly owners;
boisterous French family parties; large garden with playground.

☲ Auberge Marie Madeleine 🍷
Address and ☎ *as hotel* ☐ ☐ 🗚 🛏 🛏 *Closed Nov–May.*
Niçoise cooking, as well as alpine dishes such as *raclette* and *fondues.*

Cabris ☆
*Map **14**F13. 5km (3 miles) W of Grasse. 06530 Peymeinade,
Alpes-Mar. Population: 650 **i** Rue de l'Horloge*
☎*(93) 60–55–63.*
A very scenic route (D4) leads W from Grasse to this beautiful

old village on the spur of a hill, dominating the lush valley of the Siagne. From the terrace beside the ruined castle, and from other vantage points, the view is superb – Cap Ferrat, Cap d'Antibes, the Lérin Islands, the Ésterel and Maures massifs.

Like *St-Paul-de-Vence*, and other of the *Côte's* hinterland villages, Cabris is a sophisticated place, its narrow medieval streets lined with carefully restored houses. It has long been a favourite venue for writers, actors and others, including Gide and Marcuse, who lived here, and Jean Marais, who still does.

🔌 L'Horizon ✿
06530 Cabris ☎ *(93) 60–51–69* 🏠 *to* 🏠 *18 rms* 🛏 *11* 🚗 🏠 ☎
Closed mid-Oct to Mar.
Location: Overlooking the valley, on a quiet road on w fringe of the village.
Sartre, Camus and St-Exupéry were among past famous guests here; so too, as recently as 1979, was Leonard Bernstein. Surely it was the heart-stopping views, enough to revive the most flagging inspiration, and the lovely patio garden with its acacias and luxuriant creepers, where Bernstein would sit and compose, that drew them to such a modest hotel. Jean Roustan, the cultured young owner, talks eagerly to his guests about music, architecture and local history. His hotel is spruce and modernized; bedrooms lack character, but many have balconies with that superb view. Simple family cooking served on the patio in summer; excellent value pension terms.
🍽 📷 🐾 🌙 🎿

⚡ Lou Vieil Casteou
Pl. du Panorama ☎ *(93) 60–50–12* 🏠 *to* 🏠 🍽 🐖 🚗 🚗 *Last orders 21.00. Closed Thurs (in winter), Nov to mid-Dec.*
The name is Provençal for the 'old castle' – and aptly so, for this ravishingly pretty *auberge* has been built out of part of the 11thC castle ruins. You can eat well-cooked regional dishes, Provençal and others, in the vaulted *salle* or on the vine-covered terrace, with the mighty panorama in front.

⚡ Other restaurants: cheap outdoor restaurants and pizzerias can be found on the N side of the village, beside the Grasse road. **Le Petit Prince** is perhaps the best.

Cagnes-sur-Mer ☆
Map **15***F15. 13km (8 miles) sw of Nice. 06800 Alpes-Mar. Population: 32,000 **i** 26 Av. Auguste-Renoir*
☎ *(93) 20–61–64.*
Cagnes-sur-Mer straggles inland from the sea in three distinct parts, becoming increasingly interesting as it does so. The coastal resort of **Cros-de-Cagnes**, once a little fishing village, is today a conglomeration of highways, hypermarkets and high-rise flats – with nearby *Villeneuve-Loubet*, this is the least attractive stretch of the whole *Côte d'Azur* and has little of interest save the **hippodrome** (racecourse). 2km (1 mile) inland is **Cagnes-Ville**, notable for its **Musée Renoir**, and, just above, the tiny hilltop village of **Haut-de-Cagnes** ☆ crowned by its medieval château. Haut-de-Cagnes, like so many of the region's perched villages, is squeezed tightly into its walls creating twisting alleys and steps. Cagnes is still popular with artists, though the tourist pace is more frenetic than in Renoir's days.

Sights and places of interest
Château-Musée
Haut-de-Cagnes ☎ *(93) 20–85–57* 🖼 *Open June–July 10.00–12.00, 14.00–19.00; Apr–June 10.00–12.00, 14.00–18.00; Oct–Mar 10.00–12.00, 14.00–17.00. Closed Tues, mid-Oct to mid-Nov.*
This attractive and diverse museum is housed in the castle which

Cagnes-sur-Mer

dominates Haut-de-Cagnes. Built as a hill fortress in the early 14thC by a branch of the Grimaldi family who ruled here until 1789, it was converted by Henri Grimaldi in 1620 into an elegant Louis XIII château. In the 19thC it was bought and restored by a private purchaser and in 1939 it was acquired by the town and turned into a well laid-out museum.

Soft music plays as the visitor enters the castle via a delightful triangular inner courtyard dating from Henri Grimaldi's day, with a 200yr-old pepper tree growing on one side. Several ground-floor rooms are devoted to a museum of the olive tree, with old olive presses and many photographs, maps and books dealing with the olive industry. On the first floor, the 17thC Salle des Fêtes has a high ceiling with a *trompe l'oeil* fresco of the *Fall of Phaeton* ☆ by the Genoese Carlone, the perspective of which gives the impression that Phaeton, together with his chariot and horses, is about to come crashing to the floor.

The second floor, once the Grimaldis' private apartments, brings another abrupt change of subject – the **Musée d'Art Moderne Méditerranéen** featuring the work of artists who were either born near or drawn to the Mediterranean. They include Chagall, Dufy, Vasarely and Kisling. The former boudoir of the Marquise de Grimaldi houses a memorable oddity: 40 portraits of *Suzy Solidor*, the cabaret singer, by 40 different artists, including Cocteau, Dufy, Foujita and Van Dongen. The flamboyant free-living Solidor, never one to shun publicity, retired to Cannes in her later years.

Finally, yet another change of scene can be had by climbing up to the castle's 19thC tower for a sweeping view of sea and hills.

Event: Between June–Sept, an annual international festival of art is held in the château.

Notre-Dame-de-Protection
Below castle on NE side. Open June–Oct 14.30–18.00; Nov–May 14.30–17.00. Closed Tues, mid-Oct to mid-Nov.
In 1641 Henri de Grimaldi persuaded his cousin Honoré II of Monaco to change his allegiance to France from Spain by signing the Treaty of Peronne. To celebrate his success he had the chapel, which stands outside the walls of the town below the castle, enlarged and dedicated to our Lady of Protection. It was already decorated with interesting 16thC **frescoes** by an unknown though probably local artist, judging by their primitive style.

Renoir, Musée ☆
Les Collettes, Av. des Collettes, Cagnes-Ville ☎ *(93) 20–61–07* 📷 *Open June–Oct 14.30–18.00; Nov–May 14.00–17.00. Closed Tues, mid-Oct to mid-Nov.*
The world is full of the former homes of the great, now turned into museums; very few evoke as vividly and poignantly as this one the spirit of the man of genius who lived there. **Les Collettes** is a simple villa in a large garden full of olive trees, of which Renoir was particularly fond. Here the artist spent the last years of his life, from 1907–19. He had rheumatoid arthritis, and his brushes were tied to his paralysed fingers so that at least he could paint with the movements of his arm.

> "This was the wretched and splendid period of suffering and glory, of magnificent inventiveness. The paintbrush was slipped between his gnarled, deformed fingers. He painted non-stop, pell-mell – flowers, fruit, landscapes, nymphs, naiads, goddesses, garlanded necks, bounding bodies, expressed with a harmony ever more bold and vibrant."
> *Citation by Georges Besson on Renoir's final years, translated from the French*

Renoir's studio has been reconstructed just as it was, with his wheelchair and easel, his invalid sticks, his coat and cravat – the only addition is a life portrait of the artist at work in the same room with the same equipment, giving an eerie sense of time warp. The museum contains only one of Renoir's canvasses, but several of his drawings and sculptures, including a bronze bust of his wife and, in the garden, his bronze *Venus*. There are also letters and photos of his friends and family including his son Jean, the film director, and Gabrielle, his devoted maidservant and favourite model.

This quiet house is wrapped in a serene nostalgia; it attracts, so it seems, not numbers of impatient sightseers, but only the discerning and caring visitor.

🕭 Le Cagnard ▦
Rue Pontis-Long, 06800 Cagnes-sur-Mer ☎ *(93) 20–73–22* ▋▋▋ *to*
▋▋▋ *18 rms* 🛏 *18* 🖭 🖭 ⇌ 🆎
🅾 🆅🅸🆂🅰 *Closed Nov to mid-Dec.*
Location: In a narrow, winding alley in Haut-de-Cagnes; large cars may have difficulty. This well-known and highly sophisticated little hotel has been cleverly converted out of some 13thC houses by the ramparts of the medieval village. Some may find it a shade claustrophobic, but it is highly picturesque, and the bedrooms combine all the modern comforts with careful period decor. Some bedrooms are small, others are expensive suites. St-Exupéry and Sartre are among the many famous figures who have in the past sought repose here. (See restaurant.)
🖭 ☐ 🖭 🜄 ⟨⟨

🕭 Les Collettes
Av. des Collettes, 06800 Cagnes-sur-Mer ☎ *(93) 20–80–66* ▋▋
13 rms 🛏 *13* 🚗 *Closed Nov to mid-Dec.*
Location: On the NE outskirts of Cagnes-Ville, close to the Renoir museum. Les Collettes is very modern and functional, motel-style; but the rooms are spacious, cheerful and thoughtfully equipped, with French windows and balconies facing the sea. Most rooms have kitchenettes attached – a very useful feature in the absence

of a hotel restaurant.
🖭 🖭 ⟨⟨ ⇌ ஐ

⊏ Le Cagnard △
Address and ☎ *as hotel* ▋▋▋ ▭
▋▋ 🚗 🖭 🆎 🅾 🆅🅸🆂🅰 *Last orders 22.00 (winter), 22.30 (summer). Closed Nov to mid-Dec.*
Dine either on the terrace, with lovely views over the roof tops, or in the elegant candle-lit room that was once the castle guardroom. The *cuisine*, under the direction of M. Barel for the past 20yr, is mostly classic, with some new light touches. It is good, but not in quite the same class as the hotel (see left), and can be erratic.
Specialities: Rosace d'agneau aux fèvettes, pâté de foie gras frais, tian de St-Pierre. (See hotel.)

⊏ La Cagne Haute ✿
65 Montée de la Bourgade
☎ *(93) 20–81–52* ☐ *Closed Wed.*
Pleasant bistrot with excellent *plats du jour*.

⊏ Josy-Jo
8 place du Planastel, Haut-de-Cagnes ☎ *(93) 20–68–76* ▋▋ *to*
▋▋ *Last orders 22.30.*
An attractive spot where you can dine on a terrace under an arbour of vines. Honest cooking.
Specialities: Grillades au feu du bois (T-bone steak, etc), farcis 'grand-mère'.

Camargue, La ★

Map **8**F3. 770sq. km (300sq. miles). B.-du-R. For *i* see *Arles* or *Les Saintes-Maries-de-la-Mer*.

The symbols of the Camargue are pink flamingoes, black bulls and white horses, and they inhabit this mysterious and marshy plain, an area like no other in France, and a sharp contrast to the mountains and rocky coasts of the rest of Provence. The animals, half-wild, roam free, and are tended by tough, gypsy-like men and women called *gardians*, who live mostly out on the marshes in isolated thatch-roofed cottages, each with a cross on top. Outside the tourist season, the Camargue can be a very lonely place indeed; apart from its so-called 'capital', the seaside village of *Les Saintes-Maries*, it has no locality larger than a hamlet.

The Camargue consists of 770sq. km (300sq. miles) of the Rhône delta between *Arles* and the sea, from the Grand Rhône on the E to *Aigues-Mortes* on the W. Here land and water meet in a mesh of lagoons and salty meadows, attracting a rich variety of flora and fauna.

The sector to the N, towards Arles, has been desalinated since the war, and today is given over to rice-growing. To the S, the large Étang de Vaccarès and the maze of islands that screen it from the sea are now a **nature reserve**, where scores of species of birds live amid an equal variety of rare plants and flowers. The plain around the lake is divided into some 30 ranches, each owner having his mixed herd (*manade*) of black fighting bulls and sturdy white horses, stocky but sure-footed and extremely compliant.

The best time to see the Camargue is in spring or early summer, before the high season; in autumn mosquitoes can be a plague, and in winter the Mistral can be miserable. There are many good roads, including one along the N and E shores of the lake: but although from a car plenty of bulls and horses can be spotted, bird-watchers may be disappointed. Most of the bird wild-life is inside the reserve, which is open only to accredited naturalists and students (*apply in advance, giving reasons, to the Réserve Nationale, La Capelière, 13200 Arles ☎ (90) 97–00–97*). However, it is possible to get close to the reserve, and thus see something of the birds and flowers, by driving beyond the SE corner of the lake, then turning W to the road-end at the lighthouse of **La Gacholle**; from here you can take a long, bracing walk along the dyke (impassable in wet weather) to Les Saintes-Maries. The migratory flamingoes come in summer to the lagoons around the lighthouse, and are a wonderful sight as they rise up from the water's edge in a cloud of pink. To see them, try to arrive early in the morning, or late afternoon.

It is a profound passion, almost a religion, a faith, *La fé di biou*, or the belief in the bull, and to satisfy it, the *Gardian* will brave the elements, endure the worst fatigue and even risk his life . . . . it is a race of men apart.

Gérard Gadiot, *En Camargue*

The Camargue is ideal for a riding holiday. The ranch-hotels have their own horses (see *Les Saintes-Maries-de-la-Mer*); and numerous local establishments (details at any tourist office) take groups for long excursions on horseback through the marshes, led by *gardians*, but it is not cheap. For non-riders, there are tours by landrover. Alternatively you can see something of the Camargue's animal life by taking a 75min boat trip up the Petit Rhône from a landing-stage 3km (2 miles) W of Les Saintes-Maries (*Apr–Oct ☎ (90) 97–81–68*). The public can also attend a *ferrade*: a ranch ceremony where the young bulls are branded by *gardians*.

At **Gînes**, 5km (3 miles) N of Les Saintes-Maries on the N570, the **Camargue Information Centre** has photographs, documents and a free slide show (*closed in winter*). Next door is a small outdoor aviary, rather run-down. More interesting is the **Musée Camarguais** (**▨** *closed Tues, Sept–Apr*), installed in a handsome old farm building at the Pont de Rousty, 10km (6 miles) SW of Arles on the N570, with details of Camargue history, folklore and daily life, well set out. From the museum, there is a 3km (2 mile) signposted footpath which leads walkers into the marshes.

Méjanes is a ranch on the NW shore of Lake Vaccarès, owned by *pastis* tycoon Paul Ricard, and run by him as a holiday centre (**☎** *(90) 97–10–10*) – commercialized, but lively: horse-riding, scenic railway, mock bullfights, equestrian displays and *ferrades*.

Cannes

*Map **15**F14. 33km (22 miles) sw of Nice. 06400 Alpes-Mar.
Population: 72,688. Cannes-Mandelieu Airport
☎(93) 47-11-00. Helicopter service ☎(93) 47-15-22 i
Main station ☎(93) 99-19-77; Palais des Festivals, Bd. de la
Croisette ☎(93) 39-24-53.*

The size and splendour of Cannes' tourist industry gives the
town the air of a metropolis, even though its year-round
population is only one-fifth that of its rival Nice. It lays claim to
being the very smartest of the world's larger resorts, and
certainly all the trappings of high sophistication are much in
evidence, especially along **La Croisette**. Palm trees wave
serenely in the sea breeze and elegantly bejewelled ladies slip in
and out of the luxury hotels and shops. Yet in high summer, and
at festival time, the image becomes decidedly tarnished. Then
the town, much as any on the *Côte*, is crowded and hot, its
graciousness ruffled, making it more human, if less chic.

Rosemary sat down in the Café des Alliés on the Croisette,
where the trees made a green twilight over the tables and an
orchestra wooed an imaginary public of cosmopolitans with the
Nice Carnival Song and last year's American tune.

F. Scott Fitzgerald, *Tender is the Night*, 1939

Unlike Nice, Cannes has little history. It was still no more
than a fishing village on the day in 1834 when Lord Brougham,
a British ex-Chancellor, was forced to halt there on his way to
the Italian Riviera, as the frontier w of Nice had been closed
following an outbreak of cholera. So enchanted was he with the
pretty setting and warm climate that he built a villa where he
spent the next 34 winters. Thus he created Cannes as we know
it, for hundreds of other aristocrats and royalty soon followed
his example. The Tsar and the Prince of Wales were frequent
visitors. A modern port was built, and the great hotels grew up
along La Croisette. Cannes outshone all its rivals on the *Côte*,
and by the 1920s was arrogantly chanting the rhyme:
"Menton's dowdy, Monte's brass, Nice is rowdy – Cannes is
class!"

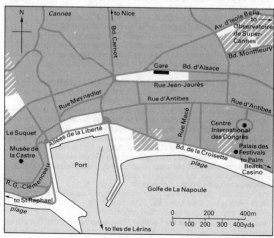

The town is in two parts. To the w is the port and the old quarter, crowned by the hill of Le Suquet with its 11thC tower, romantically floodlit at night. To the E is modern Cannes, where La Croisette sweeps round the bay to the **Palm Beach Casino** on a headland. There are miles of sandy beaches (see *Beaches*), and two marinas filled with vast, opulent yachts. The wooded hills which shelter Cannes have been marred by numerous blocks of high-rise, high-priced flats, many of them occupied by Parisians for only a few weeks in the summer. The traffic in summer is the worst element, La Croisette an endless, chaotic swarm of cars.

Not only in summer, but all year round, Cannes hums with festivals, trade fairs, conventions, regattas, tournaments, flower battles, concerts and galas. The most famous of these is the **Film Festival**, though it is not now the glamorous affair it used to be, but little more than a trade fair like any other. Its headquarters is the new Festival Hall in the vast Convention Centre for Conferences that was opened in 1982 between the port and La Croisette. This ultra-modern centre has two auditoriums, a theatre and 14,000sq.m. of exhibition space. In winter Cannes relies much on the conference trade, but it also retains a certain faithful clientele of aristocrats and genteel *rentiers* to echo former days.

Events: In Jan, the International Record and Music-Publishing Fair (MIDEM) is a major event.

In Feb, an international festival of games (bridge, chess, etc.).

In Apr, international market of television programmes.

In May, the International Film Festival; and a gymkhana.

In June, the Café-Théâtre Festival; and an international advertising film festival.

In July/Aug, the 'Nuits des Lerins'; and concerts and opera on Ile Ste-Marguerite. Also in Aug, a fireworks festival.

In Sept, an international yachting festival.

Sights and places of interest
La Castre, Musée ☆
Le Suquet ☎ (93) 39–98–98 ▣ ▨ Open July–Sept 10.00–12.00, 15.00–19.00; Oct–Mar 10.00–12.00, 14.00–17.00; Apr–June 10.00–12.00, 14.00–18.00. Closed Mon, Nov.

In the 11thC the monks of St-Honorat built a refuge and watch-tower on the hill of Le Suquet. Today it is a museum of antiquities and ethnography, donated in 1873 by Baron Lycklama Nijeholt, a Dutchman: Egyptian mummies, Chinese porcelain, vases and other objects of Persian, Greek, Roman and Etruscan origin, Polynesian and pre-Columbian artifacts, even an Inca-inspired ceramic vase by Picasso, as well as two imposing portraits of the Baron in oriental dress.
La Croisette ☆
Europe's most elegant sea promenade, signposted in gold letters, is far more the central focus of Cannes than the Promenade des Anglais is of Nice. Two long rows of palms, pines and other sub-tropical trees are flanked on one side by silver beaches, on the other by smart shops, cafés, blocks of flats and hotels such as the **Carlton** and the **Majestic**. The wide central reservation is also filled with trees and flowers. Whereas the inhabitants of Nice have deserted the Promenade des Anglais as a place to see and be seen, the locals of Cannes still flock to La Croisette. So do the tourists in summer and the boulevard is at its best out of season when the residents take their morning strolls. Three blocks inland is the **Rue d'Antibes**, Cannes' main shopping street.
Observatoire de Super-Cannes ☆
In NE suburbs, 3km (2 miles) from town centre. Leave Cannes by Av. Isola-Bella and follow signs ▨ Open daily 9.30–12.30, 13.30–17.00 (20.00 in summer); open Sat, Sun only in Nov.

One of the finest views in the South of France can be had from this purely panoramic observatory (a lift takes you to the top of the tower) on the hill of La Californie. On a fine day you can see the coast from Italy to St-Tropez, the Alps, even Corsica – and Cannes set out at your feet.

Hotels

Carlton 🏨
*58 Bd. de la Croisette, 06406
Cannes* ☎ *(93) 68–91–68*
📞*470720* ▦ *329 rms* ▭ *329* ▤
━ ▣ ▱ ━ ◎

Location: Half-way along La Croisette, overlooking the sea. The Carlton Hotel is almost as renowned as Cannes itself; its name is synonymous with grandeur and luxury. Built by the famous M. Ruhl of Nice in 1912, it is perhaps the most magnificent of the vast wedding-cake palace-hotels of the *Côte*. Like the **Négresco** in Nice it was built when the town was at the height of its *belle époque* glory. Times have changed, and so has the clientele but the Carlton still continues to provide unashamed luxury. The decor of the bedrooms and suites may be a little garish for some tastes, but their comfort is faultless and the views superb.

For so august a place, the ambience is remarkably relaxed, and the guests are an unstuffy mixture. The bar is Cannes' leading socialite centre. The hotel has its own private beach, but unfortunately no garden. It has been British-owned since 1967. (See restaurant.)
‡ ♿ ▢ ▨ ◁ ▱ ▲

La Madone
3–5 Av. Justinia, 06400 Cannes
☎ *(93) 43–57–87* ▮▯ *to* ▦
23 rms ▭ *14* ━ ▣ ▤ ◉ ◎
[VISA]

Location: In La Californie residential district, five minutes on foot from La Croisette. In a pleasant garden full of mimosa and palms, three villas have been grouped to form a very comfortable hotel; some rooms have balconies, and some have kitchenettes. Pleasant swimming pool amid greenery; no restaurant, but a big breakfast terrace.
⌂ ▢ ▨ ❧ ≋ ▱ ▲

Majestic 🏨
Bd. de la Croisette, 06403 Cannes
☎ *(93) 68–91–00* 📞*470787* ▦
to ▦ *300 rms* ▭ *300* ▤ ━
━ ▣ [CB] ◉ ◎ [VISA] *Closed
mid-Oct to mid-Nov.*

Location: At the w end of La Croisette, set back and well screened by trees. Though it may lack the **Carlton's** cachet as a social

rendezvous, and though its public rooms are less elegant, the Majestic has much to recommend it as a worthy rival. Its great advantage is its setting, lying well back from La Croisette, but enjoying the same views, with its own heated swimming pool surrounded by a garden full of sub-tropical trees in front. The bedrooms are luxurious, with modern furniture in 18thC style, and they have spacious marble bathrooms. Many rooms have wide sea-facing balconies. Built in 1926, the Majestic is no great beauty from the outside, but it lives up to its name. (See restaurant.)
⌂ ‡ ♿ ▢ ▨ ❧ ◁ ≋ ▱
▲

Mondial
*77 Rue d'Antibes, 06400
Cannes* ☎ *(93) 39–28–70* ▮▯
65 rms ▭ *50. Closed mid-Nov to
mid-Dec.*

Location: Central, in the main street. Perhaps better suited to the businessman than a family on holiday. Some rooms are rather small, but beds are large and comfortable. Service is efficient and there's a large salon with TV.
‡ ▨

Montfleury 🏨
*25 Av. Beauséjour, 06409
Cannes* ☎ *(93) 68–91–50*
📞*470039* ▦ *235 rms* ▭ *235* ▤
━ ▣ ≋ ▣ [CB] ◉ ◎ [VISA]

Location: At the foot of Californie Hill in the Parc François-André, just inland from La Croisette. For those who wish to distance themselves from the madding crowd on the sea front, who crave luxury, yet who wish to do more than lounge on the beach, this is the hotel to choose. The well-designed, dazzling white building, set in a 10-acre park, is complemented by lovely terraced gardens. Inside, it is modern and stylish, with every facility. Guests have free access to the adjacent Montfleury Sports Club: ten illuminated tennis courts, two heated swimming pools, ice-rink (in winter), gymnasium, sauna and more. There are three restaurants with fair food, a coffee shop open all day and an outdoor patio built round an ancient oak.
⌂ ‡ ♿ ▢ ▨ ❧ ◁ ≋ ❦

Les Roches Fleuries 🏠
*92 Rue Georges-Clémenceau,
06400 Cannes*
☎ *(93) 39–28–78* □ *to* ■ *24
rms* 🖃 *11. Closed mid-Nov to
mid-Dec.*

*Location: In w Cannes, up a steep
side road.* This hotel is simple and
unsmart, a good choice for anyone
wishing to avoid the bustle and
congestion of downtown, without
paying the high prices of the
Montfleury. Some bedrooms have
large shuttered windows on to
balconies with attractive sea views.
There's a small terrace with palm
tree.
🏠 ♨ ☎ ✔

Univers
*2 Rue du Maréchal-Foch, 06400
Cannes* ☎ *(93) 39–59–19*
Ⓣ*470972* ■■■ *67 rms* ☎ *67* 🖃
🍴 🚪 ᴀᴇ ᴄʙ ⓞ ⓓ ᴠɪsᴀ
*Location: Central, on the corner of
the Rue d'Antibes, close to the new
Palais des Congrès and the w end of
La Croisette.* The sixth floor roof
terrace is the main attraction of this

newly-equipped hotel. Filled to the
brim year round with tourists or
conference goers. The restaurant is
adequate.
♨ ᵬ □ ☎ ᐸᐧ

Other recommended hotels in
Cannes: **Beau Séjour** (*100 Rue
Georges-Clémenceau*
☎ *(93) 39–63–00* ■■■); **Century**
(*133 Rue d'Antibes*
☎ *(93) 99–37–64* ■■ *to* ■■■);
Château de la Tour (*Av. Font-de-
Veyre, Cannes-La Bocca*
☎ *(93) 47–34–64* ■■); **El Puerto**
(*45 Rue Petit-Juas*
☎ *(93) 68–39–75* ■■ *to* ■■);
Gray d'Albion (*38 Rue des Serbes*
☎ *(93) 48–54–54* ■■■); **Ligure** (*5
Pl. de la Gare* ☎ *(93) 39–03–11*
■■); **Molière** (*5 Rue Molière*
☎ *(93) 38–16–16* □ *to* ■■); **Ruc**
(*15 Bd. Strasbourg*
☎ *(93) 38–64–32* ■ *to* ■■);
Savoy (*3 Rue F-Einesy*
☎ *(93) 38–17–74* ■ *to* ■■);
Sofitel-Méditerranée (*2 Bd. J-
Hibert* ☎ *(93) 99–22–75* ■■■ *to*
■■■).

Restaurants

Le Bouchon 🍴 ♣
10 Rue de Constantine
☎ *(93) 99–21–76* □ *to* ■□ ▭
■ *Last orders 21.30. Closed
Mon, Jan.*
Cannes is no tourist trap if this little
restaurant is anything to judge by.
The neat kitchens and dining-room
are run with skill and enthusiasm
by young Catherine Tulasne. The
cooking is exemplary, the place
always packed. *Specialities: Aioli,
coq au vin, tarte au citron.*

La Brouette de Grand-mère
9 Rue d'Oran ☎ *(93) 39–12–10*
■■ ▭ *Dinner only. Last orders
23.00. Closed Sun, first half of
July, Nov to mid-Dec.*
A favourite bistrot with locals. Fin-
de-siècle decor and a single menu.
Wine served ad lib, and cooking
very classical. *Specialities: Pot-
au-feu aux cinq viandes, langue sauce
piquante.*

Carlton 🏠
58 Bd. de la Croisette
☎ *(93) 68–91–68* ■■■ *restaurant*
■■■ *grill room* ▭ ■ ☰ 🚪 🖃
🍴 ⓓ *Last orders 22.00
(winter), 23.00 (summer).*
Two restaurants in this lavish
hotel: the grand *salle à manger*
which has recently been renovated
to its original *belle époque* style –

eight chandeliers, huge marble
pillars, gold frescoes on the high
ceiling – and the less expensive grill
room. The Carlton's food has come
under heavy fire from critics in
recent years, and indeed the rich
and fattening classic *cuisine* is most
unfashionable and the prices are
sky high. But it is no hardship to
tuck into truffles with port and *foie
gras* or *tournedos Rossini* amid such
splendid surroundings.
*Specialities: Feuillèté de riz et
rognons de veau, suprème de loup,
crêpes soufflées Rothschild.* (See
hotel.)

Majestic 🏠
Bd. de la Croisette
☎ *(93) 68–91–00* ■■■ *restaurant*
■■■ *grill* □ ■ ☰ 🚪 🖃 ᴀᴇ
ᴄʙ ⓞ ⓓ ᴠɪsᴀ *Closed mid-Oct to
mid-Nov.*
Of the hotel's two restaurants, one,
formal and classical, aims at very
haute cuisine, with worthy if
sometimes uneven results, while
the other, the grill, is a little less
expensive and less ambitious, with
tables spilling out around the pool.
Lovely for an outdoor lunch, in
your swimsuit if you wish.
*Specialities (main restaurant):
Tourte de pigeon aux herbes, mille-
feuille de saumon frais, filet de
volaille aux morilles.* (See hotel.)

Chez Marinette
11 Rue Rebuffel, Le Cannet
☎ *(93) 38–89–46* ▢ *Lunch only.
Closed Thurs, Fri, Sat, mid-July to
Aug.*
A marvellously genuine place.
Marinette, a true local granny,
serves a superb Niçoise cuisine on
her shady terrace, and at very low
prices, You need to book.
Specialities: *Salade niçoise, osso
buco, cannelloni, mille-feuilles.*

La Mère Besson
*12–13 Rue des Frères-
Pradignac* ☎ *(93) 39–59–24*
▥ ▢ ▣ *Last orders 22.00
(summer), 21.30 (winter). Closed
Sun, June.*
This down-to-earth little place
behind La Croisette is still usually
brim-full. The decor is spartan, but
the customers noisily provide the
ambience. For fresh air and leg
room, try to book one of the few
pavement tables. Each weekday has
its special dish (for example *aioli* on
Fri), explained in English on the
menu. But take note and beware –
garlic predominates. **Specialities
(always available):** *Soupe au
pistou, pieds et paquets, salade de
mesclum.*

Le Monaco ▥ ▢
15 Rue du 24-Août
☎ *(93) 38–37–76* ▢ ▢ ▥
*Last orders 22.00. Closed Sun,
Nov.*
Georges Peisino's trattoria may be
a trifle cramped and crowded, but
the service is swift and amiable, the
food is copious and the amazingly
low prices prove that Cannes is by
no means exclusively for the rich.
The food is a mixture of Italian and
Provençal, with a good *bouillabaisse*
prepared to order. **Specialities:**
Pasta, fish dishes.

L'Oriental
*286 Av. Michel-Jourdan, Route de
Pégomas, Cannes-la-Bocca*
☎ *(93) 47–43–99* ▥ ▣ ▢ ▢
▥ ▭

A luxurious Moroccan restaurant
on a wooded hill in the western
suburbs. Decor and cuisine both
very ethnic and superb – *tajines*,
couscous etc.

La Palme d'Or
*Hotel Martinez, 73 Bd. de la
Croisette* ☎ *(93) 84–10–24* ▥
▣ ▣ ▣ ▥ ▭ ▢ ▥ ▭ *Last
orders 23.00. Closed 20 Nov–20
Jan.*
This huge dining-room of a swanky
hotel has a broad terrace giving
onto the swimming-pool and La
Croisette. Decor somewhat art-
deco. The subtle and inventive
cooking is as good as any in Cannes
but not cheap. **Specialities:** *Foie
gras chaud à la fondue de rhubarbe,
pannequets de saumon à la crème de
caviar, compote de lapereau à
l'estragon.*

Le Réfuge
13 Quai St-Pierre
☎ *(93) 39–34–54* ▢ ▢ ▥ ▭
*Last orders 22.00. Closed mid-
Nov to mid-Dec.*
Facing the port, this large bistro
with its tables spilling on to the
pavement is a good spot to rest
amid the bustle of the sea-front.
The Provençal cooking, although
not special, is good value,
particularly the fish dishes.

Royal Gray
6 Rue des Etats-Unis
☎ *(93) 99–04–59* ▥ ▣ ▣ ▣
▣ ▭ ▥ ▢ ▥ *Last orders
22.00.*
The young Jacques Chibois trained
with such great French chefs as
Michel Guérard and Roger Vergé,
and today in his own right he is one
of the gastronomic stars of the Côte
d'Azur. His cooking lends highest
distinction to this serious luxury
restaurant in a rather flamboyant
luxury hotel. **Specialities:** *Velouté
d'asperges aux lames de truffes, sauté
de langoustines aux fèvettes et aux
morilles, feuillantine de cacao à la
crème de poire et zestes d'oranges.*

Nightlife
Cannes' nightlife is livelier, more sophisticated and *outré* than
Nice's. While the **Palm Beach** and its **Jackpot** (see over) are
relatively sober and conventional, some other *boîtes* and discos
exert a much stronger pull on the fashion conscious.
Try the disco **Studio Circus** (*48 Bd. de la République, open
nightly in season*) – new, large, deafening, very in; or the **Whisky
à Gogo** (*115 Av. de Lérins*), another big place, packed out with
very trendy teenagers. At **Jane's** (*in the Hôtel Gray d'Albion*),
you can dine as well as dance, though the floor is rather small.

Cannes

Palm Beach Casino
Pl. Franklin-Roosevelt ☎ *(93) 38–25–00* ♈ ⊙ ◗ ✿ 🛇 ⋔ ⅏ ⋙
Casino open daily 20.00–4.00; dinner-dance/cabaret daily from 21.00; Jackpot disco daily 22.30 until dawn.

Cannes' summer casino is a large white building opened in 1929 which looks, as Archibald Lyall in the *Companion Guide to the South of France* (Collins, 1963) put it, "rather as though a Foreign Legion fort had had a flirtation with the Doge's palace". As is usual on the *Côte*, it houses casino, cabaret and disco under one roof.

The **casino** has less grandeur and velvet plush than at Monte-Carlo, but the clientele is smarter. The hall where the **dinner-dance/cabaret** is held opens wide on to a swimming pool, and special galas are held partly in the open air, to glamorous effect. The pool is open for daily bathing and lunches are served. The floor show and food in the evening are reasonable; ties and dresses are compulsory. At the **Jackpot** disco the advertisement urges you to *"Venez, rock n'rollez, twistez, reggaettez, discotez"*. This *franglais* frenzy takes place in a sizeable, comfortable room with moderately smart clientele.

The **Winter Casino** (*Nov–May*) is housed in the new Convention Centre.

Shopping

The most fashionable boutiques are to be found on the **Croisette**, in the **Rue d'Antibes** and in the streets between. Here are shops as chic as any in Paris. There are also some excellent shops in the **Hôtel Gray d'Albion** (*Rue des Serbes*).

For traditional and specialized shops go further w to the **Rue Meynadier**, a narrow, animated, traffic-free street behind the old port. Food shops here include **Ceneri**, at no. 22, one of the greatest cheese shops in France. It has 300 different types of cheese, ranging from a Franche-Comte monster down to tiny *boutons de culotte* (trouser-button) goats' cheese. The cellars where M. Ceneri matures his young cheeses are open to visitors in the afternoon. At no. 31 is **Aux bons Raviolis**, with a marvellous range of pastas, made on the premises. At no. 52, **Ernest**, an outstanding *charcutier*. Round the corner, at 2 Rue Louis-Blanc, the same family make and sell superb *pâtisserie* and ices. Opposite is the inexpensive and colourful **Forville market** (*open mornings only Tues–Sun*).

Beaches

Cannes possesses miles of fine sandy beach, both at **La Croisette** and to its w and E. La Croisette has one section of free public beach near its w end, but the rest is parcelled into over 20 paying beaches each with its tidy row of coloured parasols and mattresses. Several belong to the big hotels, but are open to non-residents. The **Carlton's**, opposite the hotel, is the most fashionable, followed by that of the **Gray d'Albion**. Several beaches offer swimming lessons, wind-surfing and water-skiing. For more free beaches, go a little way out of town.

Places nearby

Iles de Lérins ☆ (*Boat services from Gare Maritime, Cannes* ☎ *(93) 39–11–82, approx ten times daily in summer, five times daily in winter. 15min to Ste-Marguerite, 30min to St-Honorat*) **Ste-Marguerite** and **St-Honorat**, the two low-lying, thickly wooded islands just off the coast, have remarkable histories and are full of interest. They were first settled by the Greeks, then by the Romans. At the end of the 4thC, the monk St Honorat founded one of the first French monasteries on the island which bears his name. Pilgrims flocked there and by the 7thC it was one of the most powerful monasteries in Christendom, with 4,000 monks and a fine library; it was a major centre of religious learning in the Dark Ages. It produced 600 bishops and 20 saints, including St Patrick of Ireland, who trained there. It owned some 100 priories and castles on the mainland, and until 1788 the village of Cannes was its property, but by then the monastery was in decline and closed. In 1869 it was bought by Cistercian monks from *Sénanque* who rebuilt it and still keep it going.

Ile Ste-Marguerite takes its name from St Honorat's sister who headed a nunnery on the island. Her brother, so legend has it, only visited her once a year when an almond tree by the beach blossomed in answer to Marguerite's prayer that it would do so. Closer to fact, and our own epoch, is the story of the 17thC **fort** (*open 8.00–18.00, closed July 15–Aug 15*) built by Richelieu, which for centuries was a state prison. The most famous inmate was the Man in the Iron Mask (velvet, in fact) who was shut up between 1687–98. No one knows who this mysterious figure was – illegitimate brother of the Sun King, Louis XIV, then on the throne, says one theory. A later prisoner was the cowardly Marshal Bazaine, who in 1870 surrendered Metz to the Prussians; he escaped by bribing his guards and disguising himself as a woman. Visitors are shown the cells of both Bazaine and the Masked Man, also the statue in memory of six Huguenot pastors locked in solitary confinement after the Revocation of the Edict of Nantes in 1685; all but one went mad. From June 1 – Sept 15 a **son-et-lumière** show is held at the fort (*usually on Thurs, Sat, Sun at 21.30 – check with tourist office*). Today the fort is used as a **youth, sports and cultural centre**: in July–Aug it is reserved for 14–17yr olds, either coming individually or in groups; courses in sailing, windsurfing, scuba-diving, theatre and dance. The rest of the year (*closed Jan 6–Feb 10*) it plays host to groups of eight or more. Bed and board are provided. (*For full details apply to: Office Municipal de la Jeunesse, 2 Quai St-Pierre, 06408 Cannes* ☎ *(93) 38–21–16.*)

The **Musée de la Mer**, opened recently in the Roman foundations of the fort, contains finds from excavations on the island and from underwater research around it (Roman and Arab pottery), as well as historical documents (*open winter 10.30–11.45, 14.15–15.45 or 16.45; summer 9.00–11.45, 14.00–17.45 or 18.45; closed Mon, Jan, Feb*).

Only the cupolas of a dozen old villas rotted like water-lilies among the massed pines between Gausse's Hôtel des Étrangers and Cannes, five miles away.

The hotel and its bright tan prayer rug of a beach were one. In the early morning the distant image of Cannes, the pink and cream of old fortifications, the purple Alp that bounded Italy, were cast across the water and lay quavering in the ripples.

F. Scott Fitzgerald, *Tender is the Night*, 1939

Ste-Marguerite is 4.5km (3 miles) long, covered in pinewoods and ideal for picnics. The island is mostly uninhabited but has three restaurants including **L'Escale** which has good fish dishes and also simple bedrooms.

St-Honorat is the smaller of the two islands, 1.5km (1 mile) long. On the s side of the island, the 11thC *donjon* ☆ – keep – of the old fortified monastery stands alone by the sea looking like a toy castle in a fairy tale. Here the monks used to take refuge when Saracen marauders were sighted. Inside are 14thC

arcaded cloisters, a Roman marble cistern, and a chapel with a
high vaulted ceiling (*open June–Sept, 10.00–12.00,
14.00–17.00*). Excellent views of the coast from the
battlements.

Just inland is the large 19thC monastery, still in use. Its main
interest is the small museum, with relics and historical details of
St Honorat. Notices remind visitors that they are on holy
ground. It is a lovely island, quiet and remote, lush with flowers
and foliage – an ideal spot for idling away a summer's day.
There is one restaurant, **Chez Frédéric**.

Carpentras

*Map 4C5. 24km (15 miles) NE of Avignon. 84200 Vaucluse.
Population: 25,450 **i** Pl. du Théâtre ☎ (90) 63–00–78.*
From 1320 to the time of the Revolution, Carpentras was the
capital of the **Comtat Venaissin**, an area E of the Rhône,
corresponding roughly to the modern Vaucluse, which was
annexed by the Papacy in 1274 and did not rejoin France until
1791. Today Carpentras is the centre of a prosperous farming
district. The town is ringed by a series of boulevards on the site
of the old city ramparts, of which nothing now remains save the
Porte d'Orange.

Sights and places of interest

There is much of interest in the centre of Carpentras. Just to the
N of the town's main sight, the cathedral of St Siffrein (see
below), is a small Roman municipal **arc de triomphe**, built at
the same time as that at *Orange*: its E side is decorated with
curious low-reliefs of two captives, one wearing a tunic, the
other wearing an animal skin. Nearby is the oldest **synagogue**
in France, built in 1367, rebuilt in the 18thC; its interior (*open
10.00–12.00, 15.00–17.00, closed Sat*) is richly decorated.
Note the purification baths and the oven for unleavened bread.
The synagogue was the centre of a major Jewish colony,
especially influential when the Jews were financiers to the
Avignon Popes.

Of the town's museums, the **Musée Duplessis** (*Hôtel
d'Allemand, Bd. Albin Durand* 🖭 *closed Wed*) has works by
Provençal artists; and the **Musée Comtadin** (*also Hôtel
d'Allemand* 🖭 *closed Wed*) is devoted to local history and
folk-art. Also housed in the 18thC city mansion, Hôtel
d'Allemand, is the **Bibliothèque Inguimbertine** with a
collection of 200,000 books and MSS. The vast 18thC **Hôtel-
Dieu** (*Av. Victor-Hugo, closed Sat, Sun*), with its handsome
central stairway, is notable for its 18thC **pharmacy**, still much
in use by hospital staff; its cupboards contain Moustiers faïence
and are decorated with comic paintings of monkey
apothecaries.

St-Siffrein ☆
Rue de la République.
In the heart of the Old Town, this former cathedral has a Renaissance w
door, but the entrance is by the s door, in Flamboyant Gothic. It is
known as the Porte Juive, as Jewish converts to Christianity went
through it to be baptized. The church's interior is ornately decorated
with some fine works of art: in the choir and behind the altar, exuberant
gilded sculptures by Jacques Bernus; in the chapels of the N aisle,
paintings of saints by Mignard and Parrocel; to the left of the altar, a
triptych of St Siffrein (the town's patron) from the 15thC Avignon
school. More precious objects are in the **Trésor** (*to view apply to the
Bibliothèque Inguimbertine*).

☎ **Univers** ✿
Pl. Aristide-Briand, 84200 Carpentras ☎ *(90) 63–00–05* ⬜ *35 rms*
🛏 *21* ⚌ ⚌

Location: On a main square, close to town centre. A solid small-town commercial hotel in the best French tradition: spacious and well-modernized, and run with a cheerful, confident professionalism. Like many of its kind, the hotel is also a lively centre of local social life. Rooms at the back are the quietest.
🖼 ⛟

☎ Another good hotel in Carpentras is **Safari** (*Route d'Avignon* ☎ *(90) 63–35–35* ⬜⬜).

⚌ **Univers** ✿
Address as hotel ☎ *(90) 63–30–13* ⬜ *to* ⬜ ⬜ ⬜ 🍷 🚗 🔜 *Last orders 21.30. Closed Sat (Oct–Mar), mid-Dec to mid-Jan.*
There is a large modern dining-room, and in front a terrace on the square where the traffic is noisy but the local scene lively and watchable. The honest regional cooking, and the low-priced, varied menus, attract many local people.

Places nearby
Pernes-les-Fontaines (*6km (3¼ miles) s of Carpentras*) Capital of the Comtat before Carpentras, this ancient town has, as its name implies, a number of graceful fountains. The most pleasant spot is where the Porte Notre-Dame stands beside a former castle keep, opposite a 16thC bridge with a tiny chapel built on it. The **Tour Ferrande** is notable and worth a vis room.
the reasonably-preserved 13thC frescoes in its third-floor it for **Venasque** (*11km (7 miles) sw of Carpentras*) This old village on the foothills of the Vaucluse Plateau preceded Carpentras as the bishopric of the Comtat Venaissin, to which it gave its name. Adjoining its 13thC church is a 7thC Meringovian baptistry, not unlike those at *Riez* and *Fréjus*, save that it has only four sides. Slim marble columns with Classic capitals support its vaulted absidals. The chapel of **Notre-Dame-de-la-Vie** (*2.5km (1¼ miles) to the N on the D4*) contains the tombstone of Bohetius (died 604), said to have been Bishop of Venasque and Carpentras. It has several fine Merovingian sculptures.

Cassis
*Map **11**H8. 23km (15 miles) se of Marseille. 13260 B.-du-R. Population: 5,800* ℹ *Pl. P-Baragnon* ☎ *(42) 01–71–17.*
The most westerly resort on the *Côte d'Azur*, and also one of the most attractive, Cassis lies secluded in a deep bay, surrounded by the high limestone cliffs and hills that give this part of the coast its distinctive character. Like *St-Tropez*, it has kept its charm as an old fishing port, even if today it is submerged by tourists, and at weekends by Marseillais – many well-to-do Marseillais have villas on the lovely pine-clad slopes to the w of the port. Sadly the hillside to the N is scarred by ugly new holiday flats, but the port area is now a pedestrian zone. The municipal museum is interesting.
   Cassis has often attracted artists: Dufy, Matisse and Vlaminck, among others, have painted it. The town is also known for its white wine, which is faintly greenish, and ideal for drinking with the excellent local fish and shellfish.
   Events: First Sun in Sept, wine-harvest festival.
   July: music and ballet festival.

❧ Liautaud
2 Rue Victor-Hugo, 13260 Cassis
☎ *(42) 01–75–37* ▯▯ to ▯▯
32 rms ▭ *32* ▭ ▭ ▭ ▭
June–Sept.
Location: *Very central, on the quayside.* A busy and friendly holiday hotel, much modernized in recent years, but run by the Liautaud family for a century. The adjoining bar-café is popular with locals, so not all bedrooms are totally quiet, but the front ones have balconies facing the harbour. (See restaurant.)
▮ ৬ ▱ ⚑ ≪ ⁂ ⛱

❧ Les Roches Blanches
Route de Port-Miou, 13260 Cassis
☎ *(42) 01–09–30* ▯▯ to ▯▯
34 rms ▭ *34* ▭ ▭ ▭
Closed mid-Nov to mid-Feb.
Location: *1.5km (1 mile) sw of Cassis, alone on a rocky, pine-covered headland.* A most civilized hotel, with sophisticated owners and discerning guests. A beautifully situated, white, creeper-covered villa, its spacious garden slopes down to the sea where there is a private stone sun terrace with diving board (no sand, deep water). There are enchanting views of the port, bay and hills from the dining-room and bedrooms alike. A pity that the bedrooms' modern decor is not more alluring, and that the dining-room now confines itself to snacks and grills for residents only.
▭ ▮ ৬ ▱ ⚑ ⛱ ≪ ⁂ ⛱

❧ Other recommended hotels:
Grand Jardin (*2 Rue P-Eydin*
☎ *(42) 01–70–10* ▯▯); **Rade**
(*Av. des Dardanelles*
☎ *(42) 01–02–97* ▯▯).

⊟ El Sol
23 Quai des Baux
☎ *(42) 01–76–10* ▯▯ ▯ ▭ ⇔
⊙ *VISA Last orders 23.00 (summer), 22.30 (winter). Closed Wed, mid-Dec to Jan.*
One of the few reasonably priced restaurants along a quayside lined with expensive ones. With rustic decor and an open terrace facing the port, it is always thronged, especially by Germans (menus in German as well as French). Service is rapid, the cooking average, with Provençal dishes as well as some Lyonnaise and Norman ones.

⊟ Le Flibustier
Cap Naio ☎ *(42) 01–02–73* ▯▯ to
▯▯▯ ▯ ▭ ⇔ *Last orders 22.00 Closed Tues, Mar.*
'The Buccaneer' is a sophisticated modern restaurant overlooking the harbour entrance, with pretty decor and equally pretty views from the 'poop' (*dunette*) terrace. At night the lights are low and the mood romantic with local dishes adapted to the light *nouvelle cuisine* style. The best dishes are *à la carte*; the set menu (lunch only) is a little dull. **Specialities:** *Bouillabaisse* (*to order*), *salade de solettes de Cassis, filets de rougets*.

⊟ Liautaud
Address and ☎ *as hotel* ▯▯ ▯
▭ ⇔ *Last orders 22.00. Closed Nov.*
The hotel's dining-room, simple but cheerful, has wide windows overlooking the port. First class *bouillabaisse* which does not have to be ordered in advance. Other Marseillais dishes are on the menu, including *pieds et paquets*. (See hotel.)

Nightlife

Casino Municipal
13260 Cassis ☎ *(42) 01–78–32*
▼ ❀ ♫ ☎, *Open daily 15.00–2.00.*
In refreshing contrast to most of the *Côte's passé* Edwardian casinos, Cassis' is the most active, successful and modern on the entire coast from Cannes to Spain (Marseillais, its main clientele, are great gamblers). The new (1977) and luxurious building has marble floors, modern sculptures and a floodlat Japanese garden spread out in front – a suitably sybaritic atmosphere in which to gamble.

Discos in Cassis include **Big Ben**, near the harbour (mostly teenagers).

Places nearby

Les Calanques ★ *Calanques* means a deep creek like a small fjord, and there are several along the rugged coast w of Cassis. Flanked by limestone cliffs covered with gorse and heather, they are very beautiful. The creek of **Port-Miou** can be reached

by road from Cassis. The white rock here is quarried; its hard
stone was used to build parts of the Suez Canal. From here you
must continue on foot, along well-marked paths, to reach the
Port-Pin and **En-Vau** creeks, 2km (1 mile) further w. Or you
can take one of the frequent boat excursions from Cassis – the
best way to see the creeks.

Cap Canaille (*6km (4¼ miles) SE of Cassis*) Dominating the bay
of Cassis to the E, this craggy limestone cliff rises 360m (1,200ft)
sheer above the sea. From Cassis, the narrow D41 leads to the
top, then you can drive along the **Corniche des Crêtes** to the
Grande Tête, 396m (1,320ft), down to La Ciotat. These cliffs
are the highest in France, with wonderful views.

La Ciotat (*12km (7½ miles) E of Cassis*) Once a Greek colony,
La Ciotat is a sizeable town (population: 30,000) with shipyards
that can build or repair vessels of up to 60,000 tons. Today, like
so many in Europe, the yards are partly idle, but they are an
impressive sight, with their giant cranes lit up at night, and
behind them the strange sugarloaf outlines of the Cap d'Aigle.
Excursions can be made to the offshore **Ile Verte**, with its little
fort. There are good beaches at the resort of **La Ciotat-Plage**,
3km (2 miles) to the NE.

🛏 Two hotels in La Ciotat are: **Les Lavandes** (*38 Bd. de la République*
☎ *(42) 08-42-81* ▯ *to* ▮▯); **La Rotonde** (*44 Bd. de la République*
☎ *(42) 08-67-50* ▯).

Castellane
*Map 14E12. 63km (40 miles) NW of Grasse. 04120 Alpes-de-
H-P. Population: 1,300* **i** *Rue Nationale* ☎ *(92) 83–61–14.*

Alike from Digne or from Grasse, the N85 winds for miles over
empty highlands, then dips into the *Verdon* valley close to the
famous gorge to enter this lively little market town and tourist
centre. The **Pl. Marcel-Sauvaire** is the centre of village life,
with its terrace-cafés, shops and large buildings.

The church of **St Victor** was built in the 12thC (the side-aisles
are 16th–17thC) by monks from the abbey of St Victor in
Marseille (*ask for key at tourist office*). Behind it stands a high
pentagonal tower, vestige of the old ramparts. Castellane is
dominated by a sheer 180m (590ft) rock, on top of which is the
pilgrim chapel of **Notre-Dame-du-Roc**, accessible by a 30min
footpath climb starting behind the parish church (*for entry to
chapel, apply for key to presbytery in the town*).

🛏 **Ma Petite Auberge** ▮
8 Bd. de la République ☎ *(92) 83–62–06* ▯ *to* ▯ *18 rms* ▭ *15* 🛏
🍽 *Closed Nov–Easter.*
Location: In main square. A typical small town Provençal *auberge*, as
much a lively meeting-place for locals as a tourist hotel. Suitable for a
stop-over on the way to or from the coast.
☒ ◁€

🍽 **Ma Petite Auberge**
Address and ☎ *as hotel* ▯ *to* ▮▯ ▭ ▮ 🍴 *Last orders 21.30. Closed
Nov–Easter.*
A rustic-style dining-room with red tablecloths, or a sizeable terrace
garden, under lime trees – either makes a pleasant setting for the local
cuisine of *patron* and chef M. Tardieu. A wide range of menus and prices.

Places nearby
Castillon, lac et barrage (*5km (3 miles) N of Castellane*) The
building here in the 1940s of a large hydro-electric dam has

widened the upper Verdon river into a 11km (7 mile) long
artificial lake of bright green water, suitable for bathing. For
the best views of it, leave Castellane by the D955, then take the
hill road (D102) that climbs up from the dam to Demandolx,
which then descends in narrow hairpin bends to the high
Chaudanne dam, 3km (2 miles) E of Castellane.
St André-les-Alpes (*21km (12 miles) N of Castellane*)   At the N
end of the Castillon Lake, and on one of the two main
Digne–Nice roads, this village is a pleasant and popular
summer resort, set amid orchards and lavender fields in a wide
mountain valley with hills all round. Bathing, riding, tennis;
ideal hiking country.

≈ Closeraie Bagatelle 🏠
Route d'Allos, 04170 St-André-les-Alpes ☎ *(93) 89–03–08* ☐ *9 rms*
☐ *2* ☐ ☰ ☐ *Closed Oct, Mar.*
Location: Down a quiet road on edge of the village. For those seeking rural
peace and simplicity, a family pension with a large garden shaded by fir
and lime trees. Bedrooms basic, gaily decorated; minuscule TV lounge.
👁 ✿

☰ Closeraie Bagatelle 🍽
Address and ☎ *as hotel* ☐ *to* ☐ ☐ ▆ ☎ *Last orders 21.00. Closed
Mon (Nov–May), Sun dinner, Oct, Mar.*
Sound *cuisine familiale*, supplied by the amiable *patronne* and chef, Mme
Dubois, served either in the garden or the cheerful restaurant with
grass-green tablecloths.

≈ Other good hotels in St André are: **Grand** (☎ *(92) 89–05–06* ☐ *by
the station*); **Lac et Forêt** (☎ *(92) 89–07–38* ☐ *to* ▆ *by the lake to the
s*).

Senez (*20km (12 miles) NW of Castellane, just off N85*)   Believe
it or not, this ancient, tiny village (population: 200) was the seat
of a bishopric from the 5thC until 1790. All that today remains
of its glory is the little ex-cathedral, typically Provençal
Romanesque in style, with 17thC pulpit and choirstalls and
16th–18thC Flanders and Aubusson tapestries – all slightly
decrepit now that its many worshippers and priests have long
since departed. (*For entry, ask for the key from the curé at
Barrème, 5km (3 miles) to NW or attend Sun Mass at 11.00.*)

Cavaillon
*Map **4**E5. 27km (17 miles) SE of Avignon. 84300 Vaucluse.
Population: 21,550* **i** *Rue Saunerie* ☎ *(90) 71–32–01.*
France's leading market centre for fruit and vegetables (notably
sweet pink melons) lies in a very fertile stretch of the lower
Durance valley. In Roman times too, this was an important
trading centre, as can be seen at the **Musée Archéologique**
(*closed Tues*) with its varied collection of local discoveries
(pottery, coins, funeral urns). In the Bd. du Clos is a small
Roman arch.
   The former cathedral of **Notre-Dame-et-St-Véran** has a
Romanesque nave and cloister, with later additions; in the
side-chapels are 17thC gilded wood carvings and paintings by
Mignard and Parrocel. The nearby **synagogue** houses a small
museum of the Jewish community, once so strong in Vaucluse.

Cavalaire-sur-Mer
*Map **13**I12. 18km (11 miles) SW of St-Tropez. 83240 Var* **i** *Sq.
de Lattre-de-Tassigny* ☎ *(94) 64–08–28.*
A popular, if unremarkable, seaside resort on the Maures coast,

backed by hilly forests of oak, pine and mimosa. There are several sandy beaches, both public and private; a yachting port; and various sports and festivities all summer.

🐾 Raymond
Av. des Alliés, 83240 Cavalaire ☎ (94) 64–07–32 ▢ to ▮▮ 35 rms
▬ 28 ➡ ▥ ☰ ▤ June–Sept ⊕ ▥ Closed Oct to Easter.
Location: On the w fringe of the resort, set back from the main road and close to the beaches. The owner's white parrot helps to set the tone of relaxed informality at this rambling and unassuming holiday hotel.
▱ ⚓ ❦

🐾 Other recommended hotels are: **Calanque** (*Rue de la Calanque* ☎ (94) 64–04–27 ▮▮ to ▮▮▮); **Pergola** (*Av. du Port* ☎ (94) 64–06–86 ▮▮).

🍴 Raymond
Address and ☎ as hotel ▮▮ to ▮▮ ▭ ▤ ▥ ➡ ⊕ ▥ Last orders 21.30. Closed Wed (Sept, Easter to June), Oct to Easter.
Eat, if you can, on the side terrace rather than in the airy but dull dining-room. The whole Meunier family gears itself to the streamlined service of copious food at fair prices.

Places nearby

La Croix-Valmer (*6km (4 miles) NE of Cavalaire*) The village, set high among wooded hills, obtained its name from the vision that Constantine the Great is said to have had here, when marching to Italy to win the Empire over to Christianity: a cross appeared in the sky, with the words "thou shalt conquer by the sign." The spot is marked by a stone cross beside the N559, 2km (1 mile) SW of the village. To the E around **Gigaro** are some lovely secluded beaches.

🐾 Parc
83420 La Croix-Valmer ☎ (94) 79–64–04 ▮▮ to ▮▮ 33 rms ▬ 33 ➡
⊕ Closed Oct to Easter.
Location: In its own park just outside the village, on the D93 Ramatuelle road. At first sight this vast white mansion looks like yet another of the *Côte*'s Edwardian palace-hotels, but the institutional air and long corridors reveal the hotel's true origins – a girls' boarding school, built in 1903. Now comfortably converted, with charming staff and lovely views.
▱ ✦ ▱ ❧ ⚓ ⫻

Château-Arnoux

*Map **7**C10. 25km (15 miles) w of Digne. 04160 Alpes-de-H-P. Population: 6,250 **i** Av. Général-de-Gaulle*
☎ (92) 64–02–64.
A small town on the Durance at the junction of the highways from Marseille and Nice to Grenoble. The town has the remains of an old château, flanked by five 15thC towers. The Durance valley here is ugly, the brown river flowing sluggishly between wide mud-flats in the dry season. Industrial buildings dot the landscape, notably the large chemical and electrical works at St-Auban. 3km (2 miles) to the N is the pretty hill village of **Volonne**, crowned by two tall towers of another feudal castle.

🐾 La Bonne Étape ▦ ✿
Chemin du Lac, 04160 Château-Arnoux ☎ (92) 64–00–09 ▮▮ to ▮▮▮
18 rms ▬ 18 ➡ ▥ ☰ ▤ ☱ ▣ ⊕ ▥ ▦ Closed Jan, first two weeks in Feb.
Location: On the main road in the town, but facing open fields at the back. A 17thC coaching inn has been converted into this luxurious but unpretentious hotel, one of the most sympathetic in the famous *Relais et*

Châteaux association. The anglophile Gleize family, owners for three generations, provide all the right touches, such as homemade jams and croissants on a breakfast tray of regal elegance. Sumptuous bedrooms in Louis XIII and XV styles; lovely heated swimming pool.
□ ☑ ⚏ ⚓ ◁∈ ⇉

⇌ La Bonne Étape △

Address and ☎ as hotel ▒▒▒ *to* ▒▒▒ ⌁ ▬ ▰ ⚊ ☛ AE ⊕ ⊙ VISA
Last orders 21.30. Closed Sun dinner, Mon in winter, Jan, first two weeks in Feb.

To crown this delightful place, the food ranks as some of the best in all Provence. Joint *chefs de cuisine* are Pierre Gleize and his son Jany (who has trained with Guérard, Troisgros and other modern masters), and together they create light and subtle variations on local dishes, while Arlette Gleize serenely supervises the beautiful dining-room, with its painted silk lampshades and exquisite porcelain. *Specialities: Omelettes fraîches de legumes à la tapenade, agneau de Sisteron.*

Coaraze ☆

Map **15***D15. 06390 Contes, Alpes-Mar. 27km (17 miles) N of Nice. Population, 330* **i** *at mairie* ☎ *(93) 79–08–07.*

Steep, narrow alleys criss-crossed overhead by vaults and arches, a village square enlivened by brightly enamelled sundials – Cocteau designed the one by the mairie – and a 14thC church on the hillcrest with fine views from its terrace make Coaraze one of the most enchanting of the hill villages above Nice. Craftsmen particularly are attracted to the place; just below the church you will find **Rousselot**, a local artist who makes enamel tiles and Coaraze's modern speciality, sundials.

⇌ La Petite Auberge ❦

Domaine de la Feuilleraie, Coaraze, 06390 Contes ☎ *(93) 79–01–69* ▒▒▒ *7 rms* ▭ *7* ⌂ *compulsory in season* ▣ ⇌ ◳ *Closed middle two weeks in June, Nov to early-Dec, first two weeks in Jan.*

Location: 3km (2 miles) s of Coaraze on the D15 Nice road before Bendejun.
A diploma in French courtesy and bedrooms booked months in advance testify to the warm welcome of M. and Mme Delas at their remote, modern *auberge*. Equally enticing are the wonderful views: the village of Coaraze perched on the side of a lush, wooded valley, and beyond, a stark backdrop of mountains. The combination of real *bonhomie*, superb setting and good food (see below) has been known to lure the rich and famous as well as the humble holidaymaker.
▣ ☑ ⚏ ◁∈

⇌ La Petite Auberge

Address and ☎ as hotel ▒▒▒ ⌁ ▬ ▰ ⚒ ⚊ *Dinner for residents only. Closed Mon, middle two weeks in June, Nov to early-Dec, first two weeks in Jan.*

Only the arrival of M. Delas' excellent food and one of his modestly priced clarets can avert one's eyes from the compelling view from the shady terrace or through the huge window in the simple dining-room. Here is home cooking at its best: very simple, but using only the freshest local produce. A real treat for hungry passers-by. *Specialities: Tarte à l'emmenthal, sardines fraîches en escabèche, pâtés maison aux fruits de mer, gigot d'agneau Sisteron.*

Colmars ☆

Map **14***C12. 04370 Alpes-de-H-P. 71km (44 miles) NE of Digne, 124km (75 miles) NW of Nice. Population: 320* **i** *at mairie* ☎ *(92) 83–43–21.*

Set in the high alpine valley of the upper Verdon, against a backdrop of peaks and pine forests, Colmars is a little town bristling with fortifications and completely enclosed by 17thC

ramparts. Even the town's name is warlike – it comes from a
temple to the god Mars which once stood on the nearby hill,
Collis Martis. War remained Colmar's vocation, hence the
ramparts and the massive medieval **Fort de Savoie** (*open July,
Aug*) to the N and its twin Fort de France to the S, which
guarded the town in the 14thC when it was on the frontier of
Provence – Allos and the Barcelonnette valley having been
annexed by the Duke of Savoy.

Today Colmars is quite at peace, and makes a popular
summer resort. It is a delightful place, full of tiny traffic-free
squares, each one with a sparkling drinking water fountain.

🐾 ⟊ **Chamois** ◼ (☎ (92) 83–43–29 ▯).

Places nearby

From Colmars the road curves on up the valley, past the village
of **Allos**, with a Romanesque church, and the brash new ski
resort of **La Foux d'Allos**. Beyond La Foux the road then loops
and twists giddily upwards to the **Col d'Allos**, and down again
to Barcelonnette. Narrow and hairpin, this pass road is closed in
winter, and even in summer the drive demands quick reflexes
and a Monte-Carlo Rally spirit. For those thus equipped there is
the reward of stunning views of distant peaks and valleys from
the top of the pass.

Corniches of the Riviera ☆

Map 15E15. Alpes-Mar.
Corniche means a road along the side of a cliff, and here refers to
the three famous coastal routes linking *Nice*, *Monaco* and
Menton. The lowest, the **Basse Corniche**, N559, built by a
prince of Monaco in the 19thC, follows the contours of the
coast. The **Moyenne** (middle) **Corniche**, N7, built between
1910–14, runs past the hill village of *Èze* and has fine views.
The **Grande** (upper) **Corniche**, the D2564, also panoramic,
was first built by Napoleon on the track of the Romans' Via
Aurelia but is now a modern highway like the others: it climbs
up to *La Turbie* before dropping down to Menton. All three
corniches are connected in places by steep, zig-zagging minor
roads. A fourth and even higher through-road was added in the
1970s: the A8 autoroute connecting the *Côte* with Italy.

Digne

*Map 7C11. 153km (96 miles) NW of Nice. 04000 Alpes-de-H-
P. Population: 16,570 **i** 2 Bd. Victor-Hugo ☎ (92) 31–42–73.*
True to its name, a dignified little spa town, capital of the
Alpes-de-Haute-Provence *département*. The thermal baths, to
the SE, are recommended for rheumatism and the town's hotels
are often full of elderly *curistes*. It was in Digne that the first
chapters of Victor Hugo's *Les Miserables* were set.

Digne's main boulevard is shaded by tall plane trees, and
close by is a pedestrian zone of old narrow streets. The **musée
municipal** (◼ *closed Mon*) contains a good collection of local
natural history and archaeology, as well as paintings by local
artists. Digne's most interesting building, on the D900 in the
NE outskirts, is the yellowish 12th–13thC **Notre-Dame-de-
Bourg** (*for entry apply to cemetery keeper*), an ex-cathedral now
used only for funerals: a graceful nave in Provençal
Romanesque style, a Lombard portal and a pretty rose window.

≈ L'Aiglon
Rue de Provence, 04000 Digne
☎ *(92) 31–02–70* ▢ *33 rms*
▢ *12* ▢ ▢ ▭ ▢ AE ⓘ ⓞ
VISA *Closed Dec–Jan.*

A straightforward little place of no special charm, but suitable for a night or two's stay in the area. In the bedrooms, wallpaper and bedspreads clash merrily. The hotel's name echoes Digne's Napoleonic associations (it lies on the Route Napoléon) while an assertive mural of the dance of the eagle fills one wall of the dining-room. Sound Provençal cooking.
▱

≈ Grand Paris
19 Bd. Thiers, 04000 Digne
☎ *(92) 31–11–15* ▢▢ *to* ▢▢▢
32 rms ▢ *32* ▢ ▢ ▭ ⓞ
Closed Jan–Feb.
Location: In town centre, facing a car park. A 17thC monastery of the Brothers of the Trinity has been converted into a small, cosy hotel of some character. It is spotlessly clean and extremely well run, though the rather sombre predilection for dark colours and velvet might not suit all tastes. (See restaurant.)
⚓ ♿ ▢ ▱ ⛵

≈ Mistre
65 Bd. Gassendi, 04000 Digne
☎ *(92) 31–00–16* ▢ *to* ▢▢
35 rms ▢ *20* ▢ ▢ ▭ *Closed mid-Nov to Christmas. Restaurant: Last orders 21.00, closed Sat.*
Location: In the town centre, on the

main street. Although the bedrooms and bathrooms have been recently modernized, this sedate and spacious Edwardian hotel has the air of being somewhat past its prime; but it is friendly and comfortable and popular with the elderly French people who come to Digne for cures. The brochure in English lauds its 'insonorous rooms' and 'thrush pie'. Pleasant dining patio for summer.
▱

≈ La Chauvinière
56 Rue de l'Hubac
☎ *(92) 31–40–03* ▢ ▢ ▭ ▭
Last orders 21.30. Closed Sun dinner, Mon (Oct–Mar), second half of June, second half of Nov.
The accent is on well-prepared Provençal cooking with a number of alpine additions. Mellow lighting, soft music, quiet.
Specialities: Raclette, fondue, cheeses.

≈ Grand Paris
Address and ☎ *as hotel* ▢▢ *to* ▢▢▢
▢ ▭ ▭ ▭ ⓞ *Last orders 21.30. Closed Sun dinner, Mon (Oct–Mar), Jan–Feb.*
The best food in Digne is served either in a formal dining-room or (when fine) on a delightful terrace under shady trees. Prices are not low, but the *patron* and chef, J.J. Ricoud, deserves his accolades. Try the Vignelaure or Lirac wines.
Specialities: Mousseux de poireaux James, truite à la crème de poivrons.
(See hotel.)

Places nearby

Two roads, the D900 and D900A, wind N through impressively wild and arid **Pré-Alpes de Digne** to the **Col de Maure** and **Seyne**, on the way to Barcelonnette. Of the two routes, the westerly one on the D900A via the *clues* (clefts) of **Barles** and **Verdaches** is the most spectacular but the most narrow.

Draguignan

Map 13F12. 65km (45 miles) w of Cannes. 83300 Var. Population: 25,240 ℹ 9 Bd. Clémenceau ☎ (94) 68–63–30.
This dignified old market town has broad avenues and a floodlit fountain; the narrow streets of the old quarter are now a pleasant traffic-free zone, and above them stands the impressive 17thC **tour d'horloge** with its wrought-iron campanile. The **museum** contains some Gallo-Roman remains and Flemish and Italian paintings.

2km (1 mile) to the E, on D59, an **Allied war cemetery** holds the graves of those killed in the battles that followed the parachute drop of 10,000 at Le Muy on Aug 15, 1944. 2km (1 mile) to the NW, on D955, is the **Pierre de la Fée**, a curious dolmen 2m (6ft) high, perched on three stones.

☎ ═ **Col de l'Ange** (*Route de Lorgues* ☎ *(94) 68–23–01* **III**) and **du Parc** (*21 Bd. de la Liberté* ☎ *(94) 68–53–84* **III**) are both adequate.

Restaurant nearby
La Motte (*10km (6 miles) SE of Draguignan*)

Les Pignatelles ✿
Route de Bagnols ☎*(94) 70–25–70* ⬜ ■ ■ ═ ⌂ ➤ *VISA* *Last orders 22.00. Closed Wed.*

This fairly new and promising venture has much going for it: a *patron* and chef, Gilbert Massé, who has worked with Rostang, Outhier and Vergé; a sympathetic Provençal-style building filled with flowers and surrounded by vines; polished service under the auspices of M. Massé's brother, Georges; plus agreeably low prices both for the food and wine – the Château Minuty is excellent value. Adverse comments may include the lack of choice on the set menu, and limited choice on the *carte*, uneven cooking and a poor cheese board. **Specialities:** *Salade de saison aux écrevisses, feuilleté de grenouilles à l'ail doux, fricassée de volaille au vinaigre de vin vieux.*

Places nearby
Les Arcs (*10km (6 miles) S of Draguignan*)   The village has a Roman bridge, and in its **church** a lovely 16thC retable divided into 16 panels.
Chapelle Ste-Rosaline ✩ (*4.5km (3 miles) E of Les Arcs*)   Formerly attached to an 11thC abbey, the recently restored chapel contains 17thC gilded wood retables, 16thC choir-stalls, and modern art works, notably two by Giacometti: a lectern, and a bronze low-relief relating the saint's life.

☎ ═ **Le Logis du Guetteur** (*Les Arcs-sur-Argens* ☎ *(94) 73–30–82* **III**).

Entrevaux
*Map **14**D13. 72km (45 miles) NW of Nice. 04320 Alpes-de-H-P. Population: 700* ℹ *at mairie* ☎*(93) 05–40–04.*

This remarkable fortified village is not on a hilltop, like most in Provence, but stands beside the rushing river Var and the Nice–Digne road and railway. Vauban, Louis XIV's military engineer, built its ramparts in 1695, when the Var was France's frontier with ducal Savoy; and Entrevaux has changed little in aspect since then. It has moats and three gates, through one of which you must pass to enter the old village with its steep, shady alleys, pleasantly unspoilt. Some buildings date from the 11thC. It is worth climbing up to Vauban's fort on the hill behind.

   Events: Culture and folklore are very much alive in Entrevaux. One resident, Roger Greaves, English writer and musician, runs a two-week festival of 16th and 17thC music every Aug, with international performers and audiences.

   Another highpoint is the Fête of John the Baptist on the weekend nearest to June 24 when locals in traditional costume proceed to a chapel 12km (8 miles) away.

Ancienne cathédrale †✩
✗ *Open daily all year.*

Though it was built as a cathedral in the 17thC, this richly ornate church was demoted during the Revolution. It forms part of the 17thC ramparts, though the adjoining bell-tower is the work of the Knights Templar in the 11thC. As with many Provençal churches, the exterior is plain, even austere, and there is just one nave and no aisle. But the interior has much to please the eye: note the chancel and choir stalls, the good 17thC paintings, the antique silver ornaments and the fine altarpiece of St John the Baptist.

☎ Vauban ■ *(by the main road ☎ (93) 05–42–40 □)* offers Provençal food and simple lodging.

Places nearby
Gorges de Daluis (*16km (10 miles) N of Entrevaux*)   From Daluis at its s end to **Guillaumes** (see *Valberg* for details) at the N end, the D2202, by means of hairpins and tunnels, ascends the left side of the magnificent and giddying gorge, providing many stunning views of the towering cliffs of red rock, studded with green.

Esterel massif ☆
Map 13G13. 130sq. km (50sq. miles) between St-Raphael and La Napoule, from 8–24km (5–15 miles) sw of Cannes. Var.

The jagged red rocks of this mountain range, stretching along the coast from La Napoule to St-Raphael, are among the most haunting sights in Provence. The Esterel is thought to be one of Europe's oldest land masses – a single chunk of volcanic rock, mostly red porphyry, which has been eroded into strange craggy shapes over millions of years. It is covered with a variety of wild plants, and with forests of pine and oak, though since the war forest fires have ravaged much of the massif, where only gradually new trees are being planted.

The Romans built their Aurelian Way (from Rome to Arles), along the N fringe of the massif, and until the early 20thC this remained the only through-route anywhere near the coast. For centuries it was a route full of danger, for escaped convicts and highwaymen would use these wild ravines as hideouts. Not until 1903 was a road built along the coast, and today it is well worth taking this scenic route (N98) via *Agay* and *Théoule* to admire the many coves and cliffs and the brilliant colour contrasts of red rocks, azure sea and green trees. The spectacle is most dramatic E of Le Trayas.

There are views of the massif from the autoroute (A8) or from the parallel N7. But best of all, those who don't mind rough driving can take one of the narrow mountain roads that lead up into the lonely heart of the Esterel. From these it is possible to clamber on foot to the summit of the three main peaks: **Mont Vinaigre** (inland) and the **Pic de l'Ours** and **Pic du Cap Roux** (near the coast). All have marvellous views. Worth exploring too is the fantastic rocky gorge of the **Mal Infernet**, N of Agay.

Èze
Map 15E15. 12km (7 miles) NE of Nice. 06360 Alpes-Mar. Population: 2,064 i at mairie ☎ (93) 41–03–03.

No other of the *Côte d'Azur's* hill villages is as well-known or tourist-jammed as Èze. There are two reasons: first, because of its accessibility, close to the coast by the Middle Corniche; second, because the setting *is* spectacular, on a rocky outcrop 390m (1,300ft) almost sheer above the sea.

Èze may have become a tourist trap, but it is a good one. It has been scrupulously restored, and its numerous art and souvenir shops are not too brashly vulgar. Parking is near the entrance to the ancient village; then visitors must climb its narrow alleys on foot. If you can squeeze through the throng, climb to the summit where the remnants of a castle stand just (above the **Jardin Exotique**, full of cacti (🔲 *open daily until nightfall*). Here the coastline lies spread before you.

Today Èze is a museum, albeit a fascinating one; for a real look at Provence's hill villages, you must venture further into the hinterland.

Hotel

Château de la Chèvre d'Or 🏰
Rue du Barri, 06360 Èze-village
☎ *(93) 41–12–12* ⓘ *470673*
9 rms 🛏 *9* 🍽 🚗 🅰🅴 ⓒ 🆅🆂🅰
Closed Dec–Feb.
Location: High in the old village, facing the sea. A medieval château artistically converted into a small luxury hotel, the Chèvre d'Or has become as celebrated as many of its guests. It is run with suave efficiency by its Swiss owner, Bruno Ingold: soft music plays as you sip champagne cocktails by the pool, gazing at Cap Ferrat far below; even the telephones in the lavishly furnished bedrooms are Edwardian museum pieces. If some bedrooms are cramped, blame the 11thC architect, though the 20thC re-designers have ingeniously done their best. Rooms near the kitchens may be noisy. (See restaurant.)
🔲 🚗 ♨ ⟨∈ ≈

Château Eza
06360 Èze-Village
☎ *(93) 41–12–24* 🔲 *8 rms* 🛏 *8* 🚗 🅰🅴 🅲🅱 ⓒ ⓘ 🆅🆂🅰 *Closed Nov to mid-April.*
Perched high above the sea, a delightful place with first-class food.

Hotels nearby
Èze-bord-de-Mer

Cap Estel 🏰
06360 Èze-bord-de-Mer
☎ *(93) 01–50–44* ⓘ *470305* 🔲
47 rms 🛏 *47* 🚗 🏠 🍽 ⓒ
Closed Nov–Jan.
Location: Just off the lower Corniche, by the sea. A handsome white villa, formerly the home of a prince, has been turned into a beautiful, if rather formal luxury hotel. It stands on a promontory in a large, elegant garden. Many amenities: flats may also be rented. The cooking, though fair, does not

equal the setting, by the pool, on the terrace, or in a Louis XVI-style dining-room.
🏠 ♨ ⟨ 🚗 ♨ ⟨∈ ≈

Mimosas Cottage
06360 Èze-bord-de-Mer
☎ *(93) 01–54–82* 🔲 *40 rms*
🛏 *40* 🚗 🏠 🍽
Location: Beside the lower Corniche, close to the beach. Small, simple rooms, most of them in annexes dotted around a sub-tropical grove of orange and lemon, palm and cedar, even banana trees. Two snags: the railway is very close, and the beach is less than idyllic. Buffet breakfasts, hors d'oeuvres and good local fish dishes served on the terrace.
♨ ⟨∈ 🍴

Restaurants

Château de la Chèvre d'Or 🏰
Address and ☎ *as hotel* 🔲 *to*
🚗 🅰🅴 ⓒ 🆅🆂🅰
Closed Wed (Oct–Easter), Dec–Feb.
A beautiful restaurant filled with equally beautiful people. The chef, Elie Mazot, has worked with the Troisgros brothers and his delicate cooking shows their influence.
Specialities: Huitres chaudes au champagne, nage de poissons en blanquette, pigeonneau aux gousses d'ail en chemise. (See hotel.)

Nid d'Aigle
Rue du Château
☎ *(93) 41–19–08* 🔲 🍽 🚗
Last orders 21.00. Closed Thurs, mid-Nov to mid-Dec.
For those who do not care for M. Ingold's high prices, this is a modest but pleasing alternative. It is perched at the top of the old village, just below the garden. Good local cooking, such as *bourride* or *lapin aux herbes*; copious hors d'oeuvres trolley.

Shopping
Many artists and artisans live in Èze and sell their work there; some have studios open to the public. Among the best are **José Benito** (*Rue Principale*) for coloured glass and jewellery, and **A. Aicardi** (*Pl. du Planet*) for wrought-iron work.

Fontaine-de-Vaucluse ☆

*Map 5D6. 30km (18 miles) E of Avignon. 84800 L'Isle-sur-la-Sorgue, Vaucluse. Population: 550 **i** Pl. de l'Église*
☎ *(90) 20–31–79.*

In winter or spring, especially after heavy rain or when snows are melting, the fountain is a magnificent sight. Set in a cavern where the river Sorgue emerges at the foot of a high limestone cliff, the waters surge up over a rocky barrier in a roaring cascade of spray. In the dry season, though, the water flows normally and there is little special to see. Notwithstanding, the fountain attracts well over a million visitors every year. It is a short walk from the village of the same name which is not surprisingly tourist-orientated. Little is left of the romantic serenity that persuaded the Italian poet Petrarch to live here. He is commemorated with a stele erected in 1804 to mark his fifth centenary, and with a small **museum** of his works on the site of the house where he lived from 1337–53. There is also a **speleological museum** with fine stalactites.

   Event: A *son et lumière* is held daily at the fountain from mid-June to mid-Sept at 21.30.

⇌ Le Parc
Fontaine de Vaucluse ☎ *(90) 20–31–57* ■ *to* ■■ □ ■ 🚗 AE ⊕
Last orders 21.15. Closed Wed, Jan to mid-Feb.
Straightforward food served to hungry tourists under trees in the large garden by the river, or in the vast *salle*.
☞ The creeper and rose-covered *auberge* also has comfortable bedrooms.

Places nearby

L'Isle-sur-la-Sorgue (*7km (4 miles) W of Fontaine-de-Vaucluse*)   This cool, watery town with running streams and grassy, tree-lined banks, lies at the place where the river Sorgue divides into five branches. Its church has a richly-decorated 17thC Baroque interior, and a retable of the Assumption. The old hospital (*open daily*) has 18thC woodcarvings in its chapel and Moustiers faïence in the pharmacy.

Fontvieille

*Map 9E4. 9.5km (6 miles) NE of Arles. 13990 B.-du-R. Population: 3,000 **i** at mairie* ☎ *(90) 97–70–01.*

A small town beneath the plain of Arles and the Alpilles range, chiefly visited for its famous mill.

Moulin de Daudet
2km (1 mile) S of Fontvieille, off the D33 🚗 ✗ *Open daily Apr–Sept 8.30–12.00, 13.00–17.30.*
The windmill that 19thC writer Alphonse Daudet found so inspiring is indeed impressively situated, on a bare rocky hill with pine woods behind, amid views of the Alpilles and the Rhône valley. Despite the name of Daudet's bestselling book, *Letters from my Windmill*, he never owned the building; the letters were written in Paris where he lived, and he only used to visit the mill when staying with friends in the village. But he would go there to think for long hours, and to listen to the miller's tales, many of which he then used as his published *contes*.

   The mill is still in working order. Perched up in its beams is Daudet's 'silent tenant', the owl – now stuffed. Also in the roof are the Provençal names for the 32 winds of the region (added after Daudet's day). The basement is now a small **museum** dedicated to the author.

☞ La Régalido
Rue Frédéric-Mistral, 13990 Fontvieille ☎ *(90) 97–60–22* ■■ *11 rms*
▣ *11* 🚗 ⊟ ⊟ AE ⊕ VISA *Closed Dec to mid-Jan.*
Location: Set back from a village side street. Umbrella pines, and fig trees,

roses and magnolia, trimly-cut lawns – the beautifully kept garden is the
best feature of this luxurious little *auberge*, converted from an old oil mill.
The interior is graciously intimate and inviting. (See restaurant.)
⌂ ⌂ ⌂

Le Val Majour
Route d'Arles, 13990 Fontvieille ☎ *(90) 97–70–37* ▮▮▮ *30 rms* ▭ *27*
▭ *Closed Nov–Feb.*
Location: On the w fringe of the town, just off the Arles road. A modern
creeper-covered hotel, attractively designed in the style of a local *mas*.
Spacious, comfortable, with plenty of amenities and good views, but not
much ambience.
⌂ ⌂ ⌂ ⌂ ⌂ ⌂

La Régalido
Address and ☎ *as hotel* ▮▮▮ ▬ ▬ ⌂ ▬ AE ⓒ VISA *Last orders*
21.15. Closed Mon, Tues (lunch), Dec to mid-Jan.
The flowery patio, gently lit at night, makes a romantic setting for a
meal, or you can choose the more formal elegance of the vaulted
dining-room. Jean-Pierre Michel is a talented cook who, in the modern
idiom, produces light variations on classic *cuisine.* Good local Côte-de-
Baux wines. *Specialities: Mousseline de poissons, filet de loup en verdure,
canard braisé au poivre vert.* (See hotel.)

Forcalquier
*Map **6**D9. 59km (31 miles) sw of Digne. 04300 Alpes-de-H.-P.
Population: 3,450* **i** *Pl. Bourguet* ☎ *(92) 75–10–02.*
The town, an important feudal capital in the 12thC, is finely
situated on the slopes of a steep hill, overlooking the lush
surrounding countryside. In the central square, the stately
Romanesque **church of Notre-Dame** stands opposite a small
local **museum**. Nearby is the 13thC **Couvent des Cordeliers**,
one of the first Franciscan monasteries in France. The town's
main curiosity is its **cemetery**, 1km (½ mile) up the hill to the N:
its terraces are partitioned by tall box-hedges of clipped yew,
forming archways – a rare sight in France.

Hostellerie des Deux-Lions *(11 Pl. Bourget* ☎ *(92) 75–25–30* ▮▯
to ▮▮▮ *closed Thurs, Jan 2–Feb 10).*

Places nearby
Lure, Montagne de *(32km (20 miles) N of Forcalquier)* This
lofty ridge runs 1,800m (5,994ft) from w–e. From St-Étienne a
road leads through dense forest to the crest from where a
strenuous 15min walk leads to the **Signal de Lure** with fantastic
panoramic views as far as the coast and the Cévennes.
Observatoire de Haute Provence *(13km (8 miles) sw of
Forcalquier ✗ Wed 15.00 and first Sun of month Apr–Sept
9.30)* A major state-run astronomical research centre, with
powerful telescopes. The site was chosen because of the purity
of the atmosphere here.

Fréjus
*Map **13**G13. 40km (25 miles) sw of Cannes. 83600 Var.
Population: 32,698* ▬ *Pl. Calvini* ☎ *(94) 51–53–87.*
Lying a mile inland, on a plain just w of the *Maures massif*,
Fréjus contains some of the most fascinating traces of the
Roman era in France, and a remarkable cathedral and 5thC
baptistry. As a modern town, it has few attractions apart from
the beaches of Fréjus-Plage.
    Founded by Julius Caesar in 49BC, Fréjus *(Forum Julii)*
became an important and highly efficient naval base under

Augustus; here he moored the warships captured from Antony and Cleopatra at Actium in 31BC. Fréjus was by then a flourishing Roman town, its population, at 25,000, only a little smaller than today. But gradually, with the decline of Roman influence, the port lost its significance, and by the 3rdC AD had silted up. In the 10thC Fréjus was destroyed by Saracens, to be rebuilt by Bishop Riculphe, who elevated it to an episcopal city of some rank.

Events: The *bravade* costume procession takes place on the third Sun after Easter.

There are several bullfights in summer in the Roman Arena.

Sights and places of interest

Cité Episcopale ▥ ✝ ☆
Pl. de Formigé ▨ ▨ *For cloister, baptistry and museum. Open Apr–Sept 9.30–12.00, 14.00–18.00; Oct–Mar 9.30–12.00, 14.00–16.30. Closed Tues.*

At the entrance to this rich ensemble in the centre of town the guide opens the shutters protecting the fine **Renaissance doors** on which are carved 16 walnut panels showing scenes of the life of the Virgin and of Saracen massacres. To the left is the remarkable 5thC baptistry, one of the oldest in France. It is octagonal, with a sunken font and two doors. Baptisms in those days were conducted by bishops and reserved for adults. Catechumens would enter by one door; the bishop would wash their feet, immerse them and anoint them with oil; then, white-robed, they would pass out through the other door to their first communion in the cathedral.

The elegant little 12thC **cloister** has a colonnade of twin slender marble pillars, in the style common in Provence; in its middle is a garden with rose trees and a well. The beamed ceiling of its arcade was decorated in the 15thC with thousands of tiny painted panels of animals and grotesques, many of which were destroyed in the Revolution. Above the cloister rises the graceful bell-tower, part 13thC, its steeple covered with patterned, coloured tiles.

The rooms off the cloister house a **musée archéologique**, devoted to local Roman finds: a mosaic, discovered in 1921, and Roman sculptures and a sarcophagus. Most attractive, however, are the small Greek vases, exquisitely shaped and decorated, which the Romans brought with them on their travels.

The cathedral, part 10thC, part 12th–13thC, is of lofty and graceful dimensions, but rather austere. It has a 16thC painted wooden crucifix, and a 15thC retable of *Ste Marguerite* above the sacristy door.

Cité Romaine
The sea has receded since Roman days; Augustus' port was close to the modern town centre, just S of the Av. Aristide-Briand. It is thought to have had quays 2km (1 mile) long with a lighthouse, shipyards and warehouses. Though little remains today, there are relics enough to imagine Forum Julii in its prime. It lay astride the Aurelian Way, the highway from Rome to Arles, and was girt by 3km (2 miles) of ramparts. Its w entrance was the **Porte des Gaules**, of which one tower survives. Outside was the **arena**, the oldest in Gaul and built to seat 10,000. Today modern seating has been installed and it is still used, for bullfights and pop concerts. Inside the ramparts was a **theatre**, still partly standing. On the low hill to the SE are traces of the Roman military HQ, while the **Porte d'Orée** (*just SE of the new town*) was probably part of the old baths. The **Lanterne d'Auguste**, just E of the modern town, S of the railway, is a medieval tower built on a Roman base that is thought to have stood by the harbour entrance.

▧ Hotels worth recommending are: **Les Palmiers** (*Bd. de la Libération* ☎ *(94) 51–18–72* ▥); **Les Résidences du Colombier** (*Route de Bagnols* ☎ *(94) 51–45–92* ▥), which is modelled on the Club-Med idea with the accent on sport and get-together holiday jollity; bedrooms are in bungalows spread about the garden.

▧ **Auberge du Vieux Four** (*46 Rue de Grisolle* ☎ *(94) 51–56–38* ▥).

Beaches
There are 5km (3 miles) of sandy public beaches at **Fréjus-Plage**, 1.5km (1 mile) SE of the town centre.

Places nearby
Beside the D4 road to **Bagnols-en-Fôret** stands a **mosque** built in the First World War by soldiers from the former French Soudan. A replica of the famous Missiri mosque at Djenne, it is now empty and uncared for, and with its red paint and squat design looks like nothing so much as a big raspberry fruit cake.

Better cared for is the **Buddhist pagoda** (*3km (2 miles) NE of Fréjus, beside the N7*), built as a shrine in the cemetery of 5,000 Annamite soldiers killed in the First World War. 3km (2 miles) further up the N7, down a turning to the Tour de Mare estate, the modern chapel of **Notre-Dame-de-Jerusalem** (*often closed*) is decorated by Cocteau.

Also off the D4 Bagnols road (*the turning is 3km (2 miles) out of Fréjus, just before the autoroute*) is the **Safari de l'Esterel** (☎ *closed Tues in winter*) and the **Parc Zoologique** (☎), both with a wide variety of animals and birds in a natural environment. In the barricaded section of the safari park which contains fierce animals, mainly tigers, visitors must remain in their cars with windows shut.

Malpasset, barrage (*11km (7 miles) N of Fréjus; turn left down a track off the N7*)   A terrible tragedy occurred in Dec 1959 when this dam burst, causing flood water to sweep down through Fréjus, killing hundreds of people and causing appalling damage to the town. The ruins of the vast structure, and the enormous pieces of reinforced concrete strewn below it where they were swept by the flood are an eerie and forbidding sight.

Roquebrune-sur-Argens (*11km (7 miles) W of Fréjus*)   A pretty hill village, to the W of which is the high rocky crest of the **montagne de Roquebrune**, an outcrop of the *Maures massif*, from where there are good views (summit accessible on foot). On the N part of the same circular road (which joins with the D25), parallel with the autoroute, is the chapel of **Notre-Dame-de-la-Roquette**, well situated with a good view.

St-Aygulf (*6.5km (4 miles) S of Fréjus*)   A bustling family resort full of camping sites and shops selling buckets and spades. Pine forests fringe the bay and the beaches are sandy.

☜ **Motel St-Aygulf** (*on N98* ☎ *(94) 81–01–23* ▥), a brand new, animated, Dutch-owned beach hotel with residents' disco. Dutch-style buffet breakfast served out of doors.

☞ **La Galiote** (*St-Aygulf plage*), one of a string of beach restaurants – at this, the best, you can emerge from the sea to a plateful of enormous *gambas*, deliciously grilled in butter and herbs.

Gordes
*Map **5**D6. 38km (24 miles) E of Avignon. 84220 Vaucluse. Population: 1,500 i Pl. du Château* ☎ *(90) 72–02–07.*
One of the largest and best known of Provençal hill villages, Gordes stands on a steep rocky hillside overlooking the rolling countryside between the Vaucluse plateau and Coulon valley. Terraces of old stone houses rise sharply up to the Renaissance château on the top, visible from many miles away. Numerous craftsmen work and exhibit in Gordes: potters, weavers, painters on silk, and the like.

Sights and places of interest
Château et Musée Vasarely
■ *Open 10.00–12.00, 14.00–18.00. Closed Tues.*

Though the fortified château with its two round towers looks austere from the outside, inside it is full of elegant Renaissance touches – the fine gateway in the courtyard, the mouldings on the ceiling of the main stairway, the ornate chimneypiece on the first floor. Victor Vasarely, one of many artists and intellectuals who spend the summer at Gordes, recently restored the château in return for permission from its owners, the town council, to install there his **musée didactique** – and didactic it certainly is, even more so than his **Fondation** at *Aix*. Sliding panels give an exposé of his theories, which come alive in the two rooms filled with his vividly coloured geometric designs in the form of mosaics, tapestries and sculptures. An upper room, by contrast, contains some of his early figurative work of the 1930s.

Village des Bories ☆
3km (2 miles) sw of Gordes, off the D2, down a 2km (1 mile) rough track ■ *Open Feb to mid-Nov daily 9.00 to sunset; mid-Nov to Jan, Sat, Sun only 10.00 to sunset.*

A *borie* is a beehive-shaped primitive hut made of rough stones without mortar. In France, they are unique to the s slopes of the Vaucluse Plateau and the N slopes of the *Lubéron*, where they stand singly or in clusters. Some are thought to date from Ligurian times, but some have also been inhabited as lately as the 18thC, and one theory is that they were sometimes used by town dwellers fleeing from the plague.

This *borie* village is a group of a dozen huts, the last dwellers of which left in the early 19thC. It has now been converted into a museum of traditional rural life, well laid out and interestingly documented.

Sight nearby
Musée du Vitrail (*Museum of Stained Glass*)
5km (3 miles) s of Gordes ■ *Open 10.00–12.00, 14.00–19.00.*

A modern building beside the 16thC Bouillons olive oil mill houses a museum created by Frédérique Duran, an artist who has pioneered new techniques with stained glass tiles. Part of the museum is devoted to the history of stained glass; part is a gallery where the work of Duran and other artists is exhibited and sold.

5km (3 miles) to the N of Gordes is the abbey of *Sénanque*.

≈ La Mayanelle ❀
84220 Gordes ☎ *(90) 72–00–28* ■ *10 rms* ▣ *10* ▱ ≈ ⚌ AE ⓪ ⊙
VISA *Closed Jan–Feb.*
Location: Near the main square. A part 12th, part 17thC mansion has been converted into a sleek little hotel with bare floors and antique furniture. It's certainly gracious, but not cosy. Good local dishes are served in the dining-room. The prices are unusually modest for a Relais et Châteaux hotel. Fine views.
⌂ ☞ ⋘

≈ Les Bories
Route de Sénanque ☎ *(90) 72–00–51* ■ ▱ ≈ ⚌ ▰ *Lunches only. Closed Wed, Dec.*

On a stony plateau, 3km (2 miles) N of Gordes, a group of ancient *bories* have been transformed with great originality into a chic intimate restaurant with dim lighting, white walls and comfy chairs. *Patron* and chef Gabriel Rousselet's cooking is distinguished and often original too. *Specialities: Cassoulette de truffes aux chanterelles, chausson de queues d'ecrévisses, game (in season).*

≈ **Les Bories** also has two bedrooms which look like hovels from the outside, but inside are attractively furnished and have all modern facilities (■).

Gourdon ☆
Map 15E14. 14km (9 miles) NE of Grasse. 06620 Le Bar, Alpes-Mar. Population: 250 **i** *at mairie* ☎ *(93) 42–50–17.*

Perched high on a rock, 420m (1,400ft) above the Gorges du Loup, Gourdon vies with *Saorge* and *Les Baux* for the title of Provence's most dramatic hill village. Seen from far below, its old grey houses are barely distinguishable from the rock itself. Though spoilt by over-exposure, Gourdon is worth a visit for the majestic views from its terrace and for its **château** (📷 🅿️ *open June – Sept 11.00 – 13.00, 14.00 – 19.00, Oct – May 14.00 – 18.00, closed Tues*). Built in the 13thC on the foundations of a Saracen fortress, it has an interesting collection of armour, as well as a collection of naïve paintings, including one by Douanier Rousseau.

⇛ **Nid d'Aigle** (☎ *(93) 42–50–04* ▮▮▯).

Places nearby

Gorges du Loup ☆ Gourdon is easily reached from N or S by the D3. To the N the D3 winds down into the spectacular Gorges du Loup; you can then double back on the D6 along the green bed of the gorge, past the **Saut du Loup** (wolf leap) and two waterfalls to **Pont du Loup** where a slim railway viaduct, ruined by the Germans in the war, can be seen. Just S of Pont du Loup is the village of **Le Bar-sur-Loup**, notable for its 15thC Gothic church. It contains not only a sumptuous Bréa retable but a fascinating and devilish 15thC painting known as the *Danse Macabre* or dance of death. One lady falls, struck in the breast by an arrow from Death, the archer: beside her a man lies slain, and from his mouth a demon is pulling out his soul, a tiny naked figure. Behind, lords and ladies dance gaily, but on the head of each is a little black devil, reminder of their doom soon to come. St Michael weighs the souls, and throws them into the jaws of hell. A commentary below warns sinners to repent. Probably the anonymous painting was done at the time of the plague.

For a really good view of the whole of this lovely region, drive on to *St-Paul-de-Vence*, then to *Vence* and back to the Gorges du Loup via *Tourette-sur-Loup*.

Grasse
Map **15**F14. 17km (10 miles) NW of Cannes. 06130 Alpes-Mar. Population: 40,000 **i** Pl. de la Foux ☎ (93) 36–03–56.

"The balcony of the *Côte d'Azur*" sprawls along the southern slopes of a limestone plateau that protects it from the chilliest winds. It faces seaward across a wide vale of flowers that have brought it wealth and fame as the world capital of the perfume industry. Outside its nucleus of ancient narrow streets, modern Grasse is built in terraces with long looping boulevards, confusing at first for the motorist. Everywhere are fine views, notably from just behind the cathedral and from the broad promenade of the **Cours Honoré-Cresp**.

In the 12thC Grasse was a tiny republic on the Italian model, closely linked with Pisa. At that time its main industry was tanning. The perfume industry was introduced to Grasse from Italy at the instigation of Catherine de Medici. At first it was related to the local tanning industry because of the 16thC fashion for scented gloves. Then the cultivation of jasmin, roses and other flowers began in the valley, to provide the scent factories with their raw materials. Today, some 30 factories in and around Grasse claim to treat nearly 90% of the world's flower essence for scents. They use thousands of tons a year of local flowers and import others from 20 countries, such as patchouli from Java and eucalyptus from Australia. The factories together use annually some 490 tons of roses, 250 of jasmin, 250 of violet, 200 of orange blossom, 200 of mimosa, and 130 of lavender. This may seem a great deal, but it takes 1,000 kilos of rose petals, or 150 of lavender, to make one kilo of perfume essence.

The Grasse factories sell little of their product direct to the public. Rather, they are wholesalers, selling their essences in bulk to Dior, Chanel and the other great fashion houses in Paris, New York etc, who then blend them into their own subtle varieties with fancy names. But much of the research is done in Grasse, where one leading firm, Fragonard, has a laboratory whose experts can distinguish 1,500 different scents. This requires a nostril more finely-tuned than any wine connoisseur's palate. The skill has always been handed down from father to son, but is now in danger of dying out, so in 1981 a School of Perfumers was opened in Paris, and is doing well. Students must not smoke, drink or catch cold.

To the N and W of **Notre-Dame cathedral** is the **vieille ville** with steeply-stepped old alleys, notably the **Rue Fontette**, and the fine arcaded **Pl. des Aires**. This quarter is now largely populated by Muslim immigrants and is full of Algerian bars and cheap restaurants. On Sun, there's a lively **market** in the **Pl. Jean-Jaurès**.

In the 19thC Grasse's sheltered position made it a fashionable winter resort; Queen Victoria wintered here several times, at the now defunct Grand Hotel or in the Rothschild villa. Today, though Grasse attracts many visitors, it has a less lively life of its own than many towns of the region and is remarkably subdued at night.

Events: May, rose festival.

August, beer and jasmin festivals.

The **Centre International** (*Av. Maximin-Isnard*) holds intermittent concerts, plays and other events throughout the year.

Sights and places of interest
Art et Histoire de Provence, Musée
Rue Mirabeau. Open Mon–Fri, first and last Sun of each month 10.00–12.00, 14.00–17.00 (18.00 in summer).
Housed on three floors of this fine 18thC mansion is a collection of Provençal art and handicrafts, of various periods: faïence from Moustiers, tapestries, furniture and domestic utensils, as well as historical documents, and a room dealing mainly with local archaeology.
Fragonard, Maison ☆
Bd. Fragonard ☎ *(93) 36–44–65* 🔄 🅿️ 🔳 *factory only. Factory open May–Oct Mon–Sat 8.30–18.30, Sun 9.00–12.00, 14.00–18.00; Nov–Apr 9.00–12.00, 14.00–18.00.*
The factory mounts a skilful PR exercise, whereby expert polyglot guides give a free conducted tour to thousands of tourists every day. The three main processes of making scent from flowers – distillation, *enfleurage* and extraction – are shown and explained. The use of animal fluids as 'fixatives' is also explained, for example civet from Ethiopian cats (not specially killed) and – believe it or not – whale vomit (from live whales, not dead hunted ones) which provides the vital ambergris ingredient. The final stage of the tour is a little shop full of tempting bottles – but you are not obliged to buy. Mon–Fri are the best days for a visit, when the factory staff are at work.

The factory has its own highly-perfumed museum. This houses a varied historical array of old scent-making machines, bottles and other cosmetic aids, some 18th or 19thC, some dating back to Greek Classical times. The Molinard factory is also open to the public.
Fragonard, Villa-Musée
Bd. Fragonard. For entry details and opening times see Art et Histoire de Provence museum.
The painter Jean-Honoré Fragonard (1732–1806) was born in Grasse, but lived for most of his life in Paris where he painted his sentimental and

often sensuous canvasses. During the Terror, however, he returned to Grasse and spent a year in this pleasant little villa. Today it is a museum dedicated to the artist, but contains little of his great works. There are good copies of the panels he painted for Mme du Barry which she oddly rejected, and which he brought to Grasse with him. The originals are in the Frick Museum in New York. The staircase and landing may have been decorated by Fragonard or his son Évarist, and there are more pictures by both Fragonard and his son in the first floor rooms.

Marine, Musée de la
Hôtel de Pontèves, Bd. du Jeu-de-Ballon 🖭 *first and fourth Sun of month* 🖼 🐾 *Open Oct–June 14.30–17.00; July–Sept 14.30–17.30. Closed Sat, Sun.*

Admiral de Grasse (1722–88), born in nearby Bar-sur-Loup, was a famous French naval hero who helped America to win the War of Independence by blockading the British Army at Yorktown, Virginia. Later he was taken prisoner by Rodney and brought to London. This little museum has some interesting souvenirs of his career – maps, scenes of naval battles, models of old warships.

Notre-Dame, Ancienne Cathédrale †
Pl. du Petit Puy 🐾

With its high squat tower piercing the skyline, Notre-Dame stands grandly on a hilltop site on the edge of the Old Town. It is mostly 12thC (the facade shows Lombard influences) but was restored in the 17thC, with an 18thC curving double stairway in front. Inside, the vaulted roof is supported by unusually broad and rough stone pillars, while walls and chapels hold various works of art. Above the sacristy door is a Fragonard, *Washing of the Feet*, one of his rare religious works and with little feeling of piousness. There are also three paintings by Rubens and, in a side-chapel off the right aisle, a fine 15thC triptych, said to be by Bréa, representing St Honorat, Grasse's patron saint.

🏨 **Panorama** *(2 place du Cours* 🕿 *(93) 36–80–80* ▮▮ *36 rms* 🛏 *36* AE ⊕ 🖾 □ 🖾 🔺*)*, a hotel in modern style, opened in 1984. The rooms facing the garden are best; others look onto the main street of Grasse. No restaurant. Other recommended hotels: **Bellevue** *(14 Av. Riou-Blanquet* 🕿 *(93) 36–01–96* ▮ *to* ▮▮*)*, sedate, modernized; **Les Palmiers** ▮ *(Route Napoléon* 🕿 *(93) 36–07–24* ▮*)* with a drab front but lovely garden at the back, friendly owners and a homely atmosphere; **Le Régent** *(Route de Nice* 🕿 *(93) 36–40–10* ▮▮▮*)*, Grasse's one smart hotel, with all comforts, but formal and impersonal.

🍽 Grasse is short on good restaurants, which is odd, since taste and smell often go together. One reasonable place is **Chez Pierre** *(3 Av. Thiers* 🕿 *(93) 36–12–99* ▮*)*, crowded and a little cramped, but offering a varied Provençal choice on the set menus; another is **Maître Boscq** *(13 Rue de la Fontette* 🕿 *(93) 36–45–76* ▮*)*.

Places nearby
Auribeau *(9km (5 miles) S of Grasse)* A picturesque old hill village perched above the river Siagne, 3km (2 miles) NW of Pégomas off the D9. From the terrace beside the 18thC church (with a fine carved pulpit) on the summit there are views of the Tuscan-like landscape around, with its knobbly, wooded hills, bright green vineyards and multi-coloured flower plantations. It's best to park in the Pl. de la Libération, just below the church, before strolling down the medieval alleys.

🍽 **La Vignette Haute**
Auribeau-sur-Siagne 🕿 *(93) 42–20–01* ▮▮▮ □ ▤▤ 🚗 AE ⊕ 🖾
Mon–Sat dinner only, Sun lunch and dinner. Last orders 21.30, 22.30 (summer). Closed Mon (except July, Aug), Feb to mid-March.
In the village, an old farmhouse with rustic decor, where you dine pleasantly by the light of candles and oil-lamps, in the company of sheep and goats who are sleeping quietly in their pens, separated from the restaurant by no more than a pane of glass! The ambience is somewhat touristic, but the cooking is honest and good. A simple formula: you

choose your main dish, and the rest comes automatically – starter, entrée, etc.

🖙 ≋ **Auberge Nossi-hé** (*Place du Portail, 06810 Auribeau-sur-Siagne* ☎(93) 42–20–20 ⬛), a pleasant and comfortable village inn; sensible, inexpensive food.

Mouans-Sartoux (*7km (4 miles) SE of Grasse*) The village itself, on the main Grasse–Cannes road, has little to recommend it, save for a delightful restaurant just outside.

≋ **Palais des Coqs** ❀
Chemin du Plan-Sarrain (D409) ☎(93) 75–61–57 ⬛ to ⬛⬛ 🛏 🚗
🍴 AE VISA *Last orders 21.30. Closed Wed dinner, Thurs June 9–27 and Jan 7–Feb 1.*
A restaurant surrounded by totally unspoilt countryside and with a lovely flower-filled garden. The food is very good, and excellent value, especially on the dearer menu. Here you will find five courses which might include *pâté en croûte truffé, fricassée de queues d'écrevisses sur fondue de poireaux,* and, for dessert, *charlotte aux fruits rouges.*

Opio (*6km (4 miles) E of Grasse*) At the foot of this small village, by the D3/D7 crossroads, is the Roger Michel olive oil mill (*closed Sun*). 2km (1 mile) to the S, down an ill-signposted turning off the D3, the semi-ruined 11thC chapel of Notre-Dame-de-Brusc stands isolated amid farmland. It is closed and boarded-up, but beside it one can make out the remains of a baptistry dating from the 6thC.

≋ **Mas des Geraniums**
06650 Opio ☎(93) 77–23–23 ⬛⬛ 🛏 🚗 🍴 *Last orders 19.30. Closed Sun dinner, Oct–Feb.*
Though the prices at this charming restaurant have been creeping up of late, a meal at the Mas des Geraniums is always a delight. M. Fradois and his wife are still, after many years, producing honest food – chicken with herbs or figs, red mullet, duck or *entrecôte au poivre vert* – and can rarely have had a dissatisfied customer. Lunch is best, served in the agreeable garden with the luxury of plenty of space between the few tables. An ideal place to escape from the hectic coast, especially if you have children who can amuse themselves on the swing in the garden while you eat.
🖙 There are also seven simple but pleasant rooms available (⬛).

Pégomas (*10km (6 miles) S of Grasse*) A pleasant village on the river Siagne. All around this area are great sweeps of mimosa, both wild and cultivated, which blaze into golden blossoms in Jan and Feb.

🖙 **Le Bosquet**
06580 Pégomas ☎(93) 42–22–87 ⬛ 17 rms 🛏 15 🚗 *Closed Nov.*
Location: On the N fringe of the village, just off the D209, amid wooded hills.
The exuberant personality of the *patronne,* enchanting Simone Bernardi, and the charms of the unusual country hotel which she and her husband run, draw a faithful clientele of foreigners, mainly English, many of whom return year after year. Two red-roofed villas, one a conversion, the other new, are set in spacious, leafy grounds. Seven of the rooms have kitchenettes.
🏠 🖨 🎿 ⚓ ≈

St-Cézaire (*16km (10 miles) W of Grasse*) The village stands on a cliff above the deep Siagne gorge ☆ The terrace by the church offers excellent views of the gorge and of the mountains to the N. The village is fairly undisturbed, though many of the old houses have been restored as summer homes. The Romanesque 12thC chapel on the SE outskirts has a Roman sarcophagus.

Grottes de St-Cézaire ☆
3km (2 miles) NE of St-Cézaire ☎ *(93) 60–22–35* 🏧 💳 🅿 ♿
Open 10.00–12.00, 14.00 or 14.30–18.00 or 18.30. Closed Nov–Feb.

Formed by a glacier four million years ago, these remarkable caves plunge 60m (200ft) into the limestone plateau. They were never inhabited by prehistoric man and were discovered by chance in 1890 by a young peasant, father of the present owner. The presence of iron oxide gives the caves a reddish hue, and they have been artfully lit to show off the bizarre shapes formed by the thousands of stalactites and stalagmites. Some of the shapes have been given titles ('the vegetable garden', 'the fairy's bed', 'the skeleton', 'the gulf of hell'), as the guide reveals in his half-facetious, half-scientific patter. These chalky stalactites also have musical gifts, and the guide taps out tunes on them as if on a xylophone.

Claux de Talladoir
Route de Saint-Vallier de Thiey ☎ *(93) 60–20–09* 🛏 *22 rms* 🍴
An *auberge* secluded amid trees, ideal for a quiet holiday. Simple but comfortable, with a swimming-pool and pleasant terrace.
🖂 ≋

St-Vallier-de-Thiey (*12km (7 miles) NW of Grasse*) A summer holiday centre on a verdant plateau, with deliciously clear air, and forests and mountains behind. Amenities include walking, riding, tennis and swimming.

Le Préjoly ✿
06460 St-Vallier-de-Thiey ☎ *(93) 42–60–86* 🛏 *to* 🛏 *21 rms* 🍽 *16*
🍴 🅿 📺 🖭 🆑 🆎 💳 *Closed Tues (Oct–May), Dec, Jan.*
Location: On the main road in the village, but facing open country at the back.
Traditional Provençal hostelry at its best; an *auberge* run with skill and warmth by Georges and Arlette Pallanca. Ask for a rear bedroom overlooking open parkland; it will be quieter than those at the front.
🖾 ☇ ⇇

Le Préjoly ✿
Address and ☎ *as hotel* 🛏 *to* 🛏 🖭 🍴 🅿 🆎 💳 *Last orders 22.00. Closed Tues (Oct–May), Dec, Jan.*
A well prepared and presented menu of good home cooking with some original touches which draws people from miles around and which won the Pallancas a top prize for 'authenticity of cooking and courtesy of service' at the 1981 International Gastronomical Festival in Rome. Two drawbacks: the pressure of success has made service sometimes slow, and the pleasure of eating at the elegant front terrace is marred by the tooting traffic.

Spéracèdes (*6km (4 miles) SW of Grasse*) A quiet old village, less touristy than others in the area, and worth a visit.

La Soleillade ☕
Rue des Orangers ☎ *(93) 66–11–15* 🛏 🖭 🍽 🍴 *Last orders 21.30. Closed Wed, except July, Aug, Oct.*
In his delightful little rustic dining-room, the dryly humorous M. Forest (who for many years was a circus artist, with, among others, Britain's Bertram Mills) relies on fresh local produce to win over his guests. An excellent place, if you are exploring the delightful countryside round Grasse, to pause for a simple lunch. *Specialities: Pâté de grives avec salade aux croûtons, laperin aux herbes, caille à la romaine.*

Grimaud
*Map **13**H12. 10km (6 miles) W of St-Tropez. 83360 Var. Population: 2,550* ℹ *Pl. des Ecoles* ☎ *(93) 43–26–98.*
This dignified hill village stands on the wooded slopes of the Maures mountains, facing *St-Tropez*, and its modern

counterpart, *Port-Grimaud*. Its steep and ancient alleys have
been neatly restored, for many of these houses are now weekend
or summer residences of the well-to-do. The village is crowned
by the ruins of a feudal castle, once a Grimaldi stronghold, the
towers of which are visible for miles around. The ruins can be
explored at any time. Take a look, too, at the 11thC **Templar
church** and the arcaded **House of the Templars** beside it,
and at the **Folklore Museum**.

Coteau Fleuri
Pl. des Pénitents, 83360 Grimaud ☎ *(94) 43–20–17* 🎴 *14 rms* 🛏 *14*
▬ 🖭 ➡ *VISA Closed Nov, Jan.*
Location: On a side road in the w outskirts, facing the hills. A quiet and cosy
little *auberge* with tiled floors, a log fire in winter, and a piano that guests
can use. There is a small garden on a slope, with mimosa and olive trees,
while from the bedrooms and the dining-room there are terrific views
over the *Maures massif.* All is typically Provençal – yet the engaging
young *patronne*, Christiane Staben, comes from far-off Kiel on the
Baltic. The hotel's local *cuisine* is reliable.
🏠 📷 🛥 ⬅

Also recommended: La Boulangerie (*Route de Collobrières*
☎ *(94) 43–23–16* 🎴).

Les Santons ⬂
Route Nationale, 83360 Grimaud ☎ *(94) 43–21–02* 🎴 💬 ▬ ▬ ➡ *AE*
🄯 *Last orders 22.30 (summer), 21.00 (winter). Closed Wed, Jan, Feb,
for dinner mid-Oct to Mar.*
Silver candlesticks, red roses and an elegant Provençal decor make a
worthy setting for what is arguably the finest cooking between Marseille
and La Napoule. Service too is very stylish. Claude Girard wins
rapturous praise for a subtle blend of classic and *nouvelle cuisine*, which
varies constantly. **Specialities:** *Pâté de loup au citron, goujonettes de
St-Pierre au champagne, pigeonneau au miel.*

Also recommended: La Bretonnière (*Pl. des Pénitents*
☎ *(94) 43–25–26* 🎴); **Le Gacharel** (*7 Rue du Gacharel*
☎ *(94) 43–24–40* 🎴 *to* 🎴).

Places nearby
Cogolin (*3km (2 miles) s of Grimaud*) One of the liveliest
centres of practical handicrafts in Provence, Cogolin has kept
alive an odd variety of traditional cottage industries: carpets,
corks, briar pipes, as well as furniture, fishing-rods and clarinet
pipes; **Girodengo** (*Av. Clémenceau*) for bamboo furniture; and
Les Tapis et Tissus (*Bd. Louis-Blanc*), a carpet factory with
guided tours (*Mon–Fri*).

Clémenceau (*Pl. de la République* ☎ *(94) 56–19–23* 🎴 *to* 🎴).

La Garde-Freinet (*10km (7 miles) NW of Grimaud*) From
Grimaud, a wide road winds up through cork forests to this
unspoilt village in the heart of the *Maures massif.* The ruined
castle on the hill above (30min walk) was the last stronghold of
the Saracens who ravaged the coast in the 10thC until finally
driven out in 973 by Count William the Good. Yet the Saracens
were not just vandals: they taught medical skills to the
Provençaux, and showed them how to utilize the bark of cork
oak.
  Today, cork is still the main local industry. La Garde-Freinet
is also popular with writers and actors; Jeanne Moreau, among
others, has a villa here.

≡ **Faücado**
31 Bd. de l'Esplanade ☎ *(94) 43–60–41* ◻◻ ◻◻ ◼◼ ◻◻ ◻◻ *Last orders 22.30. Closed Tues. mid-Nov to mid-Dec.*

Behind a high wall in the main street lies a pretty garden where you can dine under parasols amid roses and wisteria, with views over the valley below. Friendly service and sound local cooking; try the *civet de porcelet à l'estouffade de pigeonneau*. Dinner, *à la carte* only, is more expensive than the set lunch menus.

Hyères

Map **12***/10. 18km (11 miles)* E *of Toulon. 83400 Var. Population: 41,050. Airport Toulon/Hyères 4km (2½ miles) to* SE ☎ *(94) 57–41–41* **i** *Pl. Clémenceau* ☎ *(94) 65–18–55.*

Hyères is the oldest resort on the *Côte d'Azur*, dating from the 18thC; Napoleon, Tolstoy, Queen Victoria and R. L. Stevenson have been among its devotees. Today, however, it has gone sharply out of fashion, though its broad avenues shaded with date-palms remain as reminders of its past glory; the name is apt – Hyères belongs to yesterday. Of most interest is the old medieval part of the town, lying 5km (3 miles) inland on a hill. The 19thC resort and modern town stretch S and E towards the sea.

Both the Greeks and Romans colonized the coast at Hyères – their archaeological remains can be seen in the **Musée Municipal** (*Pl. Lefevre, closed Tues*). In the Middle Ages the town was used as a port for visits to the Holy Land: St Louis stayed here on his return from the Seventh Crusade in 1254. The sea in those days came much closer to the town, and the port was in a place that has since silted up. Vestiges of the town's importance in medieval days can be seen in the *vieille ville*, notably around the Pl. Massillon, where a market is held on weekdays. Here is the handsome 12thC **Tour St-Blaise**, part of a former fortified church of the Templars. Steep narrow streets lead up behind it to the 12thC church of **St Paul**, flanked by an elegant turreted Renaissance house that was built above one of the medieval city gates.

In the SE suburbs, the 16-acre **Jardin Olbius-Riguier** is rich in exotic plants. West of Hyères, the main road to Toulon passes just below the high rocky crest of **Le Fenouillet** at 292m (960ft): you can climb to the summit along a footpath off the D554 to Le Crau.

Events: June, Provençal festival.
July and Aug, music and concerts in the street.

↩**Suisse** (*Av. Aristide-Briand* ☎ *(94) 65–26–68* ◻).

≡**Chez Marius** ✿ (*Pl. Massillon* ☎ *(94) 65–08–93* ◻); **Le Delphin's** (*7 Rue Dr Roux-Signoret* ☎ *(94) 65–04–27* ◼◼).

Places nearby

Giens peninsula (*11km (7 miles)* S *of Hyères*)   The peninsula would be one of the hilly *Hyères Iles*, save that it is now linked to the mainland by two strips of sand, each carrying a road: the E strip is relatively broad, covered with pines and bordered by a splendid beach on its seaward side. Here is the thriving resort of **La Capte**, where the campers' orange and yellow tents fill the pinewoods. The village of Giens stands on a hill in the centre of its lovely wooded peninsula, crowned by a ruined castle (marvellous views from its terrace). At **La Tour Fondue** to the

SE, where boats leave for Porquerolles, is a small fortress built under Richelieu. The poet St-John Perse used to live at Giens.

Le Provençal
Giens, 83400 Hyères ☎ *(94) 58–20–09* ▯ *to* ▮▮ *50 rms* ▭ *50* ⇔ ▭
▭ ▭ *mid-June to mid-Sept* ◉ ◉
Location: On a hill at the edge of the village, looking down across its large garden sloping down to the sea. Spacious, elegant and wonderfully situated, this is a large modern building, with a snugly furnished *salon* and views from the wide balconies over the rocky coast below. Plenty of amenities and a breezy holiday atmosphere. Private beach (not sand), where lunches are served in summer. Otherwise there is a panoramic restaurant serving reasonable food.
‡ ὒ ⌑ ⩊ ⇎ ⇌ ⌂ ⌒ ⛫

Hyères-Plage The plain between Hyères and the sea is remarkably ugly but full of activity. It is an important market garden centre (fruit, spring vegetables, flowers) owing to the warm winter climate. Here is Toulon/Hyères Airport; here too are a string of brash new bathing resorts, notably Hyères-Plage. Just to the s, on the isthmus leading to Giens, are the large Pesquier saltworks with their high white piles of salt.

Hyères, Iles d'

Map 12J11. Frequent boat services all year (20min) between La Tour Fondue and Porquerolles. Other services (mainly in summer) from Toulon, Hyères-Plage, Le Lavandou and Cavalaire to all three islands. For information ☎ *(94) 66–21–81/(94) 71–01–02/(94) 92–49–64.*
These three strange and beautiful islands, where the lushly sub-tropical blends with the wildly rugged, are known as the Iles d'Or, from the yellowish glint of their steep cliffs in the sunlight. Geologically, they are breakaways from the *Maures massif* to the N. In the 16thC, criminals and convicts were granted right of asylum here, but many of them became pirates, and the islands were not finally pacified until the late 17thC.
Porquerolles
To the w, this is the largest of the islands. Its one village, on the N coast, was built in the 19thC as an army garrison, and has a broad main square with the same air of a military compound as one finds all over ex-French North Africa. In the little church there is a sequence of Stations of the Cross, sculpted in wood with a penknife by a soldier with sophisticated artistic gifts.

The N coast has sandy coves, good for bathing; the s is sheer and rugged. The island is covered with pines, heather and myrtle, and is ideal for walking (or you can hire a bicycle).

Relais de la Poste
Pl. des Armes, Porquerolles, 83540 Hyères ☎ *(94) 58–30–26* ▮▯
30 rms ▣ *30. Closed Oct–Apr.*
Location: In the village square. A quiet, old fashioned *auberge* run by the same family since 1880. The atmosphere is homely and the 19thC Provençal decor real, not modern imitation.
▱ ⌑ ⌗ ⌂

Another good hotel on the island is Mas du Langoustier *(3km (2 miles) w of the village* ☎ *(94) 58–30–09* ▮▯*).*

Arche de Noé
Pl. des Armes ☎ *(94) 58–30–74* ▯ *to* ▮▯ ▭ ▬ ⇔ *Last orders 21.30. Closed Nov to mid-Mar.*
Madame Bourgue talks with wistful pride of the days when her late husband ran this famous old 19thC inn, and she will eagerly show you the

visitors' book with its dazzling signatures – King Baudouin, Chaplin, Mountbatten. . . . Today Noah's Ark may be past its prime, but it still provides many a humble visitor with an honest meal – either on the shady terrace, facing the square, or else in the ornate, dark-panelled dining-room, with its great central archway surmounted by frescoes of fish. Fish is the theme on the menu too, for example *langouste au whisky*.

☞ The **Hôtel Arche de Noé** attached has 18 spacious bedrooms, some with large balconies facing the sea (▮▢).

Port-Cros ☆

In the middle, this is the loveliest and most mysterious of the three islands. It is hilly and thickly wooded – the presence of springs explains its lush vegetation. From the tiny port, with its fishermen's cottages and few small restaurants, you can walk to the Vallon de la Solitude or the cove of Port-Man, through groves of shrubs and trees of every shade of bright green. No smoking is allowed on the island, save at the port. It is owned by the State as a National Park (nature reserve), and staff run unusual guided tours from June–Sept (▣). These include botanical rambles and underwater explorations with scuba masks to see the marine flora and fish life. (*For information* ☎ *(94) 65–32–98/(94) 05–90–17*.) Port-Cros is more for the student of nature than the casual sightseer, and it has few beaches. It is also of literary interest, having inspired several novels. D. H. Lawrence once stayed here as the guest of a young, well-bred Englishwoman who told him of her earthy affair with a local labourer. Lawrence then changed the locale – but not the theme – for his most famous novel.

☞ **Le Manoir**
83145 Ile-de-Port-Cros ☎*(94) 05–90–52* ▮▮▮ *28 rms* ▭ *28* ▭ ⇥
▭ *Closed mid-Oct to Easter.*
Location: By a creek close to the port and secluded in its own park. Pierre Buffet's family used to own the whole island. Today he is left with this graceful 18thC manor house which – to make ends meet – he runs as a hotel, though it still seems far more like a private home: no reception desk and no sign at the gate save *propriété privée*. M. Buffet and his young wife are charming, cultivated hosts; their regular visitors include theatrical directors, actors, writers and musicians. The atmosphere is precisely that of a cultured house party, not a hotel. Bedrooms are simple and spacious with 19thC furniture; food is plain but well cooked; there are few seaside amenities, save windsurfers and motor dinghies. An air of calm and romantic melancholy pervades, more Celtic than Latin, despite the palm trees.
⌂ ▱ ⚓

Ile du Lévant

This island, to the E, has high cliffs all round and dense foliage. The main part of the island belongs to the French Navy and is closed to visitors. But on the w side is the famous nudist village of **Heliopolis**, one of the early pioneers among European nudist colonies, and still popular.

Isola 2000

*Map **15**C15. 94km (58 miles) N of Nice. 06420 Isola 2000, Alpes-Mar **i** in complex* ☎*(93) 23–15–15.*
Negotiate several dozen wild hairpin bends on the D97 and high in the deserted mountains you will come across what looks like a giant space-age shopping centre: Isola 2000. This popular modern ski resort, built entirely by British enterprise, comprises one huge, snake-like complex of hotels, restaurants, apartments, shops and cafés. A central corridor connects one

end with the other, with Paris metro-style directions announcing where you are and how many 'stops' to go to your destination. It's all very far removed from the traditional alpine ski resort of one's imagination. In summer, when the slopes are dry and strewn with rocks, and the stationary ski lifts give the air of a disused mine, the place is particularly characterless. In winter the harshness of the complex is somewhat mellowed by the snow and the frenetic activity all around.

Druos ☎
06420 Isola 2000 ☎ (93) 23–12–20 ⓣ 461175 ▥ 40 rms ➤ 40 ◀
▥ AE VISA

Location: At the far end of the complex. This is the only one of Isola 2000's three purpose-built hotels that is privately owned, and the presence of the hard-working young owners, the Korosecs, does much to enliven an otherwise featureless establishment. No restaurant as such, but grills, cooked on the open fire, are served in the small lobby. Bedrooms overlooking the ski slopes are more expensive.
☎ ✹

Sports and activities

The skiing is varied, with lifts and cable cars literally on your doorstep. In summer the resort becomes a tennis centre.

Juan-les-Pins

Map **15**F14. 9km (6 miles) E of Cannes. 06160 Alpes-Mar
i Bd. Charles-Guillaumont ☎ (93) 61–04–98.

This suburb of Antibes owes its huge success as a resort to its sheltered position, facing SW across the Gulf of Juan. Juan barely existed until the 1920s, when the American millionaire Frank Jay Gould set its trend as a major fashionable resort of the inter-war years. Beside the casino, pine woods stretch down to a long beach of fine sand. This was that 'bright tan prayer rug of a beach' where Scott Fitzgerald set *Tender is the Night*.

On the back seat of the car Dick remained quiescent until the yellow monolith of Golfe-Juan was passed, and then the constant carnival at Juan-les-Pins, where the night was musical and strident in many languages.
F. Scott Fitzgerald, *Tender is the Night*, 1939

Traces of that fabled and sophisticated epoch still linger on in modern Juan, mainly in its two luxury hotels. But today this large resort is the most garish place on the whole coast. *Par excellence* it is a haunt of the young, who throng the place all summer. The nucleus of little streets off the casino is a maze of fast-food bars, pizzerias, second-rate boutiques and third-rate discos – all very lively, but certainly not chic. In winter, unlike most of the other resorts, it's dead.

Hotels

Belles-Rives ▥
Bd. Baudoin, 06160 Juan-les-Pins ☎ (93) 61–02–79
ⓣ 470984 ▥▥ 44 rms ➤ 44 ▤
▥ ➤ June–Sept AE
Closed Oct to week before Easter.
Location: On sea-front, where Juan and Cap d'Antibes merge. Of Juan's two famous luxury hotels this one

has the merit of being right on the sea with its private jetty and private beach (mostly concrete, but a stretch of sand too). It's a glamorous hotel that has carefully kept its original Gay Twenties cachet: most guests are young, smart and cosmopolitan. Beautiful outdoor dining terrace by the sea.
🕏 ☎ ⟪⟫ 🍴

Juana 🏨
Av. Gallice, 06160 Juan-les-Pins ☎ (93) 61−08−70
📞 470778 ▨ 50 rms ▭ 50 ▤
▨ ▨ ⇌ ⇲ *Closed mid-Oct to week before Easter.*
Location: In the quiet E part of Juan, facing a pine wood, 180m (200yd) from beach. The opulent leather upholstery in the bar-salon sets the style for this select and very sophisticated luxury hotel. Compared with its local rival, the **Belles-Rives**, its handicap is that it lies away from the beach (though it has its own private one), with no sea views; its ambience, too, is less breezily youthful, more sedate. But comfort and service are of the highest order, in the classic pre-war manner, with uniformed porters and waiters always on hand. The flowery garden under its shady palm trees is most elegant. (See restaurant, **La Terrasse**.)
▨ ✦ ⅋ ▢ ▨ ❧ ⅋

Mexicana
20 Av. du Docteur-Dautheville, 06160 Juan-les-Pins ☎ (93) 61−31−34 ▭ to ▨
15 rms ▭ 15 ▨ ▨ *Closed mid-Dec to early Jan.*
Location: Central, 180m (200yd)

from beach. In the heart of Juan's nightlife quarter, this is a friendly and comfortable little hotel with spacious rooms. Don't expect too much quiet in this lively location.
▨

Pré Catelan
22 Av. des Lauriers, 06160 Juan-les-Pins ☎ (93) 61−05−11 ▨ 20 rms ▭
20 ▨ ⇌ ▨ *mid-June to mid-Sept* ▨ ▨ *Last orders in the restaurant 21.30. Closed Nov to mid-Jan.*
Location: In a quiet residential street. This white-walled villa-style hotel is set in its own garden, and is well out of earshot of strident downtown Juan. Guests can lunch or dine out of doors in pleasant surroundings under creepers and gaily-coloured parasols.
▨ ▨ ❧

Some other reasonable hotels in Juan-les-Pins include: **Astor** (*Bd. Poincaré* ☎ (93) 61−07−38 ▨); **Beauséjour** (*Av. Saramartel* ☎ (93) 61−07−82 ▨); **Mimosa** (*Rue Pauline* ☎ (93) 61−04−15 ▨); **Sainte-Valerie** (*Rue Oratoire* ☎ (93) 61−07−15 ▨ to ▨).

Restaurants

Auberge de l'Esterel ❦
Rue des Iles ☎ (93) 61−86−55 ▨ ▭ ▨ ▨ *Last orders 21.15. Closed Nov to mid-Jan.*
Under separate management from the hotel to which it is attached, the restaurant has recently been taken over by two very young and enthusiastic brothers, Jacques and Christian Plumail, who have chosen the unlikely setting of a small pension for carrying out an ambitious and very successful venture in *nouvelle cuisine* at moderate prices. It's best to choose a fine day so that you can eat in the garden rather than in the dull dining-room.

Régence
2 Av. Amiral-Courbet ☎ (93) 61−09−39 ▭ ▭ ▨ *Closed Dec−Feb.*
A little family hotel on the main road, close to the beach, where the restaurant is always packed with people who appreciate the modestly priced *cuisine familiale*. The best place in town for a fairly cheap meal.

La Terrasse ⌂
Address and ☎ *as Hôtel Juana* ▨ ▭ ▨ ⇌ ▨ ▨ ▨ *Last orders 22.00. Closed lunch, July−Sept, mid-Oct to week before Easter.*
Since the hotel is closed in winter, the indoor dining-room is little used, and is severely formal and unenticing. But there is a touch of magic about the outdoor terrace by the garden, especially at night when candles flicker and soft music plays. It makes a worthy setting for a *cuisine* that is among the finest on the whole coast. The young chef, Alain Ducasse, has trained under Vergé and Guérard among others and now we too offers dishes of great subtlety and inventiveness – at a price. Dishes vary with the season and the market, and with Ducasse's creative caprice, but you can always rely on a high standard.
Specialities: Petite marinade croquante de legumes, poissons du pays à la vapeur de fenouil, gratin tiède de fraises du bois aux pignons. (See hotel, **Juana**.)

Nightlife

Most of the decibels in Juan are generated at the junction of the Bds. Baudoin and Wilson, near the casino where two huge open-fronted cafés confront each other in frenetic rivalry: the **Festival** and the **Pam-Pam Rhumerie**. Each has an ear-splitting Brazilian orchestra, each lurid lighting and flamboyant 'Brazilian' décor (especially the Pam-Pam). Each specializes in elaborate and expensive fruit cocktails and alcoholic ice-cream cups, and each nightly attracts a goggling crowd of bystanders, massed all the way down the street. This is the centre of Juan's nightlife, and no disco in town can compare with this exuberant street-theatre. All summer the show goes on till 3 or 4am: if you're booked in to a nearby hotel, bring ear-plugs.

Oddly, none of Juan's many discos is very exciting. The most select, comfortable (and pricey) is the **Chah-in-Chah**, (*Av. Gallice*). Nostalgic Iranian royalists haunt the place, the name of which is the French for their late monarch. There is also a good disco at the *Maison des Pêcheurs* (see below).

Beaches

As in Cannes, the better ones are private and paying, though free beaches can be found away from the central area. The **Maison des Pêcheurs**, at Port Gallice on the coast road to Cap d'Antibes, is a lively complex that includes beach, lido, marina, snack-bar/restaurant and nightclub.

Place nearby

Golfe-Juan   The name is nothing to do with a golf course, but refers to the deep Gulf of Juan, between Cannes and Cap d'Antibes, one of the finest roadsteads on the coast and used by the US Navy before France left NATO. Golfe-Juan today is a flourishing bathing resort with a marina and long sandy beaches (most of them free), sheltered by the hills of Vallauris with their orange and mimosa trees.

Golfe-Juan has a place in history because it was here that Napoleon landed with some 800 men on March 1, 1815, on his return from exile in Elba, and started on the *Route Napoléon* to Paris. The famous proclamation was here nailed up for the first time, 'The eagle, with the national colours, will fly from steeple to steeple as far as the towers of Notre-Dame'. Today a memorial by the harbour marks the event.

Hotels in Golfe-Juan include: **Beau Soleil** (*Impasse Beausoleil* ☎ (93) 63–63–63 ▯ *to* ▰); **De Crijansy** (*Av. Juliette-Adam* ☎ (93) 63–84–44 ▰); **Les Jasmins** (*on N7* ☎ (93) 63–80–83 ▯).

Good restaurants to try: **Nounou** (*on the beach* ☎ (93) 63–71–73 ▯ *to* ▰); **Tétou** (*Av. des Frères-Roustan* ☎ (93) 63–71–16 ▰).

Le Lavandou

Map 12I11. 41km (26 miles) E of Toulon. 83980 Var. Population: 3,800 **i** *Quai Baptistin-Pins* ☎ *(94) 71–00–61.*
The old fishing port of Le Lavandou has today swollen into a fairly large seaside holiday resort, and the charm of the attractive harbour has been somewhat eroded by the rows of high-rise holiday flats. It is not a sophisticated place, but the compensation is a coast with miles of good sandy beaches, notably to the E around **Cavalière** and **Rayol**. The wooded hills of the *Maures massif* behind make fine walking country.

Hotels

Belle-Vue
Bd. du Four des Maures, 83980 St-Clair, Le Lavandou
☎ *(94) 71–01–06* ▮▮ *to* ▮▮▮ *19 rms* ▭ *19* 🛏 🔳 ⇌ 🔳 *mid-June to mid-Sept. Closed Oct–Apr.*
Location: At St-Clair, just E of Le Lavandou, on an open hillside, just above the beach. An entrancing little villa-hotel with a not surprisingly feminine touch, since it is run by Mme Clare and her three daughters. The bedrooms are simple but pleasant with wide balconies with tables and deck chairs and views of the sea, and the bathrooms are unusually attractive. Inside, the hotel is filled with flowers; outside, blue parasols are dotted about the garden. One drawback: the food, though reasonable, is not exciting, and the *menu pension* offers no choice.
🍴 ▨ 🐾 🐾 🔆 🍷

La Calanque
Av. Général-de-Gaulle, 83980 Le Lavandou ☎ *(94) 71–00–46* ▮▮ *to* ▮▮▮ *39 rms* ▭ *39* 🛏 🔳 ⇌ 🔳 *June–Aug* AE ⓪ VISA *Closed mid-Nov to Jan.*
Location: Overlooking the harbour. A long white Provençal villa with rather heavy pre-war decor. Rooms are solidly comfortable and service attentive. (See restaurant.)

Other recommended hotels in Le Lavandou include: **Éspadon** (*Pl. Ernest-Reyer* ☎ *(94) 71–00–20* ▮▮); **Neptune** (*26 Av. Général-de-Gaulle* ☎ *(94) 71–01–01* ▮); **Résidence Beach** (*Bd. Front-Mer* ☎ *(94) 71–00–66* ▮▮▮).

Restaurants

La Bouée
Rue Ch.-Cuzin ☎ *(94) 71–11–88* ▮ *Last orders 21.30.*
Friendly service, careful cooking, good value.

La Calanque
Address and ☎ *as hotel* ▮▮ ▭ 🍴 🚗 🛏 AE ⓪ VISA *Last orders 21.00. Closed mid-Nov to Jan.*
The large beamed dining-room and its terrace both overlook the sea. The food is above average with flourishes of individuality. **Specialities:** *Navarin de loup, mousseline chaud de rascasse et saumon à la menthe fraîche.* (See hotel.)

Au Vieux Port
Quai Gabriel-Péri ☎ *(94) 71–00–21* ▮ ▭ 🍴 🚗 AE ⓪ VISA *Last orders 22.30. Closed Oct–Apr.*
The English *patron* and his chef from Alsace conspire to serve an excellent *bouillabaisse* and other local fish dishes at their gaily decorated little restaurant facing the port. The menu changes often; desserts are especially good.

Nightlife
Le Flamenco (*Av. du Général-Bouvet* ☎ *(94) 71–13–37*) is a cabaret with drag acts and also dancing. Much the best disco in the area is **Le Tropicana** (*on the beach at Le Rayol, 13km (8 miles) to the E* ☎ *(94) 05–61–50*).

Places nearby
Bormes-les-Mimosas ☆ (*5km (3 miles) NW of Le Lavandou*) One of the most elegant of all Provençal hill villages, Bormes-les-Mimosas stands on a hilltop amid mimosa and eucalyptus groves, with commanding views of the sea. The houses are painted in pastel shades of blue, yellow and pink; a

change from the austere air of most other hill villages with their streets of old grey stone.

☙ Safari
Route du Stade, 83230 Bormes-les-Mimosas ☎ *(94) 71–09–83* ▊▊▊
33 rms ▭ *.33* ➡ ⓪ ⓒ ◎ VISA *Closed mid-Oct to Mar.*
Location: Just to the E of Bormes, on an open hillside facing the sea, 2.5km (1¼ miles) away. Built in a modern functional style, this is none the less a delightful holiday hotel, cheerfully run and superbly situated. It has a garden with a grass lawn and a pleasant bar beside the heated swimming pool. The rooms, brightly decorated, nearly all have wide balconies with views over the coast and islands.
◠ ▱ ☜ ⚓ ⟨⟨ ⇝ ✎ ☝

☶ La Tonnelle des Délices
Pl. Gambetta ☎ *(94) 71–34–84* ▊▊▊ ▭ ◼ ⟁ *Last orders 21.00. Closed Oct–Apr.*
The name means 'arbour of delights' – a fitting one for this serene and intimate little place, screened from the main village square by a bower of vines and roses. The two young Gedda brothers skilfully produce their own variations on classic Provençal dishes. *Specialities: Terraieto de moules, brouillade de crêpes, pot-au-feu provençal.*

☶ **L'Escundudo** (*Ruelle du Moulin* ☎ *(94) 71–15–53* ▭) – pleasant atmosphere, authentic Provençal cooking.

Cabasson (*8km (5 miles) SW of Le Lavandou*)   A hamlet on the W side of the high promontory of Cap Benat with its wild rocky coast, best seen on a boat excursion from Le Lavandou. (Part of the Cap belongs to the military and is closed to the public.) Further S from Cabasson the fortress of **Brégançon**, built by Vauban, stands in solitary grandeur by the sea; it is now an official summer residence of the President.

☙ Les Palmiers ▬ ♣
Cabasson, 83230 Bormes-les-Mimosas ☎ *(94) 64–80–00* ▭ *to* ▭
21 rms ➡ ▱ ☶ ⟁ *mid-May to Sept. Closed Thurs dinner (winter), Jan to mid-Mar.*
Location: Near the beach on a relatively undiscovered part of the coast. A good choice for a quiet and simple seaside holiday. The Guimets run their modest family pension with real warmth, and once a week or so there is a *soirée-surprise* with a visiting orchestra or folk group. Bedrooms are more comfortable than their spartan air may suggest, and they overlook a garden filled with at least 12 different species of tree, including weeping willow, blue cedar, orange and palm.
◠ ☜ ⚓

☶ Les Palmiers ♣
Address and ☎ *as hotel* ▭ *to* ▊▊▊ ▭ ◼ ➡ *Last orders 21.30. Closed Thurs dinner (winter), Jan to mid-Mar.*
The large dining-room is rather overlit, with recorded music, but there are compensations: a rose for every lady and good value on the set menus. Simple Les Palmiers may be but it did not deter the late President Pompidou from choosing to eat *bouillabaisse* here when staying at nearby Brégançon castle.

Cavalière (*8km (5 miles) E of Le Lavandou*)   A small resort in a sheltered bay, backed by pine woods and with a splendid sandy beach.

☙ Le Club ▥
Plage de Cavalière, 83980 Le Lavandou ☎ *(94) 05–80–14* ☜ 420317
▊▊▊ *31 rms* ▭ *31* ▦ ➡ ▱ ☶ ⟁ *July–Aug. Closed late Sept to mid-May.*
Location: By the beach. The most fashionable address on the coast between *St-Tropez* and *Marseille* – and aptly named, for the ambience is that of an exclusive club. For those with plenty of money a truly

sophisticated seaside holiday awaits, including private beach and
dancing at night by the sea. Bedrooms are predictably luxurious, some in
separate bungalows with their own patios.
🏠🍴🗄️🏤🦌 ⛵ ≋ 🛥️ 🏊

☰ Le Club 🍴
Address and ☎ as hotel ▥ ☐ 🍴 ≡ 🏤 🚗 *Last orders 22.00.*
Closed Mon dinner, late Sept to mid-May.
The sumptuous hotel dining-room and seaside terrace are fit settings for
the excellent *cuisine*. The set menu (dinner only) is not unduly expensive;
but chef Alain Gigant's best creations are, on the *carte*. **Specialities**:
Loup en croûte, rillettes d'anguille et de saumon fumé aux poires.

Levens
Map **15**D15. *23km (15 miles)* N *of Nice. 06670 St-Martin-du-
Var, Alpes-Mar. Population: 1,400* **i** *at mairie*
☎*(93) 79–70–22.*
A hill village within commuting distance of Nice – hence its
liveliness. On the road just ahead of the village there are views
over the *Vésubie gorges*.

⊗ La Vigneraie ✿
Route de St-Blaise, 06720 Levens ☎*(93) 79–70–46* ☐ *20 rms* 🛏️ *6*
🚗 🅿️ ≡ *Closed mid-Oct to mid-Jan.*
Location: Standing alone, outside the village. For those who want an
inexpensive rural retreat from the hectic coast it would be hard to find
better than La Vigneraie. Owned and run by a charming elderly couple,
the Bastiens, it is a neat modern villa with a colourful garden and
excellent views. A delightful place, but rather staid clientele.
🏠🗄️🦌⛵

☰ La Vigneraie
Address and ☎ as hotel ☐ 🍴 🏤 *Last orders 20.30. Closed Oct–Nov.*
Oct–Nov.
The cheap pension menu is fairly dull, and it is on the dearer one that
M. Bastien extends himself. When fine, meals are served outdoors
under a canopy of vines. **Specialities**: *Ravioli niçoise, civet de canard,
écrevisses à l'américaine.*

Lubéron, Montagne du ☆
Map **5**E7. *24–80km (15–50 miles)* E *of Avignon. Vaucluse.*
This remarkable range of hills runs for 56km (35 miles) from
W – E between the Durance and Coulon valleys. To the E is the
higher and wilder stretch, the **Grand Lubéron**, now a national
park. The peak of **Mourre Nègre**, 1,100m (3,690ft), is
accessible by car; dizzying views from the Alps to the Rhône
delta. To the W of the Apt–Cadenet road is the **Petit Lubéron**, a
fertile plateau full of vineyards, lavender fields and beehives for
honey. From Bonnieux down to *Cavaillon*, a fine scenic road
runs along the crest of the hills, past a forest of giant cedars.
    From the 13th–16thC the Lubéron was the stronghold of an
early Protestant sect, the Vaudois. These 'heretics', if devout,
were also often violent; bands of them would burn and pillage
churches in the region. Finally in 1545 Francois 1er launched a
crusade against them, killing or capturing over 2,000.

Bonnieux
A hill village on a N-facing spur of the Petit Lubéron (as are
Ménerbes and **Oppède-le-Vieux**) with views across the Coulon
valley. On its summit is a 12thC church, now little used. The
large 19thC church down the hill is of no beauty, but is worth
visiting for the four remarkable 15thC **German paintings** ☆

behind the main altar. They depict the *Martyrdom of Christ*. Painted on wood panels in vivid reds and greens, they are fresh and well preserved. Formerly they were in the old church.

⚲ L'Aiguebrun
84480 Bonnieux ☎ *(90) 74–04–14* 🎞 *8 rms* 🖿 *8* 🚗 🚄 🚘 ⓐ ⓒⓓ
🚾 *Closed mid-Nov to Jan.*
Location: Isolated, by a stream in a narrow valley, just off the D943, 5km (3 miles) E of Bonnieux. A small 19thC manor owned by Parisian artist and ex-couturier, Roger Chastel, and furnished with taste. The enchanting setting and the quiet attract people who come to paint, write or read.
🏠 🖾 🎿 ⛷ ⭿ 🛶

🍴 L'Aiguebrun
Address and ☎ *as hotel* 🎞 *to* 🎞 🗔 🍴 🚗 ⓐ ⓒⓓ 🚾 *Last orders 21.00. Closed Mon lunch, mid-Nov to Jan.*
The chic little restaurant looks on to the valley, or you can eat under the plane and fir trees in the garden. Meals are not cheap, but the young chef shows talent. *Specialities: Figues fraîches à la crème de fenouil, gentille de saumon au buerre de tomate, poulet au safran.*

Fort de Buoux
A ruined fortress on a rocky peak above the rugged Buoux gorge. As a natural defence point, it was used in turn by Ligurians, Romans and Protestants. The **Aigue-Brun** valley, just to the E, has paleolithic cave-dwellings.

Lourmarin
A village on the S slopes of the Lubéron. Its imposing château, part 15thC, part Renaissance, has a fine main stairway and chimney pieces; classical concerts are held here in summer. The novelist Albert Camus lies buried in the village cemetery.

Ménerbes
Standing amid rocks above the valley, Ménerbes is an old village with a lively colony of artists and craftsmen. In the 16thC it was the final stronghold of the local Protestants.

🍴 Pascal 🍴
☎ *(90) 72–22–13* 🎞 🍴 🚗 🚘 *Lunches only. Closed Nov–Easter.*
Boisterous parties of Vauclusiens descend on this splendid village *auberge* to enjoy the lavish food and mountain views. There's a shady garden and three large, plain dining-rooms – all very down to earth, yet professional. Such is their popularity that the Pascals close for dinner as they say they couldn't cope with the invasion twice a day. The simple country cooking can rarely be faulted, and the five-course set menus are excellent value.

Oppède-le-Vieux
Though this medieval village, on a rocky spur overlooking the Coulon valley, had fallen into ruin, artists, writers and others have bought up some of the houses and are in the process of restoring them.

Lucéram
*Map **15**D15. 24km (17 miles) NE of Nice. 06440 Alpes-Mar. Population: 550 **i** at mairie* ☎ *(93) 79–51–83.*
Not far from Nice, yet remarkably unspoilt, this high-perched fortified village is a jumble of steep-covered stepped alleys and old houses staggered one above the other. Crowning all is the 15thC **church** with Italian Rococo decor, one of the most interesting in the Nice area, for Lucéram was a key centre of 15thC religious painting. It has six retables of the prolific Bréa school (the finest, the **retable of Ste Marguerite**, behind the

high altar, shows a touching serenity), and a collection of old silver, including the unusual statuette of *Ste Marguerite* (Lucéram's patron saint) standing on a dragon – if you require light, ask at the presbytery next door.

≈ La Méditerranée ■ ♣
Pl. Adrien-Barralis, 06440 Lucéram ☎ *(93) 91–54–54* ⬜ *8 rms* ⌂ ⇌ ⌂ ⇌

Location: A small square at foot of village. The essence of rural Provence; a very simple old village inn, run by good-hearted country people. Villagers knock back their morning tots at the bar while you breakfast. ◁€

⇌ La Méditerranée ● ♣
Address and ☎ *as hotel* ⬜ ■■ *Last orders 21.00.*

La patronne, grandmother Josephine Gaetti, and her family provide succulent home cooking at low prices – even the cheapest menu starts with a help-yourself trolley of enticing hors d'oeuvres including delicious local smoked ham. *Specialities: Ravioli niçoise, lapin provençale, gigot des Alpes, sanglier (in season).*

Places nearby

The D21 from Lucéram winds up into wild alpine scenery, amid rock-strewn forests of giant pines. The views are impressive, and the air sharp and exhilarating. Of the two little skiing and summer resorts here, **Peira Cava** is a little drab, but the **Col de Turini** has more style. From here you can drive through the lovely **Turini forest** with its towering pines and spruces to the start of a 13km (8 mile) round trip mountain drive called **Circuit de l'Aution**, to the **Pointe-des-Trois-Communes**, where the views of the Alps are dazzling. From Col de Turini there are also guided rambles in summer to the unique **Vallée des Merveilles** (see *La Brigue*).

≈ Trois Vallées
06440 Col de Turini ☎ *(93) 91–57–21* ⬜ *26 rms* ▭ *26* ⇒ ⌂ ⇌ ⌂

Location: Beside the ski lifts at Col de Turini. A spacious alpine chalet for skiers and climbers. Bedrooms have dark wood decor, some with balconies facing the forests and snow peaks. Simple, copious food for hungry *sportifs* is served in the vast dining-room. ⌂◁€

Manosque

Map **6***E9. 53km (33 miles)* NE *of Aix. 04100 Alpes-de-H.-P. Population: 19,550* ℹ *Pl. Dr. P.-Joubert* ☎ *(92) 72–16–00.*
Medieval Manosque, now a lively agricultural centre, spreads itself on a slope above the Durance valley. As at *Carpentras*, a circular boulevard has replaced the old ramparts, but two fortified 14thC gateways survive: the high **Porte de la Saunerie**, floodlit at night, is a fine sight. Inside is a maze of narrow streets lined by tall, typically Provençal town houses. Some of the streets are paved and closed to traffic. The novelist Jean Giono lived here earlier this century and both the town and the region influenced much of his writing.

≈ François Premier ■ *(18 Rue Guilhempierre* ☎ *(92) 72–07–99* ⬜ ⬤ ▨*), a clean, friendly commercial hotel, will open up for very late arrivals.*

⇌ André *(21 bis, Pl. du Terreau* ☎ *(92) 72–03–09* ⬜ *closed Mon, June), a family run auberge, popular with the locals, regional cooking.*

Marseille

Restaurant nearby
La Fuste (*6km (4 miles) E of Manosque*).

La Fuste △
Rte. de Barrème ☎ (92) 72–05–95 ▮ ⬜ ▮▬ ▭ ⬕ ⬛ (AE) ▣
⬕ (VISA) *Closed Sun dinner, Mon (mid-Sept to June), mid-Nov to mid-Dec.*
A 17thC coaching-inn, standing in its own park, has become a well-known luxury restaurant, run with style by the Jourdan family. Though seemingly remote, it is close to a main highway and easily attracts a sophisticated international clientele. Daniel Jourdan's fine cooking is an imaginative version of traditional regional *cuisine*. **Specialities:** *Truites à la nage, gigot de poulette au gingembre, cheese and desserts.*
🍴 There are nice bedrooms at the *hostellerie*, all gracefully furnished and very popular (▮▮▮).

Places nearby
Cadarache (*16km (10 miles) SW of Manosque*)   On the Durance, the Cadarache hydro-electric barrage stands adjacent to one of France's leading nuclear research centres (closed to the public).
Gréoux-les-Bains (*14km (9 miles) SE of Manosque*)   A small spa town on the river Verdon, where rheumatism, arthritis and chest troubles are treated. The waters are thought to have been used for thermal cures even in pre-Roman times. A Roman votive inscription can be seen in the modern baths.

Marseille
Map **10**H7. 777km (485 miles) s of Paris; 188km (117 miles) w of Nice. 13000 B.-du-R. Population: 914,350. Airport: Marignane 27km (17 miles) NW ☎ (42) 90–90–08 **i** 4 La Canebière ☎ (91) 54–91–11.
France's foremost port, second city and capital of the *Provence-Côte d'Azur* region is handsomely situated around a wide bay, circled by high limestone hills. It is a powerful city with a strong draw, noisy, congested, in places ugly, but with much to offer. It contrasts forcefully with the elegant smaller towns nearby such as Aix and Arles.

Marseillais are proud and hot-blooded – proud of their past, for this is the oldest town in France. Founded in 600BC by Greeks from Phocea in Asia Minor, Massilia – as it was named – soon became the main Greek colony in the west and was to play quite a role in Roman history, siding with Rome against Hannibal and then (to its cost) with the luckless Pompey against Caesar. Marseille has always lived on commerce: the period of the Crusades brought it great prosperity, when it became a trading rival of Genoa and Venice and set up posts all over the Levant. In 1721 it suffered heavily from a plague contracted from Syria, which wiped out 50,000 people. After 1789 the town welcomed the Revolution and sent soldiers to Paris, where so lustily did they sing the new *Battle Hymn of the Army of the Rhine*, composed in Strasbourg by Rouget de l'Isle, that the song was dubbed *La Marseillaise* – and the nickname has stuck.

The French conquest of North Africa in the mid-19thC, and the opening of the Suez Canal in 1869, gave Marseille its greatest era of commercial prosperity: most of the grand buildings in the city date from that period. In this century, the port has gone into relative decline, due partly to the loss of France's overseas empire and in recent years to the world shipping slump. Repair yards have closed, some docks lie idle, unemployment is above the national average. Yet this is still an active city, governed for many years with lordly *panache* by the late

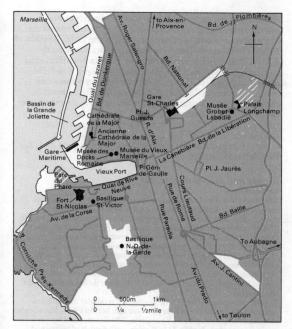

Marseille

Gaston Defferre, who was in his day Provence's most powerful
politician. As mayor he did much to modernize and develop
the city: witness the new Metro (1977) and the unlovely but
much-needed blocks of flats that now tower up on all the city's
hills. There are large universities, and many industries
(chemicals, engineering, food products and, of course, *pastis*).

Like other great Mediterranean cities (Naples, Athens,
Alexandria, etc.), Marseille is a town of contrasts – beautiful
setting, superb history and brash modern workaday reality. In
its criss-cross of drab commercial streets the traffic jams are
among Europe's worst, while the climate varies from torrid
midsummer heat to the icy blasts of the winter Mistral. The
Marseillais are industrious, volatile, rough-mannered and
earthily humorous – just as the writer Pagnol described them.
However, the rise of racial tension in France has been sharpest
here, and Marseille also still lives up to its reputation for
violence, shady dealing and mafia-style gangsterism.

A fine town, Marseille. This human ant-heap, this smutty
vulgarity, this squalor. They don't kill each other as much as it's
said, in the alleys of the Vieux Port – but it's a fine town all the
same.

Jean Anouilh, *Eurydice* (performed in US/UK as *Point of
Departure*)

Its life focuses around the main boulevard, **La Canebière**,
which slopes down to the **Vieux Port**, today used mainly by
fishing and pleasure craft (the modern port is to the N). s of
the Vieux Port, housing climbs up the slope of a broad hill around
whose western side the coastal highway, **Corniche Président-**

Kennedy ☆ winds for miles past rocks and sandy coves
and the rich villas of the bourgeoisie. Atop the hill stands the
city's most famous and evident landmark, the 19thC **Basilica of
Notre-Dame-de-la-Garde**, which is to Marseille what the
Sacré-Coeur is to Paris, only more so. Built in Neo-Byzantine
style, it is crowned by a large statue of the *Virgin*, floodlit at
night. Inside is a fascinating array of sailors' ex-votos – one
reason for going up (by car or trolley-bus) to this hideous
church, the other being the superb view ☆ from its terrace over
the city, the coast and surrounding hills.

Events: End of Nov to beginning of Jan, a picturesque
santons fair on La Canebière.

Early Apr and last two weeks of Sept, international trade fair,
Parc Amable-Chanot.

Sights and places of interest
La Canebière

This used to be one of the world's great streets, in the days before air
travel when Marseille really was 'the gateway to the east'. Its big
terrace-cafés with their orchestras were a chic social rendezvous for the
princes, sultans and maharajahs who used the port on their way to or
from Paris or London; and so there was a grain of sense in the fanciful
local boast, 'if Paris only had a Canebière it would be quite a little
Marseille'. But today the rich and mighty bypass Marseille, and the
orchestras are gone. There is now little reason to be proud of this
humdrum boulevard, lined with cut-price stores, cinemas and down-
market bars and cafeterias. But it is still the main thread that draws the
city together.

At the port end, in front of the Bourse, is a reminder that political
terrorism is no monopoly of our post-war age: here in 1934 a Macedonian
shot dead King Alexander of Yugoslavia. The Bourse itself houses a
maritime museum, **Musée de la Marine**, with models of sailing and
steamships, while 450m (500yd) to the s, in the Rue Grignan, the **Musée
Cantini** contains a good display of Provençal faïence as well as modern
sculpture by César and others. The area s of La Canebière is tolerably
smart, while that to the N, around the Rue Thubaneau, is today a squalid
red-light district, sinister at night.

Château Borély ☆
Promenade de la Plage 🚗📷 *Open 9.30 – 12.15, 13.00 – 17.00. Closed
Tues, Wed morning.*

Built as the home of a rich local merchant, Louis de Borély, this
handsome late 18thC mansion stands in a corner of the formal Borély
Park which includes a botanical garden. The château houses three
remarkable museums. On the ground and first floors, the **Musée
d'Archéologie Méditerranée** contains one of Europe's best collections
of Egyptian antiquities, including mummies, presented to the city by Dr
Clot-Bay; also Etruscan bronzes, Greek and Roman ceramics and even a
Minoan wine pitcher of the 15thC BC. The second floor brings a sharp
change of subject: here is the **Feuillet de Borsat** collection of 18thC
French drawings (slight but charming works by Greuze, Fragonard and
Ingres). The **Musée Lapidaire**, in an out-house, is rich in a diversity of
relics, Greek, Roman and medieval. Its showpiece is a reconstructed
pre-Roman sanctuary of the 3rdC BC, built up of finds made recently at
the Celto-Ligurian burial place of **Roquepertuse**, w of Aix: note the
two-headed Hermes and the portico decorated with skulls.

2km (1 mile) E of here, on the Bd. Michelet, is **L'Unité d'Habitation**,
the 17-storey 'dwelling unit' designed by Le Corbusier and built in 1952.
It was a great pioneering work in its day, and is one of the very few
buildings that the architect ever created in his adoptive land.

Docks Romains, Musée des
28 Pl. Vivaux 🚗📷 *Open 10.00 – 12.00, 14.00 – 18.30. Closed Tues,
Wed morning.*

The Roman docks of Massilia first came to light when the area N of the
Vieux Port was demolished in the war. A block of flats was then built on
top of them: but this museum on its ground floor cleverly comprises the
original docks in their actual setting – so it is less a museum than a real

Roman remain. You can see the quay and the *dolia* (grain storage jars) just as they were. Roman anchors and amphorae have been added, mostly taken from wrecks found offshore.

The museum has clear and informative maps and models of Massilia's commercial role in Greek and Roman days, and details of the retrieval of ancient wrecks carried out locally since 1952 under the supervision of the marine explorer Jacques Cousteau.

Grobet-Labadié, Musée
140 Bd. Longchamp ☎ (91) 62–21–82 ▧ Open 10.00–12.00, 14.00–18.30. Closed Tues, Wed morning.

Local musician and art-lover Louis Grobet owned this charming little 1870s house. On his death in 1919 he bequeathed it, with its remarkable contents, to the city of Marseille. The small, intimate rooms are richly furnished with the varied treasures that Grobet and his wife collected: French and Flemish tapestries of the 16th–18thC, oriental carpets, porcelain, old musical instruments, German 15thC paintings, works by Murillo and Greuze; and much else.

Despite the diversity, the overall effect is one of great harmony – a reflection of the Grobets' taste. Free leaflets give full details of all the contents of the museum.

Musée des Beaux-Arts ☆
Palais Longchamp, Bd. Longchamp ▧ Open 10.00–12.00, 14.00–18.15. Closed Tues, Wed morning.

On the first floor, the central hall displays works by Provençal painters such as Guigou and François Duparc. Here the eye is caught by **Michel Serre's** two vast canvasses of Marseille during the plague of 1721, its streets full of the dead and dying – graphic social documents, with an immediate impact.

Foreign artists on exhibit include Rubens (including an *Adoration of the Shepherds*), Annibale Carracci (a lively *Village Wedding*) and Jan Brueghel (*l'Air*, a fantasy with cupids). Two adjoining rooms are devoted to the great Marseillais sculptor Pierre Puget: details of his life and his never-realized town-planning schemes for the city; some small original works; and, notably, casts of six of his greatest sculptures (the originals are in the Louvre and in Genoa). These are imaginatively lit, in a darkened room.

On the second floor are works by French artists: Corot, Courbet, Millet, etc., and notably Daumier (who was born in Marseille) with vitriolic caricatures of Louis Philippe's supporters. On the stairways between the two floors, are two lively cartoon-like murals by Puvis de Chavannes, showing Marseille as a Greek colony and as the gateway to the East.

Muséum d'Histoire Naturelle
✱ For address and entry details see Musée des Beaux Arts.

A small aquarium of gaudy tropical fish; a large main hall with the vast skeletons of whales, elephants, rhinoceri, etc.; stuffed animals of every kind; and fossils and pre-historic remains.

Those who prefer their animals live need only walk across the broad garden behind the palace, to Marseille's **zoo**, privately-owned (▧ ▣ ✱ *open Mar–Sept 9.00–18.30, Oct–Feb 9.00–17.00*). Large, but unkempt.

Palais Longchamp ☆
Bd. Longchamp.

Built in the 1860s by the Provençal architect Henri Espérandieu, the palace is typical of the grandoise style of the period. A central colonnade links its two wings, each housing a museum (**Beaux-Arts** to the left, **Natural History** to the right). In the middle, a mighty, mossy fountain sends its waters cascading into a wide pool.

Le Port
☎ (91) 91–90–66 ▨ ✱ Visits Sun and public hols only, Apr–Sept 7.00–21.00; Oct–Mar 7.00–18.00. Entry by gate no. 2 (Arenc), no cars.

Work on the great port began in 1844, and today it contains 19km (12 miles) of quays and stretches for 6km (4 miles) N from the **Vieux Port** area. Though activity has declined, it still handles some 20 million tons of goods a year and 800,000 passengers, mostly Algerian 'guest-workers'. The port is closed to tourists, but a bird's eye view can be had by driving along the elevated Autoroute du Littoral, the fast N568B.

Marseille

St-Victor, Basilique Ⅲ † ☆
Rue Sainte 🖼 (crypt). Crypt open Mon–Sat 10.00–11.15, 15.00–18.00, Sun 15.00–18.00.

Early Christian history comes vividly alive in this ancient church. It was first built by St Cassien in the 5thC, in honour of the 3rdC martyr, St Victor. Having been wrecked by the Saracens, the existing fortified Gothic church was erected above it in the 11th–12thC: with its crenellated tower, it does look much like a fortress. Stairs lead down from the upper church to the large **crypt** which is St Cassien's original church, gracefully restored and still much in use as a place of worship. Here are catacombs with sarcophagi both early Christian and pagan (some have been transferred to the **Château Borély**). Here too, beside the main chapel, is the **tomb of two 3rdC martyrs**: this was long known to have existed, but only in 1965 were the skeletons and other relics unearthed, and dated by experts to AD250. The martyrs are thought to be Volusianus and Fortunatus, two obscure gentlemen. But a legend from the Dark Ages holds that St Lazarus and St Mary Magdalene took refuge in the grotto that is now this crypt, after bringing Christianity to Gaul (see *Les Stes-Maries-de-la-Mer*).

Vestiges, Musée des, et Jardin
Rue Henri-Barbusse 🖼 Open 8.00 to sunset.

After years of excavation, the remains of the Greek port and town of the 3rd–2ndC BC have now been ingeniously transformed into a small public garden close to the NE corner of the Vieux Port. You can walk on lawns amid the ruins: quays, ramparts, towers and a reservoir, all Greek, with some Roman additions. There are clear explanatory panels. It is a most attractive restoration, beautifully floodlit at night. To one side, excavations are still continuing.

Vieux Marseille, Musée du
Rue de la Prison 🖼 Open 10.00–12.00, 14.00–18.30, Wed 14.00–18.30. Closed Tues, Wed morning.

An absorbing folk-art museum housed in the 16thC Maison Diamantée ('diamond-studded'), so called because of its faceted facade. Ground floor: Provençal 18thC furniture, porcelain, etc. First floor: a whole room full of *santons* and Nativity cribs, of all shapes and sizes, both Provençal and Neapolitan. Mostly they are 18th and 19thC; but there is also a huge, colourful tableau of traditional local life, with hundreds of tiny *santons* made by Georges Prost. Second floor: a delightful collection of Camoin playing-cards. On all floors: maps, models and paintings of Marseille life through the centuries. The main stairway has a superb coffered ceiling, richly carved.

Vieux Port
This quay-lined inlet, full of little boats, was Marseille's port from Phocaean days till the 19thC; and today it is still in a sense the heart of the city. At its mouth stand two old fortresses: St-Jean to the N and St-Nicolas to the S, the latter built by Louis XIV to keep the unruly Marseillais under control. To the E of this fort is the **Basilique St-Victor**; to the NW, facing the sea, the public **Parc du Pharo** (fine view of the port), the château of which once belonged to the Empress Eugénie.

North of **Vieux Port** ☆ – once aristocratic, this ancient district of narrow alleys had, by the 1930s, declined into a low-life slum. In Jan 1943 the Germans, finding it uncontrollable, turned out 40,000 of its inhabitants overnight and blew up the area between the Rue Caisserie and the old port. After the war it was rebuilt with rows of soulless grey rectangular blocks. However, the area N **of the Rue Caisserie** survives intact: alleyways with five-storey houses festooned with washing like faded bunting. Around the perimeter are some beautiful buildings: the mairie with its 17thC facade; the **belfry of the Accoules**, relic of a church dating from the 12thC; the **Hospice de la Vieille Charité** with a chapel built by Puget; also the **Musée des Docks Romains** and the **Musée du Vieux Marseille**.

Just to the NW, near the new port, are the twin **cathédrales de la Major**, side by side and as different as chalk from cheese. The newer one is a vast late 19thC Neo-Byzantine folly with cupolas and striped stone, looking like a marzipan wedding-cake. Nestling in its shadow is the enchanting little **Ancienne Major** ☆ – pure 12thC Romanesque. In its ill-lit interior you can make out the porcelain low-relief by Della Robbia and, in the left transept, a 15thC altar of St Lazarus, finely sculpted (🖍 *daily 9.00–11.30, 14.30–17.00, closed Fri*).

Hotels

Concorde Palm-Beach 🛏️
*2 Promenade de la Plage, 13008
Marseille* ☎ *(91) 76–20–00*
📠*401894* ▥ *161 rms* 🛏 *161*
🖼 ⇌ AE ◐ ⊙ VISA *Open all
year.*
Location: *Right by the sea, below the
corniche road, 4km (2¼ miles) s of city
centre.* A large, fairly smart, ultra-
modern hotel, part of France's
Concorde chain but with American
overtones too, as its name implies.
While much used by business and
professional people (notably
doctors: there are about 60 medical
seminars a year), it also usefully
combines the amenities of a seaside
holiday with the proximity of the
city – and is sheltered from the
Mistral. Next door is a club and
school for sailing, windsurfing and
scuba-diving. A pianist plays at the
hotel bar, which opens on to a wide
terrace. Many bedrooms have
balconies, and it is also possible to
rent self-contained flats. Disco
(soundproofed), on the site of a
19thC spring-water thermal cure
centre. Within the hotel is Les
Voiliers, a good help-yourself
restaurant. Buffets are served by
the swimming pool during the
summer.
🖼 ‡ ♿ 🗖 🗠 ⤢ ≈ 🐾 ☷ ⊙

Frantel 🛏️
*Rue Neuve-St-Martin, 13001
Marseille* ☎ *(91) 91–91–29*
📠*401886* ▥ *200 rms* 🛏 *200* 🎚
⇌ AE CB ◐ ⊙ VISA *Open
all year.*
Location: *Close to La Canebière and
the Vieux Port.* Typical of the 30
modern luxury hotels in the
Frantel chain. Like the others, this
Frantel is geared mainly to top-
level business needs (it has ten
seminar and conference rooms),
but it could also suit the well-
heeled tourist. Outside, it is a brash
brown cube of glass and steel, but
inside all is smart, with full
amenities. It is conveniently
situated next to the Bourse
shopping centre while some of the
hotel's bedrooms overlook the
Vieux Port. (See restaurant,
L'Oursinade.)
‡ ♿ 🗖 🗠 ⤢ ☷

Ibis Prado
*6 Rue de Cassis, 13008
Marseille* ☎ *(91) 78–59–25*
📠*400362* ▥ *119 rms* 🛏 *119* 🎚
⇌ VISA *Open all year.*
Location: *In a quiet street near the
exhibition centre, 2.5km (1¼ miles) s*
of city centre. Not in fact a motel,
though it feels like one, and it is
similar to the 61 other hotels in
France's new Ibis chain: modern
and practical, modestly-priced,
geared to the basic needs of the
junior businessman, or passing
tourist. Bedrooms are small and
box-like, but neat. Cheerful
dining-room in coffee-shop style,
with straightforward cooking and
help-yourself breakfasts. All very
1980s.
‡ ♿ 🗠 ☷

Petit Nice et Marina Maldormé 🛏️
*160 Corniche Kennedy, 13007
Marseille* ☎ *(91) 52–14–39*
📠*401565* ▥ *20 rms* 🛏 *20* 🎚
🖼 ⇌ AE *Closed Jan.*
Location: *By the sea, on a small
headland between two coves, just off
the corniche road, 2.5km (1¼ miles),
sw of the city centre.* Miraculously
situated on an isolated strip of
rocky coast, yet deep within the
conurbation, this is by far the most
superior hotel in Marseille. Le
Petit Nice has had a curious
history. It was built as a private
villa in the 19thC by the Passedat
family, who turned it into a hotel in
1917 and still own and run it today
with arrogant pride. Justifiably so,
for this tiny hotel is a model of
refined enchantment: a
sumptuously decorated Hellenic-
style villa with a pretty garden
above the rocky shore. The Marina
Maldormé is a bedroom annexe
with elegant, classical-style rooms,
each with its own name
(Pompadour, du Barry . . . .) (See
restaurant.)
🖼 ‡ 🗠 ⤢ ⤢

Résidence Bompard ♣
*2 Rue des Flots Bleus, 13007
Marseille* ☎ *(91) 52–10–93* ▥
46 rms 🛏 *46* 🎚 ⇌ AE ◐
Location: *A quiet road on the high
hill s of the Vieux Port, 2.5km (1¼
miles) from the city centre.* What a
pleasant surprise to find a hotel of
rural charm, secluded in its own
extensive grounds, so close to
downtown Marseille – and at
bargain price. Run by two dynamic
Lebanese brothers, the hotel is
functional inside, but has a
pleasant English-style panelled bar
and idyllic wide patio under the
sophora trees. Twelve rooms are
bungalows with their own
kitchenettes.
🖼 ♿ 🗖 🗠 ⤢ ☷

Restaurants

Barone ✿
43 Rue Vacon
☎ *(91) 33–68–12* ▥ ▭ ▰
*Last orders 21.45. Closed Mon,
July–Aug.*
Of the hundreds of restaurants in
Marseille, almost all the best are
the most expensive. Fish,
particularly the famous
bouillabaisse, is the speciality, and
it does not come cheap, even here.
Bouillabaisse offered cheaply
(particularly in the scores of
restaurants around the SE corner of
the Vieux Port) is rarely the
genuine article. But at Barone it is.
There are no concessions to
ambience, but a fine choice on the
menu: oysters and other shellfish,
as well as cooked dishes such as
mouclade and *lotte à l'américaine*.
The house wine is excellent value.

Maurice Brun: aux Mets de Provence
18 Quai Rive-Neuve
☎ *(91) 33–35–38* ▥ ▰ ▭ ◔
*Last orders 21.00. Closed Sun,
Mon.*
A visit to *chez Brun* is an experience
not to be missed – the most
idiosyncratic restaurant in town,
also the one that is best keeping
alive the pure traditions of classic
Provençal *cuisine*. There is no sign
outside, save a modest nameplate:
you climb up a gloomy stairway, in
an old house opposite the Vieux
Port, to find the door opening into
a graceful and comfortable dining-
room. Here the founder's son,
Frédéric Brun, plays the role of
hieratic *restaurateur* – if you light a
cigarette or otherwise break his
rules, you risk incurring his wrath.
He offers no choice of food, just a
single unchanging menu, without
variations. But what a meal! For
two solid hours, the awestruck
guests eat their way through a
lavish succession of superb local
dishes – from the multiple hors
d'oeuvres via the spit-roasted
chicken and the *boeuf en daube* to
the sorbets, sweet and Provençal
pastries. The prices are somewhat
high but undoubtedly worth every
penny.

Chez Angèle ☕
50 Rue Caisserie
☎ *(91) 90–63–35* ▭ to ▥ ▭
▰ *Last orders 22.30. Closed
Mon, Christmas to early Jan.*
In a back street just N of the Vieux
Port. One of the very few cheap
eating places in town that are worth
recommending. A small, animated
bistro filled to the brim with jovial
habitués. Italo-Provençal cooking,
simple, but tasty and copious.

Michel (Les Catalans)
6 Rue des Catalans
☎ *(91) 52–64–22* ▥ ▭ ▰ VISA
*Last orders 22.00. Closed Tues,
Wed, July.*
The *bouillabaisse* here is as good as
any in Marseille – therefore it is one
of the best in the world – at this
much-praised brasserie facing the
coast on the w side of town. The
accent is entirely on serious eating –
certainly not on decor, which is very
plain, nor on ambience. Only the
view of the sea from some of the
restaurant's tables can possibly
distract you from the task in hand,
which is to relish Jeanne Visciano's
superb classical rendering of fresh
local fish.

New York/Vieux Port
7 Quai des Belges
☎ *(91) 33–91–79* ▭ to ▥ ▭
▰ ▰ AE ◔ VISA *Last orders
22.00.
Closed Sun.*
A handsome, classic fish
restaurant, much in vogue, with
tables well-spaced, pretty lighting
at night, and by day a front-of-
stalls view of the bustle around the
Vieux Port (mainly cars). The
usual local fish specialities are on
offer; or try the memorable *selle
d'agneau*.

L'Oursinade △ ✿
*Hôtel Frantel, Rue Neuve St-
Martin* ☎ *(91) 91–91–29* ▥
▭ ▰ ▰ AE CB ◔ ◔ VISA
*Last orders 22.30. Closed Sun,
Aug.*
Marseille's most luxurious
restaurant, with interesting views
over the garden of Greek ruins just
below. The food is some of the best
in town, too: the talented young
chef, René Alloin, invents light
and subtle variations on the *cuisine*
of Provence and of his native Lyon.
His special dishes are always
changing as is often the case with
nouvelle cuisine; but you are sure to
find his remarkable fish soup, the
eponymous *oursinade*, and perhaps
filet de rouget en civet or *feuilleté de
pied de mouton au basilic*. The set
menus, particularly, are
reasonably varied and worth the
price. (See hotel, **Frantel**.)

144

Petit Nice et Marina Maldormé △
Address ☎ *and* ⑦ *as hotel* ▮▮▮▮ *to*
▮▮▮▮ ▭▭ ▭ ◫ AE *Last orders*
22.30. Closed Mon, Jan, Tues
lunch (winter).
Greek statues stand guard in the
intimate, resplendent dining-room
where a pretty, curving picture-
window overlooks the sea. The
service is suitably stylish, and Jean-
Paul Passedat's cooking is
imaginative and inspired.
***Specialities:** Courgettes farcies à la
mousse de homard, marée de roche au
safran.* (See hotel.)

Nightlife

The city's nightlife is hardly distinguished. At **Au Son des
Guitares** (*18 Rue Corneille* ♪ *open 22.30 – 3.30, closed Sun*),
Corsicans sing and play guitar music. **L'Abbaye de la
Commanderie** (*same address*) is a quite comfortable bar where
typical Marseillais songs are sung and ribald jokes are told. You
need to know the *patois*.

Best discos: **L'Ascenseur** (*22 Pl. Thiers*), mainly for
teenagers; **Club 116** (*24 Rue Neuve-Ste-Catherine*), for all ages;
London Club (*73 Corniche Kennedy*), quite elegant.

The **Opera House** (*Pl. Reyer* ☎ *(91) 54 – 29 – 29*) puts on
good provincial performances all year except summer. Despite
its august presence, the streets around the opera are full of dim
bars and lolling girls.

Shopping

The streets with the smartest modern shops are the **Rue
St-Ferréol** and the **Rue de Rome**, both leading s from La
Canebière. The **Centre Bourse**, just N of Canebière, next to the
Hôtel Frantel, is a big new indoor shopping centre with 70
boutiques, including **Habitat** and **Dior**.

Some traditional shops selling local produce: **Bataille** (*18 Rue
Fontange*), a luxury delicatessen, rather like Fauchon in Paris,
selling Provençal wines and food products, including take-away
bouillabaisse; **Marrou** (*15 Pl. Castellane*), selling all regional
food products; **Les Olivades** (*Rue Moustier*) for Provençal
fabrics, *santons* etc.

Best hairdressers: **J.L. David** (*1 Pl. Général-de-Gaulle*
☎ *(91) 33 – 71 – 13*); **Hervé** (*12 Pl. Castellane*
☎ *(91) 37 – 74 – 61*).

Good open-air markets include: **Av. du Prado** for food and
clothing (*Mon – Sat mornings*); **Rue Longue-des-Capucins**
(*Mon – Sat, all day*), a varied market for food, coffee, spices, etc;
and a **fish market** along the quays of the Vieux Port (*Mon – Sat
mornings*).

Places nearby

Aubagne (*17km (10 miles) E of Marseille*) Just w of this
industrial town, off the D2 to Marseille, the **French Foreign
Legion** has its HQ, following its exit from Algeria in 1962. It
has a **museum** (*open daily June – Sept, Oct – May Wed, Sat, Sun*)
where documents, photos and other souvenirs recall the
Legion's many exploits.

Carry-le-Rouet (*27km (17 miles) w of Marseille*) The smartest
of a string of little resorts along the s side of the Estaque range
(see over): well-to-do Marseillais have villas here, and there is a
pretty fishing port.

〓 **L'Escale** △ (*Promenade du Port* ☎ *(42) 45 – 00 – 47* ▮▮▮▮) is a
sophisticated restaurant overlooking the bay and fishing-port; light, fresh
dishes based on traditional Provençal recipes.

Château d'If (◼◼ ◼◼ ◼ *open June – Sept 8.00 – 12.00, 13.30 to sunset, Oct – May 10.00 – 16.00; frequent motor-launch departures from the Quai des Belges, Vieux Port, connect with the opening times – return trip, including a visit to the castle takes approximately 90min*) An ever-popular excursion is the boat trip to this notorious fortress on a limestone islet 3km (2 miles) offshore. It was built in 1524 by Francois I as part of Marseille's defences, then long used as a state prison: its inmates included the 'Man in the Iron Mask' (see **Iles des Lérins** under *Cannes*) and (in fiction) Dumas' *Count of Monte Cristo*. You can see the carvings left by Huguenot prisoners brought here in thousands, and the memorial since erected to them; also a ghastly windowless cell where those with life sentences were flung and left to perish. It is not for the squeamish – but don't miss the view of Marseille from the highest terrace. The larger Frioul isles to the w now make up a sailing and sports centre.

Estaque, Chaîne de l' Another of the rugged limestone ranges that circle Marseille: 24km (15 miles) long, it separates the Berre Lagoon (see *Berre, Étang de*) from the sea. Its wild scenery – whitish rocks and dark pines – much impressed Cézanne, who painted it several times. In 1920, the 6km (4 mile) **Canal du Rove** was tunnelled under the mountain, to provide a shipping link from Marseille to the lake, but because of landslip, it has been out of use since 1963.

Étoile, Chaîne de l' Marseille is hemmed in to the NE by this limestone range, which has several points of interest: **Allauch**, with old windmills and a fine view over the city; splendid vistas from the **Col Ste-Anne**; **Château-Goubert** with its interesting museum of Provençal folk-art (*open Mon, Sat, Sun afternoon*); and the **caves of Loubière** – polychromatic stalactites and stalagmites (*open all day Sun, Mon, Wed – Sat afternoons only, closed Tues*).

Marseilleveyre massif These stark and craggy limestone hills frame the s side of the bay of Marseille. The *corniche* road leads round to the fishing hamlet of Callelongue. At Montredon, hardy walkers can strike inland by a stiff 90min climb to the highest peak at 430m (1,425ft) and there be rewarded with tremendous views of city and coast. From Mazargue, in the SE suburbs, other rough walks lead to the lovely creeks (*calanques*) of Sormiou and Sugiton (see also *Cassis*).

Martigues

*Map **10**G5. 40km (25 miles) w of Marseille. 13500 B.-du-R. Population: 38,350 ℹ Quai Paul-Doumer*
☎ *(42) 80 – 30 – 72.*

The former fishing village has today grown into a sizeable dormitory town, owing to its proximity to the new oil-based industries of Lavéra and Berre Lagoon (see *Berre, Étang de*). But its old quarter, where pretty houses line the canals, has not lost the charm that drew Ziem and Corot to paint it in the 19thC. The prettiest spot is the **Pont St-Sebastien** on the central Ile de Brescon, where there is also the 17thC **church of Ste-Madeleine**, fronted by Corinthian pillars, and with a fine organ loft and Baroque decor.

In the w suburbs, an imposing modern suspension bridge, 292m (330yd) long, carries an autoroute over the canal. Just N of the town, above a new hospital, the **chapelle de Notre-Dame-des-Marins** stands alone on a hilltop; from here there are views over the vast industrial complex of Berre/Fos and the limestone ranges beyond.

St-Roch (*Route d'Arles* ☎ *(42) 80–19–73* ⅢⅢ ⒶⒺ ⊕ ⱽⁱˢᵃ), a modern concrete hotel, very comfortable, mainly for businessmen; pleasant garden with an olive oil mill.

La Gousse d'Ail (*42 Quai Général-Leclerc* ☎ *(42) 07–13–26* ⅠⅠ *closed Sun, 24 Aug to mid-Sept*), an animated bistro facing the lake, popular with the locals; good *crudités*, impersonal service.

Maures massif
Map 12H11. Var.

The wooded mountain range of schistous rock follows the coast for 56km (35 miles) from *Hyères* to *Fréjus*. It is almost as ancient as the *Esterel massif* to the NE, and very much larger. Its name comes from Greek and from the Provençal word *maouro*, meaning 'dark', on account of its sombre woods of Aleppo pine and chestnut: it is not derived, as is often supposed, from *Les Maures*, the Moors (or Saracens), who occupied and ravaged the region in the 9th–10thC, having already colonized Spain.

Until the tourist boom of the 20thC this part of the coast was unpopulated, save for the old fortified port of *St-Tropez*. Today it is an unbroken string of bathing resorts, the high-rise buildings of which have only partly spoilt the lovely scenery, seen at its best on the **Corniche des Maures** between *Le Lavandou* and *Cavalaire*, and around *Ste-Maxime* (see also *Grimaud* and *Port-Grimaud*). The wild interior of the massif is still remarkably unspoilt and little-known. It is covered with a profusion of rare plants and flowers, as well as with great forests of chestnut and cork oak which provide the area with two of its industries: the making of *marrons glacés* and of corks for wine bottles.

Several scenic roads wind through the heart of the massif, offering majestic views of the coast and mountains. Take, for example, the road from Le Lavandou via the **Col de Babaou** to **Collobrières** and thence to Grimaud (with a detour to the ruined 18thC monastery of the **Chartreuse de la Verne** (*open daily, closed Tues, from Oct to June*). Or from Collobrières drive up close to **La Sauvette**, the massif's highest peak 780m (2,550ft) high and then by way of La Garde-Freinet to Plan-de-la-Tour and back to the coast at Ste-Maxime. Or, from Bormes-les-Mimosas, motor up to the rocky peak of the **Pierre d'Avenon** above Le Lavandou.

Menton ★
Map 16E16. 27km (17 miles) ᴇ of Nice, 2.5km (1½ miles) w of Italan frontier. 06500 Alpes-Mar. Population 27,500 ⓘ Palais de l'Europe, Av. Boyer ☎ *(93) 57–57–00.*

Menton is much the prettiest and least strident of the larger resorts on the *Côte*. It is also the warmest, with winters of balmy mildness due to its sheltering mountains just behind. Hence the profusion of semi-tropical fruit and plants, and the acres of lemon groves for which the town is famous.

Until the 19thC Menton was a little-known fishing port, in liege to the Grimaldis. But in the 1850s an English doctor wrote a book in which he praised the town's beneficial climate, and the English gentry descended on Menton, to retire or to winter, followed by other European aristocracy. Today, all is changed. The British resident population, once at 5,000, one of the largest on the continent, is now a mere 120 or so. The palace hotels along the sea-front, the Balmoral, the Bristol, the Majestic, have either been pulled down or converted into

holiday flats. Yet there are still echoes of the old days: the
Jardin des Colombières, Katherine Mansfield's villa, the
grandiose foyer of the ex-hotel Imperial, now flats, and the air
of faded nostalgia that envelopes the town.

Menton stands along a wide bay. To the w of the port runs the
elegant palm-lined **Promenade du Soleil** ☆ and to the E are new
beaches and marinas. Behind the port rises the picturesque
vieille ville with its bustling alleys, and from here steps lead up
to the 17thC **church of St Michel** and the nearby **chapelle des
Penitents Blancs**, which are both fine examples of Baroque
architecture.

Events: In the first half of Aug, a distinguished festival of
chamber music is held in the Pl. de l'Église, superbly floodlit.

In Feb, the famous lemon festival takes place with floats of
fruit and pretty girls.

Sights and places of interest
Cocteau, Musée
Quai Napoléon 111 🔳 ✖🍴 *Open 10.00–12.00, 14.00–18.00 (17.30 in
winter). Closed Mon, Tues, Nov.*

Installed in the harbour bastion in 1957, this small museum contains
tapestries, drawings and stage sets by the versatile painter and writer
Jean Cocteau. Most eye-catching are the gaudy harlequin paintings.

Colombières, Jardin des ☆
Bd. de Garavan (NE suburbs; ill-signposted) 🔳 ✖🍴 *Open
9.00–12.00, 14.00–18.00.*

This large Italianate garden on a steep hillside was laid out by Ferdinand
Bac, humorist writer and alleged illegitimate son of Napoleon III. It has
tall cypresses, ornamental pools, urns and statues, and in its heyday must
have been lovely, but is now sadly unkempt. The present elderly owner
can only afford one gardener, and fears the garden's days are nearly over.
The curious Villa les Colombières, which stands in the grounds, was
exuberantly designed by Bac in Hellenic-cum-Roman style, with
frescoes, arches and statues: note the elegant colonnaded atrium with a
pool in the middle, now empty and dirty. The villa has bedrooms to let,
with Roman-style baths, or you can simply take some lemon tea, gazing
out over the glorious coast below.

Just below the garden is an old **olive grove**, and further down the hill is
the **Jardin Botanique Exotique**, full of unusual shrubs and trees. Near
here is writer Katherine Mansfield's villa, Isola Bella. Further w, beyond
the road to Sospel, the **monastery of the Annonciade** stands high on its
hilltop; it's worth going up to for the views, but it is not open to visitors.

Municipal, Musée
Av. de la Madone 🔳 *Open mid-June to mid-Sept 10.00–12.00,
15.00–18.30; mid-Sept to Oct, Dec to mid-June 10.00–12.00,
14.00–17.30. Closed Tues, Nov.*

The museum is known for its pre-history and archaeology collection,
including the skull of the famous *Grimaldi Man* (c.30,000BC), found in a
cave on the shore nearby in the 19thC. Another room is devoted to local
history and popular arts; others to Italian, Dutch, French and other
paintings of the 14th–17thC; and others to minor works of such modern
artists as Utrillo, Dufy and Vlaminck.

Salle des Mariages ☆
Hôtel de Ville, Rue de la République 🔳 ✖🍴 ✗ *Open 8.30–12.00,
13.30–17.45. Closed Sat, Sun.*

This little room in the Town Hall, used for civil marriages, was decorated
by Cocteau in 1957 with a series of engagingly vivacious paintings.

Hotels

🍸 L'Aiglon
7 Av. de la Madone ☎(93) 57–55–55 🔳 *32 rms* 🛏 *26* 🚗 AE 💿 ⬤
VISA

Location: On main road, facing beach, at w end of promenade. A former
private house of the 1900 period, in a big garden with fruit trees; a
pleasant hotel with a pool and shady terraces. Some rooms have balconies.

No restaurant, but snacks served by the pool at lunchtime, and in the
bedrooms at dinner-time.
⌷ ☐ ☞ ✔ ≈ 🍴

Other recommended hotels include the following:
Auberge Provençal ■ ❖ (*11 Rue Trenca* ☎ *(93) 55−77−29* ☐);
Auberge des Santons (*Colline de l'Annonçiade* ☎ *(93) 35−94−10* ■■□);
Chambord (*6 Av. Boyer* ☎ *(93) 35−94−19* ■■□); **Londres** (*15 Av.
Carnot* ☎ *(93) 35−74−62* ■□); **Napoléon** (*29 Porte de France*
☎ *(93) 35−89−50* ■■■■); **Orly** (*27 Porte de France* ☎ *(93) 35−60−81*

Restaurants

Les Arches: chez Diana ❖
31 Quai Bonaparte ☎ *(93) 35−94−64* ■□ ☐ ■■ 🚗 VISA *Last
orders 23.00 (July−Aug), 22.00 (rest of year). Closed Wed, Nov.*
This popular quai-side bistrot is run with gusto by Englishwoman Diana
Archer. She'll happily tell you the Grand Guignolesque life story that led
her to her Menton restaurant, and after dinner regales her guests with
Piaf-style songs in many languages. In between you can sample her chef's
really good Provençal cooking, as well as English specialities like sherry
trifle and real lemon meringue pie.

Auberge des Santons
Colline de l'Annonçiade ☎ *(93) 35−94−10* ■■□ ☐ ■■ 🚗 🚗 AE
⬤ *Last orders 22.00 (summer), 21.30 (winter). Closed Sun dinner,
Mon, mid-Nov to mid-Dec.*
The best food in Menton can be found at this modern white villa
overlooking the sea. *Patron* and chef Bernard Simon continues to please
his guests with *nouvelle cuisine* prepared with tremendous finesse.
Specialities: *Escalope de saumon cru mariné au basilic, feuillété de ris de
veau sauce porto.*

Restaurant nearby
Castellar (*6km (3¼ miles)* N *of Menton*).

Auberge du Moulin ➹ ❖
Rue Garibaldi ☎ *(93) 35−99−79* ☐ ■■ 🚗 *Last orders 21.00.
Closed for dinner out of season, Tues, Mar.*
A remote, rough and ready inn in a hilltop village where you can enjoy
fresh and simple country cooking and a *pichet* of local wine under the
olive trees or by an open fire in winter.

Nightlife

Casino Municipal
Promenade de Soleil ◎ ◎ ☯ *Gaming rooms open 16.00−3.00.*
One of the *Côte's* most staid casinos. The dinner dance/cabaret is open in
summer only. On Sun afternoons there are *thés-dansants*.

Shopping
Just across the border in Italy, 11km (7 miles) away, is the vast
market at **Ventimiglia** (*Fri only*) which attracts people from
miles around with its wide choice and very cheap prices.

Places nearby
Ste-Agnès ✩ (*11km (7 miles)* NW *of Menton*)   Approached on a
winding road, this is one of the highest and most striking of all
the villages near the coast. It straddles the crest of a hill, and
behind it a track leads up a cliff to the ruined Saracen castle.
From Ste-Agnès it is possible to drive through the mountains to
the attractive villages of **Peille** and *Peillon*, and so on to Nice.
Reached by another road from Menton, the D23, is another
remarkable hilltop village, **Gorbio** ✩

Monaco (and Monte-Carlo)

≋ **Logis Sarrasin** ☻ ♣
Ste-Agnès ☎ *(93) 35–86–89* ☐ ☐ ■ ⛝ ▰ *Closed Fri, mid-Nov to mid-Dec.*

Thousands of other tourists have got here first – but don't be deterred by the crowds from eating at this well-known, old, family-run *auberge* in Ste-Agnès. Huge meals are provided for next to nothing, and there are marvellous views.

Monaco (and Monte-Carlo)

*Map **16**E16. 18km (11 miles) ε of Nice. Independent state. Population: 27,000* **i** *2a Bd. des Moulins* ☎ *(93) 30–87–01. Tourist information in English* ☎ *(93) 50–07–51.*

Prince Rainier III rules like a Medici over his wealthy and dynamic little sovereign state, a 468-acre strip of land squeezed between sea and mountains, much of it now filled up with tiers of skyscrapers. Monaco is the name of the principality, also of the 'Old Town' on its headland where the Royal Palace stands; across the harbour is the newer quarter, Monte-Carlo, gaudily glamorous, still exerting its hypnotic appeal over the world's tourists. Of Monaco's 27,000 population, most are French or Italian. Only 4,500 have the privilege of being Monegasque citizens: they do no military service, and pay no income tax.

The ruling family are the Grimaldi, who acquired Monaco from the Genoese in 1308, and in those days owned several lordships in the region, including Antibes and Cagnes. For centuries Monaco's history was a turbulent one; at various times it has been occupied by both the French and the Spanish, and a protectorate of the French and of the kingdom of Sardinia. But in 1860, when the rest of the Nice area was ceded to France by the House of Savoy, Monaco managed to hold on to its independence. Bankruptcy threatened, however, for Prince Charles III was obliged to sell Menton and Roquebrune to Napoleon III, thus losing his revenues from the lemon and olive oil trade. So he decided to build a casino; these were still banned in France, but increasingly popular in Germany. The casino opened in 1865, on a low barren rock named Monte Carlo in his honour; and, with the arrival of the railway, the aristocracy of Europe were soon crowding to Monte-Carlo to stay at the imposing new Hôtel de Paris and to indulge in the new pastime of gambling. Prince Charles had given the concession to an enterprising entrepreneur, François Blanc, who made a brilliant financial success of the new venture, so that Monaco grew rich, almost overnight.

The resplendent names – Cannes, Nice, Monte-Carlo – began to glow through their torpid camouflage, whispering of old kings come here to dine or die, of rajahs tossing Buddhas' eyes to English ballerinas, of Russian princes turning the weeks into Baltic twilights in the lost caviare days.
F. Scott Fitzgerald, *Tender is the Night*, 1939

The principality has remained rich, but only by again adapting to the times. Rainier III was only 25 when he came to the throne in 1949. Monaco was then gently on the wane, for high society gambling was no longer a solid source of wealth. But in the past 25yr or so the astute prince and his associates have totally transformed and revitalized the place, turning it into one of the most modern, efficient and high-powered pleasure-cum-business centres in the world. Big banks have arrived, attracted by the tax advantages; over 80 acres of land

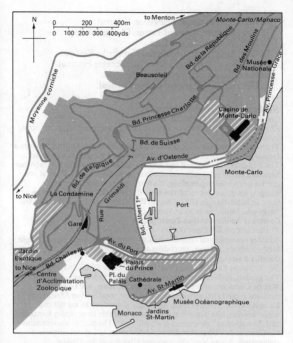

have been reclaimed from the sea to make room for a new port and heliport, two more casinos, new beaches and nightclubs. Just below the main casino is a vast ultra-modern convention centre, built out over the sea, showpiece of the prince's emphasis on 'business tourism'.

Just as Monte-Carlo in the late 19thC had an English flavour, so today it is Americanized – '*Las Vegas-plage*' is a French sneer. Yet it is a town of many facets, some of them vulgar, some chic and glamorous. It is still a magnet for the world's diamond-studded jet-setters, and its nightlife is the smartest on the coast. Here the old world meets the new in high style. For many years this union was symbolised by the marriage of Prince Rainier to Grace Kelly, Hollywood star and daughter of a Philadelphia industrialist. After her tragic death in 1982, in a car accident on the heights above the town, Monaco went into mourning and lost some of its panache. It is only now recovering.

Monaco claims, perhaps fairly, that a greater diversity of activities and tourist attractions are crammed into one small space than in any other comparable area of the globe: science (the famous **Oceanographic Museum**), culture (the Opera and a leading orchestra), sport (the Grand Prix and Rally), business . . . The firm that keeps much of these activities running smoothly is still the same one that was created by Blanc in the 1860s, the Societé des Bains de Mer (SBM) in which the principality is a major shareholder. The SBM today owns or runs four of the leading hotels, all the casinos, many of the office blocks, and most of the beaches, sports clubs and night spots.

Events: In Jan, Monte-Carlo Rally; and Festival of St Devoté, patron saint of the principality.

151

In Feb, International Television Festival.
In Apr, the International Tennis Championships.
In May, Monaco Grand Prix.
In July/Aug, the International Fireworks Festival.
In Aug/Sept, the World Amateur Theatre Festival.
In Nov, the Monegasque National Fête.
In Dec, the International Circus Festival.

Sights and places of interest

Casino de Monte-Carlo Ⅲ ☆
Pl. du Casino. Passports or identity papers are required to be shown by visitors.

The world's most famous casino raises its four towers skyward between a formal garden, full of tropical trees, and a terrace overlooking the sea. The building was designed by Charles Garnier, architect of several other Second Empire extravaganzas, including the Paris Opéra. Even if you are not interested in gambling, it's worth going inside to see the sumptuous decor and recall the days of ostrich feathers and white tie and tails. In its heyday, in 1887, Charles Wells, an Englishman, became the "man who broke the bank at Monte-Carlo".

Centre d'Acclimatation Zoologique
Pl. du Canton ▓ Open 14.00–19.00. Closed Tues, Fri.

A rather cramped and crowded zoo, with elephants, lions, tigers, bright birds, gibbons, chimps, crocodiles and fish.

Jardin Exotique
Bd. du Jardin Exotique ▓ Open 9.00–17.30 or 19.00 (summer).

The garden, built on the cliffside at the w entry to Monaco, by the Middle Corniche, offers good views over the town, just below. It contains some 1,000 different kinds of cacti, mostly from Africa and Latin America, many of them startlingly shaped; some are tall and triple-headed, like pagan totems; others resemble large, spiky footballs and are known as "mother-in-law's pillows". The garden also contains the **Grottes de l'Observatoire** which has caves full of stalactites and stalagmites, where Neolithic men once lived, and the **Musée d'Anthropologie Préhistorique** which displays relics found in these caves and at the Red Rocks near Menton, as well as Roman remains.

National, Musée (*Collection Galéa*)
Av. Princesse-Grace ▓ ⚑ 𝄐 Open 10.00–12.15, 14.30–18.30.

This graceful little villa, built by Charles Garnier, contains one of the world's finest collections of dolls and mechanical toys – set in motion only for groups, or when the museum is full. The most striking exhibit is a huge 18thC Neapolitan crib with some 300 figures.

Océanographique, Musée ☆
Av. St-Martin ▓ ⚑ ✿ Open July, Aug 9.00–21.00; rest of the year 9.00 or 9.30–19.00

The finest museum of its kind in the world belongs to Monaco thanks to Prince Albert I's passion for oceanography in the late 19thC, which he was able to finance with the profits from the casino trade. He made 24 voyages in his luxury yachts, bringing back many rare species from the ocean beds. In 1910, the imposing museum, standing on the se side of the headland, was opened, and today it is directed by Commander Jacques Cousteau, the famous underwater explorer.

The museum's aquarium is perhaps the best in Europe. Some 60 tanks contain a dazzling variety of fish, large and small, of every colour imaginable, many with delicately patterned spots and stripes. On the ground floor, a hall contains the skeletons of whales and other sea mammals. Upstairs is an elaborate display of marine technology, old and new, beautifully laid out: scientific instruments, and pictures and models of ocean beds. The adjacent hall has a large array of sea shells, some of them huge, and of objects made from the produce of the sea, from sharkskin bags and shoes to opera glasses encrusted with mother of pearl. The museum also presents daily film shows on marine subjects.

Palais du Prince
Pl. du Palais ▓ 𝄐 Open July–Sept 9.30–12.30, 14.00–18.30. Closed Oct–June.

When the palace is closed (during the times the Prince is in residence) visitors must content themselves with watching the changing of the guard (*daily at 11.55*) in the wide paved square with views over the town and coast. Or they can visit the small **Musée Napoléon** in one wing of the palace, which contains souvenirs both of Napoleon's and of Monaco's history (*closed Mon*). When the palace is open, visitors will see the fine 16thC arcaded courtyard, leading to the Throne Room and to rooms hung with pictures by Brueghel, Holbein and others. Parts of the palace are 13th–16thC, but it was extensively rebuilt in the late 19thC, hence the mock-Moorish crenellated towers, then in fashion.

Close by is the **cathedral**, also built from the Casino de Monte-Carlo's profits, from 1875–1903, in ostentatious Neo-Romanesque style. The high altar and episcopal throne are of white marble, overlaid with mosaics. The building is on the site of a 13thC church, from which it has inherited two retables by Louis Bréa, and a *Pièta* over the sacristy door.

The nearby **Waxworks Museum** (*27 rue Basse* ☎ (*93*) *30–39–05*) offers a panorama of figures from Monaco history.

Hotels

Beach Plaza 🏨
22 Av. Princesse-Grace, Monte-Carlo ☎ *(93) 30–98–80*
Ⓥ*479617* |||| *320 rms* 🛏 *320* ▦
🍴🍷 AE ⓘ ⓒ VISA
Location: On the new beach of the Casino de Monte-Carlo. This large, British-run (Trust House Forte) hotel is one of the two best for a beach holiday in the principality. It lacks the *fin-de-siècle* majesty of the **Paris**, or the **Hermitage**, but does have the advantage of a private beach and all the accompanying pleasures. One snag: the imported sand has the texture of fine gravel.
♨ ⑂ ▢ ☞ ⚓ ⧉ ⇌ 🐟 ⛱

Hermitage 🏨 ⌂
Sq. Beaumarchais, Monte-Carlo ☎ *(93) 50–67–31*
Ⓥ*479432* |||| *260 rms* 🛏 *260* ▦
🍴🍷 AE CB ⓘ ⓒ VISA
Location: Near the Casino de Monte-Carlo, just above the harbour. A marvellous Belle Époque extravagance, this sumptuous palace was built in 1899 and has been stylishly renovated by its SBM owners. Its most famous feature is the winter garden foyer with its lofty domed ceiling of glass and minty green decor. The enormous bedrooms are furnished in the style of the period; some have genuine *fin-de-siècle* blue-patterned ceramic wash-basins. (See restaurant, **Belle Époque**.)
♨ ⑂ ▢ ☞ ⚓ ⧉ ⇌ 🐟 ⛱

Loews 🏨
Av. des Spélugues, Monte-Carlo ☎ *(93) 50–65–00* Ⓥ*479435* ||||
641 rms 🛏 *641* ▦ 🍴🍷 ⇌
AE CB ⓘ ⓒ VISA
Location: Built out over the sea on piles, just below the Casino de Monte-Carlo and beside the new Conference Centre. Twice as large as any other hotel on the whole coast, Loews is a

powerful symbol of the new Monte-Carlo. It is like an autarchic state within the state, so wide are the range of its facilities: casino, restaurants, bars, shopping arcade, congress hall, heated pool on the roof, sun terrace and health centre. It's brash, efficient, airy and amusing. Rare for a hotel in this class, there are no TVs in the bedrooms – but for a cunning reason: "We don't want to distract our clients from spending their evenings in our casino."
♨ ⑂ ▢ ☞ ⚓ ⧉ ⇌ 🐟 ⛱

Monte-Carlo Beach 🏨
St-Roman, 06190 Roquebrune-Cap-Martin ☎ *(93) 78–21–40*
Ⓥ*479432* |||| *46 rms* 🛏 *46* ▦
🍴🍷 AE CB ⓘ ⓒ VISA *Closed mid-Oct to Mar.*
Location: At the E end of Monte-Carlo, just inside France, by the beach. Built in 1928 as the Old Beach Hotel, the SBM have recently given the hotel a new name and a facelift, with bedrooms redecorated in cool pastel colours. Every room has a balcony just above the sea; try for the large circular one above the foyer where Eva Peron stayed in 1947. The hotel has more charm than the vast complexes downtown, with the advantage of the **Monte-Carlo Beach** lido on its doorstep.
▦ ♨ ⑂ ▢ ☞ ⚓ ⧉ ⇌ 🐟
🐟 ⛱

Paris 🏨 ⌂
Pl. du Casino, Monte-Carlo ☎ *(93) 50–80–80* Ⓥ*469925* ||||
300 rms 🛏 *300* ▦ 🍴🍷 ⇌ AE
CB ⓘ ⓒ VISA
Location: Beside the Casino de Monte-Carlo, on the sea. Opened in 1865 to house the kings, queens and grandees who flocked to the new Casino de Monte-Carlo, the

Monaco (and Monte-Carlo)

Hôtel de Paris is still quite fashionable, though hardly as exclusive. Nowadays, flowery Bermuda shorts clash merrily with the Neo-Baroque decor in the foyer. A garden fronts the sea, and a passageway leads direct to **Les Terrasses** bathing and health centre, free to residents. (See restaurant, **Le Grill de l'Hôtel de Paris**.)

♨ ᕕ ⬜ 🖾 ⚓ ⟨⟨ ⇌ 👙

Other recommended hotels: **Balmoral** (*13 Av. de la Costa* ☎ *(93) 50–62–37* ▥▥ *to* ▥▥), traditional, family-run; **Terminus** (*9 Av. Prince-Pierre* ☎ *(93) 30–20–70* ▥▥), modestly priced, comfortable.

Restaurants

Bec Rouge ⌂
11 Av. de Grande-Bretagne, Monte-Carlo ☎ *(93) 30–74–91* ▥▥ ▭ ⌂ AE ⊚ *Last orders 23.00. Closed Mon (Jan–Apr), mid-Nov to mid-Dec.*
This sober, classic restaurant livens up in the heat of summer when the candlelit tables spill out across the street. The clientele can be eye-catching: local royals patronize the place, as does Frank Sinatra, among others. The prices can be eye-catching too, for the good, solidly traditional *cuisine bourgeoise* on offer. **Specialities:** *Gratin de langoustes, loup en feuilletage.*

Belle Époque
Address and ☎ *as Hotel Hermitage* ▥▥ ▭ ▱ ▭ ⌂ AE CB ⊚ ⊚ VISA *Last orders 21.30.*
Meals can be taken on a spacious outdoor terrace, but for once in Provence it's more amusing to eat indoors in the amazing Neo-Baroque banqueting room with its high frescoed ceiling. Ambitious and expensive *haute cuisine* with a delicate touch. **Specialities:** *Saumon cru aux courgettes, filet d'agneau à la crème fleurette et menthe fraîche.* (See hotel, **Hermitage**.)

Dominique Le Stanc
18 Bd. des Moulins

☎ *(93) 50–63–37* ▥▥ *to* ▥▥ ▤▤ AE ⊚ ⊚ VISA ▭ *Last orders 22.30. Closed for lunch Sat–Mon, and all day Mon in winter.*
The young M. Le Stanc, a Breton by origin, is regarded today as the best chef in Monte-Carlo. His very smart and prettily decorated restaurant is besieged by Monegasque high society. **Specialities:** *Raviolis au vert et aux points d'asperges, rougets au basilic et aux olives, pêche rôtie aux pistaches.*

Le Grill de l'Hôtel de Paris
Address and ☎ *as Hôtel de Paris* ▥▥ ▭ ▱ ▭ ▱ AE CB ⊚ ⊚ VISA *Last orders 22.30, 23.00 (summer). Closed Mon.*
The main restaurant and banqueting hall, the famous and fabulously ornate Empire Room with its great fresco across one wall, serves an unremarkable *haute cuisine*. Much more in vogue today is the smaller rooftop grill room. **Specialities:** *Terrine de saumon au caviar, millefeuille de moules et huîtres sauce poulette.* (See hotel, **Paris**.)

Some more moderately priced restaurants include: in Monaco, **Castelroc** (*Pl. du Palais* ☎ *(93) 30–36–68* ▥▥); and in Monte-Carlo, **Pinocchio** (*30 rue Comte Gastaldi* ☎ *(93) 30–96–20* ▥▥); **Polpetta** (*6 Av. Roqueville* ☎ *(93) 50–67–84* ▥▥).

Nightlife
Monte-Carlo at night is an incredible spectacle, with its floodlit gardens and squares, and its streets teeming with Rolls and Mercedes from which beautifully dressed women casually alight. Here the nightlife industry is the most highly organized on the Riviera, with crowded gaming rooms, super-chic discos, lavish cabarets, as well as garish slot machines.

Casino de Monte-Carlo
Pl. du Casino ☎ *(93) 50–69–31 (casino)* ☎ *(93) 50–80–80 (cabaret)* ⛄ 🍽 ⊛ ♦ ⅄ ⚓ *Public rooms open 10.00–2.00,*

American rooms open 16.00–3.00, private rooms open 16.00–4.00. Cabaret open Sept–June, dinner-dance 21.00, floor show 23.00. Closed Tues.

The *salles privées*, once reserved for high stakes and special players, are today no more private than the *salles publiques*: the entrance fee is the same, but in the former a tie is required. Some rooms have been turned over to gaming with American rules. Here the entrance is free, slot-machines click and glitter, and most of the participants are dressed very casually.

The Casino de Monte-Carlo also contains an **Opera House**, once one of the greatest in Europe; here Diaghilev created his *Ballets Russes de Monte-Carlo*. Today there is no more ballet company, but there is still an opera company which stages productions in winter and spring. More illustrious today is the **Monte-Carlo Philharmonic Orchestra** which gives concerts year round in the Convention Centre, and in summer in the Court of Honour at the Palace.

There is also a large **nightclub** for dinner-dance and cabaret, a sumptuous room with red and black Naughty Nineties decor. The clientele is most decorous, and the floor show tends to be better at **Loews**.

Loews Hotel
Av. Spelugues
🕿 *(93) 50–65–00* ☿ ⦿ ◫ ♠ ⋂
♨ ⋙ ⇌ *Casino open daily 17.00–4.00. Folie Russe dinner-dance 20.30; floor show 22.30; closed Mon; Jockey Club open 11.00–24.00.*

Just off the foyer of this enormous new hotel is a **casino** with American gaming rules. Entrance is free and unrestricted, the ambience that of Las Vegas. By contrast, Loews' dinner-dance/cabaret, **La Folie Russe**, is

most sophisticated. The **Jockey Club** is a pleasant bar.

Monte-Carlo Sporting Club
Av. Princesse-Grace
🕿 *(93) 30–71–71* ☿ ⦿ ◫ ♠ ⋂
♨ ⋙, *Sporting club open late June to early Sept and on special occasions e.g. the Grand Prix; Jimmy'z and Parady'z open from 23.00 to dawn; Salle des Étoiles open from 21.00; casino open from 22.00.*

Monaco's latest temple to the night is misleadingly named, for there are no sports here. The luxurious complex is on a 14-acre stretch reclaimed from the sea, planted with trees and romantically lit. **Jimmy'z, Chez Régine,** is generally held to be the most fashionable discotheque on the *Côte d'Azur; le très beau monde* come here in force. Dress with chic if you want to be let in. In winter the disco moves to the more modest premises in the Pl. du Casino (**Jimmy'z d'hiver**). **Parady'z**, also run by the indomitable Régine, is an outdoor disco popular with the younger smart set; you dance beside a little lake. **La Salle des Étoiles** is a huge hall with a roll-back roof, used for nightly dinner-dance/cabarets. Special galas on Fri, with evening dress compulsory, and often an international name on the bill. There's also a **casino** with nautical decor and both French and American gaming, an outdoor cinema, and **Au Maona**, a venue for dinner-dances with tropical decor and Polynesian style *cuisine*.

Other popular nightspots are **Le Café de Paris, L'X Club** and **Tiffany's**.

Sports and activities

The **Monte-Carlo Country Club** (🕿 *(93) 78–20–45*) has high quality squash and tennis courts. The **Yacht Club de Monaco** (*Quai Antoine-1ᵉʳ* 🕿 *(93) 30–23–96*) runs sailing lessons from July to Aug and deep-sea fishing expeditions from July to Oct. The **Monte-Carlo Golf Club** (🕿 *(93) 41–09–11*) has a fine 18-hole course high on the slopes of Mt Agel, just in France.

Several new **beaches** have been created by importing millions of tons of sand, and though the texture is still rather rough, it's better than shingle. There are no free beaches. The best equipped beach complex is the **Monte-Carlo Beach** (*open May–Sept*). Also good are the **Monte-Carlo Sea Club** (*May–Sept*) and the **Plage du Larvotto** (*May–Sept*). The **Stade Nautique Rainier III** is an outdoor heated sea-water swimming pool (*open Mar–Oct*). Several big hotels open their pools to the public for a fee. **California Terrace** (a beauty centre) has the best indoor sea-water pool, with an open roof.

Mons ☆
Map 13F13. 41km (25 miles) w of Grasse; 14km (8¼ miles) N of Fayence. 83440 Fayence, Var. Population: 260.
One of the most exhilarating of the hinterland villages, superbly situated at a high altitude with marvellous views, steep steps and tiny alleys leading into little courtyards. Worth a detour.

Auberge Provençale (☎ (93) 76–38–33) for simple food, marvellous views.

Places nearby
Fayence (*14km (8¼ miles) s of Mons*)   A small, pleasant town spiralling up a hill top.

☙ Moulin de la Camandoule
Chemin Notre-Dame-des-Cyprès ☎ (94) 76–00–84 ▥▥ *16 rms* ▭ *10*
�──▭ ═ *Closed Nov to late Mar or early Apr.*
Location: Beside a river, in a 15-acre park. A 17thC olive oil mill converted into a delightful hotel. Large swimming pool, pretty bedrooms. No restaurant lunch Jul–Aug, but a barbecue by the pool. A restful spot.
🖼 🖼 ⚓ ⟨⟨ ⇌

═ France ✿
1 Rue du Château ☎ (94) 76–00–14 ▭ *to* ▥▥ ▭ ▰ 🪑 *Last orders 21.00. Closed Nov–Jan (except public holidays), Wed dinner, Thurs.*
M and Mme Choisy provide food that is cooked and presented with care and that represents real value. The cheapest set menu is simple though satisfying, and the higher priced ones provide a varied choice. Eat on the terrace overlooking the street or in the calm of the neat provincial dining-room. After dinner wander across to the main square – something often seems to be happening; if it's not a fête it might be a local talent contest, a cause for great hilarity among the rapt audience of locals. *Specialities: Poulet sauté aux pignons, manchons de canard en confit, brouillade aux truffes.*

Mougins
Map 15F14. 7km (4 miles) N of Cannes. 06250 Alpes-Mar. Population: 10,197 ℹ *Pl. du Commandant-Lamy*
☎ (93) 75–82–83.
This celebrated hill village and the countryside around is today Cannes' fashionable garden-suburb: the rich and famous have houses or villas here, or come to play golf at the nearby Cannes Country Club or to eat at one of Mougins' numerous quality restaurants. The village with its narrow streets is much-restored and now very sophisticated but it keeps its charm: it has a 15thC fortified gate and remains of ramparts. The tower of the Romanesque church affords the best panoramic view over this spectacular, if over-built, sector of the *Côte d'Azur*.

Just E of the village, up a narrow bumpy track E of D3, the beautiful chapel of **Notre-Dame-de-Vie** stands alone on a hill beside an avenue of cypresses. The chapel, which was once a hermitage, has a 15thC stone cross, a 17thC porch, and Roman inscriptions. It is usually closed (*save for Mass at 11.00 on Sun*), but you can peep through the window at the fine Baroque altar and large 16thC gilded retable. The nearby *mas* of Notre-Dame-de-Vie is the house where Picasso spent his final years and died.

☙ Le Mas Candille ✿
Bd. Rebuffel, 06250 Mougins
☎ (93) 90–00–85 ▥▥ *to* ▥▥
23 rms ▭ *23* �──▭ ═ 🖼 ⒶⒺ
▭ ⅦⅠⓈⒶ *Closed mid-Nov to mid-Dec.*

Location: On a wooded hillside, just w of the village. A 17thC white-walled farmhouse, lined by cypresses, is now an enchanting country hotel, offering civilized luxury at below luxury prices. The bedrooms are very pretty, many with 17thC beams and wood fires in winter. Yet, for all the *auberge's* gracefulness, it remains refreshingly unpretentious: the young Belgian *patron*, Jean Moëns, says he prefers to keep his hotel out of the four-star luxury bracket. (See restaurant.)

🏠 🖼 🛥 🍴 ⛷ 🐾

🍽 L'Amandier de Mougins ♥
Pl. du Commandant-Lamy
☎ (93) 90–00–91 ▥▥ 🖂 ▨▨
🚗 AE ⓞ VISA *Last orders 22.00. Closed Wed, Sat lunch, Jan to mid-Feb.*

Opened in 1977 by Roger Vergé, L'Amandier is a second outlet for the master chef's style of cooking, at prices less daunting than those of his mighty Moulin. The name suggests almonds, but the restaurant is a converted 18thC olive-oil mill, and the mill-wheel still stands in the dim, low-ceilinged dining-room. On fine days, make for the upstairs terrace with its far-reaching views. Service is cordial and unfussy but efficient, and the cooking deliciously light and varied. **Specialities:** *Terrine de filets de rougets de roche, suprême de loup de pays au beurre de basilic.*

🍽 Le Bistrot de Mougins ♥
Pl. du Village ☎ (93) 75–78–34
🖂 ▨▨ *Last orders 22.30. Closed Wed (except dinner July–Aug), mid-Nov to mid-Jan.*

After working for 10yr in New York, Alain Ballatoire and J. P. Giordano have returned to their native Provence. In their gaily decorated bistro, a 17thC vaulted cellar on the village square, they are proving that Mougins' gastronomic reputation does not have to equal high prices; the set menu is excellent value. The place, not surprisingly, is always full. Service, though courteous, has become rather mechanical under pressure. **Specialities:** *Tourte aux blettes, timbale de morue, pieds et paquets, tarte aux figues.*

🍽 La Ferme de Mougins
10 Av. St-Basile
☎ (93) 90–03–74 ▥▥ to ▥▥▥ 🖂
🖵 ▨▨ 🚗 AE ⓞ *Last orders 22.30 or 21.30 (winter). Closed Mon, Thurs lunch (except summer), mid-Feb to mid-March, mid-Nov to mid-Dec.*

It is most agreeable eating on the wide covered terrace overlooking a small swimming pool, and the cushioned chairs are delightfully comfortable. Service is thoughtful (shawls are provided when scantily-clad customers become chilly) and the food, though sometimes too ambitious, is very pleasantly light and tasty.

🍽 Le Mas Candille ♥
Address and ☎ *as hotel* ▥▥ *to* ▥▥▥
🖂 ▨▨ 🚗 AE ⓞ VISA *Last orders 22.00. Closed Tues–Wed lunch, mid-Nov to mid-Dec, Jan 7–21.*

The dining-room is airy and elegant, but the hotel's best feature of all is the flower garden where you can eat in fine weather overlooking the valley. Here M. Moëns has installed a large rustic candelabrum of red flickering candles, creating a romantic effect on summer evenings. The cooking is above average and good value. Try for example the Provençal menu dubbed *'clin d'oeil sur une cuisine d'Azur'.* (See hotel.)

🍽 Le Moulin de Mougins △
424 Chemin de Moulin
☎ (93) 75–78–24 ▥▥▥ 🖂 ▨▨ ▬
🚗 AE ⓞ VISA *Last orders 22.30. Closed Mon, Thurs lunch, mid-Nov to mid-Dec, mid-Feb to March.*

In France, a great chef is as celebrated and revered as a great actor or musician; Roger Vergé is among the elite, along with Paul Bocuse, Michel Guérard and a handful of others. He certainly looks the part – handsome, tall and silver-haired, he passes majestically at the end of the meal from table to table in his neat white robes, acknowledging the applause of his guests like an opera star taking a curtain-call. A few disgruntled diners may whisper the heresy that possibly his is not the best restaurant in Provence, but such voices are still relatively rare.

In 1969, Vergé took over this 16thC olive-oil mill (SE of Mougins, on the D3), and has since built it up into the *Côte's* most fashionable eating place. Famous faces are often in evidence, as you eat from real Limoges in the spacious *grande luxe* dining-room or under parasols in the garden. The food is not easy to describe for Vergé invents 50 new dishes each year and his menu changes often, but the sauces are always light and subtle, and the salads highly coloured and unusually flavoured. The cheeses, desserts and wines are all outstanding, with prices to match. *Specialities: Poupotton de truffe noire de Valréas, fricassée de homard au sauternes, noisettes d'agneau à la*

fleur de thym.

🍴 🏨 The restaurant has five sumptuous bedrooms overlooking the gardens (▰▰▰ *to* ▰▰▰).

━━ Another outstanding restaurant in Mougins is **Le Relais de Mougins** (*Pl. de la Mairie* ☎ *(93) 90–03 47* ▰▰▰ *to* ▰▰▰).

Shopping

Roger Vergé's shop, the **Boutique du Moulin**, in the village square, sells many food and drink products bearing his name. Superb jams, liqueurs and sauces.

Place nearby

Castellaras (*5km (3 miles) N of Mougins*)   From afar this seems to be yet another old hill village; in fact, it is a modern pastiche, the work of architect Jacques Couelle who also designed Port-la-Galère at *Théoule*. He built the hillcrest 'château' as a residence for a rich American in the 1920s. In the 1960s he added a group of unusual 'sculpted houses' which blend harmoniously with the landscape. Today the complex is a luxury holiday village-cum-country club, strictly private. (*For information on renting a holiday villa write to: Castellaras 06370 Mouans-Sartoux* ☎ *(93) 75–24–13*.)

La Napoule

*Map **15**G14. 8km (5 miles) w of Cannes. 06210 Mandelieu-La Napoule, Alpes-Mar. Population: 10,250 ℹ Rue Jean-Aulas*
☎ *(93) 49–95–31.*

A thriving little seaside resort, close to the E foothills of the *Esterel massif*. Long sandy beaches stretch round the Gulf of Napoule toward Cannes, and there is an excellent marina, golf course and casino.

Fondation Henry Clews

▨ ▨ ▨ *For opening times* ☎ *(93) 49–95–05.*

La Napoule's harbour is dominated by a great medieval castle, floodlit a lurid orange at night. It was bought in 1917 by the eccentric American sculptor Henry Clews, who extensively restored it, lived and worked there and was buried there on his death in 1937. Today, part of the château is a museum of his work: his dullish paintings, and his sculptured grotesques of animals, birds and gnarled naked human figures. They were inspired, so it is said, by pre-Columbian, Negro and medieval carvings. Even if you dislike the sculptures, you will probably enjoy the gardens with their views of sea and hills.

🏨 Recommended hotels for a seaside holiday include: **Ermitage de Riou** ▰▰ (*3 Bd. du Bord-de-Mer* ☎ *(93) 49–95–56* ▰▰▰); **Parisiana** (*5 Rue de l'Argentière* ☎ *(93) 49–93–02* ▰▱).

━━ L'Oasis △

Rue Jean-Honoré Carle ☎ *(93) 49–95–52* ▰▰▰▰ ▱ ▰ ▰ 🍴 *Last orders 21.30. Closed Mon dinner, Tues, Nov to mid-Dec.*

By common consent this is one of the finest restaurants in Provence and indeed in France, fully justifying its prices. Louis Outhier, *patron* and chef, was disciple of the great Fernand Point of La Pyramide at Vienne; and he follows in the master's steps, with a repertoire that balances classic dishes with his own inventions. He flirts with *nouvelle cuisine*, while avoiding its sillier excesses. Outhier, much more retiring than most of the jet-setting top French chefs, has built up his restaurant from a humble pension. Today, the low white villa has been converted into a series of small, rather formal dining-rooms with discreet pink-orange decor. Best is the ravishing flower-filled patio with its tall palm tree (hence the name). Service is as stylish as you would expect. The food is, simply, exquisite. **Specialities (among many):** Mille-feuille de saumon, loup en croûte, foie de canard au gingembre, cheeses and desserts.

Places nearby

La Napoule is the seaside suburb of the unlovely town of **Mandelieu** lying just inland to the N, beside a sprawling modern road junction. By contrast, the narrow D92, leading W out of town climbs up through Mimosa forests to the nearby heights of the wild **Tanneron massif**, where there are wide views over the coast and the mountains behind Grasse.

Nice ★

Map 15E15. 188km (117 miles) NE of Marseille. 06000 Alpes-Mar. Population: 346,620. Airport: 7km (4 miles) W of central Nice ☎(93) 21–30–30. Recorded tourist information in several languages: English ☎(93) 85–65–83 i 32 Rue de l'Hôtel des Postes ☎(93) 87–60–60.

The *Côte d'Azur*'s capital is more than simply the doyen of Europe's sea resorts. It is also a large commercial city, excitingly diverse, at once earthy and sophisticated, whose own busy life throbs on year round, irrespective of tourists.

The city extends along the silver shore of the Baie des Anges, sheltered by the curve of steeply rising hills behind. It is in two contrasting parts. To the E of the Paillon riverbed are the port and the shadowy twisting alleys of the Old Town, crowned by the rocky hill where the castle once stood. To the W of the Paillon area is the newer post-17thC town, and the mighty **Promenade des Anglais** with its palace-hotels and palm trees. Here in modern Nice all is chic and glitter, a blend of French elegance and Mediterranean sensuality. Life is lived late, and out of doors. This is no place for a sea-bathing holiday, for the beach is shingle, but for those who are lured by the attractions of a big town, Nice is enormous fun. All year, it offers a lively parade of high-quality entertainments – opera, art exhibitions, sporting events, festivals and shows of every kind from books to dogs, culminating in the famous Lenten Carnival and the Battle of the Flowers.

Greeks from Marseille founded Nice in the 4thC BC, and gave it the name Nikêa (from *Niké*, their goddess of victory) to mark a defeat of local tribesmen. Later came the Romans, who built a major town on the hill at Cimiez, now in the northern suburbs. Cimiez was then ruined by Saracen and barbarian invasions; but after the 10thC Nice began to flourish, first under the counts of Provence, then (after 1388) under the Italian house of Savoy. Between about 1450 and 1550 it was the centre of a notable school of religious painting, led by the Bréa family, much of whose work can still be seen in the region. In 1631 Nice suffered a fearful plague, and in 1792–96 was the scene of much toing-and-froing by the armies of Napoleon. The city remained under Savoy until 1860, when it was finally annexed to France.

By this time, Nice was a thriving seaside resort, thanks largely to the English, who had begun to winter here from the late 18thC, led by the novelist Smollett in 1763. As a resort, Nice was established long before Cannes or Menton. In 1822 the thriving English colony, frustrated by the difficult access to the shore, constructed a coastal path which became the great promenade and still bears their name. Then, after the arrival of the railway in 1864, the tourist boom gathered pace: British, Russian and other aristocrats poured in for every winter season,

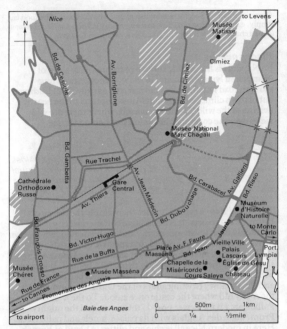

led by Queen Victoria. The Russians built their splendid cathedral, while smart hotels sprang up all along the front, with names like Westminster and West End. Today, echoes of that glory still linger: Heads of State still come to stay at the **Négresco**. But some of the other great hotels, such as the Ruhl, have gone, or have been turned into flats. Perforce, Nice today has broadened its tourist appeal since the Belle Epoque: it still has its luxury hotels of course, but now they cater more for the congress trade and package tours, than for duchesses and movie stars.

As in other big French cities, the mayor wields great power, and since 1928 Nice has been ruled by a kind of elective dynasty, the right-wing Médecin family. Jean Médecin was mayor for 37yr; on his death in 1965, his son Jacques took his place, and was re-elected for further 6yr terms in 1971, 1977 and 1983. His authoritarian style has been criticized; yet few would deny that he has done much to modernize and revitalize the city. Today it has various light industries, a new university with 15,000 students, and France's busiest international airport outside Paris. M. Médecin has built numerous road tunnels and underground car parks to cope with the very dense traffic; and he has created an elegant pedestrian zone in the heart of the modern town, near the sea.

Today, Nice is highly cosmopolitan: people come from the world over to visit or retire. But it is still dominated by its true inhabitants, the Niçois. Like most meridionals, they are at once easy-going and volatile – quick to pick a quarrel, just as quick to patch it up over a drink. Like Parisians they can be brusque at first, but it's not hard, if you make the effort, to make them smile.

160

Events: The carnival, an amazing spectacle of floats and flowers, occupies the two weeks preceding Lent, culminating in a firework display on Shrove Tues. The main Battle of the Flowers is on the day after Ash Wed on the Quai des États Unis. There are other flower battles during the summer.

In Feb, a Festival of Contemporary music takes place.

In Apr, there are the International Dog Show, Book Fair, spring Automobile Rally and Tennis Tournament.

In May, the Fêtes des Maïs is held every Sun in the Cimiez Gardens.

In July, the Grand Jazz Parade takes place in Cimiez Gardens – one of Europe's foremost jazz festivals attracting the biggest names. There is also an International Folklore Festival in the Jardin Albert-1er.

In Aug, a wine festival takes place in Cimiez Gardens.

In Oct, the Nice Philharmonic has its autumn music festival at the Opéra, and the autumn Automobile Rally is held.

Sights and places of interest
Chagall, Marc, Musée National ★
Av. Docteur Ménard ☎ *(93) 81 – 75 – 75.* 🎦 𝄪 *Open July—Sept, 10.00–19.00; Oct–June 10.00–12.30, 14.00–17.30. Closed Tues.*
For Chagall-lovers, this museum is a sublime treat. Opened in 1973, it houses the world's fullest collection of the artist's work. It was built specially for his suite of 17 large canvasses, the 'Biblical Message' painted over 13yr between 1954–67 when he was already an old man (he was born in Russia in 1887). In one large gallery, 12 of these paintings evoke the *Creation*, the *Garden of Eden*, the *Ark*, *Abraham*, *Moses*, and other biblical themes. In another, the *Song of Songs* is the inspiration for a five-part poetic series. Chagall uses bold, sensuous colours, combined with his visions of ingenuous fantasy, to convey the force of his spiritual and humanistic beliefs based on his Jewish faith. The result is a stunning combination of lyricism and seriousness of subject.

The museum has much else too, by Chagall. Outside, a large mosaic showing the prophet Elias rising to heaven in a chariot of fire; in the foyer a polychrome tapestry; in other rooms, numerous drawings, gouaches, sculptures. The graceful music room (where concerts are held each month in summer) is bathed in a deep blue light from Chagall's vivid stained-glass windows depicting the *Creation*.

The grand old man lived at St-Paul-de-Vence until his death in 1985 at the age of 97.

Château
Approach from far E end of Quai des États Unis. Ascend to castle either by 400 steps or lift.
A rocky promontory, 93m (280ft) high, forms a neat backdrop to the Promenade des Anglais. Here, the early Greeks set their acropolis, and the dukes of Savoy later built their castle. This was destroyed in 1706, on the orders of Louis XIV, by Marshal de Berwick, illegitimate son of James II of England who became a naturalized Frenchman and commander in the French armies. Today the site is a public garden, planted with trees, but is still known as the Château. On the sw side of the hill (*use the same lift*) is the **Musée Naval** in the Tour Bellanda (🎦 *open 10.00–12.00, 14.00–17.00 in winter, 14.00–19.00 in summer, closed Tues, mid-Nov to Dec*) where there are collections of historic weapons, models of old warships, paintings of Nice in the 19thC. To the E of the Château is Nice's harbour, **Port Lympia**, built in 1750 and since extended. The harbour is crammed with fishing smacks and pleasure boats and it is here that the ferries leave for Corsica.

Chéret, Musée ☆
33 Av. des Baumettes ☎ *(93) 44–50–72* 🔳 🎦 *Open June–Sept 10.00–12.00, 15.00–18.00; Oct–May 10.00–12.00, 14.00–17.00. Closed Mon, first two weeks in Nov.*
This is Nice's largest museum of art, with works ranging from Italian and Flemish primitives through to paintings by Braque and ceramics by Picasso. The Van Loo family, who worked in the area, are very well represented, as is Carpeaux, who died in Nice. There are also works by

Nice

Fragonard and by the Impressionists Monet, Sisley and Renoir,
including Renoir's *Les Grandes Baigneuses*. There are examples of the
St-Tropez school, notably by Signac, and a superb collection of the
works of Raoul Dufy who captured the sparkle of the Riviera with his gay
and witty paintings. This varied collection also includes two rooms
devoted to oriental art.

Cimiez

The hill of Cimiez in the N suburbs, with its big villas and gardens, was
once the smart residential district of Nice. At the top of the Bd. de Cimiez
there looms a titanic monstrosity in late 19thC Rococo style – the former
hotel Regina where Queen Victoria used to winter. Today it is a block of
flats and shows few traces of its former glory.

Just to the E lies the Roman settlement of Cimiez, recently excavated.
It includes a small amphitheatre and the remains of 3rdC Roman baths;
the 10m (33ft) hunk of masonry is what is left of the Temple of Apollo.
This area is now a public park, often used for festivals. On its E side
stands a former monastic church, 16thC with later additions: the *trompe
l'oeil* is pure 19thC Gothic, but inside (in the first chapel on the right, the
last chapel on the right up the nave and the chapel opposite) you will find
three of the Bréa family's finest paintings on wood. These sights are
worth a visit, but Cimiez's foremost attraction is its **Matisse Museum**
(see below).

Masséna, Musée

*65 Rue de France ☎ (93) 88–11–34. Open 10.00–12.00,
14.00–17.00. Closed Mon, two weeks in Nov.*

The imposing palace in which the museum is housed was built in the
1890s by the great grandson of Marshal Masséna, Prince of Essling, son
of an innkeeper at nearby Levens. Masséna, who was one of Napoleon's
greatest marshals, is one of Nice's foremost sons – another equally
renowned is Garibaldi – and there are memories of them both in the
museum. The palace now belongs to the Ville de Nice and its fine
Empire-style rooms on the ground floor are used for civic receptions.
Upstairs are some Bréa and Durandi primitives as well as collections of
oriental jewellery, pottery, armour, and artifacts illustrating local
folklore and customs. Especially interesting are the rooms devoted to
Nice's history: early pictures of the city, souvenirs of Napoleon,
Masséna, Garibaldi, the 1860 plebiscite and the Carnival.

Masséna, Place et Rue

The Place Masséna is the hub of modern Nice: its imposing arcaded
houses were built in the 1830s, in 17thC Genoese style. To the SW, by the
sea, is the elegant **Jardin Albert-1ᵉʳ**, used as an open-air theatre in
summer. To the W the busy Rue Masséna and a few adjoining streets have
recently been closed to traffic and paved over, with fountains and
flower-pots. With its many boutiques, open at night, pavement cafés and
pizzerias, the area attracts the *beau monde*: shopping or window
shopping, meeting friends or just strolling by.

Westward sweeps the **Promenade des Anglais**. Strident with traffic, it
has now been somewhat upstaged by the Rue Masséna as the place for
strollers to be seen. But the sea breezes and the palm trees still attract
their crowds. A mile NE of the Pl. Masséna, up the Paillon valley, is the
new and impressive **Palais des Expositions** (exhibitions centre), today
far more important to the Niçois than the sea walk that the English
built.

Matisse, Musée ☆

*164 Av. des Arènes-de-Cimiez ☎ (93) 81–59–57 ◫ ⚡ ⚔ Open
May–Sept, 10.00–12.00, 14.30–18.30; Oct–Apr 10.00–12.00,
14.00–17.00. Closed Sun, Mon in Nov.*

Henri Matisse lived and worked for much of his life in Nice and Cimiez
until his death there in 1954. He lies buried in the cemetery near to this
museum. The collection spans his working life: 30 paintings ranging
from his sober early period, through the influence of the Impressionists
to the bright colours and simple shapes of his maturity, as in *Nature
Morte aux Grenades*, 1947. There are also many of his drawings, as well as
engravings, sculpture and book illustrations. His sketches and models
for the **Chapelle du Rosaire** at *Vence* are contained in two rooms and
spread about the museum is a collection of his furniture and personal
effects.

In the same building, the **Musée Archéologique** contains pottery,
jewellery, statuary and sarcophagi found on the adjacent Roman sight.

Nice

Orthodoxe Russe, Cathédrale 🏛 ✝
Bd. du Tsarevitch 🚇 ✒ ✗ *Open 9.30–12.00, 14.30–18.00. Closed Sun morning.*

Nice's formerly large Russian colony may be dying out, but you can still hear plenty of Russian voices at their fine cathedral in the w suburbs, built in 1903. Its sumptuous exterior, with five bulbous, green-gold cupolas, is matched by the interior where rich ikons adorn the altar.

Vieille Ville

This triangle bordered by the **Château**, the sea, and the open space of the Paillon river bed makes a startling and delightful contrast to sophisticated modern Nice. The Old Town is itself in two parts: the 17thC quarter by the sea, with its orderly grid of streets; and, to the N, the older part, a maze of narrow alleys, full of little shops and bistros, teeming with its own noisy plebian life. It is very Italian – you could well be in the back streets of Genoa – and bears witness to Nice's long past as part of Italy. Today it is being restored: its façades are being repainted in the traditional ochre colours, and artists and artisans are settling there.

A stroll through the Old Town could begin with the **Palais Lascaris** (*Rue Droite* 🚇 ✗), a sumptuous 17thC Genoese-style mansion, finely restored and decked out with furniture, paintings and tapestries of the period. Northeast of the Palace is a statue to *Catherine Ségurane*, the Niçoise folk-heroine who, dagger in hand, bravely repulsed the Turkish besiegers in 1543 – or so it is said. To the s of the Palace are some fine 17th and 18thC Italian Baroque churches, notably the **Chapelle de la Miséricorde** (*Cours Saleya*); also the **Église de Gesù** (*Rue Droite*).

Visit, too, the **Opera House** (*Rue St-François-de-Paul*); the **Galerie de Malacologie** (🔲 *Cours Saleya*), with its remarkable collection of molluscs; and the markets in the **Cours Saleya**, once the home of the world-famous flower market.

Just N of the Old Town is the ambitious **Muséum d'Histoire Naturelle** (*60 Bd. Risso*) which includes aquariums full of exotic fish.

Hotels

Alfa
30 Rue Masséna, 06000 Nice
☎(93) 87–88–63 ▮▮ to ▮▮▮
38 rms 🛏 38 ▤ ▤ AE ⊕ ⊕ VISA
Location: Centrally positioned close to the sea on the attractive and traffic-free Rue Masséna. A small modernized hotel, friendly and efficiently run. Though it's in the pedestrian zone, you can park the car within 75m (80yd) to unload baggage.
✦ 🖦

Aston Concorde
12 Av. Félix-Faure, 06000 Nice
☎(93) 80–62–52 ✆470290 ▮▮▮▮
157 rms 🛏 157 ▤ ⇌ AE ⊕
⊕ VISA
Location: Central, very near the Pl. Masséna and the Vieille Ville. The most pleasing feature of this large, modern hotel is its wide terrace on the roof, with deck-chairs, parasols and panoramic views; buffet lunches are served in summer. Apart from this, it's not a hotel of any great character, though it has every comfort.
✦ ♿ ▢ 🖦 ➍ ◁ 🎬

Le Gourmet Lorrain ✿
7 Av. Santa Fior, 06100 Nice
☎(93) 84–90–78 ▮▮ 15 rms
🛏 5 ▤ ⇌ AE

Location: 2km (1 mile) N of main station in a side street in the N suburbs. Most unusual for Nice, this small hotel on the outskirts seems more like a rural inn, and is run in a personal style by the charming young owners, the Leloups (he from Lorraine, she from Dunkerque).

"We try to create a family party spirit, encouraging our guests to get to know each other," they say – and they succeed, without overdoing it. (See restaurant.)
🏠 ▢ 🖦 ➍ ➩ for children.

Négresco ▦ 🏛
37 Promenade des Anglais
☎(93) 88–39–51 ✆460040 ▮▮▮▮
160 rms 🛏 160 ▤ ⇌ AE ⊕
⊕ VISA
Location: Half-way along the promenade. This vast white wedding-cake palace, one of the world's most famous hotels, has been classified a '*monument historique*' by the French government. And justly, for its owners have been careful to restore it to the 1912 style in which it was conceived. In this temple to Edwardian grandeur, the bellboys still wear red breeches and white gloves. The huge circular **salon royal** is the setting for a Baccarat

163

chandelier that was made for the Tsar, and for 600sq. m (720sq. yd) of Aubusson carpet. Works of art by Picasso, Léger and Cocteau adorn the walls; even the ground floor lavatories, theatrically ornate, are worth a look. Upstairs, the sumptuous bedrooms are in varied styles such as Louis XIV, Empire, and Napoleon III. It goes without saying that comfort and service are beyond reproach.

Across the years, practically anyone who is anyone has stayed at the Négresco – countless film stars and many reigning monarchs. And today the hotel still attracts many of the world's top names in the arts and politics. In 1980 the then President Giscard d'Estaing stayed here with 27 African Heads of State. The 1980s may be a far cry from 1912, but the Négresco can convince you that little has changed. (See restaurant, Chantecler.)

🍴🎋♿️🅿️🗄🏊🚲◁≈🏖

Nouvel Hôtel
19 Bd. Victor-Hugo, 06000 Nice
☎ *(93) 84–86–85* 🔳 *to* 🔳
50 rms 🔳 *19* AE *Closed Nov.*
Location: In a tree-lined street not far from the Pl. Masséna and Promenade des Anglais; entry next door to the Banque de Rothschild. This is recommended among the many moderately priced hotels in Nice. Situated in a tree-lined street next to the Banque de Rothschild, the hotel is in an old, typically French town block, where the rooms have high ceilings and tall, shuttered French windows. The interior is not very modern, but it has character and is comfortable and friendly.

🏊🗄

La Pérouse
11 Quai Rauba Capeu. 06300 Nice ☎ *(93) 62–34–63*
🗄*461411* 🔳 *to* 🔳 *66 rms* 🔳 *66*
🔳🚗 AE 💳 VISA
Location: Half-way up the s side of the castle hill, facing the bay; ascend by lift. The best situated hotel in Nice is also one of the most attractive and well run. It is built high into the side of the rock in the Château gardens and many bedrooms have balconies with blissful views of the Baie des Anges below. Although there is no restaurant, light lunches are served in summer beside the heated swimming pool, or in the idyllic garden full of lemon trees. Some bedrooms have kitchenettes.

There's also a roomy bar, with a log fire in winter, a discreet sunbathing terrace, and a sauna.

🍴🎋🗄🏊🚲◁≈🏖

Relais de Rimiez
128 Av. de Rimiez
☎ *(93) 81–18–65* 🔳 *25 rms*
🔳 *25* 🔳🏊🚗
Location: Perched on a hill in the suburbs behind Nice, only 10min by car from the centre. A small modern hotel in Provençal style, surrounded by countryside and absolutely quiet. The ground-floor rooms give directly onto the garden; upper ones have balconies and a fine view. No restaurant, but a pleasant bar and tearoom.

🍴🎋🚲◁≈🍸

Sofitel Splendid
50 Bd. Victor-Hugo, 06000 Nice
☎ *(93) 88–69–54* 🗄*460938* 🔳
130 rms 🔳 *130* 🔳🏊⚡️ AE
CB 💳 VISA 🔳
Location: West-central, 350m (400yd) from the promenade. A top-class hotel with great character. The Tschann family have owned it since 1905, when German and Russian princes were often among their guests. In 1964 they totally rebuilt it, in a modern style, but they have managed to preserve in this new setting the classic tradition of personal service. All is elegance and discretion, even if the princes have long departed to be replaced by a clientele varying from Japanese bankers to British rock groups. A special delight is the swimming pool on the roof eight floors up, with splendid views. Beside it are a bar, sauna, shallow pool for children and walled-off sun-terrace.

🏊🗄🏊◁≈🏖

📖 Other hotels that can be recommended are: **Cicognes** (*16 Rue Maccarani* ☎ *(93) 88–65–02* 🔳); **Frantel** (*28 Av. Notre-Dame* ☎ *(93) 80–30–24* 🔳); **Gounod** (*3 Rue Gounod* ☎ *(93) 88–26–20* 🔳); **La Malmaison** (*48 Bd. Victor-Hugo* ☎ *(93) 87–62–56* 🔳); **Méridien** (*1 Promenade des Anglais* ☎ *(93) 82–25–25* 🔳); **L'Oasis** (*23 Rue Goudon* ☎ *(93) 88–12–29* 🔳); **Plaza** (*12 Av. Verdun* ☎ *(93) 87–80–41* 🔳); **Trianon** (*15 Av. Auber* ☎ *(93) 88–30–69* 🔳); **Victoria** (*33 Bd. Victor-Hugo* ☎ *(93) 88–39–60* 🔳); **Westminster Concorde** (*27 Promenade des Anglais* ☎ *(93) 88–29–44* 🔳).

Nice

Restaurants

Barale ♣
39 Rue Beaumont
☎ (93) 89–17–94 ▯▮ *Dinner
only. Last orders 24.00. Closed
Sun, Mon.*
A visit to Nice's most eccentric
restaurant is an instructive
experience. Mme Barale, a volatile,
elderly widow, is a lady of iron
caprice who may or may not deign
to feed you: you *must* ring up first.
You then eat what she chooses to
give you, from a set menu scrawled
on a blackboard in her large
museum/dining-room. The Barale
family have owned this place for
100yr and they surround diners
with their extraordinary collection
of bygones including two vintage
Citroens, a 19thC printing press
and cash register, and a gigantic
pair of ancient bellows. Later, the
merry widow, hot-foot from her
stove, stages an impromptu cabaret
act, taunting her guests and telling
risqué stories. The cooking,
needless to say, is archetypally
Niçois, and very enjoyable.
*Specialities: Socca, salade niçoise,
estofinado, ravioli, pissaladière.*

Le Bistrot de la Promenade
7–9 Promenade des Anglais
☎ (93) 81–63–48 ▯▮ ▤ AE ⓓ
VISA ▭ *Last orders 22.30.
Closed first fortnight Dec, latter
part of Jan.*
A big, efficient brasserie with an
open terrace. Inventive cooking and
good value. American bar at the
back, with pianist.

Boccaccio
7 Rue Masséna
☎ (93) 87–71–76 ▯▮ ▭ 🚗
AE CB ⓓ VISA *Last orders 23.00.*
The tables spill out across the
traffic-free street, and the outdoor
display of fresh shellfish looks
enticing. For the weary shopper or
sightseer in downtown Nice, this
spruce little Italian-run restaurant
offers the solace of good
bouillabaisse or *fruits de mer*. Or you
can take just the pasta.

Chantecler 🛏
*Address and ☎ and ⓣ as
Hôtel Négresco*
☎ (93) 88–39–51 ▮▮▮ ▭ ▮ 🚗
▤ AE ⓓ CB VISA *Last orders
23.00. Closed mid-Oct to end of
Nov.*
The very elegant Chantecler, the
Négresco's main restaurant, has
recently won high fame because of
the dazzling success of its young

chef, Jacques Maximin. He is a
leader of the new wave of French
chefs, apostles of *nouvelle cuisine.*
Light and very inventive, his
cooking is the best in Nice. His art
lies in his ability to take classic local
dishes and recreate them to suit
modern tastes and appetites, for
example by using a julienne of
coquilles St-Jacques as a stuffing for
ravioli. His inventiveness seems to
know no bounds. *Specialities:
Raviolis de homard au bouillon de
crustacés, loup en rôti au couli
d'olives, tian d'agneau niçois.*
(See hotel, **Négresco**.)

Chez les Pêcheurs
18 Quai des Docks
☎ (93) 89–59–61 ▮▮ ▭ ▮ 🚗
*Last orders 22.00. Closed Tues
dinner and Wed (winter), Tues and
Thurs lunch (summer), Nov to
mid-Dec.*
Dedicated to Niçois fish, this
cheerful restaurant down by the
port has roses on each table and a
tank of live lobsters by one wall.
Roger Barbate is the *'maître
cuisinier de France'*. *Specialities:
Bouillabaisse, suprême de loup a
l'estragon, filet de St-Pierre à
l'oseille.*

L'Estocaficada ☗
2 Rue de l'Hôtel-de-Ville
☎ (93) 80–21–64 ▭ ▭ ▮
*Last orders 21.00. Closed Fri
dinner, Sat.*
A very simple family-run bistro.
The name of the restaurant is
Niçois for stockfish, and the
cooking is authentic Niçois.
*Specialities: Bouillabaisse, soupe de
poisson au pistou, salade niçoise,
squid, fresh sardines, and the
eponymous dried cod.*

La Farigoula ☗ ♣
6 bis Rue de France Pietonne
☎ (93) 87–11–21 ▭ to ▯▭
▮ ⓓ VISA *Last orders 22.30.
Closed Sun.*
Situated in the smart pedestrian
zone w of the Pl. Masséna, this is
one of the best places to eat at
modest cost in the newer part of
town: neat and pretty, *auberge-*
style, it has red checked tablecloths
and a tank full of live trout. The
cooking is partly Niçois, partly
from Tourraine.

Le Gourmet Lorrain
Address and ☎ as hotel ▯ *to
▯ ▭ ▤ ▤ AE Last orders
21.30. Closed Sun dinner, Mon,*

165

Aug, first week in Jan.

Alain Leloup has justly won prizes for his cooking, served in the somewhat formal dining-room decorated in Louis XIII style. The dishes complement the surroundings for they are mainly classic – a welcome change from Niçois *cuisine*. Note the big silver duck press used for making *canard au sang*. There is, however, one notable oddity on the menu: *filet d'autruche aux cèpes* (the ostrich meat comes frozen from Australia). There is an outstanding list of 900 wines and *digestifs*, some over 100yr old, and finely-kept cigars too. **Specialities:** *Filet de boeuf bordelaise, rognons de veau aux pétales de truffes, civet de langouste*. (See hotel.)

Le Palais Jamaï
3 Quai des Deux-Emmanuels
☎ (93) 89–53–92 ▮▮▮ ▤▤ [AE] [VISA]
Last orders 22.45. Closed Mon, Tues lunch, Mar.
Excellent Moroccan cuisine served in a dream-like exotic setting, down by the harbour.

La Poularde chez Lucullus
9 Rue Gustave Deloye
☎ (93) 85–22–90 ▮▮▮ ▯ ▰▰ ▰
▤▤ [AE] [◈] [◐] Last orders 22.00.
Closed Wed, mid-July to mid-Aug.
This has long been one of the great classic restaurants of Nice, though critics are divided on its merits and it is no longer in the very top bracket. The ambience is somewhat lugubrious in the large Provençal style dining-room with its archways and dark wooden beams. But the service is attentive, and the food often excellent. Some Niçois dishes, some traditional French ones. **Specialities:** *Civet de lièvre, suprême de sole Lucullus, capilotade de volaille*.

Queenie
19 Promenade des Anglais
☎ (93) 88–52–50 ▮▮▮ ▯ ▰▰ [AE]
[◐] [◈] [◐] [VISA] Last orders 2.00
(summer), 24.00 (winter).
A popular and elegant bar/brasserie where you can eat out of doors right on the promenade, beside the palm trees, and watch the people go by (and the noisy traffic too). Or you can opt for the large indoor *salle*, cool and fairly quiet. The clientele is cosmopolitan, smart and not-so-smart. Service tends to be rather haphazard and offhand, but the cooking is fresh and varied, and

fairly reasonably priced for this part of town. **Specialities:** *Vivier de homards, langoustes et fruits de mer, magret de canard flambé, glaces maison*.

Le Safari
1 Cours Saleya
☎ (93) 80–18–44 ▮▮▮ ▯ ▰ [AE]
[◐] Last orders 23.00. Closed Mon (except July–Aug).
The locals themselves, especially young ones, flock to this very animated and informal bistro by the market place. With its loud pop music and rapid, take-it-or-leave-it service, there's more than a touch of the Boulevard St-Germain about the place; yet the cooking is varied, good and truly *niçois*, with the Piedmontese influence showing through clearly. An interesting feature is an open wood fire, for grills and pizzas. **Specialities:** *Trouchia, alouettes sans tête, bagna cauda*.

La Taca d'Oli ●
35 Rue Pairolière
☎ (93) 80–44–15 ▮▯ ▯
Last orders 23.00.
Jokey posters cover the walls, and your elbow may be in your neighbour's plate at this student-filled, Bohemian little bistro in an Old Town alley. The exuberant *pied noir* owner greets all his guests with effusive familiarity whether he knows them or not. The food is good and plentiful: the *cuisses de grenouille provençale* often seem to come from frogs the size of small chickens: the *patron* says they're from China. **Specialities:** *Pâtés au pistou, ris de veau aux coquilles St-Jacques*.

La Venta ●● ✿
4 Bd. Guynemer
☎ (93) 55–05–74 ▯ ▯ ▰▰ [◐]
[VISA] Last orders 22.00. Closed Wed, mid-Nov to mid-Dec.
Nicolas Scaltriti (who speaks perfect English) offers excellent value at his romantic and sympathetic little restaurant near the port. He cooks; his wife serves, graciously. Dim lights and Mexican style decor add to the appeal, especially in the evenings. The food is mainly Provençal (*sardines à l'escabèche, tripes niçoise*, creamy *lapin à la moutarde*), with a fine *paella aux fruits de mer* added for good measure.
Other restaurants worth trying in Nice are: **L'Ane Rouge** (*7 Quai des Deux Emmanuels* ☎ (93) 89–49–63 ▮▮▮); **Bon Coin**

Breton (*5 Rue Blacas*
☎ *(93) 85–17–01* **❚▢**); **Chez**
Puget (*4 bis Rue Gustave-Deloye*
☎ *(93) 85–25–84* **❚▢** *to* **❚❚▢**); **Le**
Madrigal (*7 Av. G-Clémenceau*
☎ *(93) 88–72–23* **❚❚▢**); **La**
Méranda (*4 Rue de la Terrasse* **❚❚▢**
to **❚❚▢**).

Restaurant nearby

St-Martin-du-Var (*27km (17*
miles) N *of Nice*).

Auberge de la Belle Route
06670 St-Martin-du-Var
☎ *(93) 08–10–65* **❚❚▢** **▢** **▬** AE
⊕ ⊕ VISA *Last orders 21.30.*

Closed Sun dinner, Mon, Feb.
Though the restaurant is set like a
roadhouse, slap beside the N202
highway, 2.5km (1½ miles) s of St-
Martin, the interior is all elegance,
with silver candlesticks and Louis
XIII chairs. Since the *patron* Jean-
François Issautier is one of the best
chefs in the area, and his wife an
excellent hostess, this is a favourite
place with the Niçois for out-of-
town dining. The menu is short
and lacks a wide choice but is
intelligent. *Specialities:*
Fleurs de courgettes à la coque,
feuillardine de loup au coulis de
poivron doux, noisettes d'agneau.

Nightlife
Those in search of exciting nightlife may find Nice a little staid
and disappointing; none of the discos are really fashionable. Not
only has the Palais de la Méditeranée casino closed down after
its long scandal of corruption, but the famous Casino Ruhl has
now closed its doors.

Nightspots in Nice include the following: **La Camargue** (*5 Pl. Charles-*
Félix **♫** **☰**); **Le Charlot** (*8 Rue St-François-de-Paul* **Y**), a gay bar;
Club 54 (*Rue des Ponchettes* **Y** **✕**); **Findlatters** (*6 rue Léponte* **❚▬**); **Le**
Musting (*19 rue Droite* **Y** **●**); **Pam-Pam** (*Pl. Masséna* **Y** **♫**); **Au**
Pizzaiolo (*4 bis Rue de Pont Vieux* **✌** **▬** **✕**).

Shopping
The main shopping streets are **Av. J. Médecin** and the
pedestrian **Rue Masséna**, the latter being full of smart
boutiques. **Galerie J. Soisson**, at no. 4, sells beautiful jewellery
and ivory, and at no. 28, **Actuel**, open every day until 22.00,
sells books and newspapers, many of them in English or
American.
   The best department store is **Galeries Lafayette**
(*Pl. Masséna*). For locally made clothes and fabrics try
La Boutique Provençale (*55 Rue de France*).
   Marotte is a good chain of hairdressers, while on the tenth
floor of the Hotel Méridien there is a health and beauty centre.
   Most traditional shops are in the Old Town. **Henri Auer** (*7*
Rue St-François-de-Paul) sells its own delicious chocolates,
pastries and crystallized fruits. Almost opposite, at no. 14,
Alziari also sells its own produce: olives, olive oil and olive-oil-
based products. At **La Confiserie du Vieux-Nice** (*Quai*
Papacino), you can watch the gaily coloured jams being cooked
and prepared for sale. Nearby, **Village Ségurane** (*28 Rue*
Ségurane) is a good antique market full of varied and tempting
stalls.
   The Cours Saleya, in the Old Town, is the home of Nice's
flower market and **fruit and vegetable market** (*open Tues–Sun,*
closed Mon) – best to go in the morning. This is a good spot to
shop for a picnic or just to gaze at the profusion of produce. In
the nearby Rue St-François is the **fish market** where you can
inspect the contents of your **bouillabaisse** in its natural state.
   Nice has its share of hypermarkets, the best of which are just
w of town. **Géant Casino** is at Magnan in the w suburbs, while
Carrefour is just N of the airport, w of N202. Just w of the
airport is **Cap 3000**, a gigantic new shopping complex,

complete with parking, restaurants, cafés and a multilingual information desk (*open 11.00–22.00, closed Sun*).

Places nearby
Several hilltops within close reach of Nice offer splendid views of the coast: **Mont Alban**, **Mont Boron** or **Mont Chauve d'Aspremont**. Close behind Nice are some pleasant hill villages, notably **Falicon** and **Aspremont** and, further away, **La Roquette**.

Nîmes ☆
*Map **8**E2. 121km (75 miles) NW of Marseille. 30000 Gard. Population: 133,950. Airport: Garons, 8km (5 miles) to S* ☎ *(66) 20–12–55* **i** *Rue Auguste* ☎ *(66) 67–29–11.*

Nîmes likes to call itself 'the Rome of France'. The parallel may be far-fetched, but the city does contain two of the best-preserved buildings of Classical Rome: the **Arena**, and the temple known as the **Maison Carrée**. The Romans came across a gushing spring here, and so founded a town. Then Augustus, after defeating Antony at Actium, settled a large colony of veterans here from the Egyptian campaign: hence the crocodile chained to a palm tree which the city still bears on its crest.

Nîmes lies at the frontier of Provence and Languedoc, and really belongs to both. Like the rest of Languedoc, it has always been strongly hostile to the central power in Paris. In the 16thC it was the headquarters of the Huguenots' 'heretics', and played a large role in the Camisard revolt after the revocation of the Edict of Nantes in 1685. Much blood was spilt – and Nîmois have neither forgotten nor forgiven.

Today this is a large commercial city of sprawling new suburbs and dusty boulevards. Apart from a small, well-restored sector of the Old Town, it is not a very elegant place. But it has a lively cultural life, though it is not a university town. Its major industries include fruit-canning, shoe-making and textiles. A rough twilled cloth for overalls was first

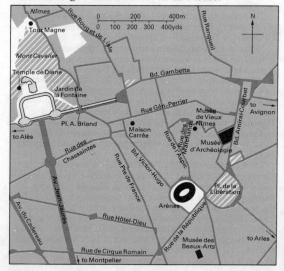

manufactured here in the 19thC and marked abroad as *'de Nîmes'*; the name was contracted to 'denim'.

Guided tours of Nîmes take place daily in July and Aug and from time to time during the rest of the year. For details ask at the tourist office.

Events: At Whitsun, Feria de Pentecôte (Whitsun Festival), five days (Thurs – Mon) of bullfights, bull races, folklore displays, concerts, dancing in the streets, etc: one of the great festivals of Provence.

In July, an international jazz festival. Also in July – Aug, an international folklore festival.

In May – Oct, bullfights take place two or three times a month in the Arena mostly on Sun afternoons. The toreadors are local and Spanish. The bulls are from the Camargue, and are fought to the death.

The last weekend in September features a wine festival, bull races and folklore displays.

As for year-round events, Nîmes is a lively and interesting cultural centre, especially for music. All summer there are frequent concerts, outdoors in the Jardins de la Fontaine or in local churches and mansions. Sometimes operas are staged in the Arena. From Nov to Mar, there are operas in the municipal theatre.

Sights and places of interest

Arènes *(Arena)* 🏛 ☆

Bd. Victor-Hugo 🚾 *One ticket covers admission to the Arènes, Maison Carrée, Jardins de la Fontaine et Temple de Diane and Tour Magne. Open July–Aug 9.00–19.00; Apr–June, Sept 9.00–12.00, 14.00–19.00; Oct–Mar 9.00–12.00, 14.00–17.00.*

This majestic arena is slightly smaller (21,000 spectators) than the one at *Arles* but otherwise very similar, and is one of the best-preserved of the 70 extant arenas of the Roman world. In the 5thC it became a fortress, and afterwards the headquarters of an autonomous corps of knights. From the 13thC it became a tenement inhabited by 2,000 poor people who built 150 houses. The Romans used it for chariot races, and for combats where gladiators fought with each other or with wild beasts. Today there are frequent bullfights there in summer.

Jardin de la Fontaine et Temple de Diane ☆

Quai de la Fontaine. Garden open daylight hours. Temple – for entry details and opening times see Arènes.

The garden was created in the 18thC, in typically French ornamental style – all urns and statues, pools and curving balustrades. At its top end, on the slopes of Mont Cavalier, the **Fontaine de Nemausus** gushes into a basin of clear water. Here the Romans built baths, a theatre and a temple: little of all this now remains, save the massive ruin of the temple, to Diana, with its great vaulted arch.

Maison Carrée ☆

Bd. Victor Hugo. Open Easter–Sept 9.00–12.00, 14.00–19.00; Oct–Mar 9.00–12.00, 14.00–17.00 (but closed Sun afternoon and May 1).

The so-called 'square house' is in fact rectangular. It is a temple, built in Hellenic style by Agrippa in c.20 BC, and is generally regarded as the loveliest of all surviving Roman temples, as finely proportioned as those of Classical Greece itself. It is well preserved, too, despite its chequered history: since the Middle Ages it has been used in turn as the town hall, a private residence, a stable, a church, and now a museum.

It stands on a raised platform, facing what used to be the Forum. Steps lead up to its peristyle of fluted columns, where the carving is superbly delicate, both on the capitals and on the frieze above them. The *cella* (interior) is walled in, and now contains a collection of local Roman finds: among them, an imposing statue of *Apollo*, and the *'Venus of Nîmes'*, found in fragments and pieced together. The original mosaic centrepiece of the *cella's* floor is in remarkable condition.

Nîmes

Tour Magne
Open Easter–Sept 9.00–12.00, 14.00–19.00; Oct–Mar 9.00–12.00, 14.00–17.00 (but closed Sun afternoon and May 1).

This massive Roman tower stands high on the wooded hill of Mont Cavalier, behind the Jardins de la Fontaine. From the garden only its top is visible: the best view of it is from the Rue Mallarmé to its E. It was built, probably as a watch-tower, near the end of the 1stC BC: originally 36m (120ft) high, it has lost its upper 10m (30ft). From the platform on its top, there are splendid views of the city, the mountains of W Provence, and even the Pyrénées on a clear day.

Vieux Nîmes ☆
The W quarter just N of the Arena is as elegant and picturesque a *vieille ville* as almost any in Provence – a contrast to the rest of dusty, workaday Nîmes. Here a few streets, notably the **Rues de l'Aspic, de Bernis** and **des Marchands**, are now a pedestrian zone, beautifully restored, lined with smart boutiques, and full of interesting surprises. Push open the door of **no. 14 Rue de l'Aspic**, and you find yourself in a private courtyard, flanked by a strikingly handsome 17thC double stairway. Look, too, at the Renaissance gateway of **no. 8** and the charming 15thC facade of **no. 3 Rue de Bernis**. The **Passage des Marchands**, off no. 12 Rue des Marchands, is a lovely Renaissance gallery with low vaulted arches and balustrades, now full of handicraft and antique shops.

Close by, the 11thC **cathedral of St Castor** was largely rebuilt in the 19thC: of the frieze on its facade, the scenes from Genesis on the left are originals but the rest are copies. Next door is the **Musée de Vieux Nîmes** (▨ *closed Sun*), housed in the former Bishop's Palace: it has furniture, pottery and costumes, and two rooms devoted to bullfighting. The **Musée d'Archéologie** (▨ *closed Sun*) has Greek pottery dating from the 8thC BC and a display of objects evoking the daily life of a Gallo-Roman family. Just to its N is the Roman **Porte d'Auguste**, built in 15BC.

The **Musée des Beaux-Arts** (*Rue de la Cité Foulc* ▨ *closed Tues*) contains some unremarkable works by Rubens, Poussin, Rodin and many others. Its star exhibit, in the centre of the ground-floor room is a huge Roman mosaic found at Nîmes in 1883 and thought to represent the marriage of Admetus.

☙ Hotels worth recommending in Nîmes are: **Impérator** ▨▨ (*Quai de la Fontaine* ☎ *(66) 21–90–30* ▮▮▮), with a vast, pompous Victorian foyer and luxuriant garden behind; **Louvre** (*2 Sq. de la Couronne* ☎ *(66) 67–22–75* ▯ *to* ▮▮), a well modernized hotel in a 17thC building, but uneven service; **Michel** (*14 Bd. Amiral-Courbet* ☎ *(66) 67–26–23* ▯ *to* ▮▮), functional but friendly with a pavement terrace; **Novotel** (*Bd. Périphérique* ☎ *(66) 84–60–20* ▮▮), an excellent modern motel, attractively designed with an inviting atmosphere.

═ Good restaurants in Nîmes are few. One is at the **Hôtel Impérator** (*Quai de la Fontaine* ☎ *(66) 21–90–30* ▮▮▮), where good classic *cuisine* is served on the lovely terrace or in the uninspiring dining-room. At **La Louve** (*1 Rue de la République* ☎ *(66) 67–33–84* ▯), a bustling bistro opposite the Arena, local dishes are served at reasonable prices.

Restaurant nearby
Garons (*8km (5 miles) SE of Nîmes*).

Alexandre
☎ *(66) 20–08–66* ▮▮▮ ▰▰ ═ ▰ ▰ *Last orders 21.00. Closed Sun dinner, Mon, Tues lunch, last two weeks in Aug.*
A luxurious restaurant, beside the airport, set in its own park. You may find the dining-room's period elegance too formal, in which case eat in the lovely garden, though it can be windy. Alexandre is a large man with an expansive personality and his *cuisine* is suitably copious and arguably the best in the Nîmes area. Dishes change seasonally but may include *petit ragoût de langoustes et de crustaces* or *tournedos Mistral*.

Nightlife
Of the ten discos and dance halls in town, the best is probably **Le Liberty** (*24 Bd. Amiral-Courbet* ☎ *(66) 21–02–15*).

Shopping

Boutique Souleïado (*5 Pl. de la Maison Carrée*) sells Provençal fabrics and costumes, including Arlesian skirts, and Camargue *gardians'* outfits. **Don Quichotte** (*10 Rue de l'Horloge*) sells local handicrafts, olive-wood carvings, ceramics, copper, *santons*. **L'Huilerie** (*10 Rue des Marchands*) sells olive oils, olive-oil soaps and local food products.

In the Old Town, E of the Maison Carrée, are many other boutiques such as these.

Place nearby

Source Perrier (*14km (9 miles) sw of Nîmes, off N113* ◻) **50min tours Mon–Fri 9.00, 10.00, 13.30, 15.30**) Perrier, the naturally sparkling mineral water, comes from an underground spring here, and from nowhere else. It was first commercialized by an Englishman, St-John Harmsworth, of the newspaper family. He bought the spring in 1903, and modelled the tapering green Perrier bottle on the Indian clubs that he used for remedial exercises after a car accident. Today, a French firm owns the spring and sells some 650 million bottles a year, half for export.

The guided tour starts with a film (in French, English or German) showing production processes including the quarrying of sand from Mont Ventoux for making the bottles. There follows a cursory visit to the plant, where 2,500 people work. One is not shown the pretty English-style mansion which Harmsworth built for himself, today used by the company as a PR centre.

Orange

Map 4C4. 31km (19 miles) N of Avignon. 84100 Vaucluse. Population: 26,468 i Cours St-Martin ☎ (90) 34–70–88.

On the site of an old Celtic capital the Romans founded a town called *Arausio*, and this is where the name Orange comes from. The town lies amid vineyards on the plain of the Rhône valley – a pleasant place, with avenues of plane trees and a nucleus of narrow streets, dominated by the Roman theatre and triumphal arch, two of the greatest monuments of the Roman world. The Romans settled a colony of veterans here, and by Augustus' day it was a thriving city with temples, baths, an arena and stadium. Later it suffered from the barbarian and Saracen invasions, and in the 13thC became a tiny principality, an enclave within the Comtat Venaissin (see *Carpentras*). Finally, in the 16thC it was inherited by William, Prince of Nassau, forebear of the present Dutch family. He found the town so agreeable that he called his dynasty the House of Orange, the title it bears to this day. And so it is, through former Dutch connections abroad, that the name of Orange is borne today by a river and state in South Africa, by towns in America and by the Protestant movement of Ulster.

The principality was annexed to France in 1713 by the Treaty of Utrecht. By then its Roman buildings had suffered heavily: when Prince Maurice of Nassau set about fortifying his city, in 1622, he used stones from the temples, baths and arena to build his château, which is why little remains of them today. The theatre and arch were spared, for they formed part of his defence system.

For the best bird's-eye view of theatre and town, drive up the Montée des Princes d'Orange-Nassau to the top of the colline St-Eutrope. The **Musée de la Ville**, opposite the theatre, has portraits of the House of Orange; Roman remains, including marble fragments of a Roman cadastral survey of the area, the only surviving example of its kind; and – most unexpectedly – paintings by the English artist Sir Frank Brangwyn.

Event: Last two weeks of July, an international music festival – operas and classical concerts – in the Théâtre Antique.

Sights and places of interest

Arc de Triomphe ☆
Av. de l'Arc de Triomphe.

This most impressive arch was built to celebrate Julius Caesar's victories over local Gauls and over the Greek fleet of Massilia which had sided with Pompey. It is the third largest extant Roman triumphal arch and one of the best-preserved, notably the N side with its elaborate low-reliefs. The frieze high above the central arch depicts battles with Gauls, while nautical emblems (anchors, prows and ropes) above the side arches mark the naval victory.

Théâtre Antique ★
Pl. des Frères-Mounet 🖼 ✗ *Open Apr–Sept 8.30–18.00, Oct–Mar 9.00–12.00, 14.00–17.00.*

Orange possesses the finest and best-preserved Roman theatre in existence, and the only one whose facade is still standing. Viewed from either side, it is an immensely stirring sight – a great wall of reddish-brown sandstone, 35m (120ft) high by 90m (300ft) long. On the inner side, the three tiers of statues and columns have gone, but the original 3m (11ft) statue of *Augustus* with his general's baton was returned to its central niche in 1935. Above, you can see the stone blocks that supported the masts carrying awnings to protect the spectators from the sun. The theatre held over 7,000 people and its acoustics were – and are – superb, as testified by the musical events still held here.

On the W side, recent excavations have laid bare the foundations of a temple, the largest found so far in Gaul, and the remains of a sports ground thought to have been 365m (400yd) long. On the slopes of the hill above stood the majestic capital, with three temples of which traces are visible. This whole ensemble of buildings must have been the most grandiose in Gaul, and a powerful reminder of the might and superiority of the Roman Empire.

🏨 There are no very exciting hotels in Orange, but **Arène** (*Pl. de Langes* 🕾 *(90) 34–10–95* 🔲 *to* 🔲🔲 *closed Nov.*) is worth mentioning. 3km (2 miles) SW of Orange, just W of the entrance to the autoroute is a lively motel with spacious grounds: **Euromotel** (*Route de Caderousse* 🕾 *(90) 34–24–10* 🔲🔲).

🍴 **Le Bec Fin**
14 Rue Segond-Weber 🕾 *(90) 34–14–76* 🔲 *to* 🔲🔲 🔲 🔲 *Last orders 21.30. Closed Thurs, Fri, Nov.*

After a long drive down from the N, this little *auberge* opposite the Théâtre may provide the first taste of the *cuisine* and ambience of Provence. The hungry traveller could do far worse: it is a good example of its genre – animated, unpretentious, with authentic local dishes. **Specialities:** *Poutargue provençale, coq au vin de Châteauneuf-du-Pape, lapereau aux trois moutardes.*

Place nearby

Châteauneuf-du-Pape (*13km (8 miles) s of Orange*) The vineyards round the village once belonged to the Popes of Avignon (hence the name) and today produce one of the finest and most celebrated of **Côtes-du-Rhônes**. In 1923 the local vine-growers won a legal battle for the right to impose regulations enabling them alone to market their wine as **Châteauneuf-du-Pape**. This led to the present system of *Appellation Contrôlée* used throughout France to guarantee the origin of good wines and to protect their quality. In the village is a small wine museum, **the Caves du Père Anselme**.

Of the summer residences built here by the Popes, only one
high tower remains. From its top there is a splendid view of the
Palais des Papes in Avignon set dramatically against a backdrop
of the Alpilles.

Château des Fines Roches (☎ (90) 83–70–23 ▮▮ *to* ▮▮▮▮) is an
excellent restaurant with a few rooms, 3km (2 miles) s of Châteauneuf-du-
Pape.

Mule du Pape (☎ (90) 83–73–30 ▢ *to* ▮▮), in the village, serves
subtle Provençal dishes at a good range of prices.

Sérignan (*8km (5 miles) NE of Orange*)   Here is the villa where
the great entomologist J. H. Fabre (1823–1915) spent the last
40yr of his life. It is now a museum (▨ *closed Tues*) housing his
varied collections.

Peillon ☆

*Map 15E16. 19km (12 miles) NE of Nice. 06440 L'Escarène,
Alpes-Mar. Population: 1,000 i at mairie ☎ (93) 79–91–04*
Of the many hilltop villages behind Nice, this is one of those
most worth a visit. Nearly all the residents are Niçois
commuters or weekenders and although this has killed Peillon's
original peasant roots, the houses have at least been restored
with care and taste – a common hill village trend.

Auberge de la Madone ♣
*Peillon, 06440 l'Escarène ☎ (93) 79–91–53 ▮▮ 19 rms ▭ 15 ▭ ▭
▤ summer only. Closed mid-Oct to mid-Dec.*
Location: On edge of village. The owners M. and Mme Millo are the
perfect hosts, cheery and relaxed, and their rural *auberge* also offers
comfort and discreet elegance, attracting a discerning clientele. For the
price, one of the very best hotels in the Nice hinterland, with the added
advantage of excellent food.

Auberge de la Madone ♣
*Address and ☎ as hotel ▮▮ ▭ ▬ ⌂ Last orders 20.30. Closed Wed
(winter), mid-Oct to mid-Dec.*
The Millos' son Christian is a chef in the best Provençal tradition, with
some successful innovations of his own. Lunch outdoors under the olive
trees with views over the valley is a particular delight. Christian's pretty
sister acts as waitress – a real family affair. *Specialities: Bouillabaisse en
gelée, jambon aux figues, poulet à l'aigre-doux.*

Places nearby

Just to the N are the **Paillon gorges**, overlooked by a huge
cement factory. 11km (7 miles) NE amid rugged scenery is the
equally fine hill village of **Peille** ☆ with an interesting 13thC
church. From here, two scenic routes lead via **Ste-Agnes** down
to *Menton*.

Pont du Gard ▥ ☆

*Map 8D3. 25km (16 miles) w of Avignon. 30210 Remoulins,
Gard i ☎ (66) 37–00–02.*
One of the noblest monuments left to the world by the Roman
Empire, this celebrated bridge was built across the Gardon by
Agrippa in 19BC, as part of the 48km (30 mile) aqueduct
carrying water from the Eure to Nîmes; and today, after some
19thC restoration, it is still in near-perfect state. It consists of
three tiers of arches, of golden local stone, harmonizing with the
landscape of rocks and forests. The lower tiers each have large

arches; the upper one, which carried the water, is a suite of 35 smaller arches. The bridge is 275m (900ft) long and 50m (165ft) high, and its blocks of stone weigh up to 6 tons each. An awe-inspiring sight, its construction is still a source of wonder to engineers.

The best view of the bridge is from the entrance to the château de St-Privat, 90m (98yd) upstream on the right bank. From near here, a path winds up to the E end of the upper tier, which can easily be walked across by those not afraid of heights. A road bridge, built in 1747, runs level with the lower tier of the Roman bridge.

Port-Grimaud ☆
Map 13H12. 7km (4 miles) w of St-Tropez. 83310 Cogolin, Var.

Port-Grimaud can well claim to be one of the most dazzling architectural achievements in post-war France, a triumph of the current return to the vernacular. On the shore of the bay of St-Tropez, the Alsatian architect François Spoerry has built a graceful small-scale Venice, a luxury holiday village where there are no roads, only broad canals and little alleys, linked by pretty arched bridges. The houses are in Provençal fishing-port style, painted in a variety of bright colours and no two looking alike. Viewed from a boat on the canals, the design is pleasing and ingenious and achieves harmony.

The houses, individually owned, appeal especially to sailing enthusiasts, for each has its own mooring by the front door. Spoerry has also conceived Port-Grimaud as a real village: around its little main square are shops, banks, cafés, a post office, and an interdenominational church. Unlike Port-Galère (see *Théoule*) the village is open to tourists (on foot). Climb the tower of the church for a fine view over *St-Tropez*, the bay and the mountains, and the port at your feet. Or tour the canals by hiring an electric self-drive boat, or taking one of the regular sightseeing cruises.

⚲ Giraglia ▥
Pl. du 14-Juin ☎ (94) 56–31–33 ◐470494 ▥ 48 rms ▭ 48 ▭ ▭
▱ ▭ July–Aug ᴁ ◑ Closed mid-Oct to Easter.

Location: On an outer arm of the new port, between a quiet canal and the beach. The glamorous, modern seaside hotel, carefully conceived in Provençal style, is part of the master design of Port-Grimaud. The hotel is built round its lovely swimming pool, beside its private beach of fine sand (wind-surfing, water-skiing, etc). The luxurious bedrooms are in a variety of period styles and the hotel's decor is gentle and sophisticated. The Giraglia is certainly artificial, but successfully so.
▨ ≑ ♿ ▢ ▱ ≪ ▭ ♨ ♟

⚲ Other hotel recommended: **Hôtel du Port** (*Place du Marché* ☎ (94) 56–38–17 ▮ to ▮▮▮), in a picturesque location at the heart of the port.

▰ Amphitrite
Address and ☎ as Hôtel Giraglia ▥ ▢ ▭ ▭ ▭ ᴁ ◑ Last orders 21.30. Closed mid-Oct to Easter.

In summer, tables are set under parasols around the pool, beside the cheerful dining-room with its views across the bay of St-Tropez. The *cuisine* is a creative blend of variations on traditional themes.

▰ Lolo's La Marina
Pl. du 14-Juin ☎ (94) 56–25–50. Last orders 1.00.
A lively and attractive place beside the water. You can enjoy *bourride*, *soupe au pistou*, spit-roast meat.

Puget-Théniers

Map 14D13. 65km (40 miles) NW of Nice; 6km (4 miles) E of Entrevaux. 06260 Alpes-Mar. Population: 1,520.

A little town huddled at the confluence of the rivers Var and Roudoule. The old quarter is largely medieval, with overhanging roofs and houses tightly pressed together. The **church**, partly 18thC, is notable for the beautiful and moving retable above the altar – St James wears a scallop shell in his hat, the sign of a pilgrim to Santiago de Compostela in Spain. Equally fine are the naïve and curious 15thC walnut woodcarvings which represent, in detail, the Crucifixion, Burial and Resurrection of Christ.

Les Acacias ♣ *(N202 ☎(93) 05–05–25 □ to ■).*

Hotel nearby
Touet-sur-Var *(9km (6 miles) E of Puget-Théniers).*

de la Poste *(☎(93) 05–71–03 □)* for good local cooking and comfy beds.

Places nearby
Gorges de la Roudoule The D16 leads N through the gorge, and past the **Pont St-Léger** suspension bridge with the old Roman bridge beneath – in a marvellous setting with good views. Further on to the right, the D416 leads to the tiny village of **La Croix-sur-Roudoule** which can be seen perched against the rock from the road below.

Riez

Map 7E10. 25km (16 miles) E of Manosque. 04500 Alpes-de-H.-P. Population: 1,630 ℹ Pl. des Quinconces ☎(92) 74–51–81.

Here is another pleasant and unassuming Provençal town which once knew days of far greater importance, being, in both Roman and early Christian times, an important religious centre. Reminders of those days include the remains of a 16thC Roman temple standing in a meadow on the town's W side: four grey granite columns with white marble Corinthian capitals.

Close by, across the river, is a 5thC Merovingian **baptistry**, not unlike those at *Aix* and *Fréjus*: its hexagonal interior has eight granite columns with marble capitals *(key available from tourist office)*. The *vieille ville*, once surrounded by ramparts, is attractive with its long alleys.

To the W stretches the wide plateau of Valensole, France's principal region of lavender cultivation. It is at its best in July, when the field and hills are a blaze of fragrant purple lavender.

Roquebrune-Cap-Martin

Map 16E16. 5km (3 miles) SW of Menton. 06190 Alpes-Mar. Population: 11,250 ℹ at mairie ☎(93) 35–62–87 and syndicat d'initiative, 20 Av. Paul-Doumer ☎(93) 35–62–87.

This sprawling commune is in three main parts: **Cap-Martin** on the coast SW of Menton; the modern resort; and the old village of **Roquebrune** high above the Upper Corniche. Cap-Martin with its woods of pine and olive has long been a preserve of the rich and famous, and is still largely given over to private villas with gardens. The Empresses Eugénie of France and Sissi of Austria used to stay here in the 19thC and first made the Cap fashionable. Later residents or regular visitors have included

Roquebrune-Cap-Martin

Churchill and van Meegeren, the forger of Vermeers; Yeats died here in 1939; and Le Corbusier, who spent many summers here, was drowned off the cape in 1965.

The medieval hill village of **Roquebrune**, one of the finest in Provence, has been gracefully restored: brash souvenir shops are not too obtrusive. Steep alleys and stairways, neatly paved, wind up under Romanesque arches to the feudal castle on the summit. The Rue Moncollet, lined by the medieval houses, is one of the most attractive.

Apart from strolling round the village, it's well worth taking the scenic footpath (approx 90min) that leads round Roquebrune Bay from the Av. Winston-Churchill on Cap Martin to Monte-Carlo Beach. It's best to do the walk with the sun behind you.

Events: A vow made by the villagers is said to have saved Roquebrune from the plague in 1467. In fulfilment, two remarkable processions have taken place annually in the old village for the past 500yr. These are held on the afternoon of Aug 5 and the evening of Good Friday. With bold pageantry and a wealth of luminous emblems, the costumed villagers enact scenes from the Passion.

Donjon 🏛 ☆

🗺 ✗ mid-July to Aug. Open May–Sept 9.00–12.00, 14.00–19.00; Oct, Dec–Apr 10.00–12.00, 14.00–17.00. Closed Fri, Nov.

Roquebrune's castle is the oldest in France, and the only Carolingian castle left standing. It was first built in the 10thC as a defence against the Saracens but the present structure is mostly 13thC. From 1350 –1848 it was owned by the Grimaldi; in 1911 an English resident, Sir William Ingram, bought it and gave it to the municipality. It is an austere building of four storeys, with walls up to 4m (12ft) thick: yet the rooms are strikingly small for so lordly a residence. On the first floor, the ceremonial hall (now roofless); above this, the guardroom, with comfortable prison beside; next, the seigneur's living quarters, with primitive kitchen. From the roof terrace, you can enjoy the anticipated marvellous views. The castle is floodlit at night and is visible for miles around.

⚓ Vistaëo 🏨

Grande Corniche, 06190
Roquebrune-Cap-Martin
☎(93) 35–01–50 ☎461021 ▥
27 rms ◨ 27 ↔ 🛏 AE ⊕ ◎
VISA Closed Nov to Mar.

Location: On cliff edge beside Upper Corniche, above Monte-Carlo. No ancient hill village is sited as theatrically as this famous modern hotel, giddily perched on its cliff 300m (1,000ft) sheer above Monte-Carlo Beach. All the trappings of extreme luxury – comfort, swift service, glamorous decor, heated pool in a garden – match the spectacular setting.

🍽 ⚓ ♿ ◻ 🖊 🏊 ⤢ ⛷ ⛰ ♨

⚓ Westminster

14 Av. Louis-Laurens, 06190
Roquebrune-Cap-Martin
☎(93) 35–00–68 ◻ 30 rms
◨ 10 ↔ 🛏 ⇆ 🛏 Dinner is compulsory June–Sept, lunches not served June to mid-Oct. Closed mid-Oct to Jan.

Location: Near Monaco frontier, just below Lower Corniche and close to the beach. A modest, efficient hotel suitable for a simple beach holiday (if you don't mind shingle). There is a railway just below the hotel, which can be rather noisy during the day, but there are few trains at night. To compensate there is a very pretty terraced garden overlooking the sea.
◻ 🏊 ⤢ ⛷ ⛰

≈ Les Lucioles ♣

12 Pl. de la République
☎(93) 35–02–19 ▥ ◻ ■ 🚗
↔ Last orders 22.00. Closed Thurs, Fri lunch, Nov to mid-Mar.

At the foot of the hill village, a restaurant with a tropical touch to the decor – the owner has lived in the Seychelles. Lovely outdoor dining terrace with views of castle and sea. The set menu presents a wide choice. **Specialities:** Soupe seychelloise, tête de veau, lapin maison.

176

Roquebrune
100 Corniche inférieure
☎ (93) 35–00–16 ▥▥▥ ⬝ ▰▰ �
🍴 AE ⬥ ⬤ VISA *Last orders
22.00. Closed Wed, Thurs lunch
(July to mid-Sept), Wed (mid-
Sept to June), early Jan, mid-Nov
to mid-Dec.*

A sophisticated restaurant situated
on the lower Corniche, near the
Monaco frontier, with pleasant sea
views from its open terrace. The
cuisine is serious and invariably
excellent. *Specialities:
Bouillabaisse, poissons du marché
frits, grillés ou en papillote.*

Roussillon

*Map **5**D7. 48km (30 miles)* E *of Avignon. 84220 Gordes,
Vaucluse. Population: 1,090.*

This is the heart of the ochre country (see also *Apt*) where pines
and heather strike their roots into the bright red earth, and the
red rocks jut out for miles around. Roussillon (meaning
'russet') is a most pretty old village on a hilltop between the
Coulon valley and the plateau of Vaucluse: its houses of local
stone are in every shade of pink, red and orange, and have long
attracted artists. All around are ochre quarries, where many
cliffs have been slashed into strange shapes and consequently
been given fancy names such as 'Giant's Causeway' and
'Needles of the Fairy Vale'.

The American sociologist Laurence Wylie lived in Roussillon
and made it the subject of his well-known book, *Village in the
Vaucluse* (1961). He described a sleepy peasant community
awaking to the modern world. Nowadays it is not so sleepy and
has become a modish centre of writers, painters (who hold
frequent art exhibitions), well-to-do summer visitors and plenty
of tourists.

Résidence des Ocres
Route de Gordes, 84220 Gordes ☎ (90) 75–60–50 ▥ to ▥▥ *15 rms*
▱ *15* ▦▦ ⬝ *Closed Feb, mid-Nov to mid-Dec.*
Location: On the edge of the village, beside a main road. A small modern
hotel, neat and well cared for. A reasonable base for exploring the area.
⬢ 🗹 ⬙

David
☎ (90) 75–60–13 ▥▥▥ ⬝ ▰▰ ⎲ *Last orders 21.00. Closed Mon, Sun
dinner, Feb, June.*
A smart, spacious village restuarant with wide windows overlooking the
valley and ochre cliffs. The *cuisine* is classic and *soigné*. *Specialities:
Feuilleté d'écrevisses, brouillade de truffes, coq en pâté.*

Route Napoléon

*Map **14**E13.*

The end of the road for Napoleon was the Battle of Waterloo,
but he must have had little inkling of the fate in store for him
when he marched triumphantly from Provence to Paris on his
return from exile in Elba. The route he and his men chose, over
the mountains to avoid armed opposition, is still proudly
commemorated and well marked.

After landing at Golfe-Juan (see *Juan-les-Pins*) Napoleon
was rejected by the garrison at *Antibes*, so he marched to
Cannes and camped by the present post office. He then roughly
followed the present N85, via *Grasse, Digne* and *Sisteron* to
Grenoble. It was a tough march in stormy weather, along tracks
in many places impassable to carriages. But the ex-emperor's
gamble paid off. The garrison at the citadel of Sisteron did not
resist, and soon he was victoriously in Grenoble. Today,
plaques mark the exact spots where he halted. The finest
scenery is on the Grasse–Digne stretch of the N85.

St-Cassien, Lac de
Map 14F13. 24km (15 miles) NW of Cannes.
Constructed after the 1959 Malpasset dam disaster (see *Fréjus*),
this large, three-fingered artificial lake has become increasingly
popular as a bathing and restricted sailing area, with
windsurfing the main attraction: the placid, velvety water and
fresh breezes make it an excellent place for both beginners and
experts, and in summer the lake is peppered with brightly-
coloured sails. Sunbathing is not so easy, as the lake's thickly-
wooded shores are very rocky.

☴ Auberge de Puits Jaubert
Route du Lac de Fondurance, Callian ☎ *(94) 76–44–48* ⅢⅡ ▭ ▆ ♨
▅ *Last orders 22.00 (summer), 21.00 (winter). Closed Tues, mid-Jan
to mid-Feb.*
An easily missed turning off the Draguignan-Grasse N562 and a very
bumpy 3km (2 mile) lane is worth negotiating to find this pleasant
restaurant situated at the w tip of the Lac de St-Cassien. The food is
served in the dining-room under 15thC stone arches or on a shady
terrace. Chef and *patron* Alain Carro (who trained under Paul Haeberlin
at the Auberge de l'Ill in Alsace) produces satisfying *nouvelle cuisine*
dishes. A good place for lunch after an exhilarating morning windsurfing
on the lake. *Specialities: Feuilleté de cuisses de grenouilles, ragoût de
rognons et de ris de veau, filet de veau aux morilles.*

St-Étienne-de-Tinée
*Map 15B14. 91km (57 miles) N of Nice. 06660 Alpes-Mar.
Population: 1,940 ℹ Rue Commune de France*
☎ *(93) 02–41–96.*
The alpine air is sharp and clear in this superbly positioned
village in the lovely **upper Tinée valley**. Once an important
religious centre, St-Étienne has a **church** with a fine
Romanesque tower and no less than three chapels with frescoes
worth seeing: **Couvent des Trinitaires**, **St-Maur** and **St-
Sébastien** (*all often locked, ask for keys at the tourist office*).

⌂ La Pinatelle ▆ ♣
06660 St-Étienne-de-Tinée ☎ *(93) 02–40–36* ▭ *14 rms* ▆ ☴
Closed Oct–Nov.
Location: On the edge of town. A modest, family-run hotel mostly
patronized by French couples seeking a very quiet country holiday.
There's a pretty orchard garden with a few tables.

☴ La Pinatelle ▆
Address and ☎ *as hotel* ⅢⅡ ▭ ▆ *Last orders 20.15. Closed Oct–Nov.*
Not exactly a rowdy place, the dining-room; conversation takes place in
gentle undertones and most eyes are on M. Martinez's very fair *cuisine
familiale*. The set pension menu will produce hors d'oeuvres, *viande
garnie, fromage, dessert,* and the more expensive one might include *crêpes
gratinées au four, daube à la provençale.*

Places nearby
Further up the Tinée valley, a turning to the left leads to
St-Dalmas-le-Selvage, a high and lonely mountain village
amid wonderful scenery, with a **church** which contains an
interesting 16thC retable of St Pancrace.
  The road along the Tinée valley finally climbs dizzily up to
Cime de la Bonnette, at 2,802m (9,200ft) one of the highest
alpine passes and open only in summer. Here in Aug the aptly
named oratory of **Notre-Dame-du-Très-Haut** attracts a
pilgrimage accompanied by a motor rally and shepherds' fête –
something for all tastes.

St-Jean-Cap-Ferrat
*Map **15**F15. 10km (6 miles) SE of Nice. 06290 Alpes-Mar.*
*Population: 2,268 **i** 87 bis, Av. Denis-Séméria*
☎ *(93) 01–36–86.*

Nearly every square metre of this lovely peninsula has long been
bought up by the rich and famous for their stately villas and
exotic private gardens. Two of the best known are **Villa les
Cèdres**, w of the port of St-Jean, which belonged to King
Léopold II of Belgium, and has a particularly fine garden, and
Somerset Maugham's **Villa Mauresque**, near the S cape where
the author spent his final years. Tourists would sometimes try
to visit him as a local 'sight' – to one, who managed to gatecrash,
he snarled in his customary style, "What d'you think I am, a
monkey in a cage?"

The profusion of flowers, palms and pines, and the many
little rocky coves and headlands, are Cap Ferrat's great assets,
but the beaches are rock and shingle (the Grand Hotel's Sun
Beach offers mattresses at medium cost to non-residents), and,
as so much of the land is private, this is poor terrain for scenic
walks. One coastal footpath does however lead round the
Pointe St-Hospice, starting from Paloma beach (allow 45min).
From the summit of the **lighthouse** by the S cape there are
sweeping views over the whole coast from Italy to the Esterel
(*165 steps up, open 9.00–12.00, 14.00–17.00 or 18.00*). **St-Jean**
itself is an animated fishing village, with little hotels, bars and
bistros.

Sights and places of interest
Fondation Ephrussi de Rothschild (*Musée Ile-de-France*) ☆
Bd. Denis-Séméria ☎ *(93) 01–33–09* ▪▪ 🏛 🈯 *Open July–Aug*
9.00–12.00 (gardens only), 15.00–19.00; Sept–June 9.00–12.00
(gardens only), 14.00–18.00. Closed Mon, Nov.
Baroness Ephrussi de Rothschild had this Italianate villa designed
especially to accommodate her treasures: the ceilings, for example, were
conceived as frames for her Tiepolos. On her death in 1934, she
bequeathed the villa and its contents to the Académie des Beaux Arts.

The collection reveals the Rothschilds' catholic tastes, and ranges
from the 14thC to the 19thC. Here you will find Renaissance and
Victorian furniture, Aubusson tapestries, Louis XVI costumes, Sèvres
and Dresden china, chinoiserie, paintings by Fragonard, Monet, Sisley,
Renoir. . . . After the guided tour, visitors are free to wander through the
villa's ornamental gardens, with their lily ponds, colonnades, exotic
flowers and shrubs, and views over the sea. On summer evenings
concerts or theatrical events are often held in the villa.
Jardin Animé (Zoo) ☆
Bd. Gén-de-Gaulle (NW of peninsula, near Villa les Cèdres)
☎ *(93) 01–31–56* ▪▪ 💻 ✳ *Open May–Sept 9.30–18.30; Oct–Apr*
9.30–17.30.
A delightful private zoo set in the lake, now drained, of King Leopold's
former domain. There's a good variety of animals, reptiles and birds in
spacious outdoor cages, and, six times daily, a chimps' tea party.

☜ Clair Logis ▦
Allées des Brises, 06290 St-Jean-
Cap-Ferrat ☎ *(93) 01–31–01* ▥▥
16 rms 🛏 *16* 🚗 AE 💳 🅱 VISA
Closed mid-Nov to mid-Dec.
Location: *In a quiet street in centre of
peninsula, near the port and sea.*
Enjoy the privileged elegance and
calm of the Cap without paying
prices that match by staying at this
villa-hotel set in its own large
garden.
🏠 🗂 🐾 🚤

☜ Voile d'Or ▦
06290 St-Jean-Cap-Ferrat
☎ *(93) 01–13–13* 🕿 *470317* ▥▥▥
50 rms 🛏 *50* 🍽 💳 📺 🚗 🚤
summer. Closed Nov–Mar.
Location: *Directly beside the harbour
and the open sea.* All is *"luxe, calme
et volupté"* at this sublime hotel,
one of the half-dozen loveliest on
the *Côte.* The long ochre building
blends perfectly with its setting,
and inside it has been modernized
with taste and rare harmony of

colour. Moreover, for all the
sophistication, the ambience is far
less affected than at some of the
Riviera's luxury palaces. Airy
salons lead out on to a glamorous
terrace-garden, which gives on to
two swimming pools with lidos,
right beside the sea. (See
restaurant.)
⌂≋♿🖼🤿⚞≋🍴🏖

☞ Other hotels in Cap Ferrat
worth mentioning are: **Brise
Marine** (*Av. J-Mermoz*
☎ *(93) 01–30–73* 📶 *to* 📶); **La
Frégate** (*Av. Denis-Séméria*
☎ *(93) 01–30–88* 📶 *to* 📶);
Grand Hôtel du Cap Ferrat (*Bd.
Gén-de-Gaulle* ☎ *(93) 01–04–54*
📶).

≋ **La Frégate** ♥
Av. Denis-Séméria
☎ *(93) 01–30–88* 📶 💬 📖 🍴
🍴 *AE Last orders 21.30. Closed
mid-Nov to mid-Dec.*
Dine overlooking the port at this
reasonably-priced restaurant, or in
a small garden at the back. Varied
local cooking; try the *crudités
provençale, or crêpes de moules St-
Jeannoise.*

≋ **Les Hirondelles** ⌂
52 Av. J-Mermoz
☎ *(93) 01–30–25* 📶 💬 ≋ 🚗
🚗 *Last orders 22.30. Closed Sun,
Mon mid-Nov to Jan.*
After 15yr, Grandmother Marie
Venturino, now over 70, still rises
early every day to go to the Nice
market, yet is in her kitchens till
late at night producing finely
prepared fish dishes in the classic
Provençal style. Her graceful
daughters work front-of-house in
the elegant restaurant near the
harbour. **Specialities:**
Bouillabaisse, sardines farcies.

≋ **Voile d'Or** ⌂
Address and ☎ as hotel 📶 💬
🍴 🚗 🍽 *Last orders 22.00.
Closed Nov–Mar.*
When it comes to the food, the *Côte
d'Azur's* luxury hotels are often
disappointing – but not the Voile
d'Or, where Jean Crépin's menu,
particularly the fish, always
delights. Meals are served in the
warm, yellow dining-room, on the
canopied terrace or, for bathers, by
the pool. **Specialities:** *Feuilleté
d'asperges et d'écrevisses, royale de
loup St-Jeannoise.* (See hotel.)

St-Martin-Vésubie ☆
*Map 15C15. 65km (40 miles) N of Nice. 06760 Alpes-Mar.
Population: 1,190 i Pl. Félix-Faure ☎ (93) 03–21–28.*
Equally popular with keen mountaineers and less hardy city
dwellers, St-Martin-Vésubie is a first-class alpine summer
resort which has an air of modern chic, yet preserves its charm –
particularly in the **Rue du Dr-Cagnoli**, a steep paved alley
flanked by graceful old houses, with a rivulet rushing down its
middle. The finely-decorated 17thC **church** is notable for its
13thC wooden statue of the *Virgin*, richly dressed: every July 2
this is taken in procession to the 14thC sanctuary of the
Madone de Fenestre, aloft and isolated in the Alps (the 12km
(8 mile) trip can also be made by car, along the D94).

☞ Small family hotels in St-Martin-Vésubie include: **La Bonne
Auberge** (☎ *(93) 03–20–49* 📶 *to* 📶); **Edward's et Châtaignerie**
(☎ *(93) 03–21–22* 📶).

≋ **La Bonne Auberge** serves local dishes in its large *salle*.

Places nearby
Le Boréon (*8km (5 miles) N of St-Martin*) Amid sensational
scenery Le Boréon marks the start of the **Réserve de Chasse du
Mercantour**. If you wish to ramble (no cars, dogs or guns
allowed) in this wildlife reserve, where you might spot chamois
or marmots, leave the car by the hotel, close to the magnificent
waterfall. This is excellent hiking country; also a centre for
mountaineering tuition in high season (*apply to the St-Martin
tourist office for information*).
Valdeblore (*10km (6 miles) W of St-Martin*) A handful of
hamlets on a sub-alpine plateau: the air is invigorating and the

scenery exhilarating, save that the place is filling up with
modern chalets and flats – tokens of its success as a new resort.
Here at **La Colmiane** you can join courses in skiing in winter
and rock-climbing or hang-gliding in summer (*for details ask the
tourist office at Valdeblore* ☎ *(93) 02–84–59*). The less athletic
can take the funicular (▧ *open all year*) from Col St-Martin to
the **Pic de Colmiane**, 1,795m (5,889ft). Spare a thought too for
Valdeblore's sad name: it derives from *'val des pleurs'* (vale of
tears), as reminder of the days when a local seigneur locked up
his wives and let them starve to death, ignoring their cries and
tears.

Venanson (*5km (3 miles) s of St-Martin*)   A quaint village high
above St-Martin, with glorious views. In a small square at the
entry to the village stands the minute **Chapelle de Ste-Claire** ☆
Don't fail to go inside, for walls and ceilings are covered in vivid
15thC frescoes, the warm colours – rusts, greens, and golds –
still excellently preserved, depicting the life and martyrdom of
St Sébastien (*keys from adjacent Bella Vista hotel*).

St-Maximin-la-Ste-Baume

*Map **11**G9. 43km (27 miles) E of Aix-en-Provence. 83470 Var.
Population: 4,580   i 23 Rue des Poilus ☎ (94) 78–02–47.*
A lively little market town with some pleasant old streets,
known above all for its famous basilica.

Ste-Marie-Madeleine, Basilique ㎡ † ☆
▧ *Open 8.00–11.45, 14.00–19.00.*

The finest Gothic building in Provence, in the town named after the saint
who is said by legend to have accompanied the three Marys from
Palestine to *Les Saintes-Maries-de-la-Mer* and then been martyred in
Aix, where he had gone to evangelize. The tombs in its crypt have been
venerated as his and Mary Magdalene's. This crypt was covered in for
safety during the Saracen period, then rediscovered in 1279; and it was
soon after this, in 1295, that the building of the abbey began, on the
orders of Charles II of Anjou. The construction took more than two
centuries, and even today the facade is not complete. The abbey was saved
from demolition in the Revolution through the lucky chance that
Bonaparte's young brother Lucien was stationed in the town and took it
over as a military warehouse.

The vaulted nave, rising to 18m (60ft), and the polygonal apse with its
high windows, are both of great beauty. Unlike many in Provence, the
church has a feeling of light and space and its many fine art works can be
seen to good effect. Among them, note the 17thC choir-screen in
sculpted wood, the fine 18thC organ, and the great 18thC pulpit carved
out of a single piece of wood. Above all, to the left of the high altar, is an
unusual 16thC retable by Antonio Ronzen of the Venetian school: his 16
painted panels portray the life and Passion of Christ against such
backgrounds as the Colosseum at Rome, St Mark's, Venice, and the
Papal Palace at Avignon.

The crypt was originally the burial vault of an early 5thC Roman villa.
Its four sarcophagi are among the oldest Christian relics in France – even
if there is little historical substance in the legend that they are the tombs
of saints. A 19thC gilt-bronze reliquary holds a skull long worshipped as
that of St Mary Magdalene.

〓 **Chez Nous** (● *3 Bd. Jean-Jaurès* ☎ *(94) 78–02–57* □ *to* ▮▮), a
simple *auberge* on the main road.

St-Paul-de-Vence

*Map **15**E14. 20km (12 miles) w of Nice. 06570 Alpes-Mar.
Population: 1,970   i Rue Grande ☎ (93) 32–86–95.*
One of the most sophisticated and cultured places in the region,
the fortified hill village of St-Paul has attracted many artists

since 1918 and is always thronged with visitors. Mosaic-paved alleys lead through pretty piazzas with fountains, to the church on the hilltop and to the ramparts. These were built in the 16thC, when St-Paul was a French frontier post facing rival Savoy across the river Var. They are still intact, and you can walk most of the way round them. The landscape immediately around the village has always been enchanting, a succession of little hills and valleys covered with flowers, orchards and pine woods; but it is now very over-built with flats and villas.

Sights and places of interest
Fondation Maeght ★
☎ (93) 32–81–63 ▥ Open May–Sept 10.00–12.30, 15.00–19.00; Oct–Apr 10.00–12.30, 14.30–18.00.

One of the most distinguished modern art museums in France, the Maeght Foundation is remarkable for its setting, its contents and the building itself, the three fusing together to create an arresting and evocative display. It was built in 1964 by the Paris art dealer, Aimé Maeght, an idealist with a zeal for spreading the love of modern art. The architect was the Spaniard J. L. Sert, whose boldly original pink and white building is topped by two inverted domes, giving it a touch of fantasy. Inside are paintings by Bonnard, Braque, Miró, Soulages and many others, including Chagall's *La Vie*, a huge colourful canvas on which the artist has expressed his ingenuously radiant joy in all aspects of human life.

In the garden, sculptures and murals have been carefully sited amid lawns, patios and pine trees, so as to be noticeable yet blend harmoniously with the natural surroundings. The effect is stunning. Sculptures by Arp and Hepworth, and mobiles by Calder, stand in the front garden. Behind the museum, Miró holds sway with a witty array of fountains, mosaics and sculptures in fanciful shapes. A courtyard is peopled with Giacomettis like giant emaciated chessmen, while the chapel has windows by Braque and Ubac.

The Foundation holds two special exhibitions a year, each usually devoted to a single artist. It has a library, a shop selling reproductions and a small cinema where films on art are shown daily (*June–Sept*).

St-Paul-de-Vence, Église † ☆
The 12th–13thC church stands at the summit of the village. Its unexciting exterior belies what appears within, for it is rich in works of art: a painting of *St Catherine*, thought to be by Tintoretto, at the end of the left aisle; a low-relief of the *Martyrdom of St Clément* on the last altar on the right; and, in the baptismal chapel, a 15thC alabaster *Madonna*.

Nearby, the **Musée Provençal** (▤ *closed Nov*) is a 16thC house which has been restored and refurbished in the style of that period.

⚲ La Colombe d'Or 🏨
1 Pl. du Général-de-Gaulle, 06570 St-Paul-de-Vence
☎ (93) 32–80–02 ▥ 24 rms
▤ 24 ▦ ▣ ▩ ▦ ⚒ ▥ ≈
Closed early Nov to mid-Dec.

Location: At the entrance to the old village. The legendary Colombe d'Or is not only a luxury hotel, occupying an old building of character, but also contains a private collection of paintings and sculpture that would be the envy of many museums. It was built up by the hotel's founder, the late Paul Roux, art connoisseur and friend of many local painters. He accepted payment in kind for his hospitality and thus acquired his works of art. They include César and Miró in the snug little lounge, Braque and Calder by the lovely pool, Matisse,

Picasso, Rouault and Utrillo in the dining-room. Here, or under white parasols on the enchanting terrace with its superb Léger mural, the cooking is enjoyable.
♿ ▢ ▥ ⚒ ≼ ≈

⚲ Le Hameau
528 Route de la Colle, 06570 St-Paul-de-Vence ☎ (93) 32–80–24
▥ 15 rms ▤ 15 ⚑ Closed Nov–Jan.

Location: 2.5km (1½ miles) sw of St-Paul, on the road to La Colle. An 18thC white-walled farmhouse with orange, lemon and apricot trees in the garden, vines overhanging the terrace, lovely views and a feeling of serenity. Inside, the furniture is sturdy and puritanical, the floors bare, with scattered rugs, the bedrooms

spacious with wide secluded
terraces, and the service friendly if
sometimes vague.
⌂ 🖼 ⛱ ⟨⟨

☜ Mas d'Artigny 🏨
Chemin des Salettes, 06570 St-
Paul-de-Vence ☎ *(93) 32–84–54*
📞 *470601* ▉▉ *82 rms* 🛏 *82* 🍽
⌂ 🍽 ⟨⟨ 🇦🇪

Location: 3km (2 miles) w of St-Paul
(off D7), secluded on a hilltop in its
own 20-acre woodland park.
Opened in 1973, here is one of the
few recent bids by the *Côte d'Azur*
to prove that its days of erecting
luxury palace hotels are not yet
over. The building is a kind of
Texan version of a Provençal
mansion, grandiosely spacious.
But the decor is modern,
sometimes tasteless, with lavish
use of marble. There is a most
elegant swimming pool and lido,
and the bedrooms have wide
balconies facing hills and sea,
while, best of all, are 26 garden-
level villa-suites, each with patio,
lawn and pool, California-style.
Much in demand for top-level
business seminars and political
conferences, this is where Giscard
d'Estaing and Schmidt met in
1976. The *cuisine* is excellent,
offering a range of regional and
new dishes, as well as delicious
outdoor barbecues.
⌂ ♨ ⛴ ▢ 🖼 ⛱ ⟨⟨ ⇌ 🏊
🎱 🅾

Other recommended hotel: **Les**
Orangers (*Chemin des Fumerates*
☎ *(93) 32–80–95* ▉▉).

⇥ La Brouette
Vieille route de Vence
☎ *(93) 58–67–17.* ▢ *to* ▉▉ 🍽
📞 🍽 ⟨⟨ ⇌ *Closed Sun dinner,*
Mon, mid-Oct to mid-Nov.
On the hills above St-Paul, and not
easy to get at, this is a most
convivial and intimate little
restaurant with pleasantly rustic
decor. It is run by two Danes, Olé
and Birgitte, who serve good
Nordic food such as Lapland
reindeer and home-smoked trout,
eel and pork . . . . well, it makes a
change from *salade niçoise* and *lapin*
aux herbes.

Nearby restaurant

La Colle-sur-Loup (*5km (3 miles)*
s of St-Paul.)

La Belle-Époque
Route de Cagnes, La Colle-sur-
Loup ☎ *(93) 20–10–92* ▉▉ 🍽
🚗 🍽 ⟨⟨ 🇦🇪 🅾 🆅🆂🅰 *Last orders*
21.30. Closed Sun dinner
(Oct–Mar), Mon, early Jan–Feb.

Flaming torches at the entrance,
carriages artfully floodlit in the
garden, a phoneboth made out of
an old calash, kitsch Belle Époque
decor – inauspicious touches you
may think, yet it is hard not to be
beguiled by this sumptuous
restaurant. The setting may be
contrived, but the warmth and
charm of the Compagnat family is
not, nor is the appreciation
of their subtle and imaginative
classic *cuisine*. **Specialities:**
Fricassée de lotte, canard de barberie
aux fruits, salade de caille aux
pleurottes.

Shopping

The village has countless art, antique and handicraft shops,
mostly rather pricey. Worth noting are: **H. and H. Dieken** (*64*
Rue Grande), painters of unusual murals and frescoes; and
L'Herbier de Provence (*Montée de la Grand Fontaine*), selling
local herbs, aromatic oils and soaps.

St-Raphael
Map **13***G13. 43km (27 miles) sw of Cannes. 83700 Var.*
Population: 23,160 **i** *Pl. de la Gare* ☎ *(94) 95–16–87.*

The sizeable, long-established bathing resort of St-Raphael
looks across the gulf of *Fréjus* to the *Maures massif*. It is a
rather sedate place, but good for families with its miles of public
sandy beach and excellent marina. Offshore lie the twin red
rocks of the Lion de Terre and Lion de Mer.
    St-Raphael was settled by the Romans at the same time as
adjacent *Fréjus*: Roman villas, of which no traces remain, once
stood on the site of the modern casino. It was in the harbour
here that Bonaparte disembarked on his return from Egypt in
1799, then later set sail for exile in Elba in 1814. St-Raphael was
then a mere fishing village. It was first developed as a resort in

the 1860s, thanks largely to the Parisian journalist Alphonse Karr, ex-editor of *Le Figaro*, who settled here and encouraged his friends to come too. One who responded was Gounod, who composed *Roméo et Juliette* here in 1866.

Set up to take in interesting finds of local diving clubs, the **Musée d'Archéologie Sous-Marine** (*Rue des Templiers* 🔲), contains old ship anchors, a wide array of Classical amphorae, and, in the garden, two 18thC warship cannons, among other objects. Next to the museum is the 12thC **Église des Templiers**, a single vaulted Romanesque building of austere simplicity.

🗫 **La Potinière**
Route des Plaines, 83700 St-Raphael ☎ *(94) 95–21–43* ▮▮▯ to ▮▮▮▮
25 rms 🔲 25 🛏 🚗 🍽 🛥 *June–Sept and Easter* AE ⊙ *Closed early Nov to mid-Dec.*

Location: In its own wooded park near the beach, 4km (2¼ miles) E of St-Raphael in the residential suburb of Boulouris. A holiday hotel in the modern style, with a youthful, sporty atmosphere. Several villas are spread out in a small park full of pines and mimosa. The very modern rooms may lack charm, but they have balconies with deck chairs, and you can park motel-style, right by your door. The hotel has its own eight-seat motor yacht with skipper, for fishing parties and short cruises. In the dining-room, try the Toulousain chef's very un-Provençal dishes.
🍴 🕭 🗖 🖼 🏊 ⇌ 🡒

🗫 Other reasonable hotels in St-Raphael include: **Beau Séjour** (*Promenade René-Coty* ☎ *(94) 95–03–75* ▮▮▯); **Pastorel** (*54 Rue de la Liberté* ☎ *(94) 95–02–36* ▮▯ to ▮▮▯); **Provençal** (*197 Rue de la Garonne* ☎ *(94) 95–01–52* ▮▯).

🍽 Restaurants worth mentioning are: **Cordon Rouge** (*11 Rue de Châteaudan* ☎ *(94) 95–64–61* ▮▯ to ▮▮▯); **Pastorel** ♥ (*16 Rue de la Liberté* ☎ *(94) 95–02–36* ▮▯ to ▮▮▯); **La Voile d'Or** (*1 Bd. Gén-de-Gaulle* ☎ *(94) 95–17–04* ▮▮▮▮).

Nightlife

Casino
☎ *(94) 95–10–59* ⊙ 🏵 ♫ 🍹 *Dancing with orchestra nightly 22.00–3.00 July–Aug; rest of year Sat, Sun only. Joker disco open all year from 22.00. Casino open daily. Closed Nov to mid-Dec.*
For a resort lacking in sparkle, the casino complex is very lively in season.

La Réserve (*Promenade René-Coty*) is the smartest disco in town.

Place nearby

Valescure (*3km (2 miles) N of St-Raphael*)   High on the slopes of the *Esterel massif*, this is a residential zone of prosperous villas scattered amid a pine forest. Valescure used to be favoured by wealthy English as a winter health resort, but times have changed, and its barrack-like Edwardian hotels now stand empty, or are used as flats. However, the famous golf course is still popular (the Grand Duke Michael founded it in 1891): for membership details apply to the **Golf Hôtel** (below).

🗫 **Golf Hôtel**
Valescure, 83700 St-Raphael ☎ *(94) 52–01–57* ☎461085 ▮▮▮▮ 40 rms
🔲 40 🛏 🚗 🍽 AE *Last orders in restaurant 21.15. Closed Nov.*

Location: Next to the golf course, in a pine wood at 550m (1,800ft) altitude. The old Golf Hôtel, built in the 1890s, is now closed. In 1981 there opened in its place this comfortable, modern super-motel, geared to sporting holidays. It owns the golf course, and offers residents cheap rates. The countryside around is excellent for walking.
🍴 ⚓ 🕭 🗖 🖼 🏊 ⇌ ℘ ✓

St-Rémy-de-Provence

Map 9E4. 21km (13 miles) s of Avignon. 13210 B.-du-R.
Population: 7,970 i Pl. Jean-Jaurès ☎ (90) 92−05−22.

The pleasant town of St-Rémy is a thriving market garden
centre, situated in a fertile plain. It was the birth-place of
Nostradamus, astrologer and seer (who later lived in *Salon-de-
Provence*). The town has two museums. One, the **Musée
Lapidaire** (*Hôtel de Sade, Rue du Parège* ▨ ▧ *closed Tues
(Apr−Sept), Sat, Sun (Mar and Oct), Nov−Feb*) is housed in
the former home of relatives of the sadistic marquis, and
contains a display of interesting finds from Glanum. The other,
the **Musée des Alpilles Pierre de Brun,** across the road (▨
closed Tues) is devoted to local folk art: costumes, *santons* and
souvenirs of Mistral and Nostradamus. There is a picturesque
market in the old town on Wed mornings. Above all, however,
St-Rémy is known for its nearby Roman monuments.

On the plain of Maillane and St-Rémy the sky can sometimes
seem more important than the earth, for here above the low
green land the dawns and sunsets quiver − magenta changing to
pale apple-green; scarlet to deep yellow − and at midday the sky
is as blue as in the tropics.

James Pope-Hennessy, *Aspects of Provence*, 1952

Sights and places of interest
Glanum and Les Antiques 🏛 ☆
*2km (1 mile) s of St-Rémy, beside the D5 ☎ (90) 92−23−79 ▨
Open Apr−Sept 9.00−12.00, 14.00−18.00 (closed Tues); Oct−Mar
10.00−12.00, 14.00−17.00 (closed Tues, Wed).*

Lying at the foot of the Alpilles, this former Gallo-Roman settlement has
been widely excavated since 1920 and is of particular interest because it
shows the diverse impact of first the Greeks, then the Romans in
Provence. In the 6thC BC it was a Gaulish settlement. Though it was
never a Greek colony, the influence of the Greeks at Marseille is clear, for
by the 2ndC BC the houses were being built to Greek design. When
Caesar colonized Provence the Romans settled at Glanum and have left
evidence of extensive building, including their customary forum, baths
and temples. In the 3rdC AD the town was destroyed by barbarian
invaders and today nothing is left standing more than a few feet high; but
the ground lay-out is clearly discernible.

To the w of a Roman-built street are Greek-style houses, notably the
house of Antes and the house of Atys, each with columns, peristyle and
fine mosaics. To the E are the Roman buildings − baths with a covered
gallery and bathing pool, a sizeable forum, and temples near its sw
corner. Further s is a nymphaeum still filled with fresh spring water, and
beside it six altars dedicated to Hercules. The Romans are thought to have
used Glanum as a hill station and spa.

Across the road from the entry to Glanum stand **les antiques**, the two
most memorable and inspiring Roman monuments in Provence. They
were obviously a part of Roman Glanum (both date from c.20 BC) but
somehow escaped the 3rdC destruction. They are not enclosed, and can
be inspected at any time.

The **arch**, the oldest in Provence, is decorated with sculptures of
captives chained to a tree and of garlands of fruit and flowers. Its top part
is missing. The **cenotaph**, however, is in a marvellous state of
preservation after 2,000yr. It was long thought to have been a
mausoleum, but scholars today hold the view that it was a memorial
erected in honour of Augustus' grandsons, Caius and Lucius, who died
young (the fine portrait bust of their mother *Julia*, is in the **Musée
Lapidaire** in St-Rémy). The square base carries elaborate bas-reliefs of
an infantry and a cavalry battle, a boar hunt, and marine emblems.
Beneath the cupola are the toga-clad statues of the two young men.
St-Paul-de-Mausole
Just N of Glanum, E of the D5. Open daily 9.00−12.00, 14.00−18.00.

A former monastery, this fine building, named after the Glanum mausoleum, has been a mental home since 1605. It was here that Van Gogh spent a year as a voluntary patient in 1889–90, after cutting off his ear in *Arles*. His cell is now closed to visitors, but you can see the bust of him in the drive, and the quiet flowery garden where he painted (his artistic powers did not diminish during this, the last year of his life), among others, his famous painting, *The Sower*. The beautiful cloister and the Romanesque chapel, both 12thC, are worth a visit in their own right.

Dr Albert Schweitzer was interned here during the First World War, for as an Alsatian he was a German citizen at the time.

≈≈ des Arts ☀
30 Bd. Victor-Hugo, 13210 St-Rémy ☎ *(90) 92–08–50* ☐☐
18 rms ☐ *16* ☐ *Closed first week in Nov, Feb.*

Location: On main street in the centre of town. This cheerful café-pension is aptly named, for the art-loving Laura family attract visiting artists and writers as well as students and locals to gossip, drink and play cards. Beamed ceilings, a pretty patio and creeper-hung terrace add to the atmosphere. Bedrooms have been modernized, while retaining their rustic charm. Just the place for the young, or the young at heart. (See restaurant.)
☑ ❤

≈≈ Le Castelet des Alpilles
6 Pl. Mireille, 13210 St-Rémy ☎ *(90) 92–07–21* ☐☐☐ *19 rms*
☐ *17* ☐ ☐ ☐ *mid-June to mid-Sept* ☐ ☐ ☐ *Closed mid-Nov to Mar 10.*

Location: On the main road just s of the town centre. An Edwardian villa converted to a sympathetic little family hotel, run by a friendly local couple. The lounge is dull, but the flowery tree-lined garden is quite idyllic. Some bedrooms are in Louis XVI style, others have balconies facing the Alpilles. (See restaurant.)
☑ ❤ ♨

≈≈ Château de Roussan
Route de Tarascon, 13210 St-Rémy ☎ *(90) 92–11–63* ☐☐ *12 rms* ☐ *12* ☐ *Closed mid-Oct to mid-Mar.*

Location: In its own 75-acre park, 2.5km (1½ miles) w of St-Rémy off the N99. The Roussan family, from Montpellier, have owned this superb, small 18thC château for 100yr as their summer residence.

Now, to make ends meet, they accept paying guests for bed and breakfast; but the atmosphere of a private home remains, and the interior with its Louis XV furniture and red-tiled floors is most gracious. Only the bathrooms are modernized. Browse in the library, explore the 16thC farmhouse once lived in by Nostradamus or stroll around the vast rambling garden, shaded by tall plane trees where pigeons flutter, swans glide in the streams and fountains cascade into pools full of goldfish. This is a noble house and park, owned by a gentle family, and steeped in romantic melancholy.
☐ ☐ ☜ ❤

≈≈ des Arts ♣
Address and ☎ *as hotel* ☐ *to* ☐☐ *Last orders 21.15. Closed Wed (Oct–Mar), three weeks in Feb, second week in Nov.*

It's usually a question of scrambling or queuing to get a table in this ever-animated and extremely popular dining-room where, despite the pressure, *la patronne* Nicole Caritoux serves her husband's *cuisine familiale*, such as *cuisses de grenouilles provençale* and *côte de boeuf aux cèpes.* (See hotel.)

≈≈ Le Castelet des Alpilles
Address and ☎ *as hotel* ☐☐ *to* ☐☐ ☐ ☐ ☐ ☐ ☐ ☐ *Last orders 21.00. Closed mid-Nov to Feb.*

In summer, try to eat on the charming terrace by the garden. Cheerful service, traditional cuisine. **Specialities:** *Bourride, gratin de crustaces, daube Provençale.* (See hotel.)

Places nearby

Maillane (*6km (4 miles)* NW *of St-Rémy*)   In this pretty village the poet Mistral was born, lived much of his life and died: he lies buried in the cemetery. The house where he lived from 1876 till 1914 is now the **Muséon Mistral**, where rooms have been preserved as they were on his death.

St-Tropez

Map 13H12. 69km (43 miles) E of Toulon. 83990 Var.
Population: 5,430 i Quai Jean-Jaurès ☎(94) 97–41–21.

That legend of our times, St-Tropez, is what you make of it. For
some it remains a charming old fishing port, loved by artists,
cradled by green hills and facing out across its blue bay towards
the Maures mountains. For others it is a haunt of high society;
or a stage for trendily Bohemian eccentrics; or a commercialized
fairground beset by trippery mobs who come in hapless quest
for that elusive legend. There's no doubt that the legend has
grown distinctly jaded, since the far-off days when, along with
Haight-Ashbury and Carnaby Street, St-Tropez embodied the
Swinging Sixties.

St-Tropez' propulsion into limelight in the 1960s was
spearheaded by a film director and his young starlet wife, but its
true beginnings stemmed from less pleasant happenings. It was
named after Torpes, a Roman officer martyred under Nero for
his Christian beliefs, whose headless body is said to have found
its way across the sea to this spot; he is venerated to this day by a
bust in the main church and by the annual *bravade* festival.
Destroyed by the Moors in 739, St-Tropez was finally rebuilt in
the 15thC by the Genoese, and for nearly 200yr was semi-
autonomous. Its citizens had a flair for naval warfare, putting a
Spanish fleet to rout in 1637, so it is fitting that France's
greatest admiral, the Bailli de Suffren, should have been born
here (statue on the Quai de Suffren).

St-Tropez' career as a centre of culture did not begin until the
late 19thC when Guy de Maupassant discovered it by chance. In
1892 the painter Paul Signac settled here, and was quickly
followed by Bonnard, Matisse and others who came for the
summer. Between the wars the town became a kind of
Montparnasse *plage* – full of artists and writers, such as Colette,
taking summer breaks from Paris. In Aug 1944 the retreating
Germans blew up the port – the pretty pink, white and yellow
houses that line the quay today are clever copies of the old ones.

In 1957, St-Tropez' post-war fortunes took another sharp
change of direction. Roger Vadim brought the little-known
Brigitte Bardot on location here to make *And God Created
Woman*. The film was a *succès fou* and started a cult for both
Bardot and St-Tropez.

Today, despite St-Tropez' tarnished reputation, it still
attracts enough lovely ladies and smooth young men from the
milieu of fashion, showbiz and the media to keep its trendy
flavour; and a surprising number of truly rich, distinguished
and famous remain loyal to St-Tropez. Among those with villas
in or near town are Bardot, Charlotte Rampling/Jean-Michel
Jarre, Herbert von Karajan and Gunter Sachs. Other celebrities
line up their yachts, stern to, along the quay, among them
Harold Robbins, Sam Spiegel, Sergio Leone, Jack Nicholson.
Nubile companions recline on deck beside the inevitable vase of
gladioli, and brazenly sip champagne under the unwavering
gaze of hundreds of tourists.

In winter, St-Tropez almost shuts down. Alone among the
Côte d'Azur's resorts, it faces N, wide open to the driving
Mistral.

Events: The folk festivals known as *bravades* are peculiar to
this part of France, and the two at St-Tropez are especially
famous. May 16–18 sees the Bravade de St-Torpes, dating from
the 16thC. The bust of the saint is taken from the church and
carried in procession round the town, with a guard of 100 men

in 18thC uniform, amid music, mirth and firing of blank
cartridges. Visitors are welcome to join in.

On June 15, there is the Fête des Espagnols, a more modest
bravade, to commemorate the victory over the Spanish fleet in
1637.

In July and Aug, there are classical concerts about once a
month in the citadel.

Sights and places of interest
Annonciade, Musée de l' ☆
Pl. Georges-Grammont ☎ (94) 97–04–01 ▨ Open June–Sept
10.00–12.00, 15.00–19.00; Oct, Dec–May 10.00–12.00,
14.00–18.00. Closed Tues, Nov.

St-Tropez' turn-of-the-century heritage as a leading artistic centre has
resulted in one of France's finest collections of paintings from that
period. It was donated to the town in 1955 by local connoisseur, Georges
Grammont. Spacious and beautifully lit, the museum contains marble
and bronze sculptures by Maillol and Despiau, and some 100 canvasses,
both by St-Tropez artists such as Signac, Matisse and Bonnard, and
many others. There are charming Van Dongen portraits of girls,
attractive bathing scenes by Manguin, cheerful Dufys, colourful
Provençal landscapes from Vlaminck and Braque. St-Tropez itself
appears time and again – in a colourful Camoin, a subtle *pointilliste*
Signac, and drawings and gouaches by Segonzac.

Citadelle
▨ Open June–Sept 10.00–12.00, 15.00–19.00; Oct, Dec–May
10.00–12.00, 14.00–16.00. Closed Thurs, Nov.

This 17thC fortress stands on a hill just E of the town, surrounded by
ramparts and a moat. In its *donjon* is a **maritime museum**, with a
reconstructed Greek galley, 17thC maps of the Mediterranean,
engravings of old St-Tropez and details of the 1944 Liberation.

Hotels

Byblos 🏨
Av. Paul-Signac, 83990 St-Tropez
☎ (94) 97–00–04 🕾470235 ▥▥▥▥
115 rms ▭ 115 ▦▦ ◨ ▬ AE ⊙
VISA Closed Nov–Mar.
*Location: On a hillside below the
Citadel, 450m (500ft) from the port.*
Today's most fashionable hotel in
the South of France, this exotic
fantasy was the dream-child of a
wealthy Lebanese with the
unlikely name of Prosper Gay-
Para. He built it in 1967 and named
it after the ancient Phoenician city
that once stood on his native shore.
The hotel is a pastiche of a
Provençal hill village: little white-
walled, red-roofed houses grouped
intimately round the swimming
pool. Inside is an ingenious
labyrinth of patios, alcoves and
archways where enough ancient
and modern *objets d'art* have been
assembled to fill a museum, mostly
from Lebanon and Syria, with
Greek and Roman touches.
Everything, from bedrooms
individually furnished with
opulent oriental fabrics and
European antiques, to the *salon
Arabe*, transferred intact from a
Beirut palace, attains a level of
studied glamour that comes near to
breaking new records even for the
Côte d'Azur. (See restaurant Le
Chabichou.)
▨ ▢ ▨ ⍦ ⫷ ⇌ ⛱

La Figuière
Route de Tahiti, 83350
Ramatuelle ☎ (94) 97–18–21
▥▥▥ to ▥▥▥ 37 rms ▭ 37 ▬
Closed Oct to week before
Easter.
*Location: In open country, amid
vineyards, close to Tahiti Beach.*
Modern villas have been grouped
around a converted 18thC
farmhouse to form a delightful
country hotel, all the more peaceful
for its proximity to St-Tropez.
▨ ▨ ⍦ ⍦ ⇌ ⌁

Lou Troupelen
Chemin des Vendanges, 83990
St-Tropez ☎ (94) 97–44–88
▥▥▥ 42 rms ▭ 42 ⊙ VISA
Closed mid-Oct to Mar.
Location: Amid vineyards on the SE
fringe of town. A new hotel,
designed in the style of an old pink-
walled Provençal *mas* and set in a
pretty garden. Rooms are simple
but comfortable, the atmosphere
cheerful and cosy.
▨ ⅍ ▨ ⍦ ⍦

Le Mas de Chastelas 🏨
Route de Gassin, 83990 St-Tropez
☎ *56–09–11* 🔲 *31 rms*
🔲 *31* 🚗 ⚡ AE ⓪ VISA *Closed*
Oct to Easter.
*Location: Secluded amid pine woods
and vineyards 3km (2 miles) w of
St-Tropez.* A 17thC farmhouse,
formerly used for breeding
silkworms, recently converted into
a select little hotel, very much in
vogue with celebrities who remain
loyal to St-Tropez but seek refuge
from the harbour area. The visitors'
book is filled with eye-catching
names from the arts world: Sagan,
Depardieu, and Nastasia Kinski.
Certainly the hotel is beautiful,
with the exact ambience of a private
house party, where guests easily
strike up friendships and return

every year. There are few greater
pleasures than sitting by the lovely
pool, or in the graceful salon,
sipping an exquisite *champagne
framboise*. Amenities at this
delightful hotel include a jacuzzi
and a children's playground. (See
restaurant.)
🔲 🔲 ⚓ ⚡ ≈ ✍

🏩 Other good hotels include: **Lou
Cagnard** (*Av. P-Roussel*
☎ *(94) 97–04–24* 🔲 *to* 🔲); **La
Mandarine** (*Route de Tahiti*
☎ *(94) 97–21–00* 🔲); **Les
Palmiers** (*26 Bd. Vasserot, 83990
St-Tropez* ⓿ *(94) 97–01–61* 🔲 *to*
🔲); **Résidence de la Pinède**
☎ *(94) 97–04–21* 🔲); **Le Yaca**
(*1–3 Bd. d'Aumale*
☎ *(94) 97–11–79* 🔲).

Restaurants

Le Chabichou
Address as hotel Byblos
☎ *(94) 54–80–00* 🔲 *to* 🔲 🔲
AE ⓪ VISA 🔲 🔲 🔲 *Last orders
23.30. Closed mid-Nov to Mar.*
The luxurious restaurant of the
Hotel Byblos (see above) serves its
dazzling array of guests with some
of the best food in the area (at fancy
prices). The set menus are better
value than the *carte*. The *cuisine* is
nouvelle, and complicated.
Specialities: *Panaché de homard et
pied de porc aux pois gourmands,
blanc de turbot en grillade, soupe de
fraises et de rhubarbe.*

Café des Arts
Pl. des Lices ☎ *(94) 97–02–25*
🔲 🔲 🚗 *Last orders 23.30.
Closed Oct–Mar.*
A simple local café until it was
taken up by the St-Tropez *beau
monde* in the early 1960s, the Café
des Arts has remained chic and
shabby ever since. It packs them
in, not for the food, which is very
ordinary, but simply as a place to
see and be seen and to have fun.

Chez Nano
Pl. de l'Hôtel-de-Ville
☎ *(94) 97–01–66* 🔲 🔲 🚗 AE
⓪ VISA *Last orders 24.00. Closed
Tues (except July–Aug), mid-Jan
to end March.*
Another intensely Tropézien

place, crowded alike with tourists
and the chic-Bohemian set. Pretty
lighting, exuberant service,
deafening chatter, even on the
terrace. The *carte* is short, simple
and so-so; but the food is not the
main reason for being there.

Le Mas de Chastelas
Address and ☎ *as hotel* 🔲
🔲 🔲 🚗 AE ⓪ VISA *Last
orders 22.30. Closed
Oct–Easter.*
Lunches, served to residents only,
are light and delicious meals served
by the pool. Dinner, also served by
the pool when fine, is more
elaborate and open to non-
residents. The cooking is excellent
– fresh and full of taste. The menus
change often. ***Specialities:***
*Volaille au citron et sa barigoule de
légumes, filet de boeuf à la crème d'ail
doux.* (See hotel.)

🍽 Other restaurants include:
Chez Fuchs (*7 Rue des
Commerçants* ☎ *(94) 97–01–25* 🔲
to 🔲); **L'Echalote** (*5 Rue Allard*
☎ *(94) 54–83–26* 🔲 *to* 🔲); **Le
Girelier** (*Quai Jean-Jaurès*
☎ *(94) 97–03–87* 🔲); **La
Marjolaine** (*10 Rue François-
Sibilli* ☎ *(94) 97–04–60* 🔲 *to*
🔲); **La Romana** (*Chemin des
Conquettes* ☎ *(94) 97–18–50* 🔲
dinner only).

Nightlife

Places to see and be seen are at: **L'Aphrodisiaque** (*Rue
Allard*); **Café des Arts** (*Pl. des Lices*); **L'Escale** (*Quai Jean-
Jaurès*); **Nano** (*4 Rue Sybille*).

La Ste-Baume, massif

Discos

Les Caves du Roy, in the Hotel Byblos, is the *Cote*'s most fashionable disco, along with Jimmy'z at Monte-Carlo; dress very modishly if you want a chance of being let in (*open mid-June to mid-Sept from 22.30*). **Le Papagayo** (*Nouveau Port*) is for anyone. **Le Pigeonnier** (*11 Rue de la Ponche*) is moderately trendy and always crowded.

Beaches

St-Tropez owes much of its attraction to its fantastic sandy beach – an unbroken 6km (4 miles), SE of the town along the **Baie de Pamplonne**. As at Cannes, almost the whole beach is parcelled into 30 privately-run sectors where you must pay. There is no road along the shore, and the beaches are accessible only via winding lanes, not always well-signposted. Some free beaches do exist, mostly further S, beyond Cap Camarat.

St-Tropez beaches are a case study in exotic hedonism. All are topless, some are bottomless; some of the sights are wonderful, others unmentionable. The beaches include: **Tahiti**, since the 1960s one of the most famous beaches in the world, though today its chic is tinged with decadence, like a late Roman orgy; **Moorea**, now more *à la mode* than Tahiti; **La Voile Rouge**, very chic; **Club 55**, also select, if less so than Moorea; **Blouch**, for nudists.

Places nearby

Gassin (*8km (5 miles) sw of St-Tropez*)   A well-known village perched high on a ridge above the plain, with marvellous views all around. Its church, floodlit at night, is a landmark for miles around. The village used to be a look-out point in the defence against Saracen pirates.

≡ **Bello Visto** ♣
Pl. des Barrys ☎ *(94) 56–17–30* 🔲 💬 ■ 🍴 *Last orders 22.00 Closed Tues, mid-Oct to Mar.*
The view alone is worth a visit, quite apart from the excellent local cooking and the entertaining company of the St-Tropéziens who pack out the place. Dishes such as *soupe au pistou* and *civet de porcelet* are served in the beamed dining-room or under giant nettle trees (common in the St-Tropez area).

Ramatuelle   The lovely Ramatuelle peninsula stretches S of St-Tropez, its hillsides cloaked in vineyards and lush woodland of oak and pine. It remains remarkably unspoilt, despite the influx of tourists to the area. Ramatuelle itself is a pleasing village on a low hill, with quiet old alleyways. The noble elm in its main square was planted in 1598.

The three ruined **Moulins de Paillas** stand 3km (2 miles) NW of Ramatuelle on a high hilltop next to a radio beacon. It's worth driving up here for the view, the best in the region.

🛏 **Le Baou** (☎ *(94) 79–20–48* ▮▮▮), a sophisticated and stunningly located modern hotel, in the style of a Provençal *mas*.

La Ste-Baume, massif de ★

*Map **11**H9. Approx. 32km (20 miles) E of Marseille. B.-du-R. and Var. Approx. 130sq. km (50 sq. miles).*
The most spectacular of all the craggy limestone massifs of Provence also breathes the mystery of early Christian legend. Its name comes from the Provençal *baoumo* (cave): here St Mary Magdalene is said to have retreated alone to a cave on the

heights and spent the last 30 yr of her life (see *Les Saintes-Maries-de-la-Mer* and *St-Maximin*).

Arid and bare on its s slopes, richly forested to the N, the range runs for 16km (10 miles) between Aubagne and *St-Maximin*. The best excursion through its wild heart is the D2 from **Gémenos**, E of Aubagne, soon passing on the right the **Parc de St-Pons** (varied, beautiful trees; remains of a 13thC Cistercian abbey). From there the narrow road loops up and up into a blasted landscape of toothy white crags. Here is the gaunt pinnacle of the **Fourcade rock**, and the sugar-loaf **Pic de Bertagne** crowned by a domed white observatory. All around are majestic views, towards Marseille to the w, the coast at Cassis to the s, and far to the N the Mont Ste-Victoire above *Aix*.

As you reach **Plan d'Aups** there's a sudden change of landscape: a mild upland plateau with neat farmsteads and cultivated fields. A little further on, to the right, is an old hostelry now run by Dominicans as a religious and cultural centre: it has a Renaissance chimney-piece and statues of *Louis XI* and his wife. Here too is the **Forêt de Ste-Baume**, famous for its giant beeches, trees rarely found in southern France. To the s the view sweeps up to the high crest of the massifs, where a stone monument crowns its topmost peak, **St-Pilon** 1,150m (3,800ft). This is holy ground, for Mary Magdalene's alleged cave is a few yards w of St-Pilon: in the 14thC kings, popes and princes would make the pilgrimage to this lonely spot, where midnight mass is still celebrated every July 22 in a chapel in the cave. From the hostelry on the main road you can walk through the lovely forest and up, along well-marked paths, to the cave and St-Pilon (views which take in Mt Ventoux, 104km (64 miles) to the N). From the hostelry, the main road winds on down through woods of silver-green trees to **Nans-les-Pins**.

Park ■ (*Vallée de St-Pons, Gémenos* ☎ (42) 82–20–34 ❚❚), a plain, modern *auberge* with a large garden, very pleasant for eating in.

Relais de la Magdeleine (*Gémenos* ☎ (42) 82–20–05 ❚❚❚❚), a most comfortable and attractive hotel in a lovely old 18thC building; many amenities.

Les Saintes-Maries-de-la-Mer ☆
*Map **8**G3. 39km (24 miles) sw of Arles. 13460 B.-du-R. Population: 2,120 i Av. Van-Gogh ☎ (90) 47–82–55.*
The only town or village in the Camargue – and hence its self-styled capital – is today a popular sea-side resort, strung out between the lagoons and the sand dunes with their miles of fine beaches. The nucleus of old alleys round the church is appealing, notably the traffic-free **Av. Victor-Hugo**. Here the **Musée Baroncelli** (▧ *closed Wed, Nov*) is devoted to the wildlife and customs of the Camargue. But folklore at Les Saintes-Maries is not relegated to museums; it is more a part of daily life than at almost any other town of Provence. Provençal is still spoken, folk groups are active, and the year revolves around the great traditional festivals.

The town is a place of pilgrimage, for it is at the heart of the legends relating to the arrival of Christianity in Provence. According to a 9thC legend, a boat without sails or oars left the Holy Land and drifted ashore here, bearing St Mary Jacobe, the Virgin's sister, St Mary Salome, the mother of James and John, St Mary Magdalene, Saints Martha, Maximin, Lazarus and Sidonius, and Sara, their African servant. The legend relates

191

that the saints then split up to evangelize Provence – Martha to *Tarascon*, Lazarus to St-Victor at *Marseille*, Maximin and Sidonius to *Aix* (see *St-Maximin*), and Mary Magdalene to *La Ste-Baume*. The two other Marys and Sara stayed on here – hence the town's name – where they built an oratory, and were buried on the spot where the great church now stands.

Events: May 23–27, Pèlerinage des Gitanes (gipsy celebration). This famous festival is the great event of the gipsy year. They converge here in their thousands from all parts of France and other countries too (mainly Spain), bringing their caravans which today are all motorized, not horse-drawn. However, the gipsies themselves are still an exotic sight, with their dusky good looks and bright clothes. On May 23 they hold a night vigil in the church crypt in honour of St Sara, whom long ago they chose as their patroness. The next day the reliquary of the two Marys is lowered from its high chapel, in a special service. Then on May 25 comes the pilgrimage: a procession of clergy, gipsies, *gardians*, Arlesiennes and flute-players, all in fine costume, carries the blue and pink statues of the two saints, in their little boat, as far as the sea. They are solemnly taken back to the church in the afternoon. The next two days are given over to Provençal fêtes, with bull races, horsemanship and folk dancing.

The same pilgrimage also takes place on the weekend nearest Oct 22 and the first Sun in Dec, but these are less colourful.

Church 🏛 † ✩
Pl. de l'Église. Crypt open Apr–Sept 7.30–12.00, 14.00–19.30; Oct–Mar 7.30–18.00.

Built in fortified style as a defence against Saracen and other attackers in the 11thC, this strange looking church does resemble a fort, with its massive walls and crenellated parapet round the roof. Above is a high five-arch belfry, visible from afar across the plain (worth climbing up, for the view). The simple, sombre nave is almost bare of decoration, save for the showcase of naïve ex-votos and, to the left of the altar, the 'boat of the Stes-Maries', carried in procession in the festivals. The reliquary allegedly holding the bones of the saints is in a chapel above the apse, kept closed. But you can visit the 15thC crypt, where the reliquary of *Sara* stands across the altar from an elaborately dressed statue of the grave-faced lady. The rows of burning candles show how much she is still venerated.

🐎 L'Étrier Camarguais
Chemin bas des Launes, 13460 Les-Saintes-Maries-de-la-Mer
☎ *(90) 47–81–14* ▥ *27 rms*
🛏 *27* 🛋 🍴 🍴 🍴 *June–Aug*
AE ⊙ ⊙ VISA *Closed mid-Nov to Easter.*

Location: In its own park, in the Camargue, 3km (2 miles) N of town, just off N570. The corner of the Camargue just N of Les Saintes-Maries has a dozen or so modern ranch-hotels, where the accent is on riding and other sports.

L'Étrier ('the stirrup') is one of the best: spacious, lively, youthful, informal. Dogs pad about in the huge log-cabin lounge with its cosy leather chairs, the barman wears a local cowboy hat, and *l'après-cheval* proves it can be as relaxing and amusing as *l'après-ski*. The hotel has 25 horses, for hire by

the hour, as well as a big swimming pool and lido, romantically lit at night with pink and orange lamps. Bedrooms, rustic and spacious, are in bungalows spread across the park.

Meals are served on the patio by the pool, or in the large dining-room, where the log fire is used for grills. The hotel has its own disco, **La Brouzetière** nearby, just out of earshot, and the best in the area.
🍴 ⚡ ▯ 🍴 🏄 ⚓ 🏊 🎿 🐎 ⛵

🐎 Mas de la Fouque ▥
Route d'Aigues-Mortes, 13460 Les-Saintes-Maries-de-la-Mer
☎ *(90) 47–81–02* ▥ *10 rms*
🛏 *10* 🛋 🍴 🍴 🍴 ⊙ VISA
Closed mid-Nov to Mar.

Location: 5km (3 miles) NW of town, in its own big park, beside a Camargue lake. Another modern

ranch-hotel: this one is smaller and more luxurious than the **Étrier**, also more formal, with an older clientele. The restaurant has large windows overlooking the lake, as does the very glamorous lounge; lunches are served by the heated swimming pool in summer. The decor is mostly Camarguais, with modern touches, for example the sumptuous en suite bathrooms.
🏠 ♿ ☑ 🐾 ⑃⑄ ➰ ⑉♨ ⮜ ♠ 🐎

🍴 Other recommended hotels in the area include: **Le Galoubet** (*Route de Cacharel* ☎ (90) 47–82–17 ▥▯); **Pont des**

Bannes et Mas Ste-Hélène (*Pont des Bannes* ☎ (90) 47–81–09 ▥▯ to ▥▯).

🍴 **Bruleur de Loups** (*Av. Gilbert-Leroy* ☎ (90) 97–83–31 ▯▯ to ▥▯) is an attractive restaurant with terrace overlooking the sea, serving delicate, if ambitious *cuisine*; **Pont de Gau** ♥ (*Pont de Gau* ☎ (90) 47–81–53 ▯▯ to ▥▯) is a down-to-earth *auberge* serving authentic *cuisine Camarguaise*. There are several lively, inexpensive restaurants around the Pl. Esprit Pioch.

Ste-Maxime

Map 13H12. 61km (38 miles) sw of Cannes. 83120 Var. Population: 6,880 ℹ *Bd. de la République* ☎ (94) 96–19–24.

Ste-Maxime's tree-lined promenade with its glittering lights and busy terrace-cafés is an elegant sight at night. It is the main focus of this sizeable modern bathing resort which – compared with its neighbours – is decidedly more fun than St-Raphael, if less exotic than St-Tropez just across the bay. Ste-Maxime has a faithful clientele of young people and of families who are drawn by the sheltered climate and the miles of public sandy beaches. It is not an expensive place. Seaside tourism is its sole industry, and there's plenty to do. Sports include water-skiing, wind-surfing, yachting (there is a good marina) and golf (9-hole course at Beauvallon, 5km (3 miles) to w). There are also a casino, six nightclubs and numerous fêtes and festivals during the summer.

🍴 Recommended hotels in Ste-Maxime are: **Beau Site** (*5 Bd. des Cistes* ☎ (94) 96–19–63 ▥▯), a family hotel with swimming pool, greenery and views of the bay; **Calidianus** (*Bd. Jean-Moulin* ☎ (94) 96–23–21 ▥▯), a quiet and very attractive modern holiday hotel; **L'Ensoleillée** ♥ (*Av. de la Gare* ☎ (94) 96–02–27 ▯▯), a clean, comfortable pension; meals are not obligatory except July–Aug; **Marie-Louise**, (*Hameau de Guerrevieille* ☎ (94) 96–06–05 ▥▯), in a lovely garden, a white villa with small, spruce bedrooms, pretty dining-room and a serene, rather wistful atmosphere.

🍴 The best restaurants in Ste-Maxime are: **Le Gruppi** (*Av. Charles-de-Gaulle* ☎ (94) 96–03–61 ▥▯), a rather pricey, formal restaurant on the promenade where very fresh fish is classically served; **La Réserve** (*Pl. Victor-Hugo* ☎ (94) 96–18–32 ▯▯), good regional dishes; **Sans Souci** ♥ (*34 Rue Paul Bert* ☎ (94) 96–18–26 ▯▯), a shining example of the kind of small family restaurant at which the French excel – simple, pretty setting, swift and smiling service, competent local *cuisine*.

Place nearby

Between Ste-Maxime and St-Aygulf lie a string of tiny resorts. At **Les Issambres**, the coast is beautiful, with sandy coves enclosed by rocks and umbrella pines waving in the breeze. The hotels are spread out at intervals, retaining their privacy.

🍴 **Rodnoi** (*Les Issambres* ☎ (94) 96–90–08 ▥▯), a simple, modestly-priced hotel beside the pines.

🍴 **La Réserve** (*Les Issambres* ☎ (94) 43–00–41 ▥▯) is a beautifully sited *auberge* above the sea serving high-quality, high-priced dishes.

Salernes

*Map 12F11. 23km (15 miles) w of Draguignan. 83690 Var.
Population: 2,520.*

Owing to its local clay deposits, this little town has a thriving
traditional industry: the making of coloured enamel tiles, for
bathrooms and other domestic uses. At some of the workshops
visitors can watch the tiles being made, and can buy samples.
Among the best: **Emphoux** on the Draguignan road, **Polidori**
on the Entrecasteaux road. The leading local firm, **Pierre
Boutal**, has a large showroom and salesroom, but the factory is
closed to visitors.

Allègre *(Rue J-J Rousseau* ☎ *(94) 70–60–30* ▯▯ *to* ▮▮▯*)*.

Places nearby

Cotignac *(13km (8 miles) sw of Salernes)*   A little town lying at
the foot of a brown cliff, pock-marked with a number of curious
caves, some of them once inhabited. To the s and e stretch miles
of vineyards.

Lou Calan *(1 Cours Gambetta* ☎ *(94) 04–60–40* ▮▮▯*)*.

Entrecasteaux *(8km (5 miles) s of Salernes)*.   A medieval village
in a narrow valley, with a 13thC humpback bridge and Gothic
fortified church. The village is dominated by its great château,
in front of which lies a formal garden by Le Nôtre, designer of
the Tuileries and Versailles gardens. It is now communal
property.

Château ✿

☎ *(94) 04–43–95* ▦ *Open daily Apr–Sept 10.00–20.00; Oct–Mar
10.00–18.00.*

The austere, prison-like castle, once strongly fortified, has, to put it
mildly, had a bizarre history, not least in recent years. It belonged to local
seigneurs, one of whom, in the 18thC, killed his young wife and then
vanished into a Portuguese jail. This event brought the family into such
disrepute and poverty that gradually the château fell into ruin. Finally it
was bought in 1974 by Ian McGarvie-Munn, avant-garde painter,
Scottish nationalist, soldier and adventurer, ex-commander-in-chief of
the Guatemalan Navy and married to the grand-daughter of a former
president of that country.

   McGarvie-Munn patiently restored the château at his own expense.
He died in 1981 and the castle is now run by his son as a museum of his
father's collections, which are at least original, if stupefyingly eclectic.
On the ground floor: Scottish bagpipes, pre-Columbian ceramics, 17thC
Chinese watercolours on silk, Murano goblets designed by the artist. In
the basement: a collection of Provençal kitchenware. Upstairs:
McGarvie-Munn's own lurid surrealist paintings. A permanent
exhibition is devoted to Admiral d'Entrecasteaux. Visitors enter through
the private kitchen and are free to wander through the living rooms. In
summer, classical concerts are sometimes held on the castle's lovely
terrace.

Fox-Amphoux *(13km (8 miles) w of Salernes)*   Superb views
over great forests of pine and oak are to be had from this old hill
village on a high plateau.

Auberge du Vieux Fox
Fox-Amphoux, 83670 Barjols ☎ *(94) 80–71–69* ▯▯ *to* ▮▮▯ *10 rms*
▭ *10* ⇔ ▬ ⇆ ▭ *June–Sept. Closed mid-Nov to Easter.*
Location: In the village square, with marvellous views. The South of France
has a fair proportion of really special hotels, ones that stand out for an
intimate quality that only the owners can provide, but they are still rare.

Here is one, run, as is often the case, by people who have forsworn the rat race for the pleasures and tribulations of running a hotel. Pierre Philippe, a furniture designer, and his wife Martine, an economist, took over this 16thC presbytery in 1975, then semi-derelict, and restored it with perfect taste. Bedrooms, inevitably small, are decorated in warm colours, each different; even the bathrooms have 16thC beams. Downstairs is a cosy salon with log fire.

◨ ▱ ⚓ ⟨⟨

⇶ Auberge du Vieux Fox
Address and ☎ as hotel ▥▯ ⌁ ▦ ⇔ ⇌ *Last orders 21.15. Closed for lunch Tues, Wed, Thurs during Apr, June and Oct; mid-Nov to Easter.*

Bach and Vivaldi play softly in the delightful dining-room, filled with flowers, and the atmosphere is convivial and amusing as Martine Philippe chats with her guests. 'Inspired amateurism' is the Vieux Fox's style, which can have its drawbacks: service can be slow and the food is sometimes erratic. Pierre Philippe's repertoire is part Provençal, partly from Béarn, where he originally hails from. (Breakfasts are delicious, with homemade fig jam and bread freshly toasted at the log fire.)

Salon-de-Provence
Map **10***F6. 55km (34 miles) NW of Marseille. 13300 B.-du-R. Population: 35,587* ***i*** *Rue des Fileuses-de-Sole* ☎ *(90) 56−27−60.*

A busy market town, its main streets lined with plane trees, and a centre of the olive oil industry since the 15thC. Today it has military connections: not only is the French Air Force's officer training school here, but a museum of French Army history, the **Musée de l'Empéri** (▧▧ *closed Tues*), is installed in the 10thC Château de l'Empéri, former residence of the archbishops of Arles, lords of Salon. The museum contains some 10,000 army souvenirs dating from Louis XIV's day to 1918. Close by is a **museum** devoted to the astrologer Nostradamus, in the house where he spent the last 19yr of his life. He is buried in the 14thC church of St-Laurent.

3.5km (2 miles) N, beside the N7, is a memorial to the greatest of French Resistance heroes, *Jean Moulin*, tortured and killed by the Gestapo, whose tomb lies in the Panthéon in Paris.

⇙ Abbaye de Ste-Croix ▥▥
Route du Val de Cuech, 13300 Salon-de-Provence ☎ *(90) 56−24−55* ◑*401247* ▥▥ *20 rms* ▭ *20* ⇌ ⇶ AE ◉ VISA *Closed Dec to mid-Jan.*
Location: Secluded in its own large grounds, on a hillside 5km (3 miles) NE of Salon. A carefully restored 12thC abbey, furnished with antiques. There are stone stairways to each bedroom, some of which look over the pretty Romanesque cloister, others over the distant hills.(See restaurant.)
◨ ▱ ⚓ ⟨⟨ ⇌ ⁓ ♠ ⚐ ♨

⇙ A more central hotel is **Sélect** ▰ (*35 Rue Suffrèn* ☎ *(90) 56−07−17* ▯).

⇶ Abbaye de Ste-Croix ◿
Address and ☎ as hotel ▥▥ ⌁ ▦ ⇔ ⇌ AE ◉ VISA *Last orders 21.30. Closed Mon lunch, Nov−Mar.*
With a new chef installed in the kitchens, the hotel's restaurant, a graceful stone-walled room lit by candles, has begun to produce excellent food: lavish, and intelligently balanced, ranging from heavier traditional dishes such as *daube de mouton*, to lighter modern ones, for example *saucisson de la mer en brioche* and *poissons crus aux herbes*. (See hotel.)

⇶ Francis Robin ✤
1 Bd. Clémenceau ☎ *(90) 56−06−53* ▯ *to* ▥▥ ⌁ ▦ AE ◉ *Last orders 21.00. Closed Sun dinner, Mon, Feb.*
Not a cheap place, but smart and comfortable, with exceptionally good

195

cooking in a modern style. ***Specialities:*** *Mille-feuille d'agneau aux légumes nouveaux, aiguillette de canard aux mangues, featherlight pâtisseries.*

≡ **Craponne** (*146 Allées Craponne* ☎ *(90) 53–23–92* ▢ *to* ▥ [VISA]).

Places nearby
Château de Barben (*8km (5 miles)* E *of Salon*) The medieval château (▥ *closed Tues*) contains paintings by Van Loo as well as the Empire-style boudoir of Pauline Borghese, Napoleon's sister, who once lived there. In the grounds are a zoo, aviary and aquarium.

≡ **La Touloubre** (*La Barben* ☎ *(90) 55–16–85* ▢ *to* ▥ [AE] [VISA]).

Lambesc (*16km (10 miles)* E *of Salon*) An old town of great charm. Beyond it, a narrow road climbs steeply on to the **Chaîne des Côtes**, a former Résistance stronghold, where a monument now stands to those killed here by the Nazis.

≡ **Moulin de Tante Yvonne**
Rue Benjamin-Raspail ☎ *(42) 28–02–46* ▥ ▭ ≡ *Last orders 21.00. Closed Mon, Tues, July 15–Aug 15.*
Treat yourself to rich and tempting fare, washed down by good Provençal wine, at this very pretty converted 15thC mill. The recipes are all local, but with a touch of luxury about them. ***Specialities:*** *Crème de poissons de roche, flan de langouste, terrine de canard, crème d'amandes glacée aux kirsch.*

Vernègue (*11km (7 miles)* NE *of Salon*) A hilltop village ruined by an earthquake in 1909. The site affords spectacular views over SW Provence.

Saorge ☆
Map **16**D16. *30km (18 miles)* NE *of Sospel. 06540 Alpes-Mar. Population: 337 (including Fontan)* **i** *at Fontan mairie* ☎ *(93) 04–50–01.*
Approached from the N204, as it finally emerges from the impressive **Gorges de Saorge**, the village of Saorge suddenly appears, soaring high above, clinging to the mountainside – a crescent of old houses, yellow, pink and grey, balanced precariously one above the other. It looks unreachable, but there is a road from Fontan 3km (2 miles) to the N. From there you must park, and climb on foot through the maze of steep stairways.

To the N of Saorge, the N204 continues to follow the Roya valley through the similar **Gorges de Bergue**, with their towering red rocks eroded into every kind of strange shape. Above the road are the numerous high viaducts of the Nice–Turin railway, a great feat of mountain engineering; the terrain is such that some tunnels make loops inside the mountain, and one can see a train entering the cliffside at one point, only to emerge minutes later directly above. The line, destroyed in the war, was only reopened in 1980.

Seillans
Map **13**F12. *31km (19 miles)* W *of Grasse. 83440 Fayence, Var. Population: 1,210* **i** ☎ *(94) 76–96–04.*
A quiet and lovely old medieval village facing SE across a valley towards the Esterel hills. It has a 12thC ruined château,

fountains and steep paved alleyways. The ramparts of the château were once used for defence against Saracen invaders, and indeed the name Seillans derives from the Provençal word meaning a pot of boiling oil. Today's more peaceful invasion is of well-to-do villa owners who find this one of the most delightful corners of Provence. Max Ernst used to live and paint here.

⌬ Deux Rocs
Pl. d'Amont, 83770 Seillans ☎ *(94) 76–87–32* ▮▮▯ *15 rms* ▭ *15* ⇌
▭ ⇌ *Closed Nov–Mar.*
Location: In a small square, opposite two rocks that stand by a gateway to the old village. An ex-biochemist from Paris, the delightful Lise Hirsch has recently converted this 18thC *maison bourgeoise* into a chic and intimate little hotel. The outside, with cream walls and brown shutters, has miniature fir trees and geraniums lining the front; while inside, the bedrooms are gaily decorated with unusual fabrics and wallpapers. As at the **Hôtel de France** (see below), the tables outside encircle a fountain, in the square. The dining-room, where the food is usually reliable, is heavily beamed and inviting; and a small private room with deep sofas leads off it.
⌂ ▱ ⚲

⌬ de France
Pl. du Thouron, 83770 Seillans ☎ *(94) 76–96–10* ▮▮▯ *26 rms* ▭ *26* ▭
⇌ *Closed Jan.*
The rooms of the long-established Hôtel de France are comfortable, if characterless, and there is a new swimming pool at the back.

⇌ Clariond
For address and ☎ *see Hôtel de France* ▮▮▯ ▭ ▆▮ ⌂ *Last orders 21.00. Closed Wed (Sept–May), Jan.*
This is the popular restaurant of the **Hôtel de France**, and all is indeed typically French at this family-run *auberge*: in summer, tables are set in a charming square, under plane trees and beside an old fountain; lunch here is a joy. M. Clariond's cooking, in the sound tradition of the hinterland, suits the mood very well. *Specialities: Civet de lièvre, poulet aux écrevisses, feuilleté de lotte, saumon soufflé, noisettes de chevreuil à la groseille.*

Shopping
Several artisans work and sell their goods here. Among the best workshops are **Castel Jehanne d'Arc** *(in the village)* for pottery and weaving; and **Poterie du Vieux Moulin** *(1km (⅓ mile) along the Mons road, D53)*.

Places nearby
Bargemon *(13km (8 miles) sw of Seillans)*   Amid equally glorious woodland scenery, this village is less quaint than Seillans, but livelier and equally popular with summer residents (the British almost outnumber the Parisians). Plane trees line its avenues, fountains play in its little squares, and there are 12thC fortified gateways. The 14thC **church of St-Étienne**, built into the ramparts, has three 17thC retables (the best is on the second side-altar on the left). The sculpted heads of angels on the high altar are by Puget.

⇌ Chez Pierrot
Pl. Philippe-Chauvier ☎ *(94) 76–62–19* ▯ *to* ▮▮▯ ▭ ▆▮ ⌂ ▭ ⊙
Last orders 22.00 (summer), 21.30 (winter). Closed Mon (except June–Sept), Feb.
In the village centre: a typical *auberge*, where you can eat in the country dining-room, or out on the square under the plane trees and watch local life go by. M. Pierrot is no pantomime figure but a serious cook who

serves basic Provençal dishes (mostly meat and poultry; there is little fish on the menu), and some Périgourdin ones such as *magret de canard au poivre vert ou aux baies de cassis, confit de canard.*

⬛ Maître Blanc
☎ (94) 76–60–24 ▯▯ to ▮▮▯ ▭ ▬▬ ⬛ *Last orders 21.00. Closed Wed, Dec, Jan.*

Considered by local connoisseurs to be just a little superior, gastronomically speaking, to **Chez Pierrot**, Maître Blanc none the less is still an ordinary village restaurant serving good local food. Sunday lunch is a great institution here. Local families – great grandmothers to babes in arms – pile in for uproarious meals that last most of the afternoon.

Sénanque, Abbaye de ⬚ † ☆
Map **5***D6. 42km (26 miles)* E *of Avignon. Vaucluse*
☎ *(90) 72–02–05* ▬▬ ✗ *June–Sept. Open June–Sept 10.00–19.00; Oct–May 10.00–12.00, 14.00–18.00*

Of Provence's three beautiful 12thC Cistercian abbeys, *Silvacane*, *Thoronet* and Sénanque, the last best exemplifies that austere Order's love of isolated sites. It stands alone in a wild and narrow valley: the access route, over rocky hills from Gordes, is far from easy. Built in 1148, Sénanque is also the best preserved of the 'three sisters', perhaps because it has had the quietest history. Its only serious drama came in 1544, when it was attacked and damaged by Protestants from the nearby Lubéron who hanged some of the monks. Later it was repaired, then sold at the Revolution like most French monasteries. But the Cistercians acquired it again in 1854 – and they still own and run it today, from their base on the Ile St-Honorat.

The main buildings are all intact, unchanged since the 12thC apart from some restoration. The arcaded cloister is enchanting; so are the chapter-house and monks' dormitory with their Romanesque vaulted ceilings. In the Cistercian manner, the large and graceful church is bare of ornamentation: but it has carpets, rows of new chairs and other signs that today it is very much in use for services and concerts.

Indeed, Sénanque's ambience is strikingly different from that of its two sisters, locked in their mystical medieval stillness. Sénanque, for all its remote setting, is full of modern bustle, for today it houses a thriving lay and religious cultural centre. There are exhibitions of contemporary art; concerts, mainly of Gregorian music; and lectures and study groups on historical and religious subjects. The former refectory has a display of Cistercian history, also an imaginative sequence of 'symbolic photographs' where bizarre landscapes are counterpointed by biblical and philosophical quotations. Above all, odd though it may seem, the **Collections Sahariennes** (Centre for Saharan Studies) has a fascinating **museum** here: details of the Tassili N'Ajjer cave paintings, of Touareg arts and lifestyles, and more.

Silvacane, Abbaye de ⬚ † ☆
Map **10***E7. 28km (18 miles)* NW *of Aix* ▬▬ ✗ *Open Apr–Sept 10.00–12.00, 14.00–18.30; Oct–Mar 10.00–12.00, 14.00–17.00. Closed Tues, Wed, Jan 1, May 1, Nov 1 and 11, Dec 25.*

Another of the celebrated trio of 12thC Cistercian abbeys in Provence (see *Sénanque* and *Thoronet*), Silvacane's setting, in the broad and ugly valley of the Durance, is less secluded and appealing than its sisters; but the harmonious purity of its Romanesque architecture is almost a match for theirs, and it follows a similar style. Its high-vaulted **church**, typically

Cistercian, is quite plain inside (note that here the side-chapels and sanctuary are not apsidal but rectangular). The **chapter-house**, built about 50yr later than the church, shows early Gothic influence in its vaulting; next door is the large, handsome **refectory**, rebuilt in the 15thC. The little **cloister** with its vaulted arcades exudes the same quiet charm as many Provençal cloisters of the period.

The abbey's name comes from *silva* (wood) and *cane* (reed), for it was built beside reed-filled marshes. In the late 12thC, with 110 monks, it was the most important of the 'three sisters' but its subsequent history was stormy. In the early 13thC the Benedictines briefly took it over by force. Then in 1357 it was pillaged by vagabonds and in 1590 was seized by bandits. For long periods it was no more than a village church. Today it belongs to the State, which is completing its restoration.

Sisteron ☆

*Map **6**C9. 39km (25 miles) NW of Digne. 04200 Alpes-de-H.-P. Population: 7,443 **i** Rue des Arcades ☎(92) 61–12–03.*
The ancient town of Sisteron forms the natural gateway to Provence from Grenoble and the Dauphiné region. It is impressively situated, at a point where the river Durance forces its way through a defile between high rocky hills. On the crest of the hill to the W stands the mighty **citadel**, while opposite is the fearsome toothy precipice of the **Rocher de la Baume**.

On Aug 15, 1944, the day of the landings in Provence, Sisteron was heavily (and some say needlessly) bombed by the Allies: 400 people were killed and many old houses destroyed. Much of the town is thus modern, but a few old medieval streets survive between the Pl. du Dr. Robert and the river. Here at 20 Rue Saunerie is the *hôtel* where Napoleon breakfasted on Mar 15, 1815, on his return along the *Route Napoléon* from Elba. The church of **Notre-Dame**, a former cathedral, is a fine example of 12thC Provençal Romanesque architecture, with a graceful nave and a portal in Lombard style. Beside it stand three isolated towers, remains of Sisteron's 14thC ramparts.

Event: In mid-July and mid-Aug, an annual festival of drama, dancing and music takes place in an open-air theatre on the N slope of the citadel hill.

La Citadelle 🏛 ☆

Open 9.00–19.00. Closed mid-Nov to mid-Mar.
"The most powerful fortress in my kingdom," said Henri IV of this massive stone edifice, towering on its rock above the town. Built in the 13th–16thC, it was badly damaged by the 1944 bombing but has since been partly restored. The long steep climb up to the top is well worth making, if only for the sweeping views from the upper terrace which show clearly that Sisteron has long been a natural frontier-point – to the S the plains and hills of Provence, to the N the rolling Dauphiné with its alpine backdrop. Points of interest in the citadel are the **tour de l'horloge** (once a prison); the 15thC Gothic **chapel** (almost totally rebuilt since 1944, with attractive modern stained-glass); and the amazing **Guérite du Diable** (Devil's Watchtower) perched precariously above the river. Free leaflets (in English, French or German) tell the citadel's story, but French speakers may also wish to listen to the dramatized record of its history broadcast continuously from the terrace. In summer the citadel is splendidly floodlit at night. At its entrance, the guardroom where French patriots were shut up by the Germans in 1940–44, is now a small museum of the local Résistance.

Two hotels in Sisteron are: **Grand Hôtel du Cours** (*Pl. de l'Église* ☎(92) 61–04–51 ▯▯ *to* ▮▮▮▮); **Tivoli** ▰ (*Pl. Tivoli* ☎(92) 61–15–16 ▯ *to* ▮▯).

Places nearby

Haute Vallée du Vançon   Cross the bridge over the Durance,
turn left, then immediately right along the D3, a narrow
mountain road that winds up to the defile of the Pierre Écrite: at
the far end of this little gorge, to the left of the road beside a
bridge, is a Roman inscription in honour of the Consul
Dardanus who opened up this route in the 5thC. The road
winds on via Authon to a dead end at the pass of Fontbelle. The
terrain of this upper valley is spectacularly mountainous.

Sospel

Map **16***D16. 06380. Alpes-Mar. 22km (14 miles)* N *of
Menton. Population: 2,150* **i** *at mairie* ☎ *(93) 04–00–26.*
A summer resort in a green valley on the Nice-Turin road with
attractive old streets and a fine medieval bridge with toll-gate.
The 17thC church, with Romanesque tower, houses a notable
Bréa retable of the *Madonna*. Sospel is a good excursion and
hill-walking centre.

des Étrangers

7 Bd. de Verdun, 06380 Sospel ☎ *(93) 04–00–09* 35 rms 13
July–Aug Closed Dec to mid-Jan.
Location: Main Turin road, on the edge of town. The ebullient Jean-Pierre
Domérégo, hotelier, cook, author and journalist, still has time for
introducing his beloved Sospel and its region to his flocks of satisfied
Anglo-American guests. After working in America, he has returned to
run this rather unattractively modernized but unpretentious little hotel
which has been in his family since 1862.

des Étrangers

Address and ☎ *as hotel* Last orders 21.00. Closed
Dec to mid-Jan.
M. Domérégo's cooking is tasty and varied. Leave room for his *glaces*
which have won prizes. **Specialities:** *Bouillabaisse de truite, cannelloni
maison, soufflées glacés.*

Shopping

Guy Pérus sculpts in local olive wood – objects ranging from
furniture to baby chess-sets (*Av. Aristide-Britan*).

Tarascon

Map **4***E4. 23km (14 miles)* SW *of Avignon. 13150 B.-du-R.
Population: 10,665* **i** *Av. de la République*
☎ *(90) 91–03–52.*
Until the death of Good King René in 1480, the Rhône was the
frontier between independent Provence and the kingdom of
France to the W. Tarascon, lying on the Rhône's E bank, was a
key strongpoint, hence its great fortified château. Here Good
King René (see *Aix*) spent much of his later life. It was he, a
lover of popular festivity, who invented the Festival of the
Tarasque for which the town has since been famous.

   The tale of the Tarasque is woven into the same 9thC legend
that the three St Marys landed in Provence having been set
adrift some years after the death of Jesus in an open boat. St
Martha, one of the party, made her way to Tarascon and found
it terrorized by an amphibious dragon which would emerge
from the Rhône to devour children and abduct their mothers.
The knights of Provence had failed to subdue this Tarasque,
but the saint did so, with the sign of the Cross. She ordered it
back to its cave in the river, and it was never seen again. St

Martha remained in Tarascon and is said to be buried in the church named after her.

Tarascon has also passed into literary history: the author Daudet made it the home town of his comic anti-hero Tartarin, in his trilogy of satiric novels. At the time, the Tarasconnais felt insulted, but today Tartarin has passed harmlessly into local folklore, even playing a role in the annual parade of the Tarasque.

Event: Last Sun in June, Fête de la Tarasque. Fascinating as a festival that has survived in a genuine form since the 15thC, the parade's focal point is the green, scaly papier-mâché monster whose head and tail are waved by young men standing inside. Costumed local figures walk beside, and there is much celebration.

Sights and places of interest
Château ★
Bd. du Château ▨ ▮ *Guided tours 10.00, 11.00, 14.00, 15.00, 16.00 (also 17.00, 18.00 Apr–Sept). Closed Tues.*
The massive walls and turreted towers of King René's castle stand proudly above the Rhône, looking across to **Beaucaire** and its own castle. The foundations and some walls are 12thC, but the main part was built by the king in the 15thC. For centuries it was used as a prison, indeed as recently as 1926. Yet it has survived almost intact, and has needed little restoration. From the outside, and even more so from within, it impresses as a perfect example of a medieval feudal castle, and is well worth a visit.

Surrounded by a moat, the castle is in two parts: the wide lower courtyard has square towers, while the *logis seigneurial* (royal dwelling) is a high compact fortress with two round towers and two square ones. Here the little inner court, elegant and intimate, has a first-floor restored loggia from where the king and his queen would watch miracle plays, jugglers and minstrels; the castle was a great centre for troubadours. The minstrels' gallery gives on to both the court and the chapel, and was used for religious services and secular singing.

From the court, a stone spiral stairway leads to the series of beautiful rooms on the three upper floors. The large banqueting hall has a fireplace for roasting and a wood ceiling covered with tiny paintings, all 15thC. But the curious graffiti on the walls, in this and other rooms, are of a later date: they are the work of prisoners, some of them English seamen captured in the 18thC. One sad little inscription reads: 'Here be three Davids in one mess/prisoners we are in distress. . . .' Upstairs is a priest's bedroom, with a hole in the wall for baking bread, and up further a chapel with separate oratories for the king and queen, built into walls which are up to 3m (11ft) thick. Finally, one arrives on the roof terrace from where supporters of Robespierre were hurled into the Rhône in 1794, when he fell from power.

The castle is bare of furniture, but there are plans to turn part of it into a museum of chivalry.
Ste-Marthe † ☆
Bd. du Château
Close to the castle entrance, this is a graceful 12thC building, restored after 1944 bomb damage. In the crypt, the 5thC sarcophagus is venerated as being the tomb of *St Martha*; above it is a lovely marble sculpture of the saint, a 17thC Genoese work. On the stairway is the fine Renaissance tomb of King René's seneschal, *Jean de Cossa*.

☞ ▦ **Terminus** ▬ *(Pl. du Colonel-Berrurier* ☎ *(90) 91–18–95* ▯ *).*

Place nearby
Abbaye de St-Michel-de-Frigolet *(6km (4 miles) NE of Tarascon, off D81)* Founded in the 10thC by the monks of Montmajour (see **Arles**), the abbey was rebuilt in the 19thC in a richly ornate style and is still actively in use (✗ *daily*); visitors can also attend the services, where the singing is very fine. The

Théoule

11thC chapel to the left of the nave has gilded wooden
sculptures, a gift from Anne of Austria in 1638.

The abbey lies in a beautiful valley just w of **La
Montagnette**, a range of rocky hills not unlike the Alpilles to
the SE.

Théoule

*Map **15**G14. 10km (7 miles) SW of Cannes. 06590 Alpes-Mar.
Population: 800 **i** 5 Pl. Général-Bertrand ☎(93) 49–28–28.*

A lively little bathing resort at the N end of the *Esterel massif*,
with reddish sandy beaches and wooded hills rising steeply
behind. Between Théoule and **Le Trayas** 10km (6 miles) to the
S, the coast is rather built up, with hotels and villas along a
succession of sandy coves. But S of Le Trayas there are no
beaches and the coast becomes wild and empty. Here the waves
dash against the bright red rocks, overlooked by the high russet
crags of the Esterel, notably the **Pic du Cap Roux**.

☎ Guerguy-La-Galère 🏨
*06590 Théoule ☎(93) 75–44–54 ▥▥▥ 14 rms ▭ 14 ▣ ▣ ⨋ Closed
mid-Nov to Jan.*

*Location: Overlooking the sea and Port la Galère, 2.5km (1½ miles) S of
Théoule.* Louis Guerguy, the *patron* and chef, is familiar with his guests
and strict with his staff. His personality enhances this already colourful
modern villa-hotel. It is superbly situated, with bedrooms, each
different, in glossy 'period' style; some have pink marble bathrooms.
One drawback: it's a steep, strenuous 10min walk down to the beach.
(See restaurant.)
▱ ▨ ▨ ⌄ ⟋

Hotel nearby
Miramar (*4km (2½ miles) S of Théoule*).

La Tour de l'Esquillon 🏨
*Miramar, 06590 Théoule ☎(93) 75–41–51 ▥▥ to ▥▥▥ 29 rms ▭ 29 ▣
▣ ▤ May–Sept. Closed Oct to Easter.*

*Location: Perched 90m (300ft) above the sea, beside the main N98 corniche
road.* A select little holiday hotel with bright modern decor and glorious
views across the bay to Cannes. Its own funicular plunges down to its
private beach just below: this consists of a concrete platform with lido (no
sand here). All the bedrooms have balconies facing the sea. As for the
food, it is classic, but not remarkable.
⚓ ▱ ▨ ▨ ⌄ ⟋ ⟋

⨋ Guerguy-La-Galère △
*Address and ☎ as hotel ▥▥▥ to ▥▥▥ ▭ ⨋ ▤ ▰ Last orders 21.00.
Closed Nov–Jan.*

M. Guerguy is, at his best, an inspired cook with a high reputation, but
his cooking can be erratic and at times uninteresting. *Specialities*:
Bourride, filet de loup en papillotte, Sachertorte. (See hotel.)

⨋ **Chez Aristide** (*46 Av. de Lérins* ☎(93) 49–96–13 ▮▮), which does
a delicious bouillabaisse; **Lei Pescadou** (*Pl. Général-Bertrand*
☎(93) 49–87–13 ▮▮), good for fish.

Place nearby
Port la Galère (*2.5km (1½ miles) S of Théoule*) Sculpted on
to a hillside, this bizarre holiday village is certainly the most
exciting post-war architectural development on the *Côte* with
the exception of *Port-Grimaud*. It is the brain-child of Jacques
Couelle, who also built Castellaras (see *Mougins*) and the Aga
Khan's new holiday complex in Sardinia. Couelle has been
called 'the French Gaudí', and with reason: his 'village' of 420

flats and villas is a honeycomb of deliberately irregular facades, pink, white and yellow, some looking like cave dwellings or as if a clever child had moulded them out of plasticine. Some people find the result hideous, others find that it does merge harmoniously with the landscape. Couelle has imaginatively blended different Mediterranean ethnic styles, to create a lavish, sensuous fantasy. Some perspectives recall Greece, or Morocco, while Couelle has also acknowledged the inspiration of Le Corbusier: the central club-house bears a startling resemblance to the great architect's chapel at Ronchamps.

Port la Galère is an exclusive private estate. It is not open to the public, unless interested in buying a villa or apartment, but a good view can be had by taking a boat offshore (the view from the road is disappointing).

Thoronet, Abbaye du ▥ ✝ ★

Map 12G11. 17km (11 miles) NE of Brignoles ▦ ✗ mid-July to late Aug. Open May–Sept 10.00–12.00, 14.00–18.00; Mar, Apr, Oct 10.00–12.00, 14.00–17.00; Nov–Feb 10.00–12.00, 14.00–16.00. Closed Tues.

In the 12thC the Cistercian monks chose three isolated spots in Provence and built the abbeys of *Sénanque*, *Silvacane* and Thoronet. The sublimely beautiful Abbaye du Thoronet reflects best of all, and to perfection, the austere and humble spirit of the Order through its architectural style of great purity and simplicity. The result is a Provençal Romanesque ensemble of exceptional harmony.

In the Cistercian manner, the **church** with its high vaulted ceiling is entirely devoid of furnishing or decoration – save for some frescoes added in the 17thC and now largely faded. The church is in the shape of a Latin cross, with narrow side-aisles opposite the altar. Outside, on the s wall, is a curious niche where local people could place their dead. On the N side a door leads to the delightful little **cloister**, entirely unadorned and very graceful, with cypresses and a hexagonal washing-house in the middle. Next door is the **chapter-house**, early Gothic, with ribbed vaulting; and beyond are the refectory, library and dormitories. Each room is finely proportioned.

The abbey has not always been in such an excellent state of repair. It fell into disrepair after the monks were expelled at the Revolution. In 1854 it was bought by the State and it has been superbly restored by the Service of Historic Monuments, using the same reddish-gold stone as the original from a nearby quarry which was reopened for the purpose.

In its secluded sylvan setting, the abbey exudes a sense of peace which visitors may find deeply spiritual. It is seen at its best in late afternoon, when the sunlight falling through bare windows gives the golden stone a soft glow. Visitors are welcome to attend vespers (*Mon–Sat 17.30, Sun 17.45*) in a plain but elegant little chapel beyond the cloister.

Toulon ☆

Map 11l9. 64km (40 miles) E of Marseille. 83000 Var. Population: 185,050. Airport at Hyères, 21km (13 miles) to E ☎ (94) 65–10–40 i 8 Av. Colbert ☎ (94) 22–08–22.

France's leading naval base is a busy commercial city in a theatrical setting: it lies around a deep natural harbour, sheltered by a ring of high hills that are crowned by Vaubanesque forts. At first it may seem a dull, workaday place; but it soon reveals itself as an exciting town of real character,

Toulon

especially in the old quarter by the port where the sailors of
many nations frequent the little bars and bistros, some less
innocent than others. Though not a place for a full holiday,
Toulon is fun to visit and a superb centre for excursions – and
prices are the lowest on the coast.

The oldest part of the port, the *vieille darse*, dates from the
16thC. But it was Louis XIV who turned Toulon into a great
naval base by building the Arsenal to the w, the *darse neuve*.
Here, in the 17thC and 18thC, convicts, Negros and political
prisoners, such as Huguenots, were forced to become galley
slaves, rowing the royal galleys, chained to their seats and
whipped by their masters into action if they slackened pace.
Passers-by would gawp and laugh at them as they shuffled,
shackled together, through the streets of Toulon.

It was at Toulon in 1793 that a young unknown artillery
captain, Napoleon Bonaparte, first made his military
reputation. The town had declared for the Royalists against the
Revolutionary government and were under the protection of an
English fleet, which set up a seemingly impregnable
strongpoint at Tamaris, on the sw of the harbour. But
Bonaparte directed on the English such a hail of cannon fire that
he forced them to withdraw. He was promptly promoted to
brigadier general.

Toulon has figured more recently in military annals. In Nov
1942, after the Allied landings in North Africa, the Vichy fleet
of 60 ships was scuttled by its own crews to evade falling into
German hands. The port was then heavily damaged by Allied
bombing in 1943–44, and in Aug 1944, after the Allied landings
in Provence, the Germans blew up the citadel and most of what
was left of the harbour, before surrendering.

Modern Toulon is divided in two by a broad boulevard
running w–e (Bd. Gén.-Leclerc, Bd. de Strasbourg). To its n is
the commercial district round the station, to its s the areas of
tourist interest: the Old Town and the harbour.

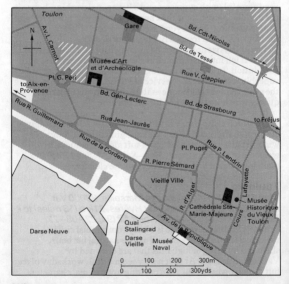

204

Events: Main annual festivals in Toulon include an Apr flower parade, and a circus performers' festival in the pedestrian zone, July–Aug.

In Nov, a fair of *santons* (Provençal clay figures) is held.

Toulon has a good theatre and opera house (*Pl. Victor-Hugo*) where frequent performances are held in winter.

Sights and places of interest

Art et d'Archéologie, Musée d'
Bd. Général-Leclerc ☎ *(94) 93–15–54. Open 10.00–12.00, 15.00–18.00. Closed Mon, Thurs.*

The paintings on display range from the 13th–20thC, with good works by Caracci, Van Loo, Fragonard, Vlaminck, Friesz and Ziem, and contemporary art too. One room is devoted to oriental art – from the Levant to Japan. Others deal with archaeology and include some interesting Gallo-Roman remains from Provence.

Le Port
Few buildings here survived the devastation of 1943–44, and today the **Quai Stalingrad** along the harbour front is lined with hideous, grey rectangular blocks thrown up hurriedly just after the war. Even so, it is a lively and amusing area, full of little bars and cafés and high-spirited sailors on shore leave. From the Quai there are frequent guided tours by boat all round the vast harbour, to **St-Mandrier**, **La Seyne** and back. On the 3hr trip the dry docks, arsenal and other installations, almost all of them modern, are explained. This is still the HQ of the French Mediterranean fleet, and also has some commercial traffic. The **Musée Naval** (🔲 *closed Tues*) housed in the Maritime Prefecture, has model ships, paintings of sea battles, and other naval mementoes.

Tour Royale
Pointe de la Mitre ☎ *(94) 24–91–00* 🔲 ✒ 📷 ☀ *Open Mar–May 15.00–18.00; June to mid-Sept 14.00–19.00; mid-Sept to Oct 14.00–18.00. Closed Mon, Nov–Feb.*

Built in the 16thC as part of the harbour defences, this sturdy stone tower stands strategically on a promontory to the E of its entrance 3km (2 miles) s of the Quai Stalingrad. It was long used as a prison: today it is an annexe of the **Musée Naval** and more interesting than its parent. There are two large black atlantes, taken from men o'war; and the cannon used by Lafayette against the British at Rhode Island. The tower's terrace provides fine views over the harbour and the coast.

Vieille Ville
Mercifully, the Allied bombers were accurate enough to hit the harbour and miss the mass of old alleyways that stretch behind it, N of the Quai Stalingrad, and today most of this area is intact. Part has now been turned into an elegant pedestrian zone, with boutiques and cafés, and little paved squares with flowers and potted palms. In the **Pl. Puget** there is the amusing 18thC **Fontaine des Trois-Dauphins**, 3m (10ft) wide and overgrown with dense foliage.

To the E is the sombre cathedral, and E again the leafy **Cours Lafayette**, filled every morning with its busy and excellent market. Here the **Musée Historique du Vieux Toulon** (🔲 *open Mon, Wed, Sat afternoons only*) might be worth a quick look – souvenirs of local history, old weapons, the works of Toulon painters, etc. Turning E again, the sadder and more sordid side of life becomes evident; here washing hangs across the alleys and Algerian children play in dirty courtyards.

🥂 La Corniche
1 Littoral Frédéric-Mistral, 83000 Toulon ☎ *(94) 41–39–53* ▮▮▮ *to* ▮▮▮ *22 rms* 🛏 *22* 🍴 🅰🅴 ⓪ 💳 🆅🅸🆂🅰

Location: 3km (2 miles) SE of city centre, facing the tiny harbour at Le Mourrillon. A cunningly designed new hotel, the central core of which is a stone flagged patio with flowering shrubs and mimosa. Inside, the rustic Provençal decor is artificial, but not unpleasing. A smell of polish lingers reassuringly. The restaurant has been constructed round three huge umbrella pines, the broad trunks of which push up through the middle of the room with extraordinary effect. Here the wine list represents remarkably good value, and the set menus are well priced.

🏠 🍴 🗖 🖼 🛥 ⚓ ◁€

Frantel 🏨
Bd. Amiral-Vence, 83000 Toulon
☎(94) 24–41–57 ☏400347 ▮▮▮▮
96 rms ▭ 96 ⬛ ▣▢ ▭ AE ⊙
⊙ VISA

*Location: 2.5km (1¼ miles) N of city
centre, high on the slopes of Mt Faron
at the foot of its funicular.* Of the
many recent additions to France's
Frantel chain, this is one of the
best, and best situated. Whether
from the airy restaurant, bedroom
balconies or outdoor bar-terrace,
the views of Toulon and its bay are
breathtaking. The hotel smoothly
gears itself to both brisk
businessmen and more leisurely
holiday-makers.
▱≢﹠◪▭◪❧⬖◉≈⬛

Other hotels worth mentioning,
both functional and efficient, are:
Amiranté (*4 Rue A.-Guiol*
☎(94) 22–19–67 ▯); **Europe** (*7
bis, Rue de Chabannes*
☎(94) 92–37–44 ▯).

Le Lutrin
8 Littoral Frédéric-Mistral
☎(94) 42–43–43 ▮▮ to ▮▮▮▮
▬▬ ▤ ⬛ AE ⊙ VISA *Last orders
21.00. Closed Sat, June.*
Admirals, diplomats and even film
stars are frequent visitors to
Toulon's smartest restaurant,
stylishly housed in a neat 19thC
villa, facing the tiny harbour at Le
Mourrillon, in the SE suburbs. But
it's by no means an exclusive place:
the owner's wife, Elizabeth Chaté,
greets even a stray tourist like an
old friend. The small dining-room
is discreetly elegant, Empire style;
or you can eat in the garden where

an old church lectern (the
eponymous *lutrin*) incongruously
stands. The *carte* is expensive but
the set menu is good value and
Bernard Chaté's careful cooking is
eclectic. **Specialities: *Soupe de
poissons de aux favouilles, boeuf à la
ficelle grand'mère.***

Madeleine ❀
7 Rue des Tombades
☎(94) 92–67–85 ▯ ▭ ▬ ▬
⊙ VISA *Last orders 21.30. Closed
Wed.*
Fanatical professional pride often
yields marvellous results: here is a
set menu that is incredibly under-
priced in relation to the quality
of the *cuisine* and represents
some of the very best value in
Provence. Francis Belloumeau and
his family rarely, if ever, take a
break, but toil away happily in
their chic 13thC *vieille ville*
restaurant. Tables are well spaced
and the service is impeccable –
even the wine is uncorked in a
professional *grand luxe* manner, yet
all is at bistro prices. M.
Belloumeau is Bordelais, and his
cooking is mainly Bordelaise and
Landaise, with Provençal
additions. On the cheap set menu,
for example, you may find a lavish
salade composée, richly dressed, or a
bisque de petits crabes; then a
bourride, or *grenadin de veau
smitane*; then excellent cheeses and
desserts.

**Also recommended: La
Véranda** (*29 Rue A.-Dumas*
☎(94) 92–81–46 ▯), excellent,
booking advised.

Beaches
There are sandy beaches at **Le Mourrillon** in the SE suburbs,
and at **Tamaris** and **Les Sablettes** in the SW suburbs.

Places nearby
Toulon is backed by an exceptionally wild and mountainous
hinterland, much of which makes excellent excursions. At
Ollioules, just off the N8, a narrow steep road winds up along
the great ridge of **Le Gros Cerveau**✩ where the views are
spectacular both over the coast and the country inland towards
the *Ste-Baume* massif. North of Ollioules, the main N8 goes
through the dry and stony **Gorges d'Ollioules**, emerging
within sight of the craggy rocks of the Grès de Ste-Anne, to the
W. Further along the N8, a turning to the E leads up to the
ruined ghostly village of **Évenos**✩ perched on a rocky cliff and
watched over by its ruined castle above. From there the D62
winds on E to the 800m (2,640ft) summit of **Mont Baume**, the
highest peak in the area, with wonderful views. The D62 then
zig-zags back, through pretty scenery, to Toulon.
Mont Faron Directly behind Toulon rises the 550m (1,800ft)

high limestone ridge, Mont Faron. From beside the **Frantel Hotel**, a funicular climbs almost to the top (*operates 9.00–11.45, 14.15–18.15*). Or you can drive up and up along a steep winding road amid pines and rocks. The view from the top is one of the grandest in Provence. All Toulon lies spread out, its great harbour full of grey warships and brown tankers, like children's toys. To the w are the Iles de Hyères; to the E stretches the coast as far as Bandol.

Just below the summit, in an old fort, is Provence's counterpart to the D-Day Museum at Arromanches in Normandy. The **Mémorial National du Débarquement**☆ (▨ ▣ ✳ *open 9.00–11.30, 14.00–17.15*) gives a full and vivid, if overblown, picture of the Allied invasion of Provence in Aug 1944, its preparation, and the battles that followed.

Close by is a small **zoo**, with monkeys and other animals (▨ *open 9.30–12.00, 14.00 to dusk*).

Solliès-Ville (*13km (8 miles) NW of Toulon, just to the W of the N97*) An old village which has a remarkable Romanesque church. It has fine 14thC and 17thC retables, and an enormously tall ciborium by the high altar. The organ, in sculpted walnut, dates from 1499 and is one of the oldest in France.

≡ At Solliès-Toucas (*3km (2 miles) NW of Solliès-Ville on the D554*) is an excellent restaurant with good value on the cheapest set menu, **Le Lingousto** (☎*(94) 28–90–96* ▯ to ▮).

Tourette-sur-Loup ☆
*Map **15**E14. 6m (4 miles) w of Vence. 06490 Alpes-Mar. Population: 890 i at mairie ☎(93) 59–30–11.*

Three old towers give this fine fortified hill village its name. From the main square, two gateways lead into the horseshoe-shaped Grande Rue, a steep medieval alley that was once the main artery. The 15thC church has a triptych by Bréa and two retables in the form of gilded wooden sculptures. Behind the high altar is the church's most curious feature: the remains of a Roman 1stC pagan shrine with the clear inscription to the god 'Mercurio'.

🛏 ≡ **Auberge Belles Terrasses** ● (☎*(93) 59–30–03* ▯); **La Grive Dorée** ● ♣ (*Route Grasse* ☎*(93) 59–30–05* ▯).

Shopping
Many artists and craftsmen have settled in Tourette. Stroll down the Grande Rue to see them at work, or visit their boutiques in ancient cellars. **Christian Massé**, for painting on silk; **A.M. and J. François** for puppets; and **Paul Badié** for ceramics – on the Vence road – are among the best.

Tourtour
*Map **12**F11. 20km (12 miles) w of Draguignan. 83690 Salernes, Var. Population: 300.*

Amid rolling woodlands of oak and olive, pine and cypress, this medieval village stands on a hill with wide vistas on all sides. Tourtour today is a smart residential centre and something of a showpiece, neatly restored; its pristine houses of local golden-brown stone have all been scraped clean. In the main square are two giant elms planted in 1638 to mark the birth of Louis XIV.

St-Pierre-de-Tourtour, 3km (2 miles) E, is a new holiday estate of chic private villas, with swimming pool, tennis courts and other amenities. Built in the local style, and carefully landscaped, it recalls **Castellaras** near *Mougins*. Close by are several smart hotels. Though not quite as gastronomic, Tourtour is certainly the upper Var's answer to Mougins.

⌂ Auberge St-Pierre ✿
St-Pierre-de-Tourtour, 83690 Salernes ☎ *(94) 70–57–17* ▥▥
15 rms 🛏 *15* 🚗 🎴 ☲ *Closed Nov–Mar.*

Location: *3km (2 miles)* E *of Tourtour, in its own 175-acre farmland, amid glorious countryside.* Claude Marcellin and his wife preside over one of the most unusual hotels in Provence, particularly suited to lovers of animals, sport and the countryside – with good riding facilities available. The solar-heated pool lies beside a wide meadow where horses and antelope graze; close by is the home farm. The hotel itself, a low-ceilinged, stone-floored 18thC manor house, is countrified and attractive, with some rather amusing touches: the chapel-turned-TV room, complete with font, and the alcoves in the lounge filled with groups of *santons*. (See restaurant.)
⌂ 🎴 ♨ ⋖ ♒ 🐎 ➝ ☲ *Oct only.*

⌂ la Bastide de Tourtour
Tourtour, 83690 Salernes ☎ *(94) 70–57–30* ▥▥ to ▥▥▥▥
26 rms 🛏 *26* 🚗 🎴 ☲ ᴁ 💳
▥▥ *Closed mid-Nov to late Feb.*
Location: *2km (1 mile)* SE *of the village, in its own pinewood grounds.* 'Bastide' is Provençal for 'farmhouse' – definitely a misnomer for this new, rather inelegant château-style hotel, albeit built with local honey-coloured stone. Inside, the effect is spacious and stylishly baronial (18thC tapestries hanging on the walls). The setting is superb, and the service attentive and impeccable. *Patron* Étienne Laurent enjoys showing his guests his intriguing collection of 200 peasant hats and bonnets. (See restaurant.)
⌂ ✦ ♿ 🎴 ♨ ⋖ ⇌ ☲

☲ Auberge St-Pierre
Address and ☎ *as hotel* ▥▥
🍽 🎴 ☲ *Last orders 20.00. Closed Thurs, Nov–Mar.*
Unfortunately, with such lovely surroundings, it's not possible to eat outdoors, but the dining-room has good views and contains a mossy fountain – this was once the manor's courtyard. M. Marcellin's cheeses and all his meat come fresh from his farm, and the menus combine Provençal dishes, such as *pieds et paquets*, with his own dishes. *Specialities*: *Beignets d'escargots*. (See hotel.)

☲ La Bastide de Tourtour
Address and ☎ *as hotel* ▥▥▥▥
🍽 🎴 ☲ ᴁ 💳 ▥▥
Last orders 21.00. Closed Tues (except summer), Nov to late Feb.
The stately, heavily-vaulted dining-room, with beamed ceilings, makes an effective medieval pastiche, or you can take lunch outdoors on the terrace. Chef Alain Anstett, who trained with the Troisgros brothers at Roanne, smoothly blends classic, *nouvelle* and regional *cuisine*. Try his *tian de légumes, rougets farcis* or *paupiettes de volaille*. (See hotel.)

☲ Les Chênes Verts
Route de Villecroze
☎ *(94) 70–55–06* ▥▥▥▥ 🍽 🍽 ☲
🎴 ☲ *Last orders 21.30. Closed Sun dinner (Oct–Apr), Wed, Jan.*
A temple to *nouvelle cuisine*, this tiny modern dining-room has just five tables, and there is little in the peaceful setting to disturb diners from the serious business of eating. The results justify Paul Bajade's dedication to his art – and his prices. The menus are without choice, but carefully thought out. Dishes often change, but might include *feuilleté d'asperges au sabayon de morilles* or *blanc de turbot*.

La Turbie
*Map **16**E16. 8km (5 miles)* NW *of Monaco. 06320 Alpes-Mar. Population: 1,830* **i** *at mairie* ☎ *(93) 41–10–10.*
An old town on the Upper Corniche 450m (1,500ft) above Monaco, with an attractive 18thC church. From the terrace by the celebrated Trophée des Alpes, there are spectacular views of the coast from Monte-Carlo to Italy, and, at night, of the glittering town below.

Uzès

Trophée des Alpes ▥ ☆
▨ ✗ mid-July to mid-Sept. Open May–Sept 9.00–12.30, 14.00–19.30; Oct–Apr 9.00–12.00, 14.00–17.30.

In 6BC, the Rome Senate decided to erect a mighty monument to celebrate Caesar Augustus' pacification of the local hill tribes who were disrupting links between Rome and Gaul. It stood 50m (164ft) by 38m (125ft) and was surmounted by a statue of *Augustus*, a salutary reminder to all of Rome's supreme power. Since then it has served as a defensive position, a staging post on the Via Julia, has been neglected, dismantled and finally blown up by the French in 1705. In more recent times the generosity of an American, Edward Tuck, has enabled it to be partially restored, with a reconstruction of the huge inscription listing the names of the defeated tribes. The adjacent **museum** has a model of the trophy in its prime, as well as relics and data about Roman Provence.

☜ ═ **Césarée** ■ ♥ (16 Av. Albert 1ᵉʳ ☎ (93) 41–16–08 ☐);
France ■ ♥ (☎ (93) 41–09–54 ☐).

Places nearby
Laghet (3km (2 miles) NW of La Turbie) Here is the 17thC sanctuary of Notre-Dame, a popular place of pilgrimage, full of curious ex-votos. The best are in the **museum** next to the church.
Mont Agel (8km (5 miles) NE of La Turbie) Near the summit is one of the best golf courses on the coast, and the most scenic.

Utelle
Map **15**D15. 50km (31 miles) N of Nice. 06450 Alpes-Mar. Population: 690 ℹ at mairie ☎ (93) 03–17–01.
The D32 winds steeply up to this largely unchanged old village with views over the Vésubie valley. The **church** ☆ on the main square is large and handsome with, inside, a Gothic vaulted roof standing on Romanesque columns. The most noticeable art works are 16thC: a life-size statue of the church's patron *St Véran* behind the altar, a sculpted wood altar front representing the *Passion*, and a lovely painted *Annunciation* above the N aisle altar.

☜ ═ **L'Hostellerie Utelloise** (Pl. de l'Eglise ☎ (93) 03–17–46 ☐), an 18thC mansion, recently converted into a pleasant, modest hotel, with bar and sun terrace on the roof. The restaurant is across the square from the hotel.

Place nearby
Madone d'Utelle (6km (4 miles) W of Utelle) The D136 zigzags up to a lonely hilltop where stands this famous sanctuary, founded in 850, rebuilt in 1806, and still the object of pilgrimage (for keys to chapel ask at any café in Utelle). From here are the most breathtaking views in the entire region of the Alpes Maritime.

Uzès ☆
Map **8**D3. 25km (16 miles) N of Nîmes. 30700 Gard. Population: 7,387 ℹ Pl. du Duché ☎ (66) 22–68–88.
The history of Uzès, a charming town of lofty towers and narrow streets, is bound up with that of its great ducal family, the House of Uzès, dating back to the time of Charlemagne. In 1632 Louis XIII proclaimed it "the premier duchy of France", a title it is still entitled to flaunt, even in today's republican age. The family continue to live in their fairytale castle in the heart of the old town, at the hub of a network of arcaded streets lined

with noblemen's houses. Towers were a great symbol of power in medieval times, and Uzès has several of them, as well as once also being heavily fortified with ramparts. But the town was a Huguenot hot-bed, and this led Richelieu to pull down its ramparts – now replaced by a circular boulevard.

Events: In the last three weeks of July, a festival of classical and modern music takes place.

Amusing country fairs are held in the Pl. aux Herbes: first Sat in Feb, pig fair; second Sat in Apr, spring fair; June 24, a garlic fair; first and second Sat in Aug, wine fair; Aug 14, general fair; Oct 11, sheep fair; Nov 17, horse and poultry fair.

Sights and places of interest

The many lovely buildings around the Château du Duché include: the 12thC **Tour de l'Horloge**; the **Hôtel Dampmartin**, with its round tower, Renaissance facade and elegant staircase; the 18thC **Hôtel de Ville**, with a fine courtyard; the **Crypte**, where one low-relief figure has glass eyes; and the 18thC colonnaded **Hôtel du Baron de Castille**. Across the road from here is the former **Cathédrale de St-Théodorit** (17thC), with a fine organ. It is flanked by a spectacular 12thC campanile, the **Tour Fenestrelle**☆ – all that remains of the Romanesque cathedral destroyed by the Huguenots. This circular six-storey tower is unique in France, though of a kind familiar in N Italy. From the **Promenade Jean-Racine** to the S (so called because the dramatist spent two years of his youth in Uzès) there is a good view over the valley.

The **Pl. aux Herbes**☆ in the Old Town is a pretty square with broad stone arcades, plane trees and a small fountain. Just to the S, in the Av. Foch, **Muséon di Rodo** (🎫 🔊 *closed Tues, Easter – Oct; open Sun afternoon only Oct – Easter*) is a vintage car and model railway museum.

Château du Duché ⅢⅢ ☆
🎫🎫 🎞 *Open 10.00–12.00, 14.30–17.00 (18.30 May–Sept). Closed Mon.*
The duke's flag flies proudly in the red and gold Occitan colours on the massive turreted castle. The building is a mixture of several different epochs and styles, as is clear on entering the courtyard. On the left is the 11thC *donjon*, the **Tour Bermonde**; next to it, the 14thC **Tour de la Vicomté**; on the right the stately Renaissance facade of the living quarters. The chapel is Gothic, but the roof of coloured tiles, emblazoned with the ducal crest, is a 19thC addition.

⌖ Château d'Arpaillargues: Hôtel d'Agoult 🏰
Arpaillargues, 30700 Uzès ☎ *(66) 22–14–48* ☏*490730* ⅢⅢ *28 rms*
🛏 *28* 🚗 🍴 ⬛ 🍴 *July–Aug* 🅿 🅭 🆅🆂🅰 *Closed mid-Oct to mid-Mar.*
Location: In its own park, 5km (3 miles) w of Uzès. The stately 18thC Château d'Arpaillargues belonged to the d'Agoult family (hence the double name), one of whom was Liszt's lover, Marie d'Agoult. Today it is a luxurious country hotel, furnished with antiques and stylishly managed. A sophisticated clientele comes here to enjoy the tennis and the large swimming pool, the views over the rolling hills, and the well-stocked library. (See restaurant.)
🏠 🅱 🎡 🌱 🎿 ⇌ ⚲ 🎣

⌖ Entraigues
Pl. de l'Evêché, 30700 Uzès ☎ *(66) 22–32–68* ⅢⅢ *19 rms* 🛏 *19* 🚗
⟿ 🅿 🅭 🆅🆂🅰
Location: Central, in a narrow street of the Old Town. The **Château d'Arpaillargues'** owner decided that Uzès had scope for a cheaper hotel in the town: so he converted this 15th–16thC mansion, once the home of a general. The result is supremely aesthetic, though hardly cosy – soft hued

stone, bare floors, and dimly-lit low-vaulted ceilings. And the hotel is enclosed, with not much of a view. Bedrooms are carpeted and attractively decorated in creams and browns. The food is deliberately simple (grills, salads, a *plat du jour*) served under 17thC beams.
🖭 ♨

🍴 **Château d'Arpaillargues: Hôtel d'Agoult** 🏨
Address and ☎ *as hotel* ▮▮▯ *to* ▮▮▮ 🖵 🛏 🍴 🚗 ⓟ ⓒⓓ 🆅🅸🆂🅰 *Last orders 21.30. Closed Wed, mid-Oct to mid-Mar.*
On fine days meals are served by the pool or on the lovely terrace by the garden. On cooler days, a log fire is lit in the baronial dining-hall. Elegance reigns supreme – and the *cuisine* makes a fair bid to compete with the setting, though its quality can be erratic. **Specialities**: *Terrine de saumon aux poireaux, volaille de Bresse au Gigondas.* (See hotel.)

Places nearby

To the s of Uzès is **Garrigues** country, typical of the s foothills of the Cévennes. *Garrigues* are low limestone hills, covered with scraggy foliage. The 13thC **Pont St-Nicolas**, 10km (6 miles) s of Uzès on the D979, is in a most attractive spot.

Vaison-la-Romaine ☆

Map **5**B6. *47km (30 miles)* NE *of Avignon. 84110 Vaucluse. Population: 5,210* 𝒊 *Pl. du Chanoine-Sautel*
☎ *(90) 36–02–11.*
Some of the most fascinating reminders of the Roman occupation in France are to be found at Vaison. Even in pre-Roman days it was a town of importance, the capital of a civilized Ligurian tribe, the Voconces. When the Romans took over, they developed it into one of the wealthiest places in Gallia Narbonensis. As excavations reveal, it was a residential centre with luxurious patrician villas, rather than a city of large public buildings, like *Orange* or *Arles*.

At the beginning of the Christian era, Vaison became a major religious centre, and later an important bishopric. The envy of the powerful Counts of Toulouse was aroused, and in the 12thC they seized the church's territory and built their own castle on the hill across the river. In the 13thC and 14thC the population would take refuge here from marauders, and gradually a medieval town grew up on the castle slopes. Later the inhabitants drifted back, and built the present 18th and 19thC town on the N bank, beside the Roman quarter. So Vaison today consists of three distinct entities, from three epochs; and they are not, as so often happens (as at *Nîmes* and *Fréjus*) jumbled on top of each other. This has made it easier to excavate the Roman town where – as at Pompeii – a lifestyle now lies revealed.

Events: Early July, an international folklore festival.
Mid-July to mid–Aug, a theatre and music festival in the Roman theatre.
In Aug, every third year, 1989, 1992 . . . ., a choral festival at Séguret.
First Sun after Aug 15, Provençal festival.
Dec 24, Provençal mystery play and Midnight Mass.

Sights and places of interest
Haute Ville
This is the medieval part of Vaison, across the river where terraces of narrow cobbled streets line the hillside below the castle. By the middle of this century the quarter was derelict and almost empty; now it has been brought back to life by the vogue for restoring old Provençal houses as summer homes. The lower part by the river is still in decay: but the

Vaison-la-Romaine

upper streets, such as the Rue des Fours, are now most elegant, with their flower-pots, creepers and neatly renovated facades. From here a steep path leads up to the 12thC château: it is empty and closed, but from beside it there is a stunning view over Mont Ventoux and the Ouvèze valley.

Notre-Dame, ancienne cathédrale 𝕸 †
Av. Jules-Ferry. Closed 12.00–14.00.

The former cathedral stands by itself to the w of Quartier La Villasse. It is 12thC Romanesque, austerely graceful, built on the clearly visible foundations of a 6thC Merovingian church. The marble high altar, table-shaped, is pre-Romanesque, and behind the present apse are traces of an arcaded 6thC apse. The attractive cloister now houses a small museum of early Christian art (*to enter, ring the bell on the N side of apse*).

Les Ruines Romaines 𝕸 ☆
𝕸 *✗ July–Sept. Open Mar–May, Oct 9.00–18.00; July–Sept 9.00–19.00; Nov–Feb 9.00–17.00.*

Two areas in the Roman town have been excavated – the Puymin Quarter and the Villasse Quarter. The former is just E of the tourist office, the latter nearer the river, by the post office.

Quartier de Puymin

The **Maison des Messii**, the home of a rich local family, has mosaic floors and tall columns. Its lay-out, with atrium, salon, baths, latrines and kitchen, is clearly discernible. Next door, the **Portique de Pompée** is an elegant colonnade with three statues; once it had a central garden with paving, murals and many more statues. Beyond are the remains of servants' and common people's houses; and above is the **Nymphée**, a covered basin above a spring that supplied the town's water. Nearby, a Roman tunnel leads to the theatre, built on the hillside facing N, away from the town. The stage, of which little survives, was cut out of the rock; the amphitheatre, better preserved, retains its rear colonnade.

The modern **museum** ☆ – containing the main finds from the local excavations – is superbly laid out, with full details in French, English and German. Look out for the marble statue of an armour-plated emperor (thought to be *Domitian*); statues of *Hadrian* and his wife *Sabina*; the silver bust of the owner of the villa in the Villasse quarter; and a delightful double-faced statuette, one side a laughing satyr, the other a bearded noble. The collection of coins, ceramics and utensils gives some idea of the daily life of the times.

Quartier de la Villasse

Here is a central street with pavements, parallel to a narrower colonnaded street once lined with shops. Next door is the huge **Maison de la Buste en Argent**, an elegant villa with paved hall, baths and peristyle; behind it are vestiges of hanging gardens. To the w, the Maison du Dauphin is similar in style.

꩜ Le Beffroi ✿
Rue de l'Evêché, Haute Ville, 84110 Vaison-la-Romaine
☎ *(90) 36–04–71* 𝍫 *to* 𝍫𝍫 *20 rms* ▭ *14* ⇔ 🖭 ⇌ AE ⦿ ⦿ VISA
Closed mid-Nov to mid-Dec.
Location: In the medieval part of town, up a steep cobbled street, beside an old belfry. No charm has been lost in converting this 16thC mansion with beamed ceilings and uneven stone floors into a comfortable, if rather folksy, little hotel. The plumbing is modern, but the antique furnishings are genuine. Informal family atmosphere and modest prices.
▱ 🖼 � 《 👥

⇌ **Le Beffroi**
Address and ☎ *as hotel* 𝍫𝍫 ▱ ▦ ⇔ AE ⦿ ⦿ VISA *Last orders 21.00. Closed Mon, Tues lunch, mid-Nov to mid-Dec, 3 Jan to mid-Mar.*
Meals are served in the cheerful red and yellow dining-room or on the panoramic terrace. Try the *râble de lapereau a l'estragon*.

Places nearby

Dentelles de Montmirail (*approx. 13km (8 miles) s of Vaison*)
The outer foothills of the Ventoux range have formed sharp, spiky crests – hence the name, lace point. The lower slopes are

covered in oak, pine and gorse, and make good hiking country.
Séguret *(10km (6 miles) sw of Vaison)* On the edge of the
Dentelles de Montmirail, this is a tiny village of cobbled streets,
beneath a steep rock. It has a 12thC church and a fine 15thC
fountain. On the plain to the w and sw lie the vineyards of some
of the best Rhône Valley *appellations*, including Gigondas.

The village today is an artistic centre. The **Atelier de
Séguret**, founded in 1956 and run by a painter from Berlin, is
an international summer pension for artists both professional
and amateur. They live communally in a group of 16thC
houses; some lessons are given, and there are lithography and
silkscreen workshops. Living conditions are Bohemian but
cheap *(open Apr–Oct. Apply: Arthur Langlet, Atelier de Séguret,
84110 Vaison-la-Romaine)*.

≡ La Table du Comtat
Séguret, 84110 Vaison-la-Romaine ☎ *(90) 36–91–49* ⅢⅢ *to* ⅢⅢⅢ 🖵
🍴 🚗 🛥 ⑩ ⑩ *Last orders 21.00. Closed Tues dinner, Wed (except
June–Sept), mid-Jan to Feb.*
The house is 15thC, finely converted, and the setting is spectacular: on a
steep hill above the Rhône vineyards, with splendid views of the valley
and of the jagged peaks of the Dentelles de Montmirail. Fully worthy of
this setting, the cooking by *patron* M. Gomez is among the best in the
region, well priced for its quality. **Specialities:** *Coq au vin de Gigondas,
millefeuille de saumon à l'oseille, gigot d'agneau en croûte.*
🛏 Le Comtat also has eight cosy bedrooms and the advantage of a
swimming pool (ⅢⅢ).

Valberg

Map **15***C14. 85km (53 miles)* N *of Nice. 06470 Guillaumes,
Alpes-Mar* **i** *Centre Administratif* ☎ *(93) 02–52–77.*
Amid the apartment blocks and chalet-style hotels of this winter
and summer resort stand an old mountain church and
tumbledown stone dwelling, reminders that Valberg was once
no more than a sparsely populated mountain pass. In summer
the modern buildings rise messily from the slopes, but in winter
they manage to blend into the snowy landscape, and it is as a ski
resort that Valberg, together with nearby *Isola 2000* and
Auron, is best enjoyed. As late as mid-Apr one can leave the
coast and go skiing less than a 2hr drive away.

Sights and places of interest
La Croix du Valberg
An energetic walk or a chair lift takes you to the Valberg (Sapet) Cross
from where there are 360° views of the mountains.
Notre Dame des Neiges †
(Apply to the tourist office for key)
This little mountain church has a simple and fresh interior with its bright
and lively decorations painted on a pale blue background between arches
that rise directly from the floor. The exterior is quite plain apart from the
murals around the door depicting Our Lady of the Snows.

🛏 Adrech de Lagas
06470 Valberg ☎ *(93) 02–51–64* ⅢⅢ *22 rms* 🛏 *22* 🛏 ⇌ ⚛ ⑩
Closed May, Oct.
Valberg's best hotel is cheerful and bright, with comfortable bedrooms,
each with a good-sized balcony. The pension terms are worth taking,
since there are no really good restaurants in Valberg and the food here is
perfectly acceptable.
🏠 ⚡ 🖵 📷 🎿 👥

Other hotels worth trying in Valberg are: **Le Chalet Suisse**
(☎*(93) 02–50–09* ⅢⅢ); **La Clé des Champs** (☎ *(93) 02–51–45* ⅢⅢ).

Sports and activities

Valberg's skiing terrain stretches up to Mont Raton at 2,025m (6,650ft) and across to Beuil and includes 19 drag lifts, 2 chair lifts and 2 ski jumps. It has excellent skiing for beginners and will keep intermediate skiers happy for several days at least.

In summer Valberg offers swimming, tennis, riding, walking, archery and shooting. Ask at the tourist office for information.

Places nearby

Guillaumes (*14km (8 miles) w of Valberg*) Take the D28 from Valberg via St-Brès for a spectacular drive to this sleepy village on the Var above the plunging **Gorges de Daluis**. Walk up to the ruined castle if you have the energy, and then down for a simple lunch in one of the café/restaurants.

The road which connects the Daluis gorges with the **Tinée valley** affords magnificent views as it twists and turns its way. After Valberg it passes **Beuil**, a pleasing village with a richly decorated church, and **Roure**, clinging impossibly to the mountainside. Finally it reaches **St-Sauveur**, surrounded by magnificent chestnut trees.

Just before Beuil the D28 drops s through the **Gorges du Cians** with their distinctive red rocks – among the finest gorges in the French Alps. For 20km (13 miles) the road follows the foot of this deep and narrow chasm: some sections of the wriggling road are one-way, carved out of the rock face. Elsewhere, there are majestic views of the jagged red rocks towering high above, their bold colour contrasting with the lush green of the lichen and bushes that cling to them, while waterfalls cascade down. Ten miles s of Beuil the gorge widens out, and a turning to the left zigzags up to **Lieuche**, a hamlet where the church contains an *Annunciation* by Louis Bréa.

More churches with remarkable retables and murals of this period (15thC and 16thC) are to be found in the lonely hamlets of the upper Var valley, NW of Valberg – at **Entraunes**, **St-Martin-d'Entraunes** and (notably) at **Châteauneuf-d'Entraunes**.

Valbonne

*Map 15F14. 13km (8 miles) N of Cannes. 06560 Alpes-Mar. Population: 2,300 **i** Av. Gambetta ☎ (93) 42–04–16.*

A seductive little town with a 17thC arcaded square and fine 13thC church. The narrow streets are, unusually for old Provence, laid out in a criss-cross grid pattern, and gaily decorated with flower pots. Valbonne lies at the heart of Cannes' opulent hinterland – a lush, rolling country of pine and olive woods, vines and flower fields, with hundreds of smart private villas and estates, and a fine golf course.

5km (3 miles) SE, to the left of the D103 to Antibes, is an ambitious new development zone that may fascinate any student of modern architecture and planning. Here the International Scientific Park of **Sophia Antipolis** marks a bid by the Government to promote this part of the *Côte d'Azur* as a centre of advanced technology. Various office and research buildings in bold modern styles lie spread out over a wooded plateau. Just across the valley, to the NW, is a newly completed private boarding-school complex, imaginatively designed in bright colours. Adjacent is a new residential estate of ochre villas rising in tiers with alleys between, a pastiche of a local hill village: the effect is a little austere.

☕ Novotel
Sophia Antipolis, 06560 Valbonne ☎ (93) 33–38–00 ⊕ 970914 ▥▥ to ▥▥ 97 rms ▭ 97 ▤▤ ▰ ▱ July–Aug ⊏⊐ ▨ AE ⊙ CD VISA
Location: In the Sophia Antipolis scientific park, facing a pine wood. The Novotel chain is excellent, and this is one of the very best. It is primarily used by businessmen, but could do equally well for a short holiday since it is quite idyllic. As in all Novotels, the bedrooms sleep three, and children under 12 are put up free of charge.
▱ ⬥ ⬤ ▭ ▨ ⛷ ⛸ ⚹ ♟

≡ Caves Saint-Bernardin ♧
8 Rue des Arcades ☎ (93) 42–03–88 ▥▯ ▬ Last orders 21.00 or 22.00. Closed Sun, Mon, Dec to mid-Jan.
Good value on the generous four-course menus makes this dark-panelled restaurant hugely popular, and it is always crowded out. The tables are tightly-packed, the chatter loud and the ventilation not ideal. But Louis Purgato's local cooking compensates.

Vallauris
Map 15F14. 6km (4 miles) NE of Cannes. 06220 Alpes-Mar. Population: 20,500 (with Golfe-Juan) ℹ Av. des Martyrs-de-la-Résistance ☎ (93) 63–82–58.
Students of Picasso will know that Vallauris owes its fame as a world centre of ceramics to him alone. Potters had been active here for centuries, but their industry was in decline by 1947 when Picasso, then living at Golfe-Juan, came on a visit. Among the many indifferent potters he found one good one, Suzanne Ramie, who ran the Madoura pottery with her husband. His enthusiasm for her work then led to his own involvement in ceramics. For the next 6yr he lived at Vallauris, and much of the time he spent decorating ceramics or twisting newly-thrown pots into imaginative shapes (many of his Vallauris ceramics are in the **Musée Picasso** at *Antibes*). The master's presence gave the local industry a new lease of life: talented young potters came from Paris and elsewhere to work in his shadow, while local craftsmen turned their skills to making reproductions of his originals. Today, alas, Picasso's influence is wearing thin: the town has many potters, but few of them are really gifted.

Musée Picasso ☆
▨▨ ▨▱ Open daily Apr–Oct 10.00–12.00, 14.00–18.00; Nov–Mar 10.00–12.00, 14.00–17.00.
The artist has left two major original works as permanent fixtures in Vallauris. One is the painting, *War and Peace*, which covers the entire walls and vaulted ceiling of this small 12thC chapel (long deconsecrated) at the top of the main street. Invited by the town council to decorate the chapel, Picasso executed the work at his studio in Vallauris in 1952, when he was 70: he painted on to plywood panels which were then fitted together. The result is one of the most haunting of all his works, reminiscent of *Guernica* in its expression of his horror of war.

To see his hands as he moulded the clay, small and feminine yet strong, gave a pleasure akin to watching a ballet, so complete was the coordination in their unhesitating movements. It seemed impossible for the clay not to obey.
Sir Roland Penrose, Picasso

Opposite the chapel, in a little square, is the second work: the curious bronze statue of a man holding a sheep, which Picasso made in Paris during the war, then donated to Vallauris. Bearded and naked, the man's stiff stance contrasts with that of the struggling sheep.

≡ Au Petit Creux (*21 Rue Clément-Bel ☎ (93) 64–22–42 ▭*).

Shopping

By far the best ceramics gallery is still the **Madoura** (*open 9.30–12.30, 14.30–18.00 or 19.00, closed Sat, Sun*), owned and run by Alain Ramie, son of Picasso's friends. This most elegant museum-shop sells the original work of its pottery – not itself open to visits – and produces copies of Picasso's ceramics. It also mounts special exhibitions.

The main street is lined with shops full of the work of local potters, mostly second-rate.

Vence ☆

Map 15E14. 22km (14 miles) w of Nice. 06140 Alpes-Mar. Population: 12,800 i Pl. du Grand-Jardin ☎ (93) 58–06–38.
The history of this mild and sizeable resort stretches back to pre-Roman times when it was an important tribal settlement. It held sway, too, under Roman rule, and as early as the 5thC it became a bishopric. Nowadays it attracts many foreign inhabitants, and is remembered as the place where D. H. Lawrence died in 1930.

Vence's Old Town, oval-shaped, is most attractive – a maze of bustling alleys, with shops selling antiques and local pottery. The **Pl. du Peyra** has an urn-shaped fountain, while the Romanesque **cathedral** is worth a visit for its 15thC choir-stalls, with human figures carved by an unknown artist with a sharp sense of satirical humour.

Chapelle du Rosaire (*Chapelle Matisse*) 🏛 ☆

Route de St-Jeannet, 06140 Vence ☎ (93) 58–03–26 ☒ ☒ Open Tues, Thurs 10.00–11.30, 14.30–17.30; or by special arrangement.
This exquisite little chapel was planned and decorated by Matisse when he was 80, in 1950. Though he was an agnostic, it was a present for the adjacent convent of Dominican nuns who had nursed him during a long illness. Through stained-glass windows of patterned greens, blues and yellows, the light falls luminously on to white ceramic walls, decorated with line-drawings of powerful simplicity.

☁ Château du Domaine St-Martin 🏚

Route de Coursegoules, 06140 Vence ☎ (93) 58–02–02 ▥▥ 15 rms �Ⅲ ☐ ☎ ▱ AE ① ⊙ VISA Closed Dec–Feb.
Location: On a hillside 3km (2 miles) NW of Vence, off D2. Aubusson and Flemish tapestries, Renaissance and Louis XV furniture, a ruined fortress in its grounds, a heart-shaped pool built at the request of Harry Truman: here is the opulence, refinement and aloofness that only great wealth can buy. Even greater wealth can buy a stay in one of the miniature villas behind the hotel – luxury indeed. Here is Relais et Châteaux at its imperious best. (See restaurant.)
🖼 ⅘ 🝙 ⅍ ⋙ 🛰 ⅍ ⅌ ⁕ 🛏

☁ Other recommended hotels in Vence include: **Floréal** (*440 Av. Rhin-et-Daube ☎ (93) 58–64–40 ▥▥*), a brand new hotel on the Grasse road, bright and brisk; **Les Muscadelles** ● (*Av. Henri-Giraud ☎ (93) 58–01–25 ▢*), a simple hotel run by a friendly Belgian couple.

═ Château du Domaine St-Martin ⌂

Address and ☎ as hotel ▥▥ ☐ ▦ ▱ AE ① ⊙ VISA Last orders 21.30. Closed Tues in winter.
There's no doubt that the food here is as distinguished as the setting – *écrevisses en cassoulette au gingembre, escalope de loup à l'infusion de cerfeuil* – but beware of the prices which are some of the highest in the region. (See hotel.)

⌇ Les Portiques

6 Rue St-Véran ☎ (93) 58–36–31 ▥▢ ☐ ▦ Last orders 1.00. Closed Sun.
Candlelight, elegant decor, friendly service, distinguish this romantic

little restaurant in the Old Town, as well as the subtle and inventive cooking of Alain and Ella Chappat, both self-taught. Excellent *menu gourmand*.

≡ A restaurant worth mentioning for a simple meal is **La Farigoule** (*15 Rue Henri-Isnard* ☎ *(93) 58–01–27* ▢).

Places nearby

Circuit of the 'clues' ★ If you have a car, try hard to make this 160km (100 mile) round trip through wild and constantly changing mountain scenery, among the finest in France. The narrow road passes close to several *clues* – rocky clefts filled by rushing torrents. (The route we here describe is a round trip from Vence, but you could equally start from another point, such as Grasse or Entrevaux.)

Leaving crowded Vence by the Coursegoules road (D2), you climb in a trice into an utterly different world – desolate *garrigue* country, a rock-strewn plateau with breathtaking views. After the **Col de Vence** comes another sudden scene shift, as you enter a land of lush meadows, then wiggle down into the wooded valley of the Loup. Stop at **Gréolières**, a typical old hill village, to admire the views. Stroll to the church with its 10thC *Virgin* in sculpted wood and its retables. From here the road twists up the side of a vertiginous gorge, on to a plateau with majestic open scenery – sub-alpine meadows and pine forests. A turning leads to the little ski resort of **Gréolières-les-Neiges**; and, farther on, another at **Thorenc**.

At the 'Chemins' crossroads, turn right along D5, up and over the **Col de Bleine** with its views to s and N of towering rock peaks. Soon comes the turning to the deep **clue de St Auban**, 6km (4 miles) to the w. It is worth the detour. To follow the circuit, take the narrow D10 that winds high along the side of the deep Estéron valley, with views of the stark Cheiron massif. It is hard to believe that Nice is a mere 32km (20 miles) as the eagle flies, for there is hardly a house, save the odd hill hamlet; hardly a soul (out of high season) but for the occasional tourist car. Only the silent uplands, rolling to far horizons. Yet the sun beats hot, and the valley vegetation is lush, with even a sign of farming on the steep terraces.

The **clue d'Aiglun** is a rock-cleft where the torrent has left clear pools for bathing. Soon to the left is the turning to the **clue de Riolan** (another detour). The circuit's route leads past the quaint village of **Roquesteron**, then dives down into a thickly wooded valley, only to climb yet again to the heights, with yet more grandiose views. Remote, deserted hill villages dot the vast landscape. Finally , at Le Broc, the 20thC returns with a shock as suddenly you find yourself sheer above the ugly urbanized plain of the lower Var. From here the road winds via **Carros**, an attractive village with castle and views of the Var, on to **Gattières** and **St-Jeannet** (see over) and back to Vence.
Gattières (*11km (7 miles) NE of Vence*) A quiet and pleasant hill village.

≡ **Auberge de Gattières**
☎ *(93) 08–60–05* ▮▮▯ to ▮▮▮▮ ▬▬ 🍴 ➳ *Last orders 21.00. Closed Wed, June, first two weeks in Dec. Dinner must be reserved before 18.00 (July–Sept).*
Daniel Darbois, from Burgundy, is a masterly cook, his wife is a charming hostess, and the food is varied and sophisticated at their classic Provençal *auberge*. Log fire for spit-roasts; elegant garden for simple summer lunches (full menu served only indoors).

La Gaude (*10km (6 miles) E of Vence* A small town in a region of flowers and orchards, now encumbered with rather too many modern villas. Just to the NE is the well-known **IBM research centre**, a star-shaped building of striking design.

≈→ ═ **L'Hermitage** (☎ *(93) 59–40–05* **Ⅱ** to **ⅢⅡ**), a family-run hostelry with a good restaurant serving Lyonnais and Provençal food, to nearby IBM staff, as well as tourists.

St-Jeannet (*8km (5 miles) NE of Vence*)   The village lies at the foot of a giant rock, the **Baou**, whose summit can be reached on foot by mule track.

═ **Auberge d'Antoine** (*Pl. St-Barbe* ☎ *(93) 24–90–06* **Ⅱ**) is an old inn run with brio by the Falstaffian Antoine Plutino, whose food is good and enlivened by his own inventions. One of the main attractions is the host himself. He loves to discuss art and life with his guests and fancies himself as an art collector; hence the contemporary paintings on the dining-room walls.

Thorenc (*42km (26 miles) NW of Vence*)   A bracing summer resort in a peaceful upland valley. Good for mountain walks in summer and cross-country skiing in winter.

≈→ ═ **des Voyageurs** ▥ (☎ *(93) 60–00–18* **Ⅱ**), a straight-forward village *auberge* with attractive garden and orchard, serving good country cooking.

Ventoux, Mont

Map 5C6. 63km (40 miles) NE of Avignon. Vaucluse.
Mont Ventoux's lonely, lofty pyramid 1,900m (6,260ft) high dominates the E side of the Rhône valley and is visible from many miles away. It is the tallest SW spur of Europe's alpine massif, and Provence's highest peak apart from the Alps themselves, 16km (10 miles) away to the E on the Italian frontier.

Beside the panorama point on the summit are a meteorological station, a TV transmitter and a military radar post. Good roads lead up, both from *Carpentras* or *Vaison* to the W, and from **Sault** to the E. The drive is well worth it, for this is the greatest viewpoint in all Provence, if not in France. The whole region lies before you, from the higher Alps to Marseille and the Cévennes: on a very clear day you can even make out the Pyrenées, 257km (160 miles) away. At night, lighthouses flash along the coast.

In summer, the best time to ascend is early morning or late afternoon, for at midday the summit is often wrapped in haze. In winter, skies may be clearer, but the Mistral howls as ferociously as the name 'Windy Mount' implies. In winter, there is skiing at **Chalet-Reynard** and **Mont-Serein**; in July, some years, the Tour de France sends its cyclists panting to the very top.

The slopes are cloaked in the usual Provençal foliage: but near the summit are alpine flowers and even polar ones, such as the hairy poppy of Greenland.

Places nearby
The Gorges de la Nesque (*8–24km (5–15 miles) SW of Sault*)   Deep, wild and dramatic. A good road runs along its N cliff, with parking points for views over the gorge and the jagged **rocher de Cire** on its S side.

s and sw from here stretches the limestone **plateau of Vaucluse**, pitted with some 200 caves, a paradise for speleologists. The s edge of the plateau dominates the Coulon valley (see *Gordes* and *Apt*).
Sault (*18km (12 miles) SE*)　A village on a rocky spur above the Nesque valley, known for its lavender and honey. Its 12thC church has a finely-vaulted Romanesque nave.

Verdon, Grand Canyon du ★

Map 7E11. Approx. 62km (45 miles) NW of Grasse, Alpes-de-H.-P.

No canyon in Europe is so deep, so long, nor so wildly impressive as Verdon. 700m (2,500ft) deep and 21km (13 miles) long, it was caused by an ancient fault in the limestone plateau that rolls for miles over this part of upper Provence. Through it the river Verdon rushes on its way to join the Durance.

The bed of the canyon is impassable. Tourist roads wind along the clifftops on both sides, and there are frequent places where you can park safely and then peer giddily into the depths where the greenish waters swirl. The roads, in some places unprotected by railings, are not broad, so cautious driving is vital. Motorists wary of precipices are advised to take the s road from w–e, or the N road from e–w. The canyon can be approached from Moustiers or Aups to the w, or from *Castellane* or Comps to the e.

On the s side of the canyon the road from Moustiers winds up through Aiguines, offering initial views over the canyon at the Col de l'Illoire and the Cirque de Vaumale. It then follows the **Corniche Sublime**, with superb viewpoints at the Falaise des Cavaliers and the tunnels de Fayet. But the best view of all is at the **Balcons de la Mescla**, just beyond the Pont de l'Artuby: from this parapet you look vertically down at the point where the Artuby and Verdon gorges meet.

On the N side, coming from Castellane, the first good view of the e part of the canyon is at the Point Sublime. Further on, a turning to the left takes you along the **Route des Crêtes** (cliff road), with its 15 belvederes overlooking the gorge.

At the Point Sublime a footpath leads down the cliff and then winds its way along a series of ledges above the river, to rejoin the Route des Crêtes at the Châlet de la Malène. This dizzily exciting walk can be made in either direction. Either way, it is an 8hr trek, recommended only for tough, experienced hikers not afraid of heights. They should take warm clothing, climbing boots and pocket torches, for tunnels are numerous. The bed of the canyon by the river is negotiable only by trained sportsmen or mountaineers, with an official guide.

Although not quite able to rival its American counterpart, this canyon is one of the most dramatic natural phenomena in Europe.

Places nearby
Aiguines　A village on the edge of the plateau, with vistas over the lake below and the plain of Valensole to the w. The pretty 17thC château has a polychromatic tiled roof.

≈ ≡ **Altitude 823** ● (☎ (94) 70–21–09 ▢ *to* ▥), basic bedrooms, good Provençal food and views of the lake from the terrace.

Comps-sur-Artuby (*16km (10 miles) e of the canyon*)　The old village stands on the bare plateau, circled by rocky escarpments. On a hill close by is a little grey limestone 13thC

church in primitive Gothic style. To the s of Comps, the large
military camp of **Canjuers** stretches for miles across the
plateau: the road to Draguignan passes its smart new army
housing.

Grand Hôtel Bain 🏠
83840 Comps-sur-Artuby ☎ *(94) 76–90–06* 🔲 *to* 🔳 *17 rms* 🔲 *8* 🔲
🍴 🚗 *Closed early-Jan to Feb.*
The name may imply some stately spa hotel, but this is a modest rural
inn, owned and run since 1737 by the delightful Bain family. Here is true
country hospitality; those not deterred by simple bedrooms would find
the Bain a good base for touring the Verdon area.
🌇 🍷 ◁⋵

Grand Hôtel Bain 🍴
Address and ☎ *as hotel* 🔲 *to* 🔳 🔳 🍴 🚗 *Last orders 20.30.*
Closed Wed in winter, early Jan–Feb.
The three rows of white-clothed tables are usually filled to bursting with
hungry tourists. Service is light-hearted and swift in the face of this
onslaught, and Mme Bain's country dishes are satisfying.

Moustiers-Ste-Marie (*6km (4 miles) N of the w end of the
canyon*) This 15thC village is strikingly situated at the foot of a
ravine 150m (500ft) deep. Between its cliffs there hangs a 210m
(700ft) iron chain with a gilded star in the middle: it is said to
have been put there by a local knight in fulfilment of a vow on
his return from the Crusades after a long captivity.

Moustiers is known for its **faïence**, the best in Provence. The
secret of its white glaze is said to have been brought by an Italian
monk from eponymous Faenza. In the 17th–18thC Moustiers
was a leading pottery centre; in the 19thC the industry
dwindled away, but was revived in the 1920s and today
flourishes modestly. Several shops sell the local produce, while
the **Faïence Museum** (*open Apr–Oct*) has a display covering
the 17th–20thC.

A 10min climb from the village leads to the **Chapel of
Notre-Dame**, up inside the ravine. It has a Romanesque porch
and tower, and a Renaissance door of sculptured wood.
Ste-Croix, Lac de At the w end of the Verdon Canyon the
river widens into an artificial lake 11km (7 miles) long, formed
in the 1960s by a new hydro-electric dam at its far end.
Trigance (*8km (5 miles) E of the canyon*) A tiny village on the
plateau, amid grandiose mountain scenery.

Château de Trigance
Trigance, 83840 Comps-sur-Artuby ☎ *(94) 76–91–18* 🔳 *to* 🔳 *8 rms*
🔲 *8* 🚗 AE 💳 🔘 VISA *Closed Nov–Mar*
Location: On a rocky hilltop above the village, circled by barren mountains.
To reach this 9th–11thC fortress (converted in 1965) you must climb a
steep rocky path – to be greeted with bonhomie by the hotelier and
seigneur, Jean-Claude Thomas, a Parisian ex-businessman. The cosy
bedrooms have stylish furnishings and marvellous views of the
mountains. In the dining-room you may find the assertive medievalism a
little oppressive; cooking is inventive but uneven.
🌇 🔲 🖼 ◁⋵

Vésubie, Gorges de la ☆
*Map **15**D15. 32km (20 miles) N of Nice. Alpes-Mar.*
Between St-Jean-la-Rivière and Plan-du-Var, the river Vésubie
plunges through 10km (6 miles) of deep and winding gorges.
One road follows the river bed: but to get the best view of this
impressive chasm, take the upper road (D19) from St-Jean to

Levens. A noted beauty spot, with a 300m (1,000ft) sheer drop below, is the point on this road that bears the sign **'Saut des Français'** (Frenchmen's Leap). The name is a grisly reminder that here, in 1793, Republican soldiers were hurled into the chasm by rebels from Nice.

Upstream, between St-Jean and the old village of Lantosque, the valley is less austere, broader and lined with steep terraces of vine and olive. Apart from *Levens*, other villages worth stopping at along the Vésubie are *Utelle* and *St-Martin-Vésubie*.

Auberge du Bon Puits (*Route de St-Martin Vésubie, Le Suquet* ☎ *(93) 03–17–65* ▮▯ *to* ▮▮) for sound home cooking in the huge dining-room; the *auberge*'s friendly ambience makes up for the bedrooms' pretentious decor.

Villefranche ☆

Map **15***E15. 6km (4 miles)* E *of Nice. 06230 Alpes-Mar. Population: 7,260* ℹ *Jardin François-Binon* ☎ *(93) 01–73–68.*

Founded in the 14thC as a customs-free port (hence its name), Villefranche today is still a lively fishing port; it lies in a deep sheltered bay, one of the loveliest on the coast. The *vieille ville* is a maze of narrow stairways and alleys, some vaulted (e.g. the Rue Obscure, dark indeed). The pretty harbour front is lined with tall, old Italianate houses, red and ochre; and with terrace-cafés and bistros from where you can laze in the sun and watch the boats. Before France left NATO, this was a US naval base; even today, it is visited by Allied warships.

Chapelle St-Pierre ▥ ☆

▨ ▨ X *Open mid-June to mid-Sept 9.00–12.00, 14.30–19.00; mid-Sept to mid-June 9.00–12.00, 14.00–16.30. Closed Fri, mid-Nov to mid-Dec.*

A 14thC chapel by the harbour, where fishermen used to store their nets, decorated by Cocteau in 1957; entrance fees now go to a charity for ex-fishermen, who run the place. Cocteau's pale pastel frescoes, depicting both religious and lay scenes, are striking, if less so than at his **Salle des Mariages** in *Menton*.

Provençal (*4 Av. Maréchal-Joffre* ☎ *(93) 01–71–42* ▮▯ *to* ▮▮) is an unsophisticated family hotel; **Welcome** (*Quai Courbet* ☎ *(93) 55–27–27* ▮▮▮) is a classic hotel of some character, well located; the cooking at its restaurant, **St-Pierre**, is interesting.

Villeneuve-lès-Avignon ☆

Map **4***D4. 3km (2 miles)* NW *of Avignon. 30400 Gard. Population: 8,980* ℹ *at mairie* ☎ *(90) 25–42–03.*

Villeneuve lies directly across the Rhône from *Avignon* ('*lès*' in French place names means 'near'). The French kings used it as a fortress town in the 13th–15thC, when the river was the frontier between France and independent Provence to the E: this explains its two great military posts, the Fort of St André and the Tower of Philippe le Bel. But this did not prevent the cardinals of the 14thC, when the Popes ruled in Avignon, from turning 'foreign' Villeneuve into a wealthy residential suburb. Finding their own city overcrowded, they built 15 grandiose mansions here. Only two survive.

Today this is a quiet little town with some splendid buildings, notably the great Charterhouse. The **Tour de Philippe le Bel**, on a rock above the river, was begun in 1293 and its watch-tower added in the 14thC (excellent views from the top, especially of Avignon and the great Palais des Papes, best seen in the late afternoon sun). The **Fort St-André**, late 14thC, is a fine example of medieval military architecture, with its twin round towers and arrogant gateway. From here too there are marvellous views.

Event: July, the International Summer Festival takes place all month in the Chartreuse. Music, ancient and modern, dancing, theatre, poetry, art exhibitions, workshops and cultural exhibitions (the exhibitions continue till end of Sept). For details apply C.I.R.C.A., B.P.30, 30400 Villeneuve-lès-Avignon ☎(90) 25–05–46.

Sights and places of interest
Chartreuse du Val de Bénédiction ⅏ ❶ ☆
Rue de la République. Municipal sector ▣ *open all the time. State sector* ▦ *Apr–Sept 10.00–12.30, 15.00–19.30; Oct–Mar 10.00–12.00, 14.00–17.00. Closed Tues.*

Covering six acres, this is the largest charterhouse in France, founded in 1356 by Pope Innocent VI. In its heyday, it housed hundreds of monks of the strict Carthusian Order with its emphasis on solitary prayer. At the Revolution, the monks were evicted and their monastery sold by lots. Today it is being restored, and has an odd variety of uses. The sw sector inside the main entrance, including the largest cloister, is today a municipal housing property, full of shops and flats. The sector to the E and N, containing the main religious buildings, is owned by the State which runs it both as an historic monument and as a scientific and cultural centre, popular for seminars. So, on your visit, you are quite likely to find, say, doctors or engineers sipping apéritifs beside the tomb of the Pope. It is a little unnerving.

In the State sector, all is very well laid out and documented, with explanatory panels in French, English and German, and pictures and diagrams of the life of the monastery in its prime. The highlights are: the graceful **tomb of Innocent VI** with its white marble effigy; the 14thC **frescoes** by Matteo Giovanetti in the chapel of Innocent VI; the two **cloisters**; and the **monks' quarters** with wash-house, bakery and barber's shop.

Municipal, Musée ☆
Rue de l'Hôpital ▦ ✒ *Apr–Sept 10.00–12.30, 15.00–19.30; Oct–Mar 10.00–12.00, 14.00–17.00. Closed Tues, Feb.*

Many of the items in the small museum, housed on the first floor of a 17thC palace, are from the **Chartreuse**: for example, a 17thC cupboard, made by the monks, the doors of which have rich panelling on their inner sides. In the same room a 17thC engraving shows the completed Pont St-Bénézet at Avignon soon before its destruction. Among the best of the paintings are a *Crucifixion* by de Champaigne, an *Entombment* by de Châlon, and a gruesome Mignard, depicting the monks being summarily hanged.

The museum's treasure is a painting of great power that stays vividly in mind. It is the *Coronation of the Virgin* ☆ by Enguerrand Charonton, often regarded as the masterpiece of the Avignon school. At the centre are the Virgin, Father and Son, all in robes of gold and crimson. Flanking them are worshippers, in strict hierarchy: saints, prophets, popes, kings and commoners. In a Flemish influenced landscape (the artist was from Laon) of mountains and cities kneels the white-robed figure of St Bruno, founder of the Carthusian Order. Below is a panorama of hell, the devil and the damned.

Notre-Dame †
Pl. J. Meissonier. Sacristy ▦ *For entry, ring bell on left of altar. Open Apr–Sept 10.00–12.00, 15.00–19.30; Oct–Mar 10.00–12.00, 14.00–17.00. Closed Tues, Feb.*

Founded in 1333, the church has paintings by Avignon artists de Champaigne and the Mignards, and a marble relief of *Christ Entombed* on the 18thC high altar. Its chief glory is in the sacristy: a 14thC polychrome ivory statuette of the *Virgin and Child* ☆ richly carved from an elephant's tusk. It follows the curve of the tusk, which is why the Virgin is leaning uncomfortably sideways.

❧ **L'Atelier** ✿
5 Rue de la Foire, 30400 Villeneuve-lès-Avignon ☎ *(90) 25–01–84* ▢
to ▢ *19 rms* 𝖵𝖨𝖲𝖠 *Closed mid-Dec to Feb.*

Location: Central, in a side street of the Old Town. A quiet and gracious
hotel, though some may find its enclosed position and severity a little
oppressive. The large bedrooms have beamed ceilings and antique
furniture, the lounge has bare stone walls and a log fire. At the back
there's a paved patio with fig trees where breakfasts are served.
🗺 📷 ⚓

❧ **Le Prieuré** 🔲
Pl. du Chapître, 30400 Villeneuve-lès-Avignon ☎ *(90) 25–18–20*
🕿 *431042* ▮ *to* ▮▮ *29 rms* ▭ *29* 🍽 🚗 🛏 � 🆎 ⊙ ⊙ 𝖵𝖨𝖲𝖠
Closed Nov–Feb.

Location: Central, in a side street close to the church. Most amenities of a
country hotel are available at this centre-of-town converted priory:
swimming pool and lido, tennis courts, shady patio and a beautiful
garden. Bedrooms in the old building have tiled floors and antiques;
those in the modern annexe, l'Atrium, are larger and more expensive,
with deep sofas and wide loggias.
🗺 ‡ ♿ ☐ 📷 ⚓ ≈ ♒ 💆

🍽 **Le Prieuré** 🏠
Address and ☎ *as hotel* ▮▮ *to* ▮▮▮ ▭ 🍷 🍽 🛏 👤 🚗 🆎 ⊙ ⊙
𝖵𝖨𝖲𝖠 *Last orders 21.30. Closed Nov–Feb.*

Everything is perhaps just a little too slick for any lasting impressions to
shine through, and though the mainly classic food is good, the prices are
very high. But it's a joy to eat on the lawn at lunch, or in the beamed
dining-room in the evening, and Ronald Searle's hilarious illustration on
the menu will keep you amused until the food (very shortly) arrives. Try
the *crêpes du Prieur*, or *sole au plat*, cooked in Vermouth and gratinéed.

Villeneuve-Loubet
Map **15***F14. 16km (10 miles) sw of Nice. 06270 Alpes-Mar.
Population: 6,870 ℹ at marie* ☎ *(93) 20–20–09.*

The coastal strip in front of the old village of Villeneuve-Loubet
has caught the full force of modern development: cranes rise up
on all sides and tower blocks emerge at frequent intervals to
ruin the skyline. There are however two good reasons for
pausing in Villeneuve-Loubet. One is the very building
development that has caused the most furore: **Marina Baie des
Anges**. Seen looming up along the shore from miles away,
these four, long, strangely curling ziggurat blocks of flats exert
a curious fascination, perhaps because of the sculptural grace of
the twisting concrete pyramids. The complex contains many
amenities including boutiques, restaurants and a
thalassotherapy (salt-water cure) centre. Apartments can be
bought or rented. The other reason is the **Fondation Auguste
Escoffier** ✫ *(3 Rue Escoffier* 🔲 *open 14.00–18.00; closed Mon).*
After a punishing Provençal lunch, a visit to a gastronomic
museum may seem insufferable, but it's worth it to see the house
where the great chef was born, and the rich array of
memorabilia, such as icing-sugar models of a Japanese pagoda
and Azay-le-Rideau château, and menus dating back to 1820.
Devotees can even buy a set of 40 colour slides about
bouillabaisse. The *cuisine* of the 'king of sauces' is today out of
fashion, but *nouvelle cuisine* master Roger Vergé is also
represented by his menus.

Sports and activities
The **Marina Baie des Anges** has moorings for 600 boats and a
public swimming pool, as well as tennis, sailing, water-skiing,
wind-surfing and deep-sea fishing.

Biographies

This list represents just some of the many people associated with the South of France. The names of great chefs – Escoffier, Thuilier, Vergé, Outhier and Maximin – as well as many other artists and writers are inextricably linked with the region.

Bardot, Brigitte (born 1934)
When director Roger Vadim made *And God Created Woman* on location at St-Tropez in 1956, he propelled both his young wife and the resort to stardom. Bardot became the archetypal sex-kitten. Today she spends little time at St-Tropez and devotes herself mainly to wildlife preservation causes.

Bonaparte, Napoléon (1769–1821)
The diminutive Corsican began his brilliant military career by driving the British from Toulon in 1793. In 1794 he commanded the defences of Antibes. When exiled, he sailed to Elba from St-Raphael in 1814, and in 1815 landed again at Golfe-Juan before marching up what is now known as the *Route Napoléon* to meet his Waterloo.

Bréa, Louis (c.1450–1522)
Pictures by the leading painter of the Nice school of the 15th and 16thC can be seen at *Nice, Antibes, Biot, Grasse* and *Lucéram*, as well as in many other hinterland village churches. They show both the influence of the Avignon school (especially the *Pièta* in the Louvre) and the Italian Renaissance. Bréa's brother Antoine and nephew François were also notable painters.

Brougham, Lord Henry (1778–1868)
A leading British politican, renowned as a law reformer and campaigner against slavery, Brougham did more than anyone to make the Riviera fashionable. He fell in love with the village of Cannes in 1834 and lived there for over 30yr.

Cézanne, Paul (1839–1906)
The leading Post-Impressionist painter, who had a fundamental influence on the art of the 20thC, was a native of Aix, where his father was a wealthy banker. Cézanne spent most of his life in Provence, painting the landscape he loved, particularly around L'Estaque and Mont Ste-Victoire.

Chagall, Marc (1887–1985)
Born in Russia, Chagall's works depict a highly personal dream world and have made him one of the most popular of 20thC artists. His later years were spent at Vence, where he died. A Chagall museum is at *Nice*.

Cocteau, Jean (1889–1963)
A brilliant and versatile poet, dramatist, painter and film-maker, and a leading figure of the avant-garde, Cocteau had a summer home at Cap Ferrat and spent much of his time in Provence. Frescoes by him are at *Menton* and *Villefranche*.

Daudet, Alphonse (1840–97)
Born at Nîmes, this writer of humorous stories of Provençal life was hugely successful in his own lifetime. From 1857 he lived in Paris, but often visited Fontvieille, the setting of *Letters from my Windmill*.

Defferre, Gaston (1910–1986)
As Socialist Mayor of Marseille since 1953, Defferre dominated the politics of post-war Provence. Staunchly anti-Communist, he was a suave, wealthy bourgeois, owning Marseille's two main daily papers. In 1981 he ceased to be president of Provence's regional council, and in 1981–4 he served as Interior Minister in Mitterrand's government.

Giono, Jean (1895–1970)
André Gide called Giono 'the Virgil of Provence'. His many novels of pastoral life, imbued with a mystical feeling for nature, were set in his beloved homeland around Manosque.

Grimaldi
One of the most powerful feudal families of medieval Provence, the Grimaldi were of Genoese origin. Monaco has been in their hands since the 15thC. The present Grimaldi ruling the principality is Rainier III.

Léger, Fernand (1881–1955)
This pioneer of abstract painting later turned to scenes of contemporary life, executed in his distinctive, simplified style. He worked first at Paris and then settled at Biot.

Matisse, Henri (1869–1954)
The leading artist of Fauvism, Matisse produced much of his finest work in Provence. He first stayed at St-Tropez in 1904, and lived at Vence and Nice from 1917 until his death.

Mirabeau, Count Honoré Gabriel (1749–91)
Although extraordinarily ugly, Mirabeau was one of the most popular leaders of the French Revolution. He spent some years in Aix and was elected to the States General as its deputy.

Mistral, Frédéric (1830–1914)
Son of a farmer, he lived his entire life at Maillane near St-Rémy, and led a revival of Provençal culture and language. In 1904 he won the Nobel Prize for his poetry.

Nostradamus (Michel de Notredame) (1503–66)
The famous astrologer and physician was born at St-Rémy. His rhyming quatrains of enigmatic predictions had a wide vogue, finding royal favour at the time, and have come back into fashion periodically ever since. He lived mainly at Salon.

Pagnol, Marcel (1895–1974)
After teaching English at Tarascon, Pagnol won fame as a writer of stage and screen comedies set in the Provence countryside or on the streets of Marseille.

Petrarch, Francesco (1304–74)
The Italian lyric poet and humanist spent many years as a churchman at the Papal court at Avignon and then lived at Fontaine-de-Vaucluse. Some of his best work was inspired by his unrequited passion for Laura, a virtuous Avignonnaise.

Picasso, Pablo (1881–1973)
Although his most creative years were spent mainly in Paris, the Spaniard's sublime genius was nourished by his native Mediterranean. In 1945 he moved permanently to Provence, living in Vallauris, Vauvenargues near Aix, and Mougins.

Puget, Pierre (1620–94)
Provence's greatest sculptor never found favour with Louis XIV and worked for much of his career in Italy, producing robust works in the Baroque style.

René, King of Naples (1409–80)
Excluded from his kingdom, Good King René became the most popular and successful Count of Provence, ruling at Aix and Tarascon. His daughter married England's Henry VI.

Renoir, Auguste (1841–1919)
After a career based at Paris, the great Impressionist spent his last 16yr at Cagnes-sur-Mer, painting with great vigour.

Van Gogh, Vincent (1853–90)
The son of a Dutch pastor, Van Gogh became a missionary in Belgium before turning to painting. He moved to Paris and then in 1888 to Provence, where he lived at Arles. The clear light of Provence inspired some of his greatest works.

Sport, leisure, ideas for children

The French are an energetic, sport-loving nation and Provence is especially well organized for most sports. The majority of clubs accept temporary members, while many resorts run courses for beginners. For details ask at the local tourist office.

Hotels in France rarely make special provision for children (though some have reduced rates). Children are expected to take all meals with their parents and to eat the same food. Most hotels, however, have a number of large bedrooms with several beds and you can economize by sharing.

The French have a typically Latin love of small children – tiny tots are welcome even in the smartest restaurants. Some hotels have children's playgrounds, ping pong, etc. A few hotels and beach lidos (*Antibes, Monte-Carlo*) employ trained *moniteurs* to take charge of small children.

Bicycling
Bicycles can be rented by the hour, day or week. Ask at the **Gare SNCF** at Antibes, Cannes, Juan-les-Pins, Aix and Avignon. In Nice try **Deux Roues Location**, and in Monte-Carlo **Autos-Motos-Garage**.

Boules
Boules (and its local variant *pétanque*) is a very popular traditional game in the south, played with small metal balls on an earth pitch. You'll see the locals playing it intently in every dusty village square. To find out more contact the **Fédération Française de Pétanque et de Jeu Provençal** (*9 Rue Duperre, 75009 Paris* ☎*4874–61–63*).

Bullfights
Real bullfights (where the bulls are killed) take place in *Nîmes* and *Arles*. The bulls and matadors come from Spain, though most of the toreadors are local. There are also less lethal *courses à la cocarde* where amateur toreadors compete to snatch rosettes from the animals' horns.

Casinos
The 'sport of kings' is today democratized (and some would say debased). American games are almost as common as continental ones, bringing more than a touch of Las Vegas. Provence's best are at *Cassis* and *Cannes* (the two big casinos in Nice closed recently). *Monte-Carlo*, however, is still the liveliest gambling centre in the South of France. Casinos are obliged by law to provide a high standard of entertainment and dining and are open year round, except public holidays. You must be over 21 and must produce a passport or identity card.

Fishing
Plenty of scope in the numerous rivers and lakes – mostly trout, also carp and perch (a permit is needed). Contact the local tourist office or the **Fédération Départementale des Associations de Pêche** (*34 Av. St Augustin, 0600 Nice* ☎*(93) 72–06–04*).

Gardens
There are *jardins exotiques* with fine collections of Mediterranean and tropical plants at *Èze, Hyères, Menton, Monaco*, and *Cap d'Antibes*.

Golf

Several clubs in the area – best are at *Monte-Carlo*, *Cannes*, **Valescure** (*St-Raphael*), and *Aix-Marseille*. Enquire at the tourist office for information.

Skiing

Most people think of the South of France in connection with sun, sea and sand. But, in early spring it is quite possible to be sunning oneself on the beach at Nice, and an hour later to be skiing high in the mountains. There are several small ski stations in the Nice hinterland, but the three best resorts are at *Auron*, *Isola 2000*, and *Valberg*. All have extensive pistes and lifts and ski schools, with provision for children. Skiing equipment can be bought or hired on the spot.

Swimming

There are bathing beaches all along the coast. But be warned – only w from Antibes are they sandy; the coast E from Antibes to Italy is shingle, apart from some not very fine imported sand at Menton and Monte-Carlo. A recent campaign against pollution has brought results. Only in the industrial zones w of Marseille and in some pockets between Nice and Menton do beaches tend to be dirty. Most smart hotels, however, have swimming pools (some heated), while every town has its *piscine municipale*.

Beaches are usually free, apart from the 'fashionable' ones at St-Tropez, Cannes, Nice and Monte-Carlo. Some hotels have private beaches. As for dress (or rather, non-dress), toplessness is now universally accepted, indeed it is the norm.

Tennis

Many of the better hotels have their own courts, but tennis clubs and public courts are numerous (all courts are hard). The **Monte-Carlo Country Club** and the **Tennis École** at *Villeneuve-Loubet* organize tennis courses.

Walking and rambling

Many tourist offices in the Alpes-Maritimes organize summer excursions into the mountains (**Sospel, St-Étienne-de-Tinée, St-Martin-Vésubie, St-Laurent-du-Var**). For further information contact the **Fédération Française de Randonnée Pedestre** (*8 Av. Marceau, 75008 Paris* ☎*4723–62–32*) and the **Club Alpin Français** (*15 Av. Jean-Médecin, 06000 Nice* ☎ (*93*) *87–95–41*).

Water sports

Sailing, water-skiing and wind-surfing at all main resorts, scuba-diving and underwater fishing at some, parascending at major ones. Ask at the local tourist office. There are good marinas and sea-port centres at *Port-Camargue*, **Bendor** and **Embiez islands** (see *Bandol*), *Port-Grimaud*, *La Napoule*, *Cannes*, *Monte-Carlo*.

For information about sailing schools contact the **Centre d'Information Jeunesse Côte d'Azur** (*Espl. des Victoires, 06000 Nice* ☎ (*93*) *80–93–93*).

Zoos and dolphinariums

Antibes has a marine park, *Bandol*, *Monaco*, *St-Jean-Cap-Ferrat*, *Toulon* and *Marseille* have zoos. The *Camargue* has a nature reserve (open only to authorized visitors), and *Fréjus* has two safari parks.

Camping

All official campsites in France have a grade of one, two, three or four stars according to regulations laid down by the government; the local *Office de Tourisme* enforces these regulations but prices in the three and four star categories are not standardized. All those sites listed (alphabetically by town, with the name of the site and postcode following) are in the three or four star category and will be in an enclosed area, marked out in pitches and guarded 24hr a day. There will be a communal area with washing facilities, often including a restaurant and/or shop. Many campsites have excellent sports and other facilities.

In the *Côte d'Azur/Provence* area prices vary enormously depending on how close the site is to the coast. In high season, campsites nearer the coast resemble high-class refugee camps rather than holiday centres, with thousands of people milling among hundreds of closely-pitched tents. Lower prices, peace and quiet and the beautiful countryside are the advantages of camping in the hinterland.

The **French Government Tourist Office** (*178 Piccadilly, London W1 (01)491–7622*) will supply you with a list of sites recommended by the **TCF** (**Touring Club de France**); and the **Camping Club of Great Britain and Ireland** (*11 Lower Grosvenor Pl., London SW1* ☎ (01) 828–1012) will supply you with any further information. Many campsites require bookings in advance, although for those sites run by the TCF this is only possible if you are a member of their club or affiliated to it.

For camping on farmland, contact the **Fédération Nationale des Gîtes Ruraux de France** (*35 Rue Godot-de-Mauroy, 75009 Paris* ☎ (1) 742–25–43).

For forest camping, contact the local **Office National des Forêts** (insurance certificate or camping permit required).

Caravans

Bringing a caravan into France may be accomplished without formality unless you plan to stay for more than six months. However, certain traffic rules must be complied with: you must have an adequate rear-view mirror; you must maintain a distance of at least 50m (55yd) between yourself and the car ahead; you may not drive through Paris whilst towing a caravan; you may not travel in the fast lane of the motorways; if the ladenweight is more than 30% greater than the weight of the towing vehicle, a 45kph (28mph) limit must be observed and you must display a plate indicating this on the back of the caravan. Many of these laws also apply to the towing of trailers.

For further information contact the **French Government Tourist Office** (address above) or your camping club.

Agay
Esterel Caravaning, 83700 St-Raphael, Var ☎ (94) 44–03–28 ⬌ ⬌ ♨ ⚓ Closed Oct to Easter.
A small, quiet campsite for caravans only, 4km (2½ miles) NW of Agay and close to the sea.

Aix-en-Provence
Chantecler, 13100 B. du-R. ☎ (42) 26–08–27 ⬌ ⬌
Large, well-shaded campsite 3km (2 miles) SE of Aix with caravans for

hire. A library, organized entertainments for adults and games for children are available.

Avignon
Pont St-Bénézet, Ile de la Barthelasse, 84000 Vaucluse ☎ (90) 82–63–50 ⬌ in summer ⚓ ⚔
A large and shady site on the Ile de la Barthelasse affording a superb view of the Palais des Papes. Additional sports are available nearby in the town itself.

228

Cagnes-sur-Mer
*Camping de l'Oasis, Av. de Grasse,
06800 Alpes-Mar*
☎ *(93) 20–75–67* 🛏
A well-run camping site, away from
the sea, but equipped with a
swimming pool.

Cavalière
*Les Mimosas, 83980 Le
Lavandou, Var*
☎ *(94) 05–82–94* 🍽 *Closed
early Oct to Easter.*
This quiet, shady campsite near
the sea is open to caravans only and
it is essential to make a reservation
in advance.

Château–Arnoux
*Les Salettes, 04160 Alpes-du-
H.-P.* ☎ *(92) 64–02–40* 🛏
🛏
A comfortable, well-equipped
campsite run by the TCF and only
1km (¼ mile) from a lake where you
can sail and fish.

Giens
*La Presqu'ile, 83400 Hyères,
Var* ☎ *(94) 58–22–86* 🍽 🛏
Closed Oct–Mar.
A small, fairly well-shaded
campsite where you can hire both
tents and caravans. Swimming
pool and riding facilities nearby.
Though close to the sea, Giens is
not quite as frenetic as the rest of
the coast in summer.

Grasse
*Caravan-Inn, 06650 Le Rouret,
Alpes-Mar* ☎ *(93) 77–32–00*
🍽 🛏 *Closed Nov.*
A small and attractive shady site for
caravans only 8km (5 miles) E of
Grasse at Opio, within easy reach
of Cannes yet providing a peaceful
retreat from the bustle. Booking is
advised in high summer. Games
laid on for children.

Grimaud
*Camping-Caravaning A-C.F., St
Pons-les-Mures, 83310
Cogolin, Var* ☎ *(94) 56–34–71*
🍽 🌺 🛏 *Closed Dec.*
An attractive and comfortable site
6km (3¾ miles) E of Grimaud and
very close to the sea.
Entertainments are provided for
both children and adults, and
sports include riding, sailing and
swimming.

Le Lavandou
*Le Domaine, 83230 Bormes-
les-Mimosas, Var*
☎ *(94) 71–03–12* 🍽 🌺 🌿
Closed Nov–Mar.

A vast (38ha) site with surprisingly
few facilities for its size, it can
accommodate 1,200 caravans or
tents. However, the site is on the
beach and sea-bathing is one of the
features.

Mandelieu-La Napoule
Les Cigales, 06210 Alpes-Mar
☎ *(93) 49–23–53* 🛏 🍃
More importance is attached to the
appearance of this pretty site than
to facilities, making it a good base
for a holiday if you want to seek
your own entertainment. Caravans
can be hired and it is advisable to
book in high summer.

Maussane-les-Alpilles
Les Romarins, 13520 B.-du-R.
☎ *(90) 97–33–60* 🛏 🌿 *Closed
Oct to mid-Mar.*
A small, quiet campsite with
modern facilities. A popular
hinterland site: reservation
recommended.

St-Paul-en-Forêt
Le Parc, 83440 Fayence, Var
☎ *(94) 76–15–35* 🍽 🛏 🌿
A small and peaceful site in an
attractive setting. Caravans and
bungalows for hire.

St-Raphaël
Douce Quiétude, 83700 Var
☎ *(94) 95–55–50* 🍽 🛏 🌺 🛏
🌿 *Closed Oct–Mar.*
As its name suggests, this camping
site, set in an attractive wooded
area, is beautifully quiet, though
close to St-Raphaël. Organized
children's games and a discotheque
are amongst the more unusual
attractions, though they don't
disturb the peace unduly. Caravans
can be hired.

Solliès-Toucas
*Les Oliviers, 83210 Solliès-
Pont, Var* ☎ *(94) 28–95–39* 🍽
🛏 🌺 🛏 🌿 *Closed mid-
Sept to mid-June.*
This small, attractive and well-
equipped site makes a good base
for seeing the art exhibitions and
workshops that are such a feature
of this area. Reservation
recommended. Tents can be hired.

Uzès
Le Moulin Neuf, 30700 Gard
☎ *(66) 22–17–21* 🍽 🛏 🛏 🌿
Closed Oct to Easter.
This is a comfortable and quiet
site, just outside Uzès in the
Provençal hinterland. It is wise to
book in advance. For those without
caravans, bungalows can be hired.

Excursion

Corsica *(Corse)*

Area: 8,800sq. km (3,400sq. miles); approx. 184km (115 miles) N–S, 84km (52 miles) E–W. Population: 294,000. The capital, Ajaccio, at the W of the island, is 320km (199 miles) SE of Marseille, 240km (150 miles) S of Nice, and 260km (162 miles) SSE of Toulon. Getting there by air: Air France and Air Inter fly regularly from Marseille and Nice to Ajaccio, Bastia and Calvi – see Basic information for Addresses and telephone numbers; maximum journey time is 1 hr; it is also possible to fly to Corsica and send your car by boat. Getting there by boat: A car and passenger service is operated by SNCM (Société Nationale Corse-Méditerranée – 61 Bd. des Dames, Marseille ☎ (91) 56–32–00; 7 Av. Gustave-V, Nice ☎ (93) 89–89–89; 21 and 49 Av. de l'Infanterie de Marine, Toulon ☎ (94) 41–25–76), linking Marseille, Nice and Toulon with Ajaccio, Bastia, L'Ile-Rousse, and Propriano; journey time 5–10hr depending on destination. Getting around on the island: Regular bus, train and air services link the major towns; all major towns have car hire companies; mopeds and bicycles can also be hired.

Corsica is the most thinly-populated of the larger Mediterranean islands, but it is probably the loveliest – a rugged land of bright, contrasting colours where the mountains sweep grandly to the sea, and flowers and forests fill the lonely valleys. This scenery, Corsica's potent individuality and tradition, and prices that are generally lower than on the mainland, have made it one of Europe's most attractive tourist destinations.

Its history has been long and stormy. Invaded by Phoenicians, Greeks, Romans and other maritime powers, it came under Genoese rule until its attachment to France in 1768, the year before Napoleon was born in its capital, Ajaccio. The Corsicans, an exceptionally proud and hot-blooded people, have always felt very different from the mainland French, whom they derisively call *'les continentaux'*. Since the last war, a separatist movement has developed and there have been several instances of terrorism. Since 1981, however, this has been assuaged by the Socialist Government's offer of internal autonomy.

Corsica's flavour is in some ways as much Italian as French. The people, largely of Italian ancestry, have Italian-sounding names and speak a semi-Italian dialect. They have long been prone to violence, and long-running family feuds were habitual – the word *vendetta* is Corsican – but in recent years they have become tamer. The drama of elections (where a little cheating and bribery is all part of the fun) is still relished, however, as is the celebration of religious festivals. And although Corsicans are by and large fun-loving and noisy extroverts, they are also islanders, and as such can seem to be cautious at first towards outsiders.

The 960km (600 miles) of coastline is nearly all beautiful, with its succession of sandy beaches, rocky coves, pine-clad headlands and tiny fishing ports. Everywhere, jagged granite peaks break the skyline, some rising to over 2,440m (8,000ft) even though only a few miles from the sea. The NW coast, from Porto to Bastia, is the loveliest area, where crimson rocks, azure sea, lush green foliage and white houses create an almost psychedelic effect.

The countryside is wild. Livestock roam free on the pastures, and the air is scented with honeysuckle and lavender, mint and myrtle, pine-resin and eucalyptus – no wonder this is called 'the Scented Isle'. Much of it is covered with dense undergrowth that is known as *maquis*, a traditional hiding place for bandits, and the origin of the name by which the French *Résistance* was known during World War II. Compared with Provence, Corsica has relatively few museums and fine churches, but the many old fortresses, picturesque hilltop villages, and imposing medieval towns such as Bonifacio and Corte more than make up for that lack.

Happily, few ugly modern high-rise hotels or blocks of holiday flats have been built on the island, which is still relatively underpopulated.

Ajaccio
153km (96 miles) sw of Bastia. 20000 Corse-du-Sud. Population: 51,770 i Hôtel de Ville ☎ (95) 21–40–87.

Corsica's capital is a lively and appealing old town, with palm-lined boulevards, squares full of open-air cafés, a yacht-crammed harbour, a casino, and a splendid quayside fish market. Ajaccio lies in a bay, guarded by an old citadel and backed by wooded mountains. It was for long a Genoese colony, but is best known as the birthplace of Napoleon. There are several statues to him; in the cathedral is the font where he was baptized; and the town hall and the house where he was born contain museums devoted to him. The **Palais Fesch** has a notable collection of early Italian paintings.

☜ **Albion** (*Av. Gén.-Leclerc* ☎ (95) 21–66–70 ▮▮▯), close to the beach and town centre, but fairly quiet and very comfortable; **Eden Roc** (*8km (5 miles) w of town on Route des Sanguinaires (95) 52–01–47* ▮▮ *to* ▮▮▮), a beautiful, secluded, modernized hotel, with garden, heated pool, and all rooms with sea views, *pension* compulsory; **Napoléon** (*4 Rue Lorenzo-Vero* ☎ (95) 21–30–01 ▮▯ *to* ▮▮), useful and very centrally located.

🍽 **L'Amore Piattu** (*8 Pl. du Gén.-de-Gaulle* ☎ (95) 51–00–53 ▮▮▯), small, intimate and very personal, more like dining in a private house; lovely regional food; dinners only; **Chez Maisetti** (*at Baleone* ☎ (95) 22–37–19 ▮▯), authentic Corsican cooking at its best, at this big, traditional eating-house just out of town; **Pardi** (*60 Rue Fesch* ☎ (95) 21–43–08 ▯ *to* ▮▯), central and reliable; basic Corsican fare.

Hotel nearby
Porticcio (*on coast 19km (12 miles) to SE*).

Le Maquis (☎ (95) 25–05–55 ▮▮ *to* ▮▮▮), a charming old manor with its own sandy beach, sophisticated, quiet and comfortable, good food and friendly owners.

Bastia
153km (96 miles) NE of Ajaccio. 20200 H.-Corse. Population: 52,000 i 35 Bd. Paoli ☎ (95) 31–02–04.

Just larger than the capital, Ajaccio, this is Corsica's biggest town and main commercial port. Between the Vieux Port and the wide esplanade of the Pl. St-Nicolas is a picturesque maze of narrow old streets. South of the Vieux Port, the 19thC Genoese citadel includes a museum (formerly the Governor's Palace) and two interesting churches: the 15thC Ste-Marie (note the silver statue of the Virgin) and the chapel of Ste-Croix (note the blue Louis XV ceiling).

Excursion to Corsica

North from Bastia stretches the long finger of the mountainous peninsula of **Cap Corse**: its narrow, zig-zagging 112km (70 mile) coastal road passes through dazzling scenery – rocky coves, deep mountain valleys, olive groves, old Genoese watchtowers on hilltops. The w coast is especially beautiful, around the tiny port of Centuri and the high-perched villages of Nonza and Pino.

≋ **Pietracap** (*3km (2 miles) to* N, *at Pietranera* ☎ *(95) 31–64–63* ▥▥ *to* ▥▥), attractive modern hotel, set in an olive grove, with heated swimming pool but no restaurant; **Posta Vecchia** (*Quai des Martyrs* ☎ *(95) 32–32–38* ▥▥), modern and central, facing the port.

≋ **Chez Assunta** (*4 Pl. Fontaine-Neuve* ☎ *(95) 31–67–06* ▥▥), a former chapel, now an elegant restaurant, with a range of excellent local dishes, especially good fish and Corsican wines; **Chez Mème** (*Quai des Martyrs* ☎ *(95) 31–44–12* ▥▥), and **La Taverne** (*9 Rue du Lycée* ☎ *(95) 31–17–87* ▥▥), two good, cheap bistros near the attractive Vieux Port.

Hotel nearby
Centuri-Port (*on Cap Corse*).

Le Vieux Moulin (☎ *(95) 35–60–15* ▥▥), a simple and charming little *auberge* down by the port, with very good food.

Bonifacio ☆
150km (94 miles) SE *of Ajaccio. 20169 Corse-du-Sud. Population: 3,015* i *Rue Longue* ☎ *(95) 73–03–48.*
Bonifacio lies isolated at the far s tip of the island, approached across an arid chalky plateau. Widely regarded as Corsica's most picturesque town, it is a medieval fortress perched dramatically on a narrow headland of 51m (167ft) limestone cliffs. It has cobbled alleys, sometimes pungent – but the local people are lively and fun. The citadel was often under siege: witness the 187 steps cut into the cliff in a single night by the troops of the King of Aragon, in a 15thC siege. The **Partusato** lighthouse, 5km (3 miles) SE, has superb views, with Sardinia a mere 13km (8 miles) away.

≋ **Club des Pêcheurs** (*at Ile de Cavallo* ☎ *(95) 70–36–39* ▥▥▥); **Résidence du Centre Nautique** (☎ *(95) 73–02–11* ▥▥), an attractive place beside the yachting port, offering studios and duplexes; **Solemare** (☎ *(95) 73–01–06* ▥▥).

Calacuccia
104km (65 miles) NE *of Ajaccio. 20224 H.-Corse. Population: 1,100.*
This mountain resort on a lake is the starting point for the long ascent (by car and on foot) of **Monte Cinto**, 2,710m (8,900ft), Corsica's highest peak, always snow-covered.

A well-known folk festival, on Sept 8, is at nearby **Casamaccioli**.

Calvi
93km (58 miles) SW *of Bastia. 20260 H.-Corse. Population: 3,684* i *Chemin de la Plage* ☎ *(95) 65–05–87.*
This old fortified port on the NW coast has a citadel on a headland, built by the Genoese in the 15thC. It was often besieged, and in the Napoleonic Wars the British took the town in 1794 after a long battle in which Nelson, then a young

captain, lost his right eye. Calvi today is a popular summer resort with fine beaches backed by pine forests. The 13thC church of St-Jean-Baptiste has a sumptuous interior, while the former Governor's palace is now a Foreign Legion HQ. Calvi is one of several European towns claiming to be the birthplace of Christopher Columbus. Splendid views can be seen from the hilltop chapel of Notre-Dame de la Serra, 6.5km (4 miles) to the SW.

Grand Hôtel (*Bd. du Prés.-Wilson* ☎ *(95) 65–09–74* ▮▮▮▮), well run and very central, with panoramic views from the restaurant; **Le Magnolia** (*Pl. du Marché* ☎ *(95) 65–19–16* ▮▮), beautiful and rather expensive, housed in former sous-préfecture of Calvi, in heart of town; **Résidence des Aloès** (*1.5km (1 mile) SW of town, in Donatéo district* ☎ *(95) 65–01–46*), unpretentious, secluded, near the beach, good views.

Ile de Beauté (*Quai Landry* ☎ *(95) 65–00–46* ▮▮ *to* ▮▮▮▮), an elegant setting and imaginative cooking, good for fish and local dishes, with *nouvelle cuisine* touches too.

Cargèse
48km (30 miles) NW of Ajaccio. 20130 Corse-du-Sud. Population: 915 i Rue du Docteur Dragacci ☎ *(95) 26–41–31.*
Greeks fleeing from Turkish rule founded this little west coast fishing port in 1663. It is now a popular resort, with good beaches close by. Cargèse lies on a headland on the Gulf of Sagone, N of Ajaccio.

Hélios (*2.5km (1½ miles) E of village* ☎ *(95) 26–41–24* ▮▮), a friendly and enticing modern hotel by the beach; **Thalassa** (*at Plage du Pero, 1.5km (1 mile) to N* ☎ *(95) 26–40–08* ▮▮), right on the beach, with sea and mountain views from some rooms and good local cooking.

Cervione
32km (20 miles) S of Bastia. 20230 San-Nicolao. H.-Corse. Population: 1,450.
A pretty townlet near the E coast; with a 16thC cathedral, and chapel of Ste-Christine with 15thC frescoes. The mountain villages behind, such as **La Porta**, have surprising Baroque churches.

Corte
85km (53 miles) NE of Ajaccio. 20250 H.-Corse. Population: 6,060.
The island's main inland town and its former capital, Corte, today retains a more potent 'Corsican' flavour than anywhere else, perhaps because it has long been isolated in its lonely setting of granite mountains. It stands boldly on a rock above two rivers: there are steep cobbled streets, a 15thC citadel, murmuring fountains, and fine views. Just W are the grandiose gorges of the **Tavignano** and the **Restonica**. The lonely hill village of Sermano, to the E of the Restonica gorges and pine forests, is worth an expedition, not least for its astonishing fresco, dating from the Middle Ages, in the village church.

Sampiero Corso (*Av. du Prés.-Pierucci* ☎ *(95) 46–09–76* ▮▯) is modern and central.

Auberge de la Restonica (☎ *(95) 46–08–58* ▮▯ *to* ▮▮▯), a big country inn, not itself very beautiful but with a splendid view over the valley and good, copious Corsican food.

Excursion to Corsica

Evisa
70km (44 miles) N *of Ajaccio. 20126 Corse-du-Sud.*
Population: 725.
Though only 22km (14 miles) from the coast at **Porto**, this little
resort is 825m (2,700ft) up in the mountains. The scenery all
round is superb, notably the deep **Spelunca** gorge to the W and
the forest of **Aitone** to the E. Beyond is the **Col de Vergio**,
Corsica's highest mountain pass.

🚄 **Scopa Rossa** (☎ *(95) 26–20–22* ▯), small, quiet and modern.

Ghisoni
79km (50 miles) NE *of Ajaccio. 20227 Corse-du-Sud.*
Population: 650.
Two sheer rocks tower high above this inland mountain village.
35km (22 miles) SW is **Monte Renose**, 2,312m (7,750ft). Its
summit can be reached by a 4hr walk, offering sublime views.

L'Ile-Rousse
68km (42 miles) W *of Bastia. 20220 H.-Corse. Population
2,650* i *Pl. Paoli* ☎ *(95) 60–04–35.*
A smart resort on the N coast, with a mild climate and good
beaches. Its name ('Red Island') comes from the group of
red-coloured rocks offshore. In the mountains to the SW are the
medieval fortified villages of **Sant'Antonino** and
Montemaggiore, and the old town of **Corbara**, which has a fine
15thC monastery.

🍴 **A Pastorella** (*at Monticello, 3km (2 miles) to* SE ☎ *(95) 60–05–65*
▮), on a hill high above the port and beach, is a simple, cheery family
place, truly Corsican, run by an ex-shepherd – meals are copious and
low-priced; **La Pietra** (*Route du Port* ☎ *(95) 60–01–45* ▮), a quiet and
comfortable modern hotel built out on the rocks above the sea, with good
views and first-class fish.

Porticciolo
178km (111 miles) NE *of Ajaccio. 20228 H.-Corse.
Population: 100.*
A small yachting harbour on the E side of the lovely Cap Corse
peninsula (see under Bastia).

🍴 **Caribou** (☎ *(95) 35–00–33* ▯ *to* ▰), very highly praised as an
atmospheric hotel with a lovely personal warmth to it, set right by the sea
amid flowers and trees, with swimming-pool, shady terrace, and excellent
food.

Porto
83km (52 miles) N *of Ajaccio. 20150 Corse-du-Sud.
Population: 600* i ☎ *(95) 26–10–55.*
The deep gulf of Porto is arguably the loveliest part of the whole
Corsican coast. Its colours are unforgettable: bright blue sea,
reddish cliffs and lush green foliage. Between the village of
Porto and the hill resort of Piana lie forests of sweet chestnut
and the famous 'Calanche', a fantasy of red and orange rocks in
bizarre shapes, where the coast forms tiny coves. At Porto itself,
the river runs into a lagoon anchorage and houses are huddled
attractively around it beneath a rocky backdrop.

🍴 **L'Aiglon** (*6.5km (4 miles)* N *by D81* ☎ *(95) 26–10–65* ▮), quiet
and secluded near Bussaglia beach with fine views; **Les Flots Bleus** (*at
Porto Marine* ☎ *(95) 26–11–26* ▮), on a rock by the sea, modern and
comfortable.

Porto-Vecchio
131km (82 miles) SE of Ajaccio. 20137 Corse-du-Sud.
Population: 7,800 i 2 Rue Mar-Juin ☎ (95) 70–09–58.
On the SE coast, this busy port and resort lies amid cork-oak
forests at the head of a deep, narrow gulf, with sandy beaches
and coves all around. Above stand the ruins of an old Genoese
citadel.

Cala Verde (☎ (95) 70–11–55 ▮▮), a modern hotel in a quiet
location, all rooms with balconies, some with sea views, others looking
onto the mountains. No restaurant; **Stagnolo** (6.5km (4 miles) NE, Route
de Cala Rossa ☎ (95) 70–02–07 ▮▮ to ▮▮), a series of villas scattered
among the cork oaks, with views over the gulf – total calm;

Lucullus (*Rue Gén.-de-Gaulle* ☎ (95) 70–10–17 ▮▮), rustic-style
bistro with sound local cooking.

Propriano
74km (46 miles) SE of Ajaccio. 20110 Corse-du-Sud.
Population: 2,940 i 2 Av. Napoléon ☎ (95) 76–01–49.
A busy little tourist resort in a deep and lovely bay, with miles of
sandy beaches. Greeks, Phoenicians and Etruscans traded here.
At **Filitosa ☆** 20km (12 miles) NW in the beautiful Taravo
valley, is Corsica's leading prehistoric religious site (c.6000BC;
carved menhirs; museum). **Sartène**, a medieval town in the
mountains, 13km (8 miles) SE of Propriano, has remarkable
Holy Week processions; striking views, too.

Miramar (*Route de la Corniche* ☎ (95) 76–06–13 ▮▮ to ▮▮), an
enchantingly furnished and attractively decorated modern hotel close to
the beach, with a flower-filled garden, swimming-pool and lovely sea
views.

Restaurant nearby
Sartène (*13km (8 miles) SE of Propriano*).

La Chaumière (*13 Rue du Capitaine Benedetti* ☎ (95) 77–07–13 ▮▮),
the *patronne*, a Parisienne, offers Corsican specialities in her small family
restaurant.

Quenza
84km (53 miles) SE of Ajaccio. 20122 Corse-du-Sud.
Population: 800.
A village on a wooded plateau at the foot of the rocky Bavella
peaks, with a remarkable church. To the NE, the **Col de Bavella**
and **Monte Incudine** are well-known beauty spots.

Sole e Monti (☎ (95) 78–62–53 ▮▮). Margaret Thatcher has stayed
at this small, friendly, modern hotel on the edge of the village; fine views,
good local cooking.

Venaco
*71km (43 miles) NE of Ajaccio. 20231 H.-Corse. Population:
1,500.*
A big village on the slopes of Monte Cardo, high in the heart of
the island. Spectacular views, notably from the **Col de
Bellagranajo** to the N.

Paesotel E Caselle (*5km (3 miles) to SE by D43* ☎ (95) 47–02–01
▮▮), a tranquil retreat amid the *maquis*, rustic in style, but modern in
comfort, with riding and tennis facilities.

WORDS AND PHRASES

A guide to French

This glossary covers the basic language needs of the traveller: for pronunciation, essential vocabulary and simple conversation, finding accommodation, visiting the bank, shopping, using public transport or a car, and for eating out.

Pronunciation

It is impossible to give a summary of the subtlety and richness of the French language, but there are some general tips about pronunciation that should be remembered.

French tends to be pronounced in individual syllables rather than in rhythmic feet, so that the word *institution* has four stresses in French and only two in English. In French the voice usually rises at the ends of words and sentences whereas it drops in English. French vowels and consonants are shorter, softer and more rounded than their English counterparts.

The French language is full of characteristic sounds – the r, the u, the frequent eau sound and the nasal sounds (e.g. an, en, ien, in, ain, on, un). The best way to acquire these is to speak English whilst mimicking a strong French accent. The great poet Verlaine used this method with his English pupils.

Vowels

a		short, as in hat; e.g. haricot
	before i	long, as in hay; e.g. aimer
	before m,n	as the o in hot; e.g. dance
e	at beginning of word	as the e in let; e.g. exemple
	at end of syllable	as the ir in irk; e.g. repas
	before m,n	as the a in arm; e.g. emploi
	before r or z at end of word	as the a in lady; e.g. chercher, venez
é		as the a in baby; e.g. bébé
è		as the ai in air; e.g. frère
i		as the ee in seek; e.g. rire
	before m,n	as the a in pan; e.g. vin
o		short, as in song; e.g. tomate
	before i	as the wh in white; e.g. soif
	before n	as the or in torn; e.g. Londres
u		as the u in tune; e.g. jupe

Consonants

c	before a,o,u	hard, as in cat; e.g. canard
	before e,i,y	as the s in sight; e.g. cèpe
	before h	as the sh in shock; e.g. chic
ç		as the c in facet; e.g. façon
g	before a,o,u	as in gun; e.g. gaz
	before e,i,y	as the dg in ledge; e.g. Gigi
	before n	as the n in onion; e.g. Cognac
h		never sounded
j		as the s in leisure; e.g. jupe
m,n	at end of word	not sounded, except with slight nasal twang; e.g. nom —
r		rolled in back of throat
s	at end of word	usually silent; e.g. Paris
t	at end of word	usually silent; e.g. tôt
x	at end of word	usually silent, e.g. prix

Letter Groups

(e) au (x)	as in oh; e.g. gâteaux
ail (le)	as in eye; e.g. volaille
(a) (e) in	as in pan, plus nasal twang; e.g. pain
(a) (e) ine	as en in men; e.g. Madeleine
il (le) at end of word	usually ee as in see; e.g. rouille (except ville, pronounced "veel")
ine	as in green; e.g. poitrine

236

Reference words

Monday	lundi	Friday	vendredi
Tuesday	mardi	Saturday	samedi
Wednesday	mercredi	Sunday	dimanche
Thursday	jeudi		

January	janvier	July	juillet
February	février	August	août
March	mars	September	septembre
April	avril	October	octobre
May	mai	November	novembre
June	juin	December	décembre

1	un	11	onze	21	vingt-et-un
2	deux	12	douze	22	vingt-deux
3	trois	13	treize	30	trente
4	quatre	14	quatorze	40	quarante
5	cinq	15	quinze	50	cinquante
6	six	16	seize	60	soixante
7	sept	17	dix-sept	70	soixante-dix
8	huit	18	dix-huit	80	quatre-vingts
9	neuf	19	dix-neuf	90	quatre-vingt-dix
10	dix	20	vingt	100	cent

First	premier, -ière	Half-past . . . . et demie	
Second	second, -e	Quarter to . . . . moins le/un	
Third	troisième	quart	
Fourth	quatrième	Quarter to six six heures moins le	
. . . . o'clock	. . . . heures	quart	
Quarter-past	. . . . et quart		

Mr	monsieur/M.	Ladies	dames
Mrs	madame/Mme	Gents	hommes/messieurs
Miss	mademoiselle/Mlle		

Basic communication

Yes	oui (si, **for emphatic** contradiction)	Good	bon, bonne
No	non	Bad	mauvais, -e
Please	s'il vous plaît	Well	bien
Thank you	merci	Badly	mal
I'm very sorry	je suis désolé/pardon, excusez-moi	With	avec
		And	et
Excuse me	pardon/excusez-moi	But	mais
Not at all/you're welcome	de rien	Very	très
		All	tout, -e
Hello	bonjour, salut (**familiar**), allo (**on telephone**)	Open	ouvert, -e
		Closed	fermé, -e
Good morning	bonjour	Left	gauche
Good afternoon	bonjour	Right	droite
Good night	bonsoir/bonne nuit	Straight on	tout droit
Goodbye	au revoir, adieu (**final or familiar**)	Near	près/proche
		Far	loin
Morning	matin (m)	Up	en haut
Afternoon	après-midi (m/f)	Down	en bas
Evening	soir (m)	Early	tôt
Night	nuit (f)	Late	tard
Yesterday	hier	Quickly	vite
Today	aujourd'hui	Pleased to meet you.	Enchanté
Tomorrow	demain	How are you?	Comment ça va?
Next week	la semaine prochaine	(Formal: comment allez vous?)	
Last week	la semaine dernière	Very well, thank you.	Très bien, merci.
. . . . days ago	il y a . . . . jours		
Month	mois (m)	Do you speak English?	Parlez-vous anglais?
Year	an (m)/année (f)	I don't understand.	Je ne comprends pas.
Here	ici		
There	là	I don't know.	Je ne sais pas.
Over there	là-bas	Please explain.	Pourriez-vous m'expliquer?
Big	grand, -e		
Small	petit, -e	Please speak more slowly.	Parlez plus lentement, s'il vous plaît.
Hot	chaud, -e		
Cold	froid, -e		

Words and phrases

My name is .... Je m'appelle ....
I am English/American. Je suis anglais, -e/americain, -e.
Where is/are? Où est/sont ....?
Is there a ....? Y a-t-il un, une ....?
What? Comment?
How much? Combien?
That's too much. C'est trop.
Expensive cher (chère)
Cheap pas cher/bon marché
I would like .... je voudrais ....

Do you have ....? Avez-vous ....?
Just a minute. Attendez une minute. (On telephone: *ne quittez pas!*)
That's fine/OK. Ça va/OK/ça y est/d'accord.
What time is it? Quelle heure est-il?
I don't feel well. Je ne me sens pas bien/j'ai mal.

Accommodation
Making a booking by letter

> Dear Sir, Madam,
> *Monsieur, Madame,*
> I would like to reserve one double room (with bathroom), one twin-bedded room
> *Je voudrais réserver une chambre pour deux personnes (avec salle de bain), une chambre avec deux lits*
> and one single room (with shower) for 7 nights from
> *et une chambre pour une personne (avec douche) pour 7 nuits à partir*
> 12th August. We would like bed and breakfast/half board/full board,
> *du 12 août. Nous désirons le petit déjeuner/la demi-pension/pension,*
> and would prefer rooms with a sea view.
> *et préférerions des chambres qui donnent sur la mer.*
> Please send me details of your terms with the confirmation.
> *Je vous serais obligé de m'envoyer vos conditions et tarifs avec la confirmation.*
> Yours sincerely,
> *Veuillez agréer, Monsieur, l'expression de mes sentiments distingués.*

Arriving at the hotel

I have a reservation. My name is ....
J'ai une réservation. Je m'appelle ....
A quiet room with bath/shower/WC/wash basin
Une chambre tranquille avec bain/douche/toilettes/lavabo
.... overlooking the sea/park/street/back.
.... qui donne sur la mer/le parc/la rue/la cour.
Does the price include breakfast/service/tax?
Ce prix comprend-il le petit déjeuner/la service/les taxes?
This room is too large/small/cold/hot/noisy.
Cette chambre est trop grande/petite/froide/chaude/bruyante.
That's too expensive. Have you anything cheaper?
C'est trop cher. Avez-vous quelque chose de moins cher?
Where can I park my car? Où puis-je garer ma voiture?
Is it safe to leave the car on the street? Est-ce qu'on peut laisser la voiture dans la rue?

Floor/storey étage (m)
Dining room/restaurant salle à manger (f)/restaurant (m)
Lounge salon (m)
Porter portier/concierge (m) porteur (station)
Manager directeur (m)
Have you got a room? Avez-vous une chambre?
What time is breakfast/dinner? À quelle heure est le petit déjeuner/dîner?
Can I drink the tap water? L'eau du robinet est–elle potable?
Is there a laundry service? Y a-t-il un service de blanchisserie?
What time does the hotel close? À quelle heure ferme l'hôtel?
Will I need a key? Aurai-je besoin d'une clé?
Is there a night porter? Y a-t-il un portier de nuit?
I'll be leaving tomorrow morning. Je partirai demain matin.
Please give me a call at .... Voulez-vous m'appeler à ....
Come in! Entrez!

238

Shopping

Where is the nearest/a good . . . .? Où est le . . . . le plus proche?/Où y a-t-il un bon . . . .?
Can you help me/show me . . . .? Pouvez-vous m'aider/voulez-vous me montrer . . . .?
I'm just looking. Je regarde.
Do you accept credit cards/travellers cheques? Est-ce que vous prenez des cartes de credit/chèques de voyage?
Can you deliver to . . . .? Pouvez-vous me le livrer à . . . .?
I'll take it. Je le prends.
I'll leave it. Je ne le prends pas.
Can I have it tax-free for export? Puis-je l'avoir hors tax pour exportation?
This is faulty. Can I have a replacement/refund? Celui-ci ne va pas. Voulez-vous me l'échanger?
I don't want to spend more than . . . . Je ne veux pas mettre plus de . . . .
I'll give . . . . for it. Je vous donne . . . .
Can I have a stamp for . . . .? Donnez-moi un timbre pour . . . .s'il vous plaît.

Shops

Antique shop antiquaire (m/f)
Art gallery galerie d'art (f)
Bakery boulangerie (f)
Bank banque (f)
Beauty salon salon de beauté (m)
Bookshop librairie (f)
Butcher boucherie (f)
Horse butcher boucherie chevaline (f)
Pork butcher charcuterie (f)
Tripe butcher triperie (f)
Cake shop pâtisserie (f)
Chemist/pharmacy pharmacie (f) /drugstore (m)
Clothes shop magasin de vêtements/de mode (m)
Dairy crèmerie (f)
Delicatessen épicerie fine (f)/ charcuterie (f)
Department store grande surface (f)/grand magasin (m)
Fishmonger marchand de poisson/poissonier (m)
Florist fleuriste (m/f)
Greengrocer marchand de légumes/primeurs (m)

Grocer épicier (m)
Haberdashery mercier (m)
Hairdresser coiffeur (m)
Hardware store droguerie (f)
Jeweller bijoutier/joaillerie (f)
Market marché (m)
Newsagent marchand de journaux (m)
Optician opticien (m/f)
Perfumery parfumerie (f)
Photographic shop magasin de photographie (m)
Post office bureau de poste (m)
Shoe shop magasin de chaussures (m)
Souvenir shop magasin de cadeaux/souvenirs (m)
Stationers papeterie (f)
Supermarket supermarché (m)
Tailor tailleur (m)
Tobacconist bureau de tabac (m)
Tourist office syndicat d'initiative (m)
Toy shop magasin de jouets (m)
Travel agent agence de voyage (f)

At the bank

I would like to change some pounds/dollars/travellers cheques.
Je voudrais changer des livres/dollars/chèques de voyage.
What is the exchange rate?
Quel est le taux?/le cours du change?
Can you cash a personal cheque?
Pouvez-vous encaisser un chèque personnel?
Can I obtain cash with this credit card?
Puis-je obtenir de l'argent avec cette carte de crédit?
Do you need to see my passport?
Voulez-vous voir mon passeport?

Some useful goods

Antiseptic cream crème antiseptique (f)
Aspirin aspirine (f)
Bandages pansements (m) bandes (f)
Cotton wool coton hydrophile (f)
Diarrhoea/upset stomach

pills comprimés (m) pour la diarrhée/l'estomac dérangé
Indigestion tablets comprimés pour l'indigestion
Insect repellant anti-insecte (m)
Laxative laxatif (m)
Sanitary towels serviettes hygiéniques (f)

Words and phrases

Shampoo shampooing (m)
Shaving cream crème à raser (f)
Soap savon (m)
Sticking plaster sparadrap (m)
String ficelle (f)
Sunburn cream crème écran solaire (f)
Sunglasses lunettes de soleil (f)

Suntan cream/oil crème solaire (f)/huile bronzante (f)
Tampons tampons (m)
Tissues mouchoirs en papier (m)
Toothbrush brosse à dents (f)
Toothpaste (pâte) dentifrice (f)
Travel sickness pills comprimés pour les maladies de transport

Bra soutien-gorge (m)
Coat manteau (m)
Dress robe (f)
Jacket veste/jaquette (f)
Pants slip (m)
Pullover pull (m)
Shirt chemise (f)

Shoes souliers (m)/ chaussures (f)
Skirt jupe (f)
Socks chaussettes (f)
Stockings/tights bas/collants (m)
Swimsuit maillot de bain (m)
Trousers pantalon (m)

Film film (m)/pellicule (f)
Letter lettre (f)
Money order mandat (m)

Postcard carte postale (f)
Stamp timbre (m)
Telegram télégramme (m)

Motoring

Service station station de service (f)
Fill it up. Plein, s'il vous plaît.
Give me .... francs worth. Donnez m'en pour .... francs.
I would like .... litres of petrol. Je voudrais .... litres d'essence.
Can you check the .... ? Voulez-vous vérifier ...?
There is something wrong with the .... Il y a quelque chose qui ne va pas dans le ....

Battery batterie (f)
Brakes freins (m)
Exhaust échappement (m)
Lights phares (m)

Oil huile (f)
Tyres pneus (m)
Water eau (f)
Windscreen pare-brise (m)

My car won't start. Ma voiture ne veut pas démarrer.
My car has broken down/had a puncture. Je suis tombé en panne/J'ai eu une crevaison.
The engine is overheating. Le moteur chauffe.
How long will it take to repair? Il faudra combien de temps pour la réparer?

Car rental

Is full/comprehensive insurance included? Est-ce que l'assurance tous–risques est comprise?
Is it insured for another driver? Est-elle assurée pour un autre conducteur?
Unlimited mileage kilométrage illimité
Deposit caution (f)
By what time must I return it? À quelle heure devrais-je la ramener?
Can I return it to another depot? Puis-je la ramener à une autre agence?
Is the petrol tank full? Est-ce que le réservoir est plein?

Road signs

Aire (de repos) motorway layby
Autres directions other

Centre ville town centre
Chaussée déformée irregular surface
Déviation diversion
Passage à niveau level crossing
Passage protégé priority for vehicles on main road
Péage toll point
Priorité à droite priority for

vehicles coming from the right
Ralentir slow down
Rappel remember that a previous sign still applies
Route barrée road blocked
Sortie de secours emergency exit
Stationnement interdit no parking
Stationnement toléré literally, parking tolerated
Toutes directions all directions
Verglas (black) ice on road

Other methods of transport

Aircraft avion (m)
Airport aéroport (m)
Bus autobus (m)
Bus stop arrêt d'autobus (m)

Coach car (m)
Ferry/boat Ferry/bâteau/bac (m)
Ferry port port du ferry/bâteau/bac (m)

240

Hovercraft hovercraft/
  aéroglisseur (m)
Station gare (f)
Train train (m)
Ticket billet (m)
Ticket office guichet (m)
When is the next . . . . for . . . .? À quelle heure est le prochain . . . .
  pour . . . .?
What time does it arrive? À quelle heure arrive-t-il?
What time does the last . . . . for . . . . leave? À quelle heure part le
  dernier . . . . pour . . . .?
Which platform/quay/gate? Quel quai/port?
Is this the . . . . . for . . . .? Est-ce que c'est bien le . . . . pour . . . .?
Is it direct? Where does it stop? C'est direct? Où est-ce qu'il s'arrête?
Do I need to change anywhere? Est-ce que je dois changer?
Please tell me where to get off? Pourrez-vous me dire ou je devrai
  descendre?
Take me to . . . . . Conduisez-moi à . . . . .
Is there a buffet car? Y a-t-il un wagon-restaurant?

Single billet simple
Return billet aller-retour
Half fare demi-tarif
First/second
  class première/seconde classe
Sleeper/couchette wagon-lit (m)

Food and drink

Have you a table for . . . .? Avez-vous une table pour . . . .?
I want to reserve a table. Je veux réserver une table.
A quiet table. Une table bien tranquille.
A table near the window. Une table près de la fenêtre.
Could we have another table? Est-ce que nous pourrions avoir une
  autre table?
Set menu Menu prix-fixe
I did not order this Je n'ai pas commandé cela
Bring me another . . . . Apportez-moi encore un . . . .
The bill please L'addition s'il vous plaît
Is service included? Le service, est-il compris?

Breakfast petit déjeuner (m)
Lunch déjeuner (m)
Dinner dîner (m)
Hot chaud
Cold froid
Glass verre (m)
Bottle bouteille (f)
Half-bottle demi-bouteille
Beer/lager bière (f)/lager (m)
Draught beer bière pression
Orange/lemon squash sirop
  d'orange/de citron (m)
Mineral water eau minérale (f)
Fizzy gazeuse
Still non-gazeuse
Fruit juice jus de fruit (m)
Red wine vin rouge (m)
White wine vin blanc
Rosé wine vin rosé
Vintage année (f)

Dry sec
Sweet doux (of wine)
Salt sel (m)
Pepper poivre (m)
Mustard moutarde (f)
Oil huile (m)
Vinegar vinaigre (m)
Bread pain (m)
Butter beurre (m)
Cheese fromage (m)
Milk lait (m)
Coffee café (m)
Tea thé (m)
Chocolate chocolat (m)
Sugar sucre (m)
Steak biftek (m)
  well done bien cuit
  medium à point
  rare saignant
  very rare bleu

Menu decoder

Agneau lamb
Agneau de pré salé young lamb
  grazed in fields bordering the sea
Aiglefin haddock
Aigre–doux sweet and sour
Aiguillettes thin slices
Ail garlic
Ailerons chicken wings
Aïoli garlic mayonnaise
Allumettes puff pastry strips
  garnished or filled
Alouette lark
Ananas pineapple
Anchoïade anchovy paste,
  usually served on crispy bread

Anchois anchovies
Andouillette chitterling sausage
Anguille eel
Arachides peanuts
Artichaut artichoke
Asperges asparagus
Assiette assortie mixture of cold
  hors d'oeuvre
Baguette long bread loaf
Banane banana
Barbue brill
Barquette pastry boat
Basilic basil
Baudroie monkfish
Belons flat shelled oysters

Words and phrases

Betterave beetroot
Beurre butter
Biftek beefsteak
Bignorneaux winkles
Bisque shellfish soup
Blanchailles whitebait
Blanquette 'white' stew thickened with egg yolk
Bombe elaborate ice cream
Bouchée tiny vol-au-vent
Boudin (noir ou blanc) (black or white) sausage pudding
Bouillabaisse Mediterranean fish soup which must include fresh fish and saffron
Bouillon broth
Bourride Provençal soup of mixed fish with aïoli
Brandade de morue purée of salt cod, milk and garlic (Provençal dish)
Brioche soft bread made from a rich yeast dough
(à la) Broche spit roasted
Brochet pike
Brochette (de) meat or fish on a skewer
Cabillaud cod
Calmar squid
Canard duck
Carré (d'agneau) loin (of lamb)
Cassis blackcurrants
Cassoulet casserole from Languedoc with haricot beans, confit d'oie and pork
Cèpes prized wild, dark brown mushrooms
Cervelles brains
Champignons mushrooms
Chanterelles, girolles yellow-coloured type of mushroom
Chantilly whipped cream with sugar
Chicorée curly endive
Chou light puff pastry/cabbage
Choucroute pickled white cabbage/sauerkraut
Choufleur cauliflower
Citron lemon
Citron vert lime
Civet de lièvre jugged hare
Colin hake
Concombre cucumber
Confit meat covered in its own fat, cooked and preserved
Confit d'oie preserved goose
Confiture jam
Contre-filet sirloin steak
Coquillages shellfish
Coquille St Jacques scallops, usually cooked in wine
Côte, côtelette chop, cutlet
Coupe ice cream dessert
Crabe crab
Crème cream
Crêpe thin pancake
Cresson watercress
Crevettes grises shrimps
Crevettes roses prawns

Croque-monsieur toasted cheese and ham sandwich
Croustade small bread or pastry mould with a savoury filling
(en) Croûte cooked in a pastry case
Cru raw
Crudités selection of raw sliced vegetables
Cuisses (de grenouilles) (frogs) legs
Cuit cooked
Culotte de boeuf topside of beef
Darne thick slice, usually of fish
Daube meat slowly braised in a rich wine stock
Daurade sea bream
Dindon turkey
Écrevisses freshwater crayfish
Émincé thinly sliced
Endive chicory
Épaule (d'agneau) shoulder (of lamb)
Éperlans smelts
Épices spices
Épinards spinach
Escabèche various fish, fried, marinated and served cold
Escargots snails
Estouffade a stew marinated and fried then slowly braised
Estragon tarragon
Faisan pheasant
Farci stuffed
Faux filet sirloin steak
Fenouil fennel
Feuilleté light flaky pastry
Filet fillet
Flageolets kidney beans
Flétan halibut
Foie liver
Foie gras goose liver
(au) Four cooked in the oven
Fourré stuffed
Frais, fraîche fresh
Fraises strawberries
Framboises raspberries
Frappé surrounded by crushed ice
Fricadelle kind of meat ball
Frit fried
Frites chips
Fritots fritters
Fruits de mer seafood
Fumé smoked
Galantine cooked meat, fish or vegetables served cold in a jelly
Galette flaky pastry case
Gambas large prawns
Garbure very thick soup
Garni garnished
Gâteau cake
Gibier game
Gigot (d'agneau) leg (of lamb)
Glace ice cream
Glacé iced, frozen, glazed
(au) Gratin crispy browned topping of breadcrumbs or cheese

Grenouilles   frogs
Grillé   grilled
Grive   thrush
Hachis   minced
Harengs   herrings
Haricot   stew with vegetables/beans
Haricot verts   green beans
Homard   lobster
Huile (d'olive)   (olive) oil
Huîtres   oysters
Jambon   ham
Laitue   lettuce
Langouste   spiny lobster or crayfish
Langoustines   Dublin bay prawns
Langue (de bœuf)   (ox) tongue
Lapin   rabbit
Légumes   vegetables
Lièvre   hare
Loup de mer   sea bass
Magret (de canard)   breast (of duck)
Maïs   sweetcorn
Maquereaux   mackerel
Marcassin   young wild boar
Marrons   chestnuts
Matelote   freshwater fish stew
Merlin   whiting
Morilles   edible dark brown fungi
Morue   cod
Moules   mussels
Moules marinière   mussels cooked with white wine and shallots
Museau de porc   pig's snout
Navarin   stew of lamb and young root vegetables
Noix   nuts, usually walnuts
Noix de veau   topside of veal
Oeufs   eggs
Oie   goose
Oignons   onions
Oseille   sorrel
Oursins   sea urchins
Palourdes   clams
Pamplemousse   grapefruit
(en) Papillote   cooked in oiled or buttered paper
Pâte   pastry
Paupiette   thin slices of meat or fish rolled up and filled
Pêche   peach
Perdreau   partridge
Persil   parsley
Petit salé   salted pork
Petits fours   tiny cakes and sweets
Petits pois   peas
Pieds de porc   pigs' trotters
Pignons   pine nuts
Piments doux   sweet peppers
Pintade   guinea fowl
Pissaladière   bread dough or pizza covered with tomatoes
Pissenlits   dandelion leaves, used in salads
Pistou   vegetable soup with a paste of garlic, basil and oil

Poché   poached
Pochouse   fish stew
Poire   pear
Poireaux   leeks
Poisson   fish
Poitrine de porc   belly of pork
Pomme   apple
Pomme (de terre)   potato
Porc   pork
Poularde   capon
Poulet   young spring chicken
Poulpe   octopus
Poussin   very small baby chicken
Primeurs   young vegetables or wines
(à la) Provençale   with tomatoes, garlic, olive oil, etc
Quenelles   light dumplings of fish or poultry
Queue de bœuf   oxtail
Quiche   egg- and milk-based open flan
Radis   radishes
Raie   skate
Raifort   horseradish
Ris (de veau)   (calf's) sweetbreads
Riz   rice
Rognons   kidneys
Romarin   rosemary
Rôti   roast
Rouget   red mullet
Rouille   garlic and chilli sauce usually served with fish soups
Safran   saffron
Saint Pierre   John Dory
Salade Niçoise   salad including tomatoes, beans, potatoes, black olives and tunny
Sanglier   wild boar
Saucisses   fresh wet sausage
Saucisson   dry sausage (salami-type)
Sauge   sage
Saumon   salmon
Selle (d'agneau)   saddle (of lamb)
Suprême de volaille   chicken breast and wing fillet
Tapenade   purée of black olives and olive oil
Tête (de veau)   (calf's) head
Thon   tunny fish
Thym   thyme
Timbale   dome-shaped mould or the pie cooked within it
Tournedos   small thick round slices of beef fillet
Tourte   covered tart
Tranche   slice
Truffes   truffles
Truite   trout
Truite saumonée   salmon trout
(à la) Vapeur   steamed
Veau   veal
Viande   meat
Vinaigrette   oil and vinegar dressing
Volaille   poultry
Vol-au-vent   puff pastry case

243

Glossary of art and architecture

Aedicule Niche framed by columns

Apse Semicircular or polygonal termination to E end of church

Arcade Range of arches supported on piers or columns

Atlante Carved male figure used as a column

Atrium Central room or court of pre-Christian house; forecourt of early Christian church

Balustrade Ornamental rail with supporting set of balusters

Baptistry Building, often separate from church, containing font

Barrel vault Continuous vault of semicircular or pointed section

Basilica Rectangular Roman civic hall; early Christian church of similar structure

Campanile Bell tower, generally free standing

Capital Crowning feature of a column or pilaster

Cartoon Full-size preparatory drawing for a painting, fresco or tapestry

Caryatid Carved female figure used as a column

Chancel Part of church reserved for clergy and containing altar and choir

Choir Part of church where services are sung, generally in w part of chancel

Ciborium Altar canopy; casket for the Host

Cloisters Covered arcade around a quadrangle; connects the monastic church to the domestic parts of the monastery

Colonnade Row of columns supporting arches or an entablature

Column Vertical cylindrical support, usually with base, shaft and capital

Crenellate To indent or embattle

Crossing Space at intersection of chancel, nave and transepts in a cruciform church

Diptych Work of art on two hinged panels

Donjon Castle keep (inner stronghold)

Entablature Upper part of a classical order, between capitals and pediment

Ex-voto Work of art offered in fulfilment of a vow

Facade Exterior of a building on one of its principal sides; usually incorporates main entrance

Faïence Glazed earthenware used for pottery or to decorate

buildings; originally from Faenza in Italy

Flying buttress Arch or half-arch built on a detached pier abutting against a building to take the thrust of a vault

Fresco Technique of painting onto wet plaster on a wall

Frieze Continuous band of relief around the top of a room or building; middle section of entablature

Greek cross Cross with arms of equal length

Low relief Sculpture that is attached to its background and projects from it by less than half its natural depth

Mosaic Surface decoration made of small cubes of glass or stone set in cement

Nave Main body of a church w of crossing; more specifically the central space bounded by aisles

Pediment Triangular gable above window, door or classical entablature

Pier Heavy masonry support, like a column only thicker, often square in section

Pilaster Rectangular column projecting from wall

Polyptych Work of art on more than three hinged panels

Presbytery Part of cathedral or church E of the choir in which the main altar is situated

Retable Painted wooden screen above the altar

Ribbed vaulting Arched ribs built across the sides and diagonals of the vaulted bay to support the infilling

Sacristy Repository for sacred vessels in a church

Sarcophagus Stone or marble coffin or tomb, usually decorated with inscriptions or sculpture

Stele Commemorative stone slab often bearing an inscription

Terra cotta Baked unglazed clay used for construction and decoration

Transept Transverse arms of a cruciform church

Triptych Work of art on three hinged panels

Triumphal arch In Roman architecture, monumental arch usually erected in honour of a victorious commander

Tympanum Triangular space enclosed by a classical pediment

Vault Arched ceiling or roof of stone or brick

Index and gazetteer

Within this index and gazetteer are listed towns, villages and places of interest covered in this book; major entries, important sights and general categories such as hotels, restaurants and places nearby form sub-entries. Map references refer to the maps at the end of the book. Important sights and places of interest are also listed separately, both under their most common names and in general categories such as Museums or Hill villages. Important artists, novelists etc. are also listed. Specific hotels and restaurants are not indexed individually but are easily located within A–Z entries.

Page numbers in bold indicate the main entry.

Index and gazetteer

Baie des Anges, Nice, 159;
Map 15F15
Marina, 25, 44, 223
Bandol, 36, 40, 81–3;
Map 11I8–9
hotels, 81–2
nightlife, 82
places nearby, 82–4
sports and activities, 82
zoo and gardens, 81
Banks, 11
French phrases, 239
Le Bar-sur-Loup, 42, 121;
Map 15E14
Barbentane, 39, 81;
Map 9D4
Château, 39, 81
Bardot, Brigitte, 187, 224
Bargemon, 42, 197–8;
Map 13F12
Barjols, 84; Map 12F10
Le Barthelasse island,
Avignon, 78
Bastia, Corsica, 231
Bastide (country house),
18
Les Baux, 21, 27, 29, 36,
37, 39, 84–7; Map 9E4
hotels and restaurants,
85–6
Midnight Mass on
Christmas Eve, 85
places nearby, 86–7
Bauxite mining, 18, 90, 91
The Bearing of the Cross,
retable (Avignon), 78
Beaucaire, 21, 87;
Map 9E4
annual fête, 87
bullfight, 87
Château, 87
Beaulieu-sur-Mer, 45,
88–9; Map 15E15
Bendor island, 82–3;
Map 11I8
Benedict XII, Pope, 75,
77
Bennett, Gordon, 88
Berre *see* Etang de Berre
Beuil, 214; Map 15C14
Bibliothèque
Inguimbertine,
Carpentras, 104
Bicycling, 226, 230
Biographies, 224–5
Biot, 27, 36, 44, 51, 90;
Map 15F14
Bizet, Georges, 68
Blanc, François, 150, 151
Bonifacio, Corsica, 232
Bonnard, Pierre, 27, 187
Bonnieux, 39–40, 135–6;
Map 5E7
Le Boréon, 44, 180;
Map 15C15
Bormes-les-Mimosas, 37,
40, 41, 133, 133–4;
Map 12I11
Bouillabaisse, 47
Boules, 29, 226
La Brague (near Antibes);
Map 15F14
Marineland, 64
Bravades, 29, 187–8

Bréa, Louis, 26, 63, 214,
224
Brignoles, 18, 41, 91; Map
12G10
La Brigue, 36, 44, 91–2;
Map 16C17
Brougham, Lord Henry,
224
Le Brusc, 84; Map 11I9
Buddhist pagoda (near
Fréjus), 119;
Map 13G13
Bullfights, 68, 87, 118,
169, 226
Bull-rearing, 18, 96
Bureaux de change, 11
Bus services, 8, 10

C

Cabris, 37, 43, 51, 92–3;
Map 14F13
Cadarache, 138; Map 6E9
La Cadière-d'Azur, 51,
83; Map 11I9
Café-Théâtre Festival,
Cannes, 98
Cagnes-sur-Mer, 27, 36,
42, 57, 93–5;
Map 15F15
Cagnes-Ville, 93
campsite, 229
festival of art, 94
Haut-de-Cagnes, 93
hotels and restaurants,
95
sights and places of
interest, 93–4
Calacuccia, Corsica, 232
Les Calanques, 36, 40,
106–7; Map 10H–I7
Calendar of events, 34
Calissons (almond cakes),
48, 60
Calvet, Musée (Avignon),
76
Calvi, Corsica, 232–3
La Camargue, 36, 38, 39,
95–6, 191; Map 8F3
Camping, 228–9
Canal du Rove, 146;
Map 10H7
La Canebière, Marseille,
139, 140
Canjuers military camp,
220; Map 7E11
Cannes, 19, 36, 37, 41, 43,
97–104; Map 15F14
airport, 9, 97
beaches, 102
events, 98
Film Festival, 22, 98
golf club, 43
hotels, 99–100
Iles de Lérins,
102–4
nightlife, 101–2
restaurants, 100–1
Royal Regatta, 98
shopping, 102
sights and places of
interest, 98–9
Cap Canaille, 107;
Map 11H8

Cap d'Aigle, 107;
Map 11H8
Cap d'Antibes, 28, 36, 43,
65–6; Map 15F15
see also Antibes
Cap Ferrat, 28, 36, 45;
Map 15F15
Cap-Martin, 175–6;
Map 16E16
La Capte, 127; Map 12I10
Caravans, 228–9
Cargèse, Corsica, 233
Carpentras, 23, 37, 40,
104–5, 137; Map 4C5
Carros, 217; Map 15E14
Carry-le-Rouet, 145;
Map 10H7
Cars/motoring:
accidents, 15
breakdowns, 15
documents required, 7
driving in South of
France, 10
French words and
phrases, 240
from Paris, 8–9
renting, 8, 10
insurance, 7
parking, 10
routes, 38–45
Casinos:
Aix-en-Provence, 60
Beaulieu-sur-Mer, 88
Cannes (Palm Beach),
98, 102, 226
Cassis, 106, 226
Juan-les-Pins, 132
Menton, 149
Monte Carlo, 22, 150,
152, 154–5, 226
St Raphael, 184
Cassis, 36, 40, 105–7;
Map 11H8
hotels, 106
nightlife, 106
places nearby, 106–7
Castellane, 43, 107–8;
Map 14E12
Castellaras, 158;
Map 15F14
Le Castellet, 37, 83;
Map 11I9
Castillon artificial lake,
43, 107–8; Map 14E12
La Castre, Musée
(Cannes), 98
La Caume, 86; Map 9E4
Cavaillon, 40, 108;
Map 4E5
Cavalaire-sur-Mer,
108–9; Map 13I12
Cavalière, 134–5; Map 12I11
campsite, 229
Cervione, Corsica, 233
Cézanne, Paul, 26, 61, 224
Atelier at Aix, 56–7
Chagall, Marc, 224
Museum in Nice, 27, 161
Chaîne de l'Estaque, 146;
Map 10H7
Chaîne de l'Etoile, 146;
Map 10H7
Chaîne des Côtes, 196;
Map 10F6

Index and gazetteer

Index and gazetteer

250

Index and gazetteer

Index and gazetteer

SOUTH OF FRANCE

1

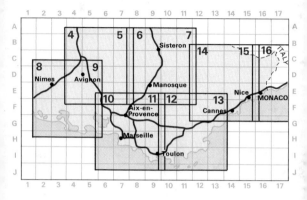

LEGEND

0 5 10 15 20 Km	
═O═	Motorway (with access point)
═══	Main Road-Dual Carriageway
━━━	Other Main Road
━━━	Secondary Road
───	Minor Road
───	Scenic Route
A8	Road Number
─ ─ ─	Ferry
═══	Railway
✈	Airport
✦	Airfield
▓▓▓	International Boundary
─ ─ ─	National Park Boundary
⛪	Church, abbey
∴	Ancient site, ruin
♜	Château
■	Other Place of Interest
⚐	Good Beach
10 ➤	Adjoining Page No.

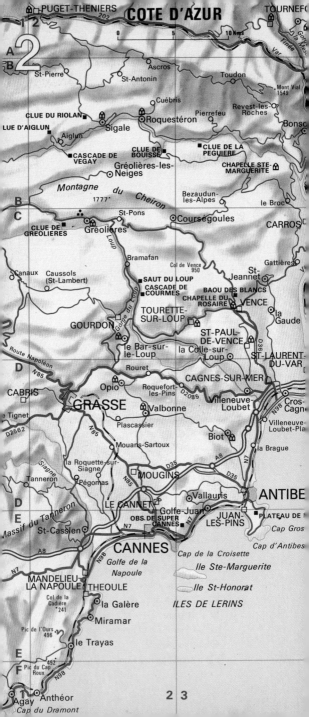

CÔTE D'AZUR

TOURNEFO

PUGET-THÉNIERS 202

Var

0   5   10 Kms

A

B

2

Ascros

Toudon

St-Pierre

St-Antonin

Mont Vial 1549

Revest-les-Roches

Cuébris

Pierrefeu

CLUE DU RIOLAN

Bonso

LUE D'AIGLUN

Sigale

Roquestéron

Aiglun

CLUE DE BOUISSE

CLUE DE LA PÉGUIÈRE

CASCADE DE VÉGAY

Gréolières-les-Neiges

CHAPELLE STE-MARGUERITE

Montagne du Cheiron 1777

Bezaudun-les-Alpes

le Broc

B

CARROS

C

St-Pons

Courségoules

CLUE DE GRÉOLIÈRES

Gréolières

Loup

Gattières

St-Jeannet

Canaux

Caussols (St-Lambert)

Bramafan

Col de Vence 950

SAUT DU LOUP

Gorge du Loup

CASCADE DE COURMES

BAOU DES BLANCS

CHAPELLE DU ROSAIRE

VENCE

la Gaude

TOURETTE-SUR-LOUP

GOURDON

le Bar-sur-le-Loup

ST-PAUL-DE-VENCE

la Colle-sur-Loup

ST-LAURENT-DU-VAR

D36

Route Napoléon

N85

Rouret

CAGNES-SUR-MER

D

CABRIS

Opio

Roquefort-les-Pins

D2085

Villeneuve-Loubet

Cros-Cagn

N98

e Tignet

GRASSE

Valbonne

Villeneuve-Loubet-Pla

D2562

N85

Plascassier

Biot

la Brague

N7

Mouans-Sartoux

A8

Siagne

la Roquette-sur-Siagne

D35

Tanneron

Pégomas

MOUGINS

D35

Massif du Tanneron

N85

Vallauris

ANTIBE

D

LE CANNET

Golfe-Juan

E

St-Cassien

OBS. DE SUPER CANNES

JUAN-LES-PINS

PLATEAU DE

N7

Cap Gros

A8

CANNES

Cap d'Antibes

Cap de la Croisette

MANDELIEU-LA NAPOULE

Golfe de la Napoule

Île Ste-Marguerite

N7

THÉOULE

Col de la Cadière 241

la Galère

Île St-Honorat

ÎLES DE LÉRINS

Miramar

Pic de l'Ours 496

le Trayas

E

Pic du Cap Roux 452

F

N98

Agay

Anthéor

2   3

Cap du Dramont

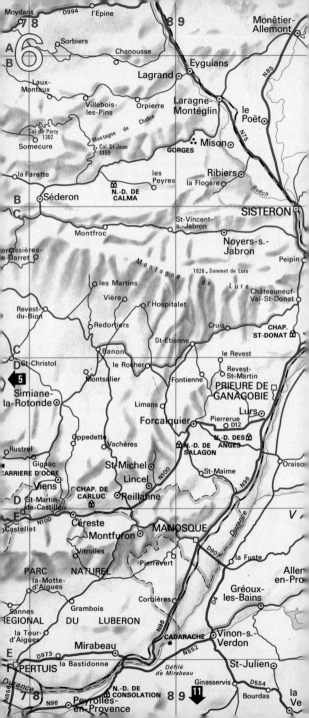

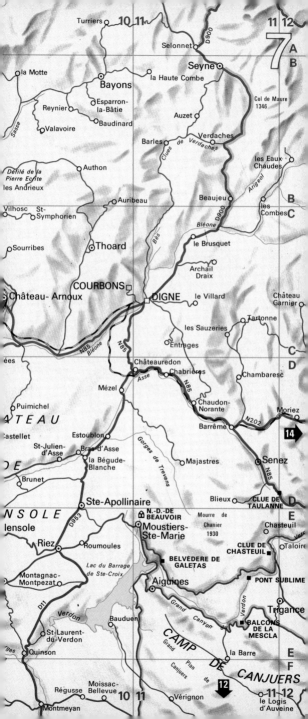

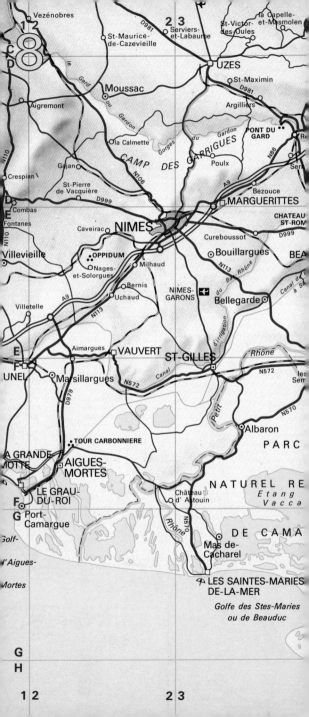

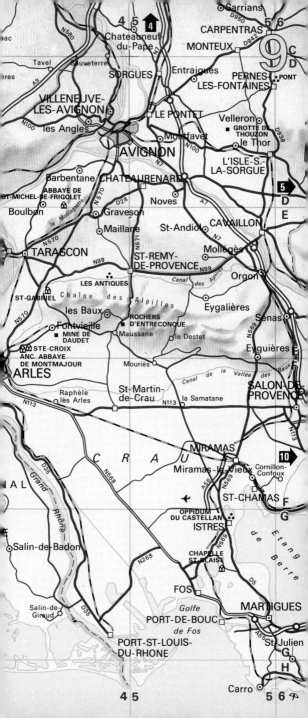

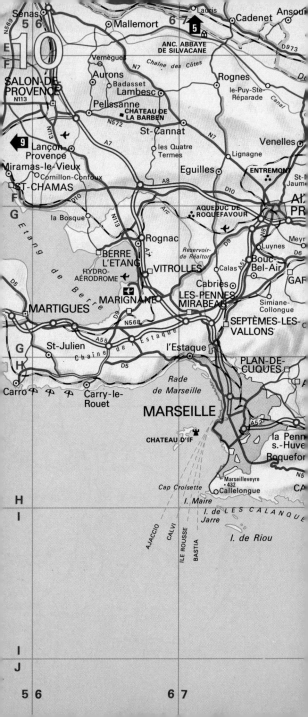

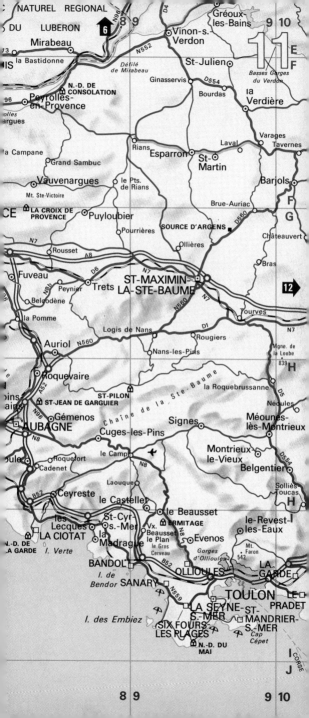

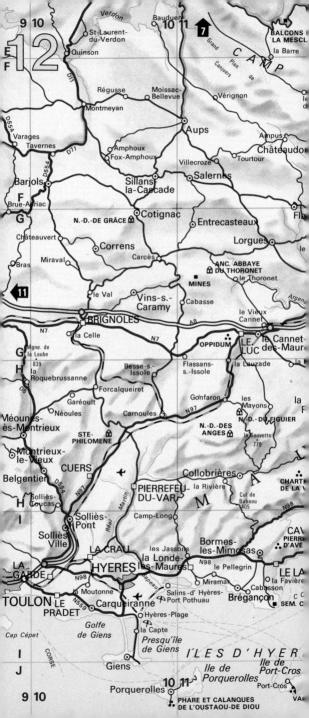

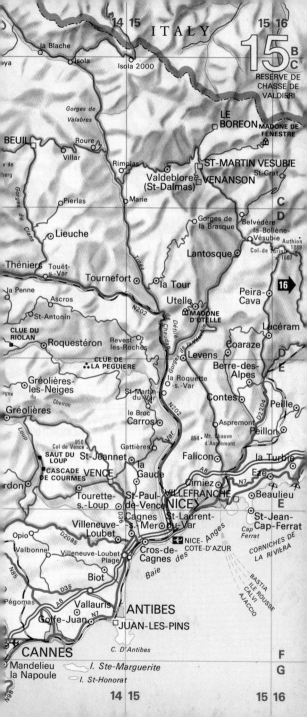